GODS
AND
KINGS

THE RISE AND FALL OF

ALEXANDER MCQUEEN

AND JOHN GALLIANO

DANA THOMAS

PENGUIN PRESS | NEW YORK | 2015

PENGUIN PRESS
Published by the Penguin Group
Penguin Group (USA) LLC
375 Hudson Street
New York, New York 10014

USA · Canada · UK · Ireland · Australia
New Zealand · India · South Africa · China

penguin.com
A Penguin Random House Company

First published by Penguin Press, a member of Penguin Group (USA) LLC, 2015

Excerpts from transcripts of Charlie Rose broadcasts: interview with Alexander McQueen
(November 17, 1997) and with John Galliano (June 13, 2013). Courtesy of Charlie Rose Inc.

Photograph credits appear on page 385–86

ISBN 978-1-59420-494-4

Printed in the United States of America
1   3   5   7   9   10   8   6   4   2

Designed by Gretchen Achilles

For my parents,

Charles H. Thomas
and
Susie S. Thomas

GODS

AND

KINGS

On the evening of February 24, 2011, thirty-five-year-old Géraldine Bloch, the head of exhibitions at Paris's Institute of the Arab World, and her boyfriend, forty-one-year-old Philippe Virgitti, who worked as a receptionist, were sitting on the terrace of the Paris café La Perle, chatting over a couple of beers, when the man next to them yelled to quiet down. Realizing that he was drunk—his eyes were glassy and his speech was slurred—they brushed him off. But he kept needling them.

"Your voice is annoying me," he snarled. "You're speaking too loudly."

The drunk man's bodyguard, standing a few feet away, saw that the situation was quickly devolving into a fight and Bloch was getting upset. He rang his boss's lawyer on a cell phone and tried to pass the phone to Bloch so the lawyer could calm her down, but she refused to take the call. A security guard suggested she move to another table.

Before she could, the drunk man grabbed her hair and shouted, "Dirty Jew face, you should be dead." She screamed in pain. "Shut your mouth, dirty bitch," he snapped. "I can't stand your dirty whore voice."

He then turned his anger toward Virgitti and yelled: "Fucking Asian bastard, I'll kill you!" As Bloch continued to shriek, the drunk told her: "You're so ugly. I can't bear looking at you. You're wearing cheap boots, cheap thigh boots. You've got no hair, your eyebrows are ugly, you're ugly, you're nothing but a whore."

Then he let her go, stood up, struck a rock star–like pose and proudly declared in a posh English accent: "I am the designer John Galliano!"

WHEN THE NEWS BROKE the next morning that the creative director of the esteemed French couture house Christian Dior had been arrested for fighting and shouting anti-Semitic slurs—an act that is considered a hate crime in France—no one in fashion knew quite what to think. Dior's owner Bernard Arnault and the company's chief executive Sidney Toledano—a French Jew who is one of the most respected executives in the business—responded cautiously by simply suspending Galliano pending the police investigation.

But a few days later—in the thick of Paris Fashion Week—the British tabloid *The Sun* published a video on its Web site of Galliano at the same café several months earlier, obviously plastered and spewing decidedly more virulent anti-Semitic insults, including "I love Hitler," at a couple of patrons, neither of whom were Jewish. The video went viral and the international Jewish community was outraged. Abraham Foxman, national director of the Anti-Defamation League, called Galliano "a serial bigot."

It was more than Arnault and Toledano could accept. Within twenty-four hours, they fired Galliano from both Dior and his namesake brand John Galliano. The news of his sacking played on front pages around the world, right next to the revolt in Libya.

Though personally wounded by Galliano's vicious racist outbursts, Toledano chose to go ahead with the Dior women's wear show as scheduled, in a large tent pitched in the Musée Rodin's gardens. As the lights went down, he came out and told the audience: "What has happened over the last week has been a terrible and wrenching ordeal for us all. It has been deeply painful to see the Dior name associated with the disgraceful statements attributed to its designer, however brilliant he may be." With that came a charming, commercial collection of hippie-inspired clothes, and at the close, in Galliano's absence, Dior's hardworking atelier hands, mostly older women, dressed in white smocklike coats, stepped into the spotlight and humbly took the bow.

Galliano's flameout came almost a year to the day after his competitor and compatriot, the forty-year-old British designer Alexander McQueen, was found dead in his London flat. After years of serious drug abuse and profound depression that his psychiatrist Dr. Stephen Pereira later testified was caused by work pressures and accentuated by the death earlier in the week of his devoted mother Joyce, McQueen hanged himself in his wardrobe.

The coincidence in timing was both disturbing and poignant. Galliano and McQueen had arrived on the international fashion stage almost simultaneously in the mid-1990s, when the dominant style was minimalism, and together they shook the industry out of its boring, bourgeois stupor with their innovative, complicated, and deeply seductive designs.

Galliano and McQueen had similar personal stories. Both grew up in working-class London—Galliano, the son of a plumber; McQueen, the son of a cabdriver—with doting mothers who nourished their love of fashion. Both discovered as boys that they were gay and were bullied by homophobic school-mates, which pushed them to develop violent tempers and mouthy retorts as retaliation. Both apprenticed in the costume departments of London theaters, where they cultivated a taste and an eye for elaborate stage production. Both became regulars on the London nightclub scene and partook in its vices. And both attended Central Saint Martins, a then-little-known but respected art school in London, where they put on exceptional graduation shows.

Galliano and McQueen weren't simply driven and gifted. They wanted to revolutionize fashion in a way no one had in decades. With little money, vol-unteer helpers, and sheer will, they turned out landmark collections in mes-merizing, theatrical shows that retailers and critics still gush about and designers continue to reference.

Galliano led the way with his sensual bias-cut gowns and his voluptuous hourglass tailoring, which he presented in romantic storybook-like settings. "Everything John did was touched with artistry and meaning," explained Amanda Harlech, who served as his creative partner and muse for the first decade of his career. "He created whole worlds for every woman—no, for every girl, boy, woman, man to explore."

Galliano's zenith came in March 1994 with his São Schlumberger show—so named because it was staged in the Portuguese socialite's empty eighteenth-century Paris mansion. Out of business for the third time in ten years, Galliano landed at the last minute a deep-pocketed American banker to back him. Working day and night for two weeks, he and his team pulled together eighteen Japonism-inspired mini-kimonos and fluid gowns cut from the same bolt of cheap black satin and topped off with secondhand furs and Harry Winston diamonds on loan. Everyone—the world's top models, the hair-dressers and makeup artists, the shoe designer Manolo Blahnik, the milliner Stephen Jones—agreed to work for free, because, as Harlech said, "We all believed in John."

Since the space was small the guest list was limited, but those who did attend were agog at the beauty, glamour, and poetry of the clothes, worn so sensually by twenties-like sirens in such a resplendent setting. "What the hell!" howls *Vanity Fair* fashion and style director Michael Roberts twenty years on. "It was like being on a major drug trip. You were transported completely for twenty-five minutes." More important, with the Schlumberger collection, then–French *Vogue* editor Joan Juliet Buck explained that Galliano launched "a new way of looking, an affirmation of femininity that you could see in the cut."

At the same time, McQueen, though nearly ten years younger than Galliano, was also changing the way the world was dressing, but more profoundly. For his first official collection, in March 1993, at the tender age of twenty-three, McQueen did what few in fashion ever achieve: he invented a new silhouette. Called the Bumster, it was a pair of flat-front pants with a waistline slung so low it revealed the top of the pubis and derriere. "I wanted to elongate the body, not just show the bum," he explained. "To me, that part of the body—not so much the buttocks, but the bottom of the spine—that's the most erotic part of anyone's body, man or woman."

He presented the Bumster in various incarnations—flared, cropped, as part of a suit, or zippered to a bodice as a jumpsuit—in a series of disturbing shows, such as "The Birds," based on Alfred Hitchcock's spooky thriller, with models covered with greasy tire tracks, and "The Highland Rape," which was inspired by England's violent clearing of the Scottish highlands and featured models in torn garments, running down the catwalk as if escaping their oppressors.

Before long, every designer was dropping waistlines and eliminating front pleats, making flat-front hip-huggers the dominant pant silhouette for two decades now and running. Throughout his early shows, such as "Nihilism," which featured fierce models in faux blood-smeared microminidresses worn without underwear, revealing their naked pubes; "The Hunger," with prim dresses slashed violently across the torso; and "Dante," with gowns and suits printed with war photographer Don McCullin's brutal black and white images of combat, McQueen brought confrontation and raw sex into mainstream fashion and made it not only appealing and desirable but also acceptable. It took a while for the fashion writers to pick up on McQueen—his East End ruffian persona frightened them—but when they did, they understood the magnitude of his talent. As *Guardian* fashion writer Alix Sharkey declared: "Alexander McQueen is unquestionably the most gifted, influential and innovative fashion designer this country has produced since John Galliano."

McQueen and Galliano "were constantly in motion. Constantly creating something, destroying it, turning it around, changing all the time," says the fashion hairdresser Eugene Souleiman, who worked with both men over the years. "They were out there on their own, trailblazing. Their only competition was themselves, getting better and better."

And though their approach to fashion was wildly different—Galliano began as an illustrator, McQueen as a Savile Row tailor—their forthright designs seemed to complement each other, like yin and yang.

As McQueen once explained: "John's a hopeless romantic and I've become a hopeless realist.

"But you need both in the world."

WHEN GALLIANO AND MCQUEEN STARTED, in the mid-1980s and early 1990s respectively, "fashion wasn't a big industry as it is now," remembers Rifat Özbek, who back then was one of London fashion's shining stars. "We wanted to make beautiful things and have fun along the way. There wasn't the pressure to do handbags, shoes, perfumes. It was about the clothes—the shape, the feel, the colors."

In strode Bernard Arnault, the French tycoon who owned Christian Dior as well as LVMH, a group of more than fifty luxury companies including Louis Vuitton, Moët & Chandon, Guerlain, and Givenchy. Arnault was a former real estate developer from the north of France who had maneuvered his way into the luxury industry in the late 1980s with aggressive business strategies that earned him the press nicknames "the Terminator" and "the Wolf in Cashmere."

He had big plans for his group: following the business model created by the Wertheimer family when they hired Karl Lagerfeld in 1982 to modernize Chanel, Arnault wanted to "renovate" his musty old houses and turn them into multibillion-dollar global brands. But he needed dynamic, young designers to make that happen.

He dared to hire Galliano and McQueen to run two of his best-known *maisons de couture*, Givenchy and Christian Dior, while allowing both men to keep working for their namesake companies. It seemed like a smart move for all three at the time: Arnault got Galliano and McQueen's superior talent and magnetic personalities to liven up those near-dead brands, and Galliano and McQueen got Arnault's money and the best seamstresses in the business to execute their ideas.

With their appointments to Dior and Givenchy, Galliano and McQueen joined a new generation of fashion designers—which included Marc Jacobs at Louis Vuitton and Tom Ford at both Gucci and Yves Saint Laurent—who made their international reputations by working for established companies rather than solely for themselves. With their street smarts, their wildly theatrical shows, and their hedonistic audacity, these guns-for-hire made fashion youthful, vibrant, and sexy again.

In return, their corporate benefactors swathed them with big-league perks such as chauffeur-driven sedans 24/7, Concorde or private jet travel, decent expense accounts, and fat paychecks. The designers became as famous as rock stars—complete with groupies and, at times, bodyguards—and the press regularly referred to them as "kings." Galliano so embraced the title he had himself photographed sitting on a throne, wearing a crown.

The ceaseless fashion cycle—which required a fresh crop of designs every four to six months—wasn't new: "I've made a rope to hang myself with," Yves Saint Laurent complained back in the 1970s. "I'd love to be able to do fashion when I want, but I'm a prisoner of my own commercial empire."

What was new was the corporatization and democratization of the industry, and the phenomenal expansion on every front. For more than a century, luxury fashion—the world of handcrafted leather goods and made-to-measure couture—had been made up of small businesses run by their founders or the founders' heirs. They were niche businesses catering to a niche clientele. A handful of companies eventually blossomed into international brands—in the 1950s, Dior was known as the General Motors of fashion—but they all remained privately held and were primarily run by executives who specialized in producing and selling clothes, leather goods, and perfume.

In the late 1980s and throughout the 1990s, many of these companies were acquired—in friendly buyouts or hostile takeovers—by tycoons and financiers such as Bernard Arnault and François Pinault who had little or no experience in fashion but knew how to make serious money in business. The tycoons listed the companies on the international exchanges, which made the businesses more fiscally responsible but also vulnerable to economic cycles and beholden to shareholders who expected continuous increases in profits and dividends.

To spur sales growth, the tycoons decided to target the burgeoning middle market, a sprawling consumer group newly flush from the 1990s economic boom. And to reach these new customers, the tycoons rolled out stores by the score. They hired executives from outside the industry—one Givenchy executive had previously worked for Whirlpool and Nike; a Gucci Group CEO was recruited from Unilever's frozen food and ice cream division—to come up with new marketing strategies. Focus groups and designing by committee replaced intuition and creative integrity. The designers-for-hire were tasked with generating ideas that could be spun off into affordable high-profit items such as perfumes and accessories and drumming up media hype with provocative catwalk shows and splashy red carpet events that would make the brands' names as recognizable and desirable as Nike, Apple, and Coca-Cola. In less than two decades, what had been an informal club of family-owned businesses had grown into a $200-billion-a-year global industry.

The tycoons relished their success and riches: they posed for covers of business magazines, bought grand homes and yachts, and built museums to show off their impressive private art collections. In 2006, Bernard Arnault landed on the *Forbes* list of the world's richest individuals—at number seven, with a net worth of $21.5 billion—and has remained in the top twenty ever since. His employees, including his inner circle of lieutenants, took to referring to him as *Dieu*, or God, as in: "What would God think?"

But from the designers' point of view, luxury fashion under its modern corporate leadership had become "dehumanized," said Nicolas Ghesquière, a French designer who in 2012, after fifteen years on the job, quit his post as creative director of the Pinault-owned brand Balenciaga. "There are people I've worked with who have never . . . actually grasped that [fashion] isn't yogurt or a piece of furniture," he said. "They're transforming it into something much more reproducible and flat."

The compromises the designers were forced to make in the name of commerciality were soul crushing. "You would see McQueen's show, and then you would walk into department stores and see his rack and think, 'What are these clothes? Where did they come from?' Because they had nothing to do with him," says a longtime McQueen supporter and former British *Vogue* editor. "I could see why he was having a hard time reconciling it. The product they kept churning out didn't have anything to do with his work."

The go-go pace was unsustainable and the wreckage it caused astounding: Jacobs wound up in rehab, twice; Tom Ford was pushed out of Gucci—in part because board members felt he was running out of ideas—and suffered a bout of depression; French designer Christophe Decarnin reportedly abandoned his post at Balmain after being hospitalized for a nervous breakdown; Galliano's trusted assistant Steven Robinson died of a cocaine-induced heart attack at thirty-eight; Galliano became a severe alcoholic and prescription drug addict who inevitably imploded; and McQueen killed himself.

The designers were also all substantially oversubscribed, workwise. When Galliano first started back in the mid-1980s, he produced two collections annually. At the time of his termination in 2011, he was overseeing—at the Dior and John Galliano brands combined—an astounding thirty-two collections a year. And as he pointed out, "You're only as good as your last collection. . . . [It's] an enormous pressure."

"Fashion is fast forward, frenetic," *Vogue* contributing editor André Leon Talley told me in the days after Galliano's implosion. "There are too many collections, too many seasons. How can designers keep up?"

ALL CREATIVE BUSINESSES—fashion, music, theater, art, cinema, literature, photography, and others—have at one time or another endured battles between art and commerce. But the conflict of these opposing forces escalated during the era of globalization, particularly in fashion, where the bottom line became more important than the hemline. Innovation gave way to marketing and technology; quality to quantity. As Bernard Arnault's son Antoine Arnault, CEO of LVMH menswear brand Berluti, told me quite frankly, there is no room for art in fashion today. "If designers wanted to be artists, they would paint or sculpt," he said. "But they design clothes or leather goods or products that are made to be sold in large quantity."

"Fashion doesn't want eccentrics anymore," says John McKitterick, the former designer of Red or Dead and one of McQueen's first employers. "It wants bland people. It wants art directors. It wants employees. The companies don't even want a designer really. Everyone is turning out the same old things. You can't tell now who is designing what. It's all the same."

FASHION PEOPLE LIKE TO TALK about having a "moment." It could be when an utterly delicious dress comes down a runway. It could be when a model in exactly the right outfit, hair, and makeup strikes a perfect pose. It could be when a designer reaches the ne plus ultra of his or her career. Usually it's brief, a flash.

In 1996, a reporter asked Galliano: "How would you define fashion?"

"For me," he responded, "it's a fleeting moment."

Looking back on the last thirty years of fashion, as I have for this book, I would say the business experienced a long, fabulous moment—a magical moment—that began with Galliano's St. Martins graduation show in 1984 and came to a definitive two-step close with McQueen's suicide in February 2010 and Galliano's dismissal one year later.

"With Galliano you got a sense of the flamboyant possibilities of fashion—beautifully absurd, he intoxicated us with excess. And there was always a fusion and a dissonance between the present and the past, as if you were witnessing fashion history through the immediacy of the moment," says Claire Wilcox, senior curator, department of furniture, textiles, and fashion for the Victoria and Albert Museum. "With McQueen, there was a sense of danger—you went to his shows and didn't know what to expect—and you felt you were witnessing the future."

So powerful was McQueen's impact not only on fashion but on society that when the Metropolitan Museum of Art's Costume Institute mounted a retrospective of his work a year later, in a show titled "Alexander McQueen: Savage Beauty," it had more than 660,000 visitors in three months, ranking it the eighth most popular show in the history of the Met, and the Costume Institute's most successful fashion exhibition ever.

And the Institute—now known as the Anna Wintour Costume Center after the influential *Vogue* editor—chose to mount "Chinese Whispers: Tales of the East in Art, Film, and Fashion" as its summer blockbuster for 2015, with several of Galliano's Chinoiserie-style designs from throughout his career as well as a sidebar on the Peking opera, featuring his Christian Dior spring–summer 2003 haute couture collection, inspired by the celebrated performer Mei Lanfang.

Galliano and McQueen had longer staying power than most of their peers—their magical moment carried on—simply because they were two of the strongest and the most determined of fashion's many egoists.

During their twenty-year reign, they poured their creative souls into fashion, helping companies turn into not only megaconglomerates but also names that will stand for decades to come. In return they were sacrificed in the name of capitalism.

They were indeed kings, the sort history later hails as The Great.

But kings come and kings go.

And Gods remain.

I

Tangier is a city as ancient as the gods, the point where Europe and Africa meet, where the Atlantic and the Mediterranean kiss. It is a labyrinth of narrow streets "thronged with the phantoms of forgotten ages," Mark Twain wrote in 1869, and "a basin that holds you," Truman Capote observed, where "the days slide by less noticed than foam in a waterfall."

In the early 1960s, a young boy from Gibraltar named John Charles Galliano passed through Tangier by ferry with his Spanish mother, Anita, on his way to and from school in Spain—an exotic commute made necessary by a long-standing diplomatic feud between his father's homeland and his mother's. Galliano delighted in their stopovers in this strange, curious place. "The souks, the markets, woven fabrics, the carpets, the smells, the herbs, the Mediterranean color," he reflected years later. This, he mused, was "where my love of textiles comes from."

Galliano was born on November 28, 1960, the middle child of three; sister Rose Marie was five years older, and Maria Inmaculada, three years younger. His father, John Joseph, was a plumber who "came from a long line of rather serious and practical men, such as tailors and carpenters, all of whom traditionally began to earn a living from the age of fourteen," he said.

His mother, Ana Guillén Rueda—known as Anita—hailed from La Línea de la Concepción, the Spanish town across the border from Gibraltar. The Guillén family had long lived in the rural farming region next to the British territory. "They were renowned for their passion for flamenco and a temperament that was utterly fiery and wild," Galliano said. She grew up under Spanish dictator General Franco's totalitarian regime—a pro-nationalist and ultra-Catholic society where anti-Semitism flourished. After she married and moved to Gibraltar, she maintained close ties to her homeland, and made sure her young son was educated in the same culture as she had been.

The Galliano family resided at 13, Serfaty's Passage, a small lane named for the local Jewish population, where the Esnoga Grande, Gibraltar's principal synagogue, has been located since the early eighteenth century. Gibraltar has had an uneasy relationship with the Jewish community for centuries. Following their expulsion from Spain in 1492, much of the Spanish Jewish diaspora—known as the Sephardim, after the Hebrew word for Spain—passed through Gibraltar on their way to settlements in North Africa. They were given the right to a permanent settlement in 1749 and the population flourished quietly until World War II, when all its residents were evacuated from the two-and-a-half-square-mile territory.

The Gallianos were devout Catholics who attended mass regularly. Galliano was baptized at the Cathedral of St. Mary the Crowned, the baroque seat of the Roman Catholic diocese of Gibraltar, before the same altar where his parents wed. He adored growing up in Gibraltar, mesmerized, he said, by the "bright alleyways, sunshine, blue skies and a main street bustling with sailors."

But John Joseph wanted more for his children: in 1967, he moved the family to South London, so six-year-old Galliano and his sisters could receive a better education. Galliano remembered thinking how brave his mother was "to depart with three young children to a completely foreign country where she did not speak a word of the language." They eventually settled in the middle-class neighborhood of Peckham, where they lived in a tan brick Victorian row house at 128, Underhill Road.

London was in the throes of the Swinging Sixties, when the Beatles, the Rolling Stones, and other British Invasion bands were topping the pop music charts; fashion designer Mary Quant was liberating women with the miniskirt and hot pants; film directors Tony Richardson and Richard Lester were turning out cool, ironic comedies like *The Knack . . . and How to Get It*; and photographers David Bailey, Terence Donovan, and Harry Benson were capturing it all for *Harper's Bazaar*, *Vogue*, and *Life*. "In a decade dominated by youth," *Time* magazine pronounced in its landmark cover story on the city's cultural renaissance, "London has burst into bloom. It swings; it is the scene."

The Galliano family wanted no part of that London. Instead Anita, a striking redhead with an olive complexion and a good figure, did what she could to keep the scents, the colors, and the music of southern Spain alive in cold, gray, rainy England. She cooked traditional Mediterranean meals and encouraged her young son to sing—he had a lovely, pitch-perfect voice—and to dance the flamenco. "On tabletops," he later explained, because "it makes more noise."

"I knew pretty soon that I had inherited this whole Spanish pride thing from my mother—the way you look and the way you walk and dress," he admitted. "I never knew anyone with more outfits than her. She was the sort of woman who would dress herself and her children up to the nines and scrub us all with baby perfume until we sparkled just to go out down the road for a coffee. I can still remember all the heads turning as she walked by."

John Joseph—a fairly short and stocky, fair-skinned, balding man—ran his own plumbing business, and taught his son some of the basics, like how to use a blowtorch. "I would sometimes go out with him on jobs and I was struck by how he always had to have the most perfect finish and the cleanest joint, and how sad it was that all that craftsmanship would never be appreciated," Galliano said. His father's profession—which was very low on the English class scale—eventually became a sore spot for him: "People are always talking about how I am a plumber's son," he complained. "I am my father's son primarily. What he chose to do as a career was his choice and he did it very, very well." Galliano's mother worked as "dinner lady" in a local school cafeteria. He never made mention of it publicly.

Throughout the home there were souvenirs of their pre-London life, such as a Spanish fan and pictures of Gibraltar. Galliano spoke Spanish with his mother and English with his father. "Other boys' houses always seemed to smell of dogs and musty carpets," he said, "whereas ours smelt of garlic and clean laundry and fresh flowers."

As in Gibraltar, the Galliano family attended mass regularly. On some Sundays, Galliano would serve as an altar boy at the 9:30 service and play guitar for the Latin mass. He was particularly captivated by "all the pomp and ceremony, the clouds of incense, the Holy Communion outfits," he recalled—an infatuation that would later surface in his fashion shows. For his first communion, he said, "I arrived in this dazzling white suit, bedecked with rosary beads and gold chains and ribbons with all the saints on." The other boys were in their conservative school uniforms. "I knew I was different," he admitted, "and I ended up being photographed with all the girls. But it didn't bother me. I always liked being with the girls, and I also liked looking cool."

Galliano readily allows that his parents instilled a strong set of values, "like the need for discipline and honesty, the notion that things were only worth doing if you did them to the best of your ability, and the importance of a deep religious faith," he said.

Later in life, however, Galliano disclosed that underneath the appealing veneer, there lurked unspoken darkness and fear. His father "was pretty strict and I was always afraid of him," he said. "If I went a little bit too off—*slap!* It was Dad's upbringing and it was Victorian, and that's the way he was." One time, when he found his father's authority too suffocating, he said, "I flew into a rage [and] took the guitar I had been practicing on and smashed it down the stairs, just missing my father's head. Everyone looked utterly horrified, and . . . I can remember the sick feeling I had, until I could finally go to confession and get rid of all the badness that I felt."

GALLIANO WAS A GOOD STUDENT and passed the entrance exams for Wilson's Grammar School, a state-run boys' middle and high school. Back then, grammar schools were a cross between private school and public school: students wore uniforms and the education was a rigorous, advanced curriculum, but the tuition was state-funded. Students came from all backgrounds, particularly what one Wilson's alum described as "hardcore middle-class families who pushed their kids to do well on the exams." For the less privileged, such as Galliano, attending grammar school was a ticket to a better life.

He quickly discovered "what the whole place was going to be about," he said. "The first-year pupils were bullied by the sixth-formers; they would do it very slyly, like suddenly winding you with a blow to the stomach, which would leave you gasping, on the way to assembly, while the teachers would more or less turn a blind eye." Eventually, he made a small circle of friends and participated in creative school activities, such as theater.

Small and thin with a dark Mediterranean complexion, he had little in common with the other boys in such a heavily Protestant culture—a gypsy-looking imp in the midst of a clan of freckle-faced roughhousers. He wasn't much of an athlete—he only excelled at tennis, a sport he'd keep up in adulthood. He wasn't too masculine either, opting to sass up his conservative uniform with mod shoes and cut his hair in a stylish wedge. "John stood out and was camp," says a former schoolmate. "He definitely got picked on."

"I developed cunning because of it," Galliano later said. "I would work out what earlier trains to get and what carriages to ride in to not be beaten by the boys. Hiding the bruises, hiding the cuts, going home and not being able to talk about it, because if I did I would get another good beating." Instead of complaining he escaped, he said, "into my own world of daydreams."

He also fought back—with words. "Some of the boys, I think, found [Galliano] a bit of a challenge to their gender identity [and] they did make his life difficult," says David Jefferson, Wilson's school chaplain at the time. "He responded with spirit. I thought he was a brave boy, [though] not always particularly wise. . . . It may be that it is sort of his character that when he's provoked, he retaliates."

DURING THE MID-1970S, Britain was seized by social and economic upheaval: in 1975, inflation reached a record 26.9 percent; the following year, the world's once-greatest empire humbly accepted financial aid from the International Monetary Fund. Unemployment was on a steep rise, reaching 1.6 million in 1977.

Out of this upheaval emerged "punk": a pop-culture movement driven by the rejection of all things bourgeois and establishment. Contemporary historians believe that punk was born in the early 1970s downtown Manhattan music scene—in particular rockers Richard Hell and Tom Verlaine, their band Television, and the New York Dolls, most of whom played at the rock club CBGB. But punk hit its stride in Britain, thanks to a relentless, press-savvy English entrepreneur named Malcolm McLaren, who, after a visit to New York, put together and managed a new band in London called the Sex Pistols. Their music was aggressive and, at the time, shocking; twenty minutes into their first concert—at St. Martins School of Art in Soho in November 1975—they were thrown off stage.

London punks were far more raw, primal, and combative than the New York breed. They came from all classes—a social revolution in itself—since everyone, from the East End council-housing kids to the private-school-educated posh set, suffered from the country's economic woes and general malaise. Their look was vulgar and violent: safety pins through cheeks; gothic eye makeup; bleached spiky hair; torn, disheveled clothing often with offensive statements blasted across the front. It was an utter rejection of all that was considered aesthetically beautiful or appealing, of all that was English reserve and gentility.

The epicenter for the movement was SEX, a shop that McLaren and his girlfriend Vivienne Westwood had on King's Road. There they sold Westwood-designed clothes that combined Third Reich style and symbolism with bondage, Dickensian poverty, Surrealism, Dadaism, and downtown New York rock and roll. There were T-shirts with outrageous slogans and rude images; trousers in shiny fabric with zippers on the sides or along the crotch seam; and shirts made of parachute fabric, with straps and rings. "They were powerful, those clothes," said Sex Pistols drummer Paul Cook, who regularly dressed in Westwood's designs. "You had to have balls to wear them. You'd get confronted in the street and you'd have to stand up for yourself."

At Wilson's Grammar School, this all played out gently. Since it was a school with uniforms, the boys couldn't really rebel in their manner of dress or appearance; they followed the movement by reading *Melody Maker* and *New Musical Express*, by listening to the music, by partying on weekends—for them it was more part-time recreation than a life philosophy. As immigrants, the Gallianos cautioned their children not to renounce their new culture and instead taught them to earn respect through hard work. For Galliano, that meant attaining good grades, helping his father on plumbing jobs, and working at a car wash.

In 1979, Margaret Thatcher was elected prime minister after five years of political and economic crises under leftist Labour Party rule. During her three terms in office, the Iron Lady introduced a series of reforms, such as deregulation of the financial business and privatization of state-owned companies, all of which she deemed necessary to modernize Britain and lift it out of its economic morass. Simultaneously, the policies opened doors for social mobility and created opportunities that encouraged entrepreneurialism.

Galliano, the son of a working-class immigrant, was coming of age in this era. In pre-Thatcher Britain, chances are he would have been stuck in his station for the rest of his life, unable to move up the social or economic ladder. Thatcherism and punk changed all that by boosting the economy and breaking down Britain's entrenched class barriers. Galliano wasn't a Thatcherite and he wasn't a punk. But he benefited from both movements: they provided a way out of Peckham, gave him a sense of possibility, and would allow him to fulfill his potential.

AT SIXTEEN, Galliano left Wilson's, having passed several of his O-level—or Ordinary Level—exams, the British standardized tests for the basic level of the General Certificate of Education. He thought of studying foreign languages—he was quite gifted in language, so much so that his mother hoped he "would become a great interpreter in a courtroom somewhere," he said. But a quiet passion for art tugged at him, so he enrolled in the design and textile program at City and East London College in Whitechapel. He still lived at home on Underhill Road and he kept up his church and family commitments, including going to confession regularly until he was eighteen. He stopped, he said, because "whatever I had to confess, I need to confess only to myself."

For pocket money, he took on a part-time job as the "Saturday Boy"—or Saturday sales assistant—for the Howie's concession at Topshop on Oxford Circus. Galliano enjoyed the retail side of fashion, though since it was a Saturday morning job, there were times when his supervisor Heather Lambert had to "tell him off for being late because he had been out clubbing the night before," she recalls now. Once he did arrive, fashion PR maven and Howie's co-owner Lynne Franks reports that "he was incredibly professional and worked very, very hard."

At the end of his second year at the college, his teachers advised him to apply to St. Martins School of Art for its year-long foundation course—a survey of the school's various offerings—so he could, as he put it, "sort out in my mind what I would specialize in."

St. Martins was founded in 1854 by the parochial authorities of the St Martin-in-the-Fields church to add art education to the church school curriculum. In the 1980s, the British government "was giving education grants more freely than today," remembers Hamish Bowles, a British-born American *Vogue* editor who also attended St. Martins then. That allowed for more of a melting pot of students from all social classes. But St. Martins was also quite a competitive school that was reputed for educating rising stars such as restaurateur Michael Chow, designers Paul Smith and Rifat Özbek, the writer A. A. Gill, and Pierce Brosnan, who studied commercial illustration before going into acting. For Galliano to have been accepted to the school was a real achievement.

At last, he had found his sort of people, and he reveled in it. "You could move across the disciplines and keep abreast of what was happening in, say, the film or sculpture department," he said. "Fashion wasn't put into a ghetto. Some of my closest friends were graphic artists. . . . I found it inspiring popping in to see my mates painting or sculpting or whatever. It was a real traditional art school where we could all intermix with style."

As at his previous schools, Galliano was shy and a loner. St. Martins teacher Sheridan Barnett remembers him as "a quiet little mouse, off on his own working quietly, always in the library looking at books." He dressed inconspicuously in jeans, T-shirts, and Doc Martens boots or in vintage 1950s suits, crisp white shirts, and often a tie, and he still wore his thick hair in a gelled wedge—"with a quiff in the front, like Elvis," remembers his classmate John Cahill.

Trailblazing fashion professor Bobby Hillson says that she and her colleagues quickly realized that Galliano was "terribly talented" and he "worked incredibly hard." At first, Galliano studied graphics, filmmaking, fine art, and fashion illustration, and, he said, "I found I really enjoyed drawing." In his third year, he decided to specialize in design, and later confessed, "even then I had my head set on being an illustrator." His drawings were very detailed and precise, often in pen and ink and watercolor, and rather elegant in their style. "Phenomenal," remembers his schoolmate and friend Sara Livermore. "You'd put them on the walls."

One of the design teachers, Hanna Weil—pronounced "vile," which students used to crack was appropriate—gave her class an elaborate fashion project to do in a short time. Just before they were to present their projects, Weil said, "I want to show the portfolio of one of the students to give you the idea of the standard I expect." She opened the dossier and, Hamish Bowles remembers, "it was page after page of the most exquisite drawings you have ever seen. The imagination was so fecund, the concepts were so thoughtfully realized and executed. The penmanship was just exquisite. We were all quaking in our boots." It was Galliano's portfolio. "He was clearly the star," Bowles says, "and rightly so."

For St. Martins students, the most important activity outside of class—and maybe the most important activity of all—was nightclubbing. Students would spend all week designing and pulling together their outfits for club nights.

In early 1980s London, there were several different youth fashion movements happening at the same time: the New Wave, a less scary and political descendent of punk; Buffalo, created and shaped by influential stylist Ray Petri, where kids of mixed race or ethnicities wore classic 1950s looks like leather bomber jackets, pressed dungarees, white T-shirts, tailored overcoats, and porkpie hats with what Petri described as "a hard attitude"; and the New Romantics, a group of young outsiders—often homosexual—who rebelled against society through resplendent costumes, outrageous posing, and excessive partying. All the groups intermixed strikingly at the city's popular dance clubs. "Only the coolest got into the clubs, and your rite of passage was the way you dressed," remembers Mitzi Lorenz, who was a club kid and indie magazine stylist at the time.

The New Romantics' favorite stop was Blitz, a once-a-week nightclub in a wine bar in Covent Garden run by a young impresario named Steve Strange and his friend the deejay Rusty Egan. "It was red-and-white gingham tablecloths and all dark wood—like Joe Allen in New York and Paris, a real saloon," remembers Fiona Dealey, a St. Martins student who became a successful designer. An eccentric kid from the Warren Street squat named George O'Dowd—known at the club as Boy George—worked in the cloakroom. Strange was at the door, judging who was worthy enough to enter—the more outrageous the outfit the better. "You'd have Clark Gable coming through the door, and Marilyn Monroe," says Steve Dagger, a London School of Economics student who went on to manage the pop group Spandau Ballet.

The club regulars became known as Blitz Kids and their style influence was far reaching. The fast fashion retailer Topshop sold knockoffs of the look. Princess Di, Cyndi Lauper, and Madonna in her initial Boy Toy phase were New Romantics. So was "everyone in John Hughes's movies," such as *Pretty in Pink* and *The Breakfast Club*, Dagger says. "The Blitz spirit totally entered the culture."

Blitz gave birth to a flurry of other clubs. There was the Cha-Cha club, which was in the back room of another, bigger club called Heaven. "There was a woman named Scarlett Cannon who sat at the door," Bowles recalls. "She had a hatchet face, like a character from Otto Dix—this very narrow face, with peroxide hair that at one point was cut into the shape of the New York skyline. She had marvelous style and was absolutely terrifying, a young Gorgon. She was infamous for having a hand mirror and she would hold up the mirror to someone she deemed inappropriately dressed for admission and say, 'Would you let yourself into this club?' She was all powerful."

And there was Taboo, a private night on Thursdays at a club called Maximus in Leicester Square cofounded by the Australian-born performance artist Leigh Bowery. If Blitz launched the New Romantic poseur movement, Taboo made it de rigueur. "It was important to have your way-out look," explains Boy George, who by then had developed his own eccentric style of dress, with layers of oversized tunics, Cleopatra eye makeup, bits of rags and ribbons in his hair, and big, exotic hats.

Galliano told me that back in the eighties he was a "club demon" and his favorite was Taboo. He'd hang out there with all the regulars, such as the filmmaker John Maybury, the singer Billy Idol, the aspiring actor Tim Roth, the milliner Stephen Jones, and Boy George, who remembered him as "quite introverted" until he'd "have a drink and become Shirley Bassey." Taboo "was the place to be," Galliano later said. "It became harder and harder to get in, and the harder it was the more people would try, and that made it even more exclusive." He described Taboo as "quite notorious," adding, "there was a lot of drug use."

Cocaine, poppers, pills, and heroin were all part of the scene. Fiona Dealey, who worked the door at Le Beat Route, a club on Friday nights on

Greek Street in Soho, remembers that many of the clubbers "were speed freaks, coming in pie-eyed. Then they went to heroin, because it was cheaper than speed and drink—a gram for forty to fifty pounds." Most kids who did heroin back then smoked it—a practice called "chasing the dragon"—which had the same nauseous effect as shooting it intravenously. "There were a lot of drugs and chemicals," Boy George confirms. "It was very frenzied and people partied hard. It was a real time of excess."

Galliano concurred: "Any kid in the eighties used drugs," he said. "I am glad I did. And I am glad that, somehow, I got through it. It helped me evolve."

THE ONLY THING MISSING in Galliano's life was love. Then he met John Flett.

Three years Galliano's junior, Flett grew up in Crawley, Sussex, not far from Brighton. Of Jewish descent, he was five-foot-ten, slim and striking with an aquiline nose. His father, Bill Owen, was a civil engineer and a compulsive gambler from South London; his mother, June Owen, worked at a local Boots pharmacy. When John was seven, his father was killed in a car crash that some family members have long thought was suspicious and perhaps related to the gambling. At eleven, he was diagnosed with epilepsy. About that time, his mother married for a third time to a kind man named Allan Flett, who was a cashier at a garage; he officially adopted the boy. Despite the more stable household, teenage John Flett had run-ins with the police, and was once arrested for soliciting. He briefly ran away from home to London.

Thankfully, he had a keen interest in fashion, which would eventually take him away from Crawley and give him purpose. When he and his childhood friend John Puddephatt were teens, they worked at a taxi stand in Gatwick airport and to while away the day Flett would study the women who walked by and identify the brands they were wearing. Both young men later attended West Sussex College of Art and Design in nearby Worthing—Flett with a full grant. Afterward, they went to St. Martins. Puddephatt was in Galliano's class; Flett was a year behind them.

What most remember about Flett back then was his innate talent, his prickly nature, and his profound arrogance. "He was very preternaturally self-assured, and had a lot of charisma," says Bowles, who eventually became one of Flett's best friends. "He was one of those people who could take a pair of shears, cut into a piece of fabric and create something without a pattern." Another classmate, Deborah Bulleid, says: "John Flett was very self-possessed—rather scarily so—and always falling out with people."

Soon, Galliano was spending much of his free time at Flett's—a second-floor apartment in a mid-nineteenth-century house on Cromwell Road that he shared with fellow St. Martins student Sara Livermore, a fun blonde from Essex. It was a grungy student flat, furnished with street and junk shop finds, and it was located around the corner from Earl's Court, which was then the center of London's gay community, with leather bars and clubs. This, remembers one friend, suited Flett's "naughtiness."

Flett was wildly funny—"He could make you cry with laughter," Livermore says—and he had great style. "He was the first person I saw wearing a tailored Armani jacket with slashed jeans, classic brogues, a cravat, and a cigarette—always a cigarette," she recalls.

Galliano, on the other hand, "was a romantic, a historian, a charming gentleman who had a great love for his mum and dad—his mum still called him 'Juan Carlos,'" she says. "He was shy and grounded and kind, and he had to find an alter ego. John Flett had a spirit, and he pulled Galliano's spirit out, too." Puddephatt agrees: "Flett was Galliano's driving force. He really pushed Galliano out of his timid self, and pushed his creativity."

To MAKE SOME EXTRA MONEY, Galliano got a part-time job as a dresser at the National Theatre. He was assigned to Dame Judi Dench, Sir Ralph Richardson, and Zoë Wanamaker when they appeared in such National Theatre productions as *The Importance of Being Earnest* and *Inner Voices*. "I would be in the right place at the right time even if it meant lying under a fucking stage for two hours until the actor made his entrance," he said. The actors "taught me very much about bodies and clothes. And how they commanded their space," he explained. "It helped shape my view of drama, of clothing, of costume—the way people dress."

Fellow dresser Ralph Mills was so charmed by Galliano's enthusiasm that he took Galliano on a tour of the costume atelier. Galliano bombarded the designers with questions about the process of making costumes, the material they used, how they distressed the fabrics to make them look old. "He never missed a trick," Mills says. "Always scribbling and sketching in a notebook, with a fag in his mouth." He loved going out in the front of the house "to see how it looked on the stage, with the lights, to see how it was all put together—the theatrical side of it," Mills remembers. "You could see his hunger and love for theater."

In addition to his duties at the National Theatre, Galliano learned tailoring as an intern for Tommy Nutter on Savile Row, a house known for dressing Mick Jagger and Elton John.

When not at school or work, Galliano immersed himself in fashion history books at libraries and pored through the fashion archives at the Victoria and Albert Museum. During his research he discovered a post–French Revolution royalist movement called les Incroyables, which, like the New Romantics centuries later, used frilly clothing to flaunt social and political disregard. The men sported wide pantaloons, giant neckties, oversized earrings, and monocles; and they wore their hair long, to their shoulders or pulled back with a comb. The women, known as les Merveilleuses—or the Marvelous Women—dressed in gowns and tunics inspired by the Greeks and Romans, often made of transparent linen or gauze, which shocked Paris high society.

Les Incroyables informed Galliano's lifestyle as well as his studies. "I was looking like this down-and-out French tramp," he said. "Living it, breathing it. Drawing by candlelight. Producing parchment paper soaked with bits of bread that are then stained with tea. Drawing with a calligraphy pen and sepia ink in this very kind of curious light. I could just imagine these fantastic creatures marching, running across the wet shiny cobblestones of Paris." Galliano's professor told him he should use all of this for his graduation collection. "My tutor Sheridan Barnett and I had decided there should be a return to something gentler after [Giorgio] Armani's mannish styling of the time," he said.

IN PARIS, there was a startling new movement from Japan: a group of avant-garde designers including Yohji Yamamoto, Kansai Yamamoto, Issey Miyake, and Rei Kawakubo of Comme des Garçons, who were blowing apart French bourgeois conventions by showing deconstructed clothes—a first in fashion—in outsized shapes, mostly in black. Hems and seams were unfinished and left to fray; sleeves didn't always match in size or length; shoulders were padded amply and sometimes unevenly; jackets buttoned asymmetrically.

St. Martins assigned its fashion students to go to Paris for the official ready-to-wear shows in the tents at the Cour Carrée of the Louvre, the central courtyard of the museum, and then report back what they saw. And though the students didn't have invitations, they'd manage to sneak in. "We'd go in the back way, backstage where the models were," Livermore says. "We looked fabulous—dressed in an Edwardian twenties feel that we were cutting at school—and we'd walk right in."

They saw collections by Chloé, which Livermore remembers as "a bit cheesy," Jean Paul Gaultier, "which was awesome," and Yohji Yamamoto, which she describes as "seminal. It was harnesses and bare feet and white faces—strong and new. There wasn't anything chichi about it. The clothes were exquisitely cut and challenged balance. It changed our view completely."

Inspiration also came from the new crop of hip British youth culture magazines, such as *Blitz*, *The Face*, and *i-D*, which spotlighted unknown talent in fashion, photography, music, and art, and used models of mixed race—another first in fashion—who were tough looking and unconventionally beautiful and usually photographed in the street.

The most important influence for British fashion students back then, however, was Vivienne Westwood, who had become a full-fledged designer. Mainstream fashion's leaders were Ralph Lauren, who was reinterpreting preppy chic, and Calvin Klein and Giorgio Armani, who were modern minimalists known for their gray-beige palette and feminist power dressing to compete in a man's world. Westwood was anti all of that. She took historical clothes and copied them in cheerful colors such as marigold, vermilion, tangerine, and cornflower blue. The trousers were low-slung, loose-fitting hip-huggers—the opposite of the popular high-waist, form-fitting pants. "I wanted that rakish look of clothes which didn't fit," she explained.

Her shows were just as radical; she staged one called "Pirates," during London Fashion Week fall–winter 1981–82, with models dressed as marauders wearing Walkmen and bopping down the runway through clouds of dry ice as cannons fired in the background. It was a fashion happening like no one had seen before.

In March 1984, Galliano and Flett caught Westwood's fall–winter 1984–85 Clint Eastwood show, which spoofed Sergio Leone's spaghetti westerns. The clothes were a mixed bag of ideas including Day-Glo trenches, a revival of her 1970s punk bondage pants, nylon jackets, and Velcro-closure belts—a long way from the avant-garde intellectualism of Yamamoto and Kawakubo, and even farther away from the bourgeois ladylike clothes that Yves Saint Laurent and Hubert de Givenchy were showing in Paris that week. Canada-born shoe designer Patrick Cox made platform shoes for the collection. Galliano liked them, and Cox, and made a mental note.

GALLIANO BEGAN TO WORK on his graduation collection, designing eighteenth-century-style clothes—frock coats, waistcoats, romantic blouses, pantaloons—that were exaggerated, tattered, and droopy. "I knew I had to put together an extremely wicked show for my last year at St. Martins," he said, "but because I knew it was so wicked, whenever any of the tutors came round—apart from Sheridan Barnett, who was my only ally—I hid all of my designs under the table. I was doing coats that could be worn inside out or upside down, and although I was quite aware of how you tailored correctly, I wanted all my buttons to look like they were hanging off. But how do you explain that to the sewing teacher? I was sure that what I was doing was strong and right, but at the same time I did not want anyone coming up to stop me or to say: 'Well, that is just a load of old rags, John.'"

Those who did see what Galliano was doing were amazed by what he was up to. "Every detail was phenomenal—the illustrations were all burned on the edges so they looked like old scrolls," Livermore says. "I remember him tea-staining shirts in our bath. We never got the tea stain out afterward."

Eventually, Galliano enlisted a handful of fellow students to help him. Deborah Bulleid sewed on mother-of-pearl buttons. Another student named John McKitterick assisted making jersey tubular skirts. "They had three tubes, and we were wrapping them up around our body," McKitterick says. Flett helped Galliano figure out designs and cut and sew the clothes, which, Livermore says, was an "advantage for Galliano, because Flett cut so beautifully." Galliano's teacher Bobby Hillson says she was impressed by how Galliano "had this talent of getting people to do things for him. He had the capacity to inspire people."

While Galliano was excited about the work he was creating, once he completed his studies, he said, "I had my heart set on being an illustrator." In fact, he had already found an illustration job in New York to begin after he graduated. Not everyone thought this was a good idea. Lydia Kemeny, then the head of St. Martins fashion department, and Sheridan Barnett "advised [me] to change my mind, or at least think seriously about what I wanted to do," he said. "His work was so modern and so wonderful and there was nothing else like it. It was a one-off—really genius," Barnett told me. "And you have to support genius."

The degree shows were scheduled for the end of the school term—July 1984—at Jubilee Hall in Covent Garden. Each graduating fashion student staged a short catwalk presentation of a half dozen or so looks, one after the other, three times during the day, in order of preference by the teachers, the best coming last. The fashion staff chose Galliano for the finale.

For the runway models, Galliano enlisted several club kids and fellow students including Paul Frecker, Camilla Nickerson, Lorraine Piggott, and Lizzie Tear, who was dating club deejay Jeremy Healy. A girl named China did their makeup—white faces, somewhat Kabuki-like, as if an homage to the Japanese designers in Paris. Galliano told the models: "Be fierce!" St. Martins students and London club kids had heard about Galliano's collection and turned out en masse. When St. Martins Bobby Hillson arrived for the show with top London retailer Joan Burstein of Browns and Burstein's women's wear fashion director Robert Forrest, they couldn't find a seat; eventually Hillson asked a couple of students in the front row to move for Burstein. The atmosphere was "so exciting," Burstein says. The crowd watched about two dozen student collections, one after another, to whistles and cheers. "Some were pretty bad," she recalls. "Then, all of a sudden, these wonderful pieces came out."

It was Galliano's collection. There were billowing eighteenth-century blouses with frilly neckerchiefs and jodhpurs with knee-high black riding boots; oversized trenches in pale gray and ivory with shoulders down by the elbows; huge kimono-like coats over soft, ample pajamas; deconstructed black frock coats with waistcoats and fitted white shirts with high collars tied up in a poofy bow.

You could see Galliano's love for all things old and historic. But there were also splashes of Boy George and Culture Club—their studied disheveled look—and what the Japanese were doing in Paris: the large proportions, the deconstruction. Galliano finished off the ensembles with kitschy accessories like silk sashes, red-white-and-blue ribbon medallions, watch chains, and do wraps; some students marched down the catwalk waving sabers in the air.

The models vamped it up in a way that was unusual for shows back then—not only playing to the audience but also portraying the role of snooty, rebellious French aristocrats. At first, "there was a quietness," Barnett says. "And then suddenly everyone was screaming and clapping—like a delayed reaction." It was, as fashion folk like to say, a moment.

"The clothes were overblown—just fabulous—and everything was wearable," Burstein remembers. "You just wanted them."

"It was totally different, it was on another planet," Barnett concurs. "It really was."

Directly after the show, several important fashion players went backstage to meet Galliano.

"We'll have it all," Burstein told him. "I would like to give you a window at Browns because I think it's just stunning, just stunning."

It appeared that Galliano's plans of moving to New York following graduation to work as an illustrator would be put on hold.

II

The day after his triumphant debut, Galliano took his collection to Browns. He was too broke to pay for a taxi, so he loaded everything onto a rolling clothes rack and pushed it across town, from St. Martins in Soho to South Molton Street in Mayfair. "Wheeled it through Oxford Street," he recalled. "[Joan's husband and Browns co-owner] Sidney Burstein liked that, I think."

Scoring Browns was a coup for Galliano. Founded by Joan and Sidney Burstein in 1970, it was known as the "Buckingham Palace of fashion." The

Bursteins were the first in Britain to carry major foreign brands such as Calvin Klein, Ralph Lauren, Giorgio Armani, and Donna Karan, and were longtime champions of new talent. The singer Diana Ross saw a Galliano coat in the window and went straight in and bought it. "John's collection was so different. Just marvelous," Joan Burstein says. It sold out "just like that."

Unfortunately, once his graduation collection was sold, that was it: no more Galliano. "He couldn't repeat," Burstein says. "There was no backup." Galliano realized he had started something important and he had to follow up fast, so he got to work, sewing clothes in his parents' home. He relied on friends, such as Flett and Bowles, to help sew buttons on jackets and do whatever else was needed. And whenever there were finished pieces, Browns sold them. "Looking back, it was so amateur," he said. "But, God, it was fun."

SHORTLY AFTER HIS SHOW, a junior fashion editor at *Harpers & Queen* magazine named Amanda Grieve was looking for a baroque collection to photograph with a then-unknown Peruvian fashion photographer named Mario Testino. A friend who worked for Lynne Franks PR suggested Galliano. Grieve rang him up and invited him to tea at the house where she had a room.

He arrived with his portfolio of designs under his arm. "What was meant to be tea ended at two in the morning," she recalled. The next day, she had a freelance project to do: designing the cover for Malcolm McLaren's new album, *Fans*. "And suddenly I realized I couldn't do it without [John]," she said. "So he took over and made this fantastic fan out of torn-up pieces of Japanese newspaper. He went to Soho and got the actual thing, then scribbled in gold and blood red ink." She was enchanted.

Grieve, a regal, slim brunette with ethereal green eyes, had a privileged London upbringing—the utter opposite of Galliano's. She grew up on Regent's Park, the oldest of three children of Alan Grieve, a successful solicitor, and his stylish wife, Anne. As a child, she loved dressing up—she once cut up one of her mother's couture gowns to make a witch costume (her mother approved)—and often played dolls with her neighbor Jasper Conran, the son of interior designer Terence Conran. She read English at Oxford and planned to pursue a doctorate. Her proposed thesis: Henry James and moral bankruptcy.

Instead, she fell in love with a dashing aristocrat: Francis Ormsby-Gore, son of David Ormsby-Gore, fifth Baron Harlech (pronounced "Har-leck"), who was a former member of Parliament and had served as British ambassador to the United States during the Kennedy and Johnson administrations. Grieve divided her time between Ormsby-Gore's farm in Shropshire in the Midlands, his family seat in Wales, and London, where she swirled in the fashion scene. *Harpers & Queen* hired her as an editorial assistant, and she was soon promoted to junior editor.

Four years on she met Galliano. In him, she found a kindred spirit: someone who was as idealistic, perfectionist, romantic, and daydreaming as she was. He relished everything about her: she was well born, well bred, well educated—a true Lady—and her beauty captivated him. She was enchanted by his boundless creativity, relentless drive, and wild imagination. They fell hopelessly for each other in a platonic relationship that was full of true love. "My feelings were: 'I don't want to let him go, I can't possibly exist without him,'" she said, "because he electrified everything that I had felt."

ONE AFTERNOON THAT SUMMER, a handsome, twenty-four-year-old Ghanian-Dane named Johann Brun, who ran a clothing boutique in Copenhagen, was shopping on South Molton Street with his sister Brigitte when she spotted a Galliano coat in the window. They went in so she could try it on, and there was Galliano, meeting with customers. They were so impressed with the collection that Brun asked Galliano if he could place an order for his shop. Galliano graciously declined, explaining that he barely produced enough to keep Browns stocked. When they left the shop, Brigitte told her brother, "You should go into business with him."

A few weeks later, Brun met with Galliano at a pub near the Baker Street tube station to discuss what they could do together. "We were clearly on the same wavelength," Galliano later said. Brun proposed to bankroll Galliano—it would be a modest operation, with local production. Galliano was thrilled and immediately accepted. "That was our start," Brun says. "We didn't have a contract. We shook hands and we were in business." The company was officially called John Galliano/Brun Ltd. but the label would read *John Galliano*. They set up shop in an old warehouse on Earl Street in East London: a two thousand square foot, first-floor studio that they shared with fashion photographer Tom Mannion.

Galliano's first goal was to get a collection together—spring–summer 1985—to present during the upcoming London Fashion Week in October. He called Brun in Copenhagen and said that he needed 3,000 pounds—$3,900 at the time—to produce clothes and put on a presentation at the fashion week trade show staged at Olympia, London's imposing Victorian exhibition hall. Brun agreed, and wired the money to Galliano's bank account. As for his degree show, Galliano had a theme and title for the collection: "Afghanistan Repudiates Western Ideals." His inspiration was a 1920s cartoon from *Punch* magazine that he found of an Afghan in traditional dress poised to stomp on a British bowler hat. It was a commentary on the Afghan king Amanullah Khan, who ruled from 1919 to 1929 and, after visiting London, encouraged his subjects to dress Western-style as part of his social modernization movement. Conservative opposition to his reforms eventually led to his abdication.

Galliano then called Grieve.

"Would you, could you, will you please style my first show?"

"Yes!" she cried.

Grieve quit her job at *Harpers & Queen*, which allowed St. Martins student Hamish Bowles—who was an intern—to take it over. Grieve didn't have a specific job per se, nor much of a salary; she simply wanted to be there, next to Galliano, helping him. They'd talk every day and see each other when they could.

With his new assistant, Michael Collins, who had worked for Westwood, Galliano scrambled to make the clothes in time—hand-dyeing and bleaching fabrics in the studio bathroom, cutting everything himself, and fitting the clothes on his body. "I'm a perfect size ten," he'd boast—size ten then being the standard British size for women's fashion. He hired a woman part time to break old eyeglasses in half and tape them back together—the idea being that they were a symbol of people's resistance to change. It was, he admitted, "all very ad hoc."

Galliano worked through the night leading up to the presentation. The next morning he, Grieve, and Brun arrived at Olympia to stage the twenty-piece collection on mannequins at their stand, which was next to the fire exit. There were gauzy Eastern-like robes in saffron, curry, and a deep red moiré and georgette mixed with classic pinstripe tailoring, in an East-meets-West silhouette. "I like the idea of the tension and romance of wearing two different cultures," he explained. Grieve accessorized—or "styled"—the outfits with the taped eyeglasses and belts strung with pots and pans and wooden spoons.

"My clothes are a reaction against all the hard Milanese androgyny we've seen in the last year, against simple shapes by Armani and other designers," Galliano told *The New York Times*. "[They are also] a reaction against the way we were taught in school: that colors have to be put together a certain way. That you cut fabric a certain way. That you can't do this or that. I want to mix things up, fabrics, masculine and feminine. It's been drummed into us that certain things are right and certain things are wrong. It's usually the wrong things that are more fun."

Excited by what they had heard about Galliano all summer, editors and retailers descended on Galliano's stand in a flurry. "[New York retailer] Susanne Bartsch had said to me, 'Have you heard of John Galliano? He just did the greatest collection at St. Martins,'" Bloomingdale's then–associate fashion director Roberta Wagner recalls. "So I sought him out." Wagner was overwhelmed by what she saw on the mannequins. "Sweaters in the most amazingly sophisticated colors. Like a sandy brown with a mauve-y lavender. And the construction of the garments was absolutely impeccable."

Despite Galliano's unkempt appearance—he obviously hadn't slept or bathed in days, his fingernails were grimy from dye, and, one visitor remembers, "He smelled. It was horrible. You could smell it throughout Olympia"—retailers were furiously negotiating with him to carry his clothes. "I can't articulate the frenzy surrounding him at the Olympia," one retailer recalls. "Everybody was in a lather, offering him things that were just incredible to have the collection at their store." Among those who placed orders were Browns; Bazaar, which was also on South Molton Street; Alan Bilzerian in Boston and Chicago; Susanne Bartsch; and Bloomingdale's, which ordered pieces for the New York flagship.

Respected British fashion writer Colin McDowell reflected on what Galliano was trying to achieve, later writing that the collection not only triggered "fundamental re-thinking of the nature of dress" but also contained "layers of social and sartorial subversion." He applauded Galliano for creating something of such "remarkable originality and maturity of vision" a mere four months out of school.

———

FOLLOWING THE PRESENTATION, Galliano told Brun, "We need a PR"—a public relations person who would organize interviews and send clothes out to fashion shoots. Brun scratched his head. "I had never heard of a PR to tell you the truth," he says now. "I thought you just got press because you were good. John said, 'No, no. We have to organize this.'"

They hired Jean Bennett, a public relations leader in London fashion, and with her help, Galliano's clothes appeared in several fashion magazines, including British *Vogue*. Retail prices were about 100 pounds ($130) for a pair of trousers, 400 pounds ($520) for an unlined cotton coat, which Brun points out "was a huge amount of money" at the time. Nevertheless, they sold surprisingly well. The sales turnover was about 45,000 pounds ($66,150) and the company made a profit—almost unheard of for a first season in fashion.

Galliano wanted more than good sales. He wanted prestige. He was pleased to sell to Bloomingdale's, which was one of the world's most influential stores at the time. But it wasn't enough. Despite his quiet, shy demeanor, Galliano was an extremely ambitious young man, and he was willing to take risks to achieve his goals. His most immediate was to sell his clothes at the esteemed New York retailer Bergdorf Goodman, even if that meant alienating Bloomingdale's.

Bergdorf's was in the midst of a dazzling renaissance. Founded in 1901, and located in its stately edifice on the corner of Fifty-seventh Street and Fifth Avenue since 1928, it had for most of its history been synonymous with upscale luxury shopping. But in the mid-1970s, Bergdorf's had fallen behind the times. In response, the store's new head, Ira Neimark, and new fashion director, Dawn Mello, launched a $15 million renovation that included putting down plush carpeting, installing escalators, adding a new entrance on Fifth Avenue and bringing in sophisticated fashion. Neimark and Mello targeted unknown, rising companies in Italy, Paris, and London, such as Fendi and Jean Paul Gaultier—brands that wanted a retail outlet in New York but were too new or small to be picked up by major department stores. Bergdorf's made this its mission. "It took years to develop and get going," Mello says. But once it did, Bergdorf's became a real competitor with Bloomingdale's.

"Behind the scenes on a retail level, there was a heated battle going on between Bergdorf's and Bloomingdale's," explains Andrew Basile, who worked as fashion director for both during his retail career. "Bloomingdale's was known for being trendy and discovering new talent, but Bergdorf's had discovered its voice and pulled itself out of the gray-haired ladies demographic and become more on trend. They were willing to throw big money [to create in-store] shops and corners and spaces, and they had a great location."

Galliano became so obsessed with selling to Bergdorf's that he didn't deliver that first season's order to Bloomingdale's. He lost Bloomingdale's but the gamble paid off: he got Bergdorf's.

TO KEEP UP WITH the increased workload, Galliano brought on several more assistants, including Deborah Bulleid, an intern from St. Martins who was a friend of Flett's; Gail Downey, a former model who specialized in knitwear; Bill Gaytten, a Manchester-born pattern cutter who had studied architecture before moving into fashion; and Paul Frecker, another St. Martins pal who knew Flett from Brighton.

Most important, Galliano found a muse: Sibylle de Saint Phalle, a Paris-raised French aristocrat and London It Girl who was the niece of French pop art sculptor Niki de Saint Phalle. Sibylle grew up in the posh sixteenth arrondissement, attended all the right schools, and as a teen became a regular at the famed Le Palace nightclub—Paris's version of Studio 54. Once she finished her studies, she ran off to London, where she modeled, worked for the milliner Stephen Jones, and went to nightclubs a lot. Galliano met her at one and he fell for her on the spot. She was fair and petite with a moon face, rosebud lips, and the long white blond hair of a fairy princess. If Grieve was Galliano's creative soul mate, Saint Phalle embodied all that he and Grieve dreamed up together.

Saint Phalle's role at the Galliano studio was a bit blurry. As one assistant explained, "She'd come around and exist"—often in a post-nightclub haze. She could be "slightly patronizing," the assistant says, but it was easy to understand why Galliano adored her: "She was like a cute little doll you could dress up. And John did."

Though there were more hands to help, Galliano's company was still a fledgling operation. "One gas burner. Bacon sandwiches," Gaytten recalls. "It was all on a shoestring." The team was paid a pittance, or nothing. Everyone was young, fun, idealistic, optimistic, and did whatever it took to make it work—from tea-staining fabric to packing up orders. "This was pre-computers and I had a friend who worked in an office nearby who typed up the invoices for us, and then we'd photocopy them and pack the boxes and send them to Bergdorf's," Bulleid remembers. "We'd have to fill in the customs declarations—stuff we didn't learn at St. Martins—while the shipping guy waited downstairs."

Brun, whom Galliano affectionately referred to as "Yo-Yo," short for Johann (pronounced "Yo-hahn"), was hands-off as a backer; he traveled from Copenhagen to London once every four to six weeks to see what was going on. Otherwise, he received updates from Galliano by phone. The relationship worked for Galliano: he had financial stability with Brun's backing, yet he also had the freedom to run the company as he wished.

JAZZED BY HIS IMMEDIATE SUCCESS, Galliano decided to go bigger and bolder: For the fall–winter 1985–86 collection, he wanted to put on a full-fledged fashion show during London Fashion Week in mid-March 1985. Like his two previous collections, it had a title: "The Ludic Game," an allusion to the public games of ancient Rome, which were known as *ludi*. The show's narrative was based on Angela Carter's 1984 book, *Nights at the Circus*, about a nineteenth-century winged aerialist named Sophie Fevvers, mixed with Celtic, pre-Raphaelite, and Victorian references. "A Brueghel painting cavorts around the maypole of a village green in Dorset" was how the press handout described it.

For the silhouette, Galliano continued down the path he began at St. Martins, making deconstructed clothes that could be worn upside down or interchangeably as skirts or jackets. "Imagine a roomful of kids and a box of clothes," he said. "Put a shoe on your head. It's a wonderful, naïve approach to dressing."

Ideas came from everywhere. One night, while out with Brun at the club Heaven, he saw Paul Frecker wearing a 1930s double-breasted evening jacket with a cool back that Frecker had reworked into a pleated, 1880s-style bustle. Galliano was so dazzled by it, he turned to Brun and declared: "That's my new shape."

He also reinterpreted a theme that had been introduced by French designer Jean Paul Gaultier a year earlier: skirts for men. But it wasn't simply any old skirt. Galliano saw Frecker wearing a pair of Yohji Yamamoto pants that were a skirt-pants hybrid. "He got me to put it on, putting my legs through the middle instead of the trouser part, and had me walk back and forth, and from that came the trousers of 'The Ludic Game,'" Frecker says. "They were made of green and black stripe fabric, dark and tight, and with big windowpane checks in white that were slightly fleecy. The green and black stripes were supposed to evoke plowed fields as seen from above and the windowpane check with white fluff was meant to be sheep's wool on barbed wire. They were inspired by countrywomen who throw a coat on over their pajamas to drive their kids to school. It was all crazy creative. Just fabulous."

The day before the show, the makeup artist William Casey worked out the models' look: Japanese-like with shadowing in deep green—"green like a Tanqueray gin bottle," he says—on snow-white faces and kohl eyes.

For the soundtrack, a friend of Casey's told Galliano about an Italian horror movie she had recently seen. "You have to use the music from that for the opening sequence," she said. "You have to!" He listened and agreed. Casey, the son of an Irish couple, suggested some Irish rebel songs too. Neil Mersh, a photographer's assistant from the studio upstairs, mixed the soundtrack with a few additions of his own. Galliano loved it. "John wasn't as dictatorial as people think," Casey says. "Everybody put out ideas, and he was quite willing to listen, and say, 'All right, let's give it a go.' He would just do it."

The show was held on Monday, March 15, at 6:30 P.M. in Pillar Hall at Olympia, and there was such a demand for invitations that Galliano and Brun decided to stage it twice. Galliano wanted to change the way clothes were shown—to put on an artfully acted production, like what Vivienne Westwood had done with "Pirates." He told the models to think of themselves as storybook characters and to dance a jig down the runway. For a last-minute flourish, he decorated their hair with ivy that Bulleid had pulled off trees in a nearby park.

There were more than one hundred outfits and it went on for a good half an hour—the crowd, which included Vivienne Westwood, cheering the entire time. The look was sort of Yohji Yamamoto–meets-hobo, with oversized clothes layered and askew. For the finale, there was an accordion player dressed like Charlie Chaplin's Little Tramp and a frizzy blond model flinging real mackerels into the audience. One came close to hitting Westwood. Another landed in Joan Burstein's lap.

The reviews were uneven. Richard Buckley of the menswear trade paper *Daily News Record* declared Galliano "London's hottest fashion ticket" and the "stylistic successor to Vivienne Westwood," adding, "Galliano aggressively pushes the limits of shape and construction, actively questions the social implications of fashion and bends genders into complicated knots."

But Bill Cunningham, who covered the shows for *Details*, then a hip downtown Manhattan monthly, wrote: "Galliano never convinced us that he was designing clothes for any other purpose than youthful eccentric display [and] the echoes of the Westwood vocabulary embittered her followers and disappointed those who hoped to discover in the Galliano collection a new London direction. What they discovered was an extraordinary imagination creating costumes that might be better placed on the stage of the ballet or theater."

Cunningham asked Westwood for her reaction.

"I never thought of my ideas being carried this far," she responded.

Despite the negative reviews, the sales stand at Olympia "was a mob," Gail Downey recalls. She and Galliano simultaneously modeled the clothes and took orders. Brun says the company eventually sold 66,000 pounds, or roughly $70,000 worth, wholesale, thereby turning a profit.

Galliano was utterly overwhelmed by the response. "I didn't know if I was teetering on the brink of huge success or a nervous breakdown," he said. "There was quite a high chance that I'd crash and burn."

WHEN BRUN WAS IN TOWN, he would spend time at the studio, meeting with retailers and helping with shipping and deliveries. "John was very normal," he says. "He would stay until eleven at night. And after everyone left, we'd sit there in the studio and drink Coca-Cola and he'd sweep up."

What Brun and others didn't realize was how compartmentalized Galliano kept his life. Brun, for example, didn't learn that Flett was Galliano's boyfriend until a mutual friend mentioned it. "I thought they were just best friends," he recalls.

And then there were Galliano's partying ways—about which Brun had barely a clue. "I don't drink [alcohol], so he didn't drink around me. I don't do drugs, and he wouldn't do drugs, at least not in front of me," Brun says. "He

would talk about it from time to time—'Oh, we did this and this and this'—
and I said, 'I bet you make this up to shock me.'"

What Brun did notice was a manic-depressive-like pattern in Galliano's
day-to-day life. "John would run on highs and lows," he says. "After every
show he would crash for a minimum three days. It was so sad. Physically and
emotionally drained, almost like a death. Crumpled up in the studio. He'd
lock the door and wouldn't come out."

The company's PR rep Jean Bennett told him one day, "Have you heard
the rumor that John is on drugs?"

"No, I didn't know," Brun responded.

"I just thought you should know," she said.

"I didn't take what Jean said seriously," Brun says now. "Because John
worked so hard. If someone is working until eleven or twelve every night, you
don't think something's wrong. I thought, 'People are making up nasty stories' and because he is so sensitive, I didn't want to upset him so I didn't bring
it up."

THAT SUMMER, John Flett concluded his studies with a degree collection of
loose-fitting, hobo-chic clothes in muddy colors that was so lauded it was
picked up by several retailers, including Bloomingdale's. He decided that he
too wanted to have his own label and through Paul Frecker he found a backer:
Miles Gill, a Bristol-based businessman who owned a furniture company
called Elephant, with five shops around England.

Soon Gill was sucked into the Galliano-Flett vortex and he was appalled
by their behavior—as if they were "demigods, not to be questioned," an observer recalls.

One night, at a fancy-dress dinner party to celebrate Frecker's birthday,
several guests including Flett were smoking heroin at the table and taking
turns to go to the loo to vomit.

They were at their worst, however, when they'd critique people they saw.
"Though Flett and Galliano weren't terribly good-looking, they regarded
themselves as the paradigm of beauty and everyone else as being ugly," a
friend of theirs says. "'Ugly' was really the worst put-down they could use and
they used it regularly against a lot of people."

———

FOR HIS NEXT COLLECTION—spring–summer 1986, to be presented during London Fashion Week in mid-October 1985—Galliano chose, once again, to riff on post-Revolution France. "I am quite obsessed with the eighteenth century," he admitted. "I have some kind of an affinity for that century. . . . The different quirks of fashion, how people wore clothes and why they wore them that way." He decided to call the collection "Fallen Angels."

The women's wear was ethereal and romantic: sheer and draped, in soft colors, with Empire waists. The menswear was tailored and deconstructed and featured sleeves that were cut in big circles and buttoned closed around the arm—an interesting new design technique that many of Galliano's friends and staff attribute to Flett. Since Galliano and Flett lived together, there was an obvious cross-pollination between the two creatively.

Galliano's genius was that he could take raw ideas from eighteenth-century France, Westwood, Kawakubo, Yamamoto, and Flett, and, as with the French modern artist Marcel Duchamp's "readymades," he could fiddle with them—by using a new cut, a new color, an interesting twist or turn—and make them his own. The designs might not always have been new, or practical, or even wearable, but they were, for the most part, decidedly Galliano.

It was Amanda Grieve, however, who made Galliano's work sing. It might have been a historic reference that she'd brought to his attention, or a story that they'd make up together, or something from a book she'd read or a film she'd seen. Like Flett before her, she would push Galliano's creativity further, open wide his mind. "John would say, 'I've got this idea for little pinstripe suits,' and I'd say, 'Well, they're little honcho girls and they're there in the bar, and they've rubbed up against the brick of the wall—and the brickwork made a mark at the back of their jacket,'" she once explained. "That's how we worked together."

"Galliano was very strong about his vision," says jewelry designer Vicki Sarge, who worked with Galliano in the 1980s and 1990s. "But Amanda was really genius too, and they both shared the same fantasy, a sort of fairy tale, and they created that fairy tale together."

As "Fallen Angels" started to take form, Galliano reached out to Patrick Cox for shoes. Cox designed a round-toed boot with a square extended sole and white mattress ticking hanging out the back like that of a hobo, and a round-toed shoe with the big toe cut out and a piece cut out of the back.

As usual, Galliano and his team stayed up until all hours finishing the collection. But when it was time for the show, in a tent on the lawn of the Duke of York's Barracks on King's Road, he was focused and oversaw everything. Casey applied white clay on the models' faces and their hair, which he slicked back to create the shaved-head look of the Elizabethan era—a Grieve idea. Galliano said he wanted the models to bear his name on their foreheads—as if they had been branded—so Casey had a rubber stamp made of the Galliano logo and stamped it on their brows in water-soluble ink.

Galliano decided minutes before the show that the shoes were too clean and instructed the models to go outside to the running track in the rain and drag the shoes through the mud. When Cox confronted Galliano about it, Galliano shrugged: "Don't worry," he told Cox. "They are worth more money now because it's designer mud, darling." Boy George later recalled the scene and said, "Patrick was in tears."

Galliano had Saint Phalle open the show looking like a pre-Raphaelite Ophelia, dressed in a putty-colored loose-fitting gown hitched up at the hem and an oversized black bolero worn askew, walking hand-in-hand with a male model in a long black military-style coat, to Henry Purcell's march *Lillibullero*. The models were a real mix—black, Asian, and Caucasian; short and tall; men and women—dressed in baggy coats, waistcoats, ample white blouses with billowing sleeves, gray jersey jumpsuits reminiscent of old-fashioned men's underwear, and sexy, tight ivory knit dresses. For the finale, Galliano doused the models with water to make the draped muslin gowns cling to their naked bodies seductively; the ink on their foreheads ran down their faces. Galliano had come up with the idea from reading about muslin disease, an early-nineteenth-century epidemic triggered by French women's wearing sheer, wet dresses to look like Greek goddesses and contracting pneumonia. "People thought [dousing the sheer dresses] was meant to be attention-grabbing," Galliano later said. "I thought it was very beautiful."

The critics hated it. Suzy Menkes of *The Times* of London declared that it "looked like the cast of *Les Misérables* photographed by Bruce Weber." *The New York Times*'s Bernadine Morris jabbed: "This presentation looks as tired as the handful of punks of King's Road with their spiky hairdos and studded leather clothes." *The Guardian*'s Sarah Mower called it "a ghostly tribe of mentally disturbed eighteenth-century refugees."

Most troubling, however, were charges that Galliano had plagiarized Vivienne Westwood—most notably by *Details*' Bill Cunningham.

"John cried for days," Cox said. "But it was true."

"There were times Galliano sent things down the runway and I'd cringe: 'Oh my God, it was such a direct copy,'" Paul Frecker remembers. "And John would say he was 'inspired' by Westwood, that it was an 'homage' to Westwood. 'No, John, that's called copying.' He admired her enormously but he needed to find his voice and his confidence, and he let other people influence him too much."

RETAILERS WERE HESITANT to place large orders, because, as Jim Griebenow, then-vice president and fashion merchandising director for Marshall Field's in Chicago, explained, "When fashion becomes advanced contemporary (such as Galliano) at designer prices, it's a tough sell." Those who did order reported to Brun that they were experiencing "fit problems"—meaning the clothes didn't fit customers' bodies and either needed alterations or didn't sell. Galliano was still fitting clothes on his own body; he wasn't terribly keen on the shape of a woman's body—at least a curvaceous woman's body. Around that time, a British fashion writer named Louisa Young sat next to Galliano at a dinner. "We got talking about tits, as you do," she recalled. "'You don't like them much, do you?' I suggested. He looked a little sheepish, and then whispered: 'No. They spoil the line.'"

"Retailers were telling us: 'You have to address this,'" Brun says.

He brought the issue up with Galliano, and Galliano turned dark and argumentative. "If we get the press, we can sort out these issues, and the orders will follow," Galliano insisted.

"But," Brun says, "the orders didn't follow because the clothes didn't fit. I heard from retailers who said, 'I bought several pieces and only twenty percent sold at full price and the rest went on sale because they didn't fit.'"

Galliano was spending recklessly as well, and Brun's budgets were getting blown to bits. "John was not a mathematician. He didn't know anything about costing," Brun says. "He would give an estimate of, say, three thousand pounds and it would turn out to be eight thousand. And then you'd see a roll of fabric, and if it was the wrong roll, it would be kept, instead of sent back, and we'd have to pay for it. He'd eventually use it—he used everything—but still, we'd have to pay for it when we didn't budget it." As Brun tightened budgets and shot down Galliano's expensive ideas, Galliano and his staff began to consider him the enemy.

To complicate matters, Galliano was getting fussy with editors. "One time an American fashion editor wanted to put a Galliano outfit in the magazine, and she had one idea, and John had another," Brun says. "And she said, 'That might be your version, but this is America and the girl is going to look beautiful and sexy because we're trying to sell the collection.' And then she called back and said, 'I can't give you the cover because I checked with Bergdorf's and you don't have a high enough sell-through.' That's the first time we realized there is a link—the way [editors and retailers] would talk together. And John got very upset and angry about that—*very* upset and angry." Brun was beside himself: he saw sales, and profits, slipping away.

"I don't want to be commercial now," Galliano told Brun. "I can be commercial twenty years from now."

GALLIANO WASN'T SIMPLY out of touch with how business worked. He was starting to live in a self-created bubble—distancing himself from the hoi polloi—in part because of his shyness, in part because of his passionate, blinding focus on his work, and in part because of an increasing sense of self-entitlement. He had started to believe the hype. Brun hosted a Christmas party for the company at a bar in Long Acre that was a bit spartan because of budget constraints. Galliano was so bored that he left for an hour and a half and went to a gay club around the corner—evidence to at least one assistant of how dismissive Galliano could be toward Brun as well as his team. "John didn't want to party with the people he worked with," the assistant said. "We were just staff."

After all those years of commuting to school on buses and trains, Galliano had grown to loathe public transportation, and though he was scraping for money, he could almost always find a way to pay for a cab. "One day he had to go for a meeting in Covent Garden, which was five stops on the tube from Liverpool Street station," Casey remembers. "[Seeing Galliano's reluctance,] I said, 'It's all right, John, I'll go with you.' When we got in the station, John stood up against the wall, hoping no one would notice him. He was shocked that there were people wearing trainers [sneakers].

"'God, everyone wears trainers!'

"'Yes, John, people wear them when they walk around during the day,' I told him. This was a revelation to him because he never went out during the day. He only went out to clubs, to home, and to work. There was his inner sanctum, and then there were the other people."

Galliano worked through the holidays—he spent Christmas Day at the studio. Once the team was back to work in the New Year, he focused intently on his next collection, the fall–winter 1986–87 season, to be presented in March 1986. It was called "Forgotten Innocents" and, as with "Fallen Angels" the season before, women were depicted as fragile victims of society's whims, in particular, man's twisted, contrived image of perfection. The idea, Galliano said, was to evoke feral children, like those in *Lord of the Flies*, playing dress-up in the attic. The use of children as a central theme was appropriate given that Grieve was in her second trimester of pregnancy with her first child.

While working on the collection, Galliano sat for an interview with *The Guardian*'s fashion writer Sarah Mower, one of the industry's most powerful writers. British journalists often interject first-person opinions into features—and it is not always kind. This practice is particularly prevalant in fashion coverage. Forever in search of the new, fashion writers will embrace and champion a rising talent in hopes that they have found—or created—a new king. But then, a few seasons later—out of disappointment, frustration, or enmity—they will turn on the designer and take him or her down publicly.

Now it was Galliano's turn to be hazed by the press. In her report, Mower echoed the press's hard turn against him. "He is a volatile mix of the best and some of the worst tendencies in British fashion," she wrote. "His shows are confrontational fantasies on historical themes, deliberately freakish, self-consciously theatrical. . . . Some [believe], at twenty-five, he has already had too much publicity and is suffering from it. . . . [He gets] defensive when chided about his outlandish presentation and often confounding garments."

To show what she meant, Mower explained that it took half an hour to figure out how to put one of his "octopoid" limbed outfits on a model for the accompanying fashion shoot. "[Galliano] says he is a designer of clothes, not fashion," she continued. "It smacks, I am afraid, of that arty, Dada-ist stage of postgraduate development best explored behind closed doors rather than trumpeted abroad as a major, mold-breaking insight. It will pass, and Galliano will find out that if he is not a fashion designer, he is nothing."

THOUGH THE CRITICISM STUNG, Galliano did his best to remain focused on his work. To convey the youthful spirit of "Forgotten Innocents," he cast several teenage models, some as young as fourteen. For the press handout, he had photographer Robert Erdmann shoot a fresh-faced nineteen-year-old aspiring actress named Helena Bonham Carter, her hair wet and stringy, her face as sweet as a cherub's. Like Grieve, Bonham Carter was a British blue blood with a smart upper-class accent—in other words, everything that Galliano idolized and adored.

Galliano and Grieve styled the looks joyfully, putting small naïf crowns that Grieve made with tarot cards and other found objects on the models' long, wavy pre-Raphaelite-like hair. The clothes were wispy Empire-waist frocks, like Victorian nightgowns, mostly in white and brown, wrapped around the body in disheveled ways, as if they were all too big and belted to fit. The makeup was light and simple, with rosebud lips, "to make the models look like children, like china dolls," Casey says.

"It was very erotic," Galliano admitted. "But there was a point." Namely, he said, "breaking down preconceived ideas of how things could be worn." *Details'* Bill Cunningham found genius elements amid the madness. "If John Galliano had shown only his balloon-shaped coats it would have been enough to secure his position in the design hierarchy of London," he wrote. "Etched into the memory was style number 05-603 of grey fleece. Built with a balloon shaping Charles James would have admired, it broke at the center back with a cross-grain swooping fishtail . . . I later saw the coat being worn in Paris by one of Galliano's models. It looked even better off the runway."

Brun was still tearing his hair out about fit problems. He was so concerned that he went to New York and met with buyers. "Show me the sales figures," he told them. "There must be an error." But there wasn't. "They explained to me that sixty, seventy percent of the collection wasn't selling," Brun recalls. "I saw that knitwear was selling, so I said, 'Order knitwear.' They did. For ["Forgotten Innocents"], that's all they ordered. And John got so angry. But I said, 'You know what, John? Otherwise they wouldn't have ordered a thing.'" Galliano believed that all the glossy magazine coverage was going to pull them out of the financial abyss. "I understood John's point of view," Brun says. "But I also got the buyer. It's business. And John didn't know about business."

It became apparent to Brun that the only solution was to shut down the company. He called an attorney he knew who advised him to hold on to everything—the patterns, the samples, the unused bolts of fabrics, sewing machines—because they were the company's assets and would be needed to pay off creditors in liquidation. Brun went to the studio to look at the archives and realized that they had already been somewhat plundered. He called a locksmith, had the locks changed, and went home.

In June 1986, they made a joint announcement in the *Daily News Record* declaring the dissolution of their partnership. Galliano's spokeswoman said that the split was by mutual agreement, adding, "The arrangement did not suit either of them." Galliano reportedly informed some of the company's customers that nothing from "Forgotten Innocents" would be delivered in the fall. "We wanted to do it as quickly as possible so retailers would not be inconvenienced," the spokesman said.

Galliano went to the studio and found the locks had been changed. He wanted what he felt were *his* archives, so he talked assistants Gail Downey and Nick Michaels into climbing along onto the eighteen-inch-wide ledge and entering the studio through an unlocked window to take as much as they could.

Later, at night, after partying at Taboo, Galliano and a crew of pals that included Flett and Frecker went back, shimmied along the ledge to the open window again, and finished cleaning out the place. "We ran up and down the ledge, so high up, off our faces, and got bags and bags of clothes out," Frecker says. "John said, 'It's my collection.' He believed, 'I designed it, therefore it belongs to me.' He had no idea how a company works"—that the clothes were actually a business asset.

Galliano was later asked by a friend if there was anything he wished he'd learned at St. Martins that would have helped him in his career up to that point. "I wish I'd been more equipped on the business side of things," he answered. "I was thrown in the deep end and had to learn fast."

III

Galliano was so broke he was sleeping on the floor of Saint Phalle's London flat. But he didn't let that squash his spirit. He was determined to find a new backer and get his business running again. He was briefly in talks with the Giorgio Armani company in Milan and had even sewed up some sample garments at his friend Sara Livermore's studio to show the Armani team, but the deal never came together. Then he heard that a Danish-born, British-raised oilman named Peder Bertelsen, who had a fashion company called Aguecheek—named for a character in Shakespeare's

Twelfth Night—was actively looking for young British designers to finance. Galliano understood the potential: "[Bertelsen] was the only man I knew who had money," he said.

He drew a collection and went to see Bertelsen to present the sketches as well as a business plan. "I wanted a big studio and machinists," Galliano said, referring to employees who work on machines. "I wanted to get the best finish I could. I wanted to work with people who understood my things, to deliver on time. I wanted to do it properly."

As Bertelsen reviewed Galliano's sketches he asked himself, "Would my wife wear them? No. Would my friend's wife wear them? No."

Bertelsen told Galliano: "We can't see its commercial value. Can you draw something commercial?"

A few days later, Galliano came back with a new set of sketches.

"I didn't alter what I'd designed," Galliano later admitted. "I drew differently. I drew really straight women, with bobs, with earrings . . . for him. They were the sort of drawings you'd do for your bank manager."

Bertelsen and his staff liked them, and decided to draft an agreement. Galliano was pleased with it: "I keep my own identity and we really have to look after our own affairs," Galliano said. "But . . . there are certain ways of doing things and before I didn't see that. It's no good fighting from the outside. If you become part of the establishment, a lot more people sit up and take notice. You have to work how they expect you to work, as long as you get what you want by the end of it. One day I'll be able to do—" He paused, and exhaled. "Pure Galliano."

"John Galliano was not a sensible choice," Bertelsen admitted. "What he has is talent and a certain insouciance."

Galliano's deal with Aguecheek Ltd. was announced in the fashion trade papers in July 1986. An Aguecheek spokeswoman emphasized that the agreement was only for one season—spring–summer 1987—to be shown during London Fashion Week in October 1986. In return, Galliano promised he would rein in his wild imagination. "My next collection will be much more disciplined—it has to be," he declared. "I finally have gotten to where I want to be in the design sense and I now have disciplined and harnessed my creativity. I am making my designs much more accessible and commercial."

FOR GALLIANO, the Aguecheek deal was the fresh start he needed, and he took it seriously. He cleaned up his appearance, trading in his dungarees and T-shirts for tailored suits and polished shoes and cutting his now-shoulder-length hair short and conservatively. "John wanted to be luxury, he wanted to be more real, more commercial," Patrick Cox says. "He wasn't trying to impress twenty students he went to St. Martins with anymore. He was looking at a wider public [and] bought into the fame and all the rest of it."

But he was under the gun, time-wise: he had six—maybe eight—weeks to get the collection designed, sourced, and produced; to hire the models; and to stage the show. To find fabric at such short notice was not easy and he needed more help. He rang up knitwear designer Gail Downey—whom he fondly called "Dolly"—and asked her to return. He told her that since he had bigger backing he could pay her more than the 60 pounds ($80) a week she earned during the Brun era. The studio was temporarily in the basement stockroom of Aguecheek's warehouse space on Berkeley Square.

Galliano's key inspiration for the new collection was Australian director Peter Weir's recent movie *Witness*, a thriller starring Harrison Ford and Kelly McGillis about an Amish boy who witnesses a cop killing. Galliano became obsessed with the film, as if it were an allegory for his life. In it, the boy and his mother, played by McGillis, arrive at Philadelphia's monumental Thirtieth Street Station from Lancaster, Pennsylvania, dressed in their traditional, homespun garb and seem quite out of place, as Galliano and his family were when they immigrated from Gibraltar to London.

Galliano not only seized upon the themes of the film, he told his assistants that he wanted to adapt the Amish style of dress too. "When John has an idea for a collection it's called The Word," said Amanda Harlech—she had recently married and taken her husband's name. "It's then passed around to his whole team, each member adding and giving. It was always the most extraordinary experience."

To help him realize his vision, Galliano hired a theatrical costumer named Karen Crichton, who worked for the English National Opera. Together, they came up with a dress silhouette with a proper corsetlike bodice with boning and a full skirt that was "hitched up in the back," she says, like a little bustle.

Galliano was so pleased with how it turned out that he and Crichton came up with several more versions. To further evoke the Amish look, Galliano had the models' hair styled to resemble the organdy *kopp* head covers that Pennsylvania Dutch women wear, with side locks in the place of dangling tie straps. "A lot of women don't want to look aggressive," he explained. "What I design reflects the look of fresh young girls." Though it didn't have an official name, it became known at the studio as the "Witness" collection.

London Fashion Week, it seemed, had finally evolved into what *Washington Post* fashion editor Nina Hyde described as a "new maturity." The British fashion industry exported some 1.3 billion pounds ($2.4 billion) of clothing and accessories each year, the majority by household name brands such as Burberry, Aquascutum, and Jaeger. But it was the smaller, more avant-garde companies that drew retailer and media attention. More than 7,500 fashion professionals attended British Fashion Week. The fashion shows had a much more businesslike setup, with the three hundred design and accessory brands on display in the Olympia exhibition hall and a big tent pitched on and adjacent to the parking lot for the shows. Attendees discovered that the clothes were better designed, better made, and more salable than previous seasons.

Galliano's Aguecheek debut was scheduled for Sunday, October 12, in the British Fashion Council (BFC) tent behind Olympia at 1:45 in the afternoon—not a great time for a designer whose shows whooped it up, party-style. One of the models was a striking Afro-Jamaican teenager named Naomi Campbell who was born in Streatham, not far from where Galliano grew up. She arrived backstage directly from high school, still dressed in her school uniform. It was Campbell's first fashion show, Cox says, "And she was nervous as hell, terrified to go out, shaking with fear. John and I kept telling her, 'You're beautiful, you're beautiful.'"

To the eerie sound of birdcalls in the darkness, a model dressed in a sheer black blouse that revealed her small breasts and black crepe high-waist skirt came out and slowly cavorted like a macaw. (Galliano once told a reporter: "The moment you put on my clothes you should feel as proud as a bird and move accordingly.") The music—a mix of Go-Go drum rhythms and house techno by Jeremy Healy and Neil Mersh—kicked in and models marched in groups of two and three purposefully and quickly, swishing their black Amish-like pinafores down the catwalk. Occasionally, there was a smart 1930s-like suit with broad shoulders—an homage to Marlene Dietrich, a favorite Galliano inspiration—and a tinge of orientalism, with long, tight sheaths with obi-like drum bows on the back.

The show was a hit. *The New York Times* said that Galliano had left behind his "clothes that looked as if they stepped out of Sherwood Forest and instead, amid his fairy-tale designs for romantic Alice in Londonland, he scattered perfect blazers, skirts, simple black dresses and a plain T-shirt or two, clothes that will surely sell well."

It seemed, at least for the moment, that Galliano and Aguecheek were a good fit.

THAT FALL, GALLIANO JOINED a half dozen designers, including Alistair Blair and Jasper Conran, on a British Fashion Council–sponsored trip to New York. The tone of the trip was set before the plane touched down in the United States when Galliano started excitedly running up and down the aisle of economy class, where they were seated.

Galliano had a ball in New York. Over dinner one night with *New York Times* fashion writer Michael Gross at Il Cantinori, he confessed that he'd hit so many clubs he couldn't remember them all.

Another night, during an AIDS benefit at Barneys downtown, he ran up to B-52's singer Kate Pierson, who was modeling in the event's celebrity fashion show, and pulled off her auburn beehive wig. As Pierson stood there shrieking, Alistair Blair's fashion coordinator Limpet O'Connor says, "I saw two security guards walking out, with John dangling in between them."

During the trip, Galliano—who had recently split with Flett—launched into a full-fledged romance with Jasper Conran. O'Connor figured it out when she commented on a nice pair of cuff links that Galliano was sporting and he responded slyly, "Jasper gave them to me."

Flett was crushed. Shortly after Galliano dumped him, he went to see his former St. Martins teacher Bobby Hillson. "You don't know John," he told her. "There are two sides. You think you know him, but you've only seen this side. There's another side you wouldn't want to see."

Though they had only two months to get it together and show it, Galliano's first collection for Bertelsen was indeed a commercial success—so much so that Bertelsen had Galliano sign a five-year contract. To make everything run more smoothly, Galliano hired Lorraine Piggott, a young Londoner who had modeled in "Les Incroyables" and later worked for Westwood, as studio manager. Piggott beefed up the staff, bringing on former intern Deborah Bulleid as a studio assistant, a freelance pattern cutter named Sue Bottjer, and a twenty-one-year-old retail assistant from Browns named Sean Dixon to work as production assistant. Dixon had attended Wilson's Grammar School at the same time as Galliano, though he was five years younger.

"I remember you got picked on there," he told Galliano.

"I did," Galliano responded. "And you know, I see a lot of those guys who picked on me in the gay clubs now."

In early 1987, Galliano and his team moved out of the Aguecheek basement digs and into the big, light-filled space on the top floor of a converted warehouse on Shelton Street, around the corner from St. Martins. There, he and his team had a proper studio as well as a business office; it was a real luxury for such a small company to have both under the same roof. Like back at the old Earl Street studio, Galliano worked hard and long, paying particular attention to his pattern cutters, who were trying to turn his complicated creations into something manufacturing-ready. "John liked that one-on-one interaction," Dixon remembers. "He loved the hands-on."

Everyone was dedicated, and sometimes at the end of a workday, they'd sit down together and have a beer—except Galliano, who'd have a Coke and a cigarette—and laugh and joke and horse around. Galliano would start to mimic folks he knew, some of them right there in the room, which didn't go over well, even if it was spot on. But usually the jokes were good-natured, and he would erupt into fits of giggles.

GALLIANO ALSO HAD A NEW HOME: he moved into Conran's Regent's Park Terrace house, a "warm, cozy, and tasteful" place, as one friend recalls, with original decor by famed interior designer and former silent picture star William Haines. The pair regularly hosted dinners for their friends and colleagues—Conran cooking while Galliano entertained everyone with his jokes, impressions, and tales. For vacations, Conran whisked them off to far-flung places that Galliano could never previously afford. "Jasper was grown up," a Galliano friend remembers. "He had his own company, a house, a dog."

"John was happy then," remembers another. "Really happy."

But Galliano's inner circle wondered aloud what the relationship truly was about, since they were such an odd pairing. Says one: "Jasper wanted to be cool and John wanted to be rich."

Once Galliano settled into Conran's home, friends immediately noticed a change in his comportment: he became more mannered and proper, and he replaced his South London accent with something far more posh and affected. "I thought, 'Bloody, how are you going to keep that up?'" John Puddephatt says. "But he did." Flett found Galliano's transformation so ridiculous that he started to refer to Galliano as "the duchess."

Conran was crazy about Galliano, thought of him as a sprite, a will-o'-the-wisp of the woods, with a generous heart, no concept of money, and a wicked sense of humor. "The funniest guy I ever met," he once said. One time on vacation, Galliano and Conran were on a beach and Conran was reading a book. Galliano decided to read one too, and every time Conran turned a page, Galliano turned a page. After a few turns, Conran realized something was up and looked at Galliano: his book was upside down. "What's going on?" Conran asked. "This is the reason I'm such a visual person—I can't read," Galliano confessed with sincerity. He went on and on, for ten minutes or more, describing his frustrations in school, how he hid his illiteracy from others. Conran was amazed and saddened by the story and asked how he could help. "Got you!" Galliano cracked, and broke out into his high-pitched laugh.

Galliano's relationship with his family was far less lighthearted. He compartmentalized his life completely, the Thames serving as a definitive border between his pre-fashion youth in poor South London and his new fabulous existence in the center of town. He never talked with friends or colleagues about his family or his childhood, he never had any members of his family to the home he shared with Conran, and he never took Conran to his parents' house.

When he and Conran would go out on the town, to parties or clubs, the paparazzi would try to photograph them together—fashion's two It Boys as an It Couple. The pair dodged the camera flashes or entered and left separately to spare Galliano's family any shock or embarrassment. Eventually, Conran quietly spoke to the photographers and explained that publishing a picture of them together with a cutline describing them as a romantic couple would effectively "out" Galliano to his deeply Catholic family. The photographers backed off—for a while.

WHILE GALLIANO'S NIGHTS were filled with men, his days were all about women. He surrounded himself with beautiful, smart women—assistants, muses, the studio was teeming with women. They inspired him, nourished him, coddled him, and helped him make extraordinary clothes.

The two most important were Saint Phalle and Harlech. Unfortunately, Saint Phalle had so alienated fellow staff that eventually Piggott asked Galliano to do something about it: "You have to talk to her," she told him. "She's your friend. That's why she is here." Galliano did. And Saint Phalle decided to leave the company.

Harlech, however, was both adored by the staff and seemingly irreplaceable: she generated themes and ideas for the collections; assistants traveled to her hilltop home, The Mount, in Oswestry, Shropshire, or the Harlech family's grander estate, Glyn Cywarch, an early-seventeenth-century manor in Wales, to have her approve fabrics, colors, and other technical details; she styled looks before the show, mating stockings, shoes, and accessories with just the right outfit. "Amanda had an amazing eye," remembers one Galliano assistant.

Harlech would also send things by mail—poems, pictures, a pebble, or a dried flower—to stimulate Galliano's thoughts, spark new ideas. "She was incredibly important to the creative process—strong, inspirational," the assistant says. "She was beautiful inside and out."

Galliano adored everything about Harlech: her beauty, her refinement, her kindness and generosity, her taste and style, and now that she had married a Lord, her title. "You know, she's a Lady, she's a *Lay-dee*," he would tell his assistants.

Her life embodied the bohemian aristocracy lifestyle. In Shropshire, she was blessedly far removed from the fashionable cosmopolitan life of London. She would ride with the local hunt, cook up meals with the bounty from her kitchen garden, and look after her children in the grand house, with its faded paint, peeling wallpaper, velvet curtains, and attic full of fabulous old clothes.

In Wales, at Glyn Cywarch, the old stone manor filled with Harlech ancestors' portraits, shelves of books, and original seventeenth-century furnishings, she would run with the children on the nearby beach and keep her Fendi fur in the walk-in refrigerator next to dead pheasants from recent shooting parties. Galliano adored all of this, and spent weekends with Harlech and her family at their estates, soaking in the history and properness. He described their relationship as symbiotic: "If I do the notes, then Amanda does the symphony."

Harlech's input was becoming increasingly necessary to Galliano as his self-importance and phobias were turning him into a social recluse. He had no idea how the average consumer dressed—what was being distilled from high fashion down to mass market—because, Gail Downey says, "John was above all that. He didn't shop. He didn't go in the High Street." He rarely had cash on him, relying instead on others to pay his way. One night when he and Downey were out in Mayfair together and he stuck her with the bill, she teased him: "Oh, kings don't carry money, do they, John?"

FOR EACH COLLECTION—and therefore each fashion show—there was always a narrative: In the beginning he used historical themes or movements, like les Incroyables and the 1920s Afghan revolts. But since joining Aguecheek, that mechanism had evolved into something more allegorical: He was latching on to stories, such as *Witness*, that allowed him to portray his life through clothing design. For his spring–summer 1988 collection, Galliano chose Elia Kazan's film of Tennessee Williams's blistering play *A Streetcar Named Desire*.

The story fit perfectly with Galliano's creative and emotional state. In his collections and shows, there was a powerful male character, which represented him, and a vulnerable female figure, which represented his muse. In *Streetcar*, the main male character is Stanley Kowalski, a working-class son of a Polish immigrant who drinks too much and has a lightning-quick, violent temper. Both on stage and in film the role was played by Marlon Brando. "John probably saw himself as Marlon as Stanley Kowalski," said an assistant who worked on the collection.

And in *Streetcar*, there are not one but two female leads in the story: Stanley's stable, devoted brunette wife, Stella, played in the film by Kim Hunter, and her psychologically unstable, boozing blond sister, Blanche DuBois, played by Vivien Leigh. When Blanche arrives for an extended visit in the Kowalskis' slumlike apartment, her presence and madness throw Stella and Stanley's mutually dependent relationship off-kilter.

Harlech was like Stella, strong, able, and addicted to the Galliano/Kowalski dominant male. And like Stella, Harlech was pregnant again (the baby was due in the spring). Saint Phalle was the more fragile Blanche, and seemed, at least to the staff, to have been a self-absorbed and destabilizing presence in the studio. In the play and film, Blanche eventually suffers a mental breakdown and is taken away to a mental asylum. At the Galliano studio, Saint Phalle had been banished.

Galliano was drawn to Williams's writing and the films based on his plays. He could relate to the family dynamics—the strong, scary patriarch, the proud women who still were subservient to their tyrannical spouses, and the hardworking, misunderstood young men—as well as the brutal environment heavy with alcohol and physical abuse.

For his designs, he borrowed greatly from the travel trunk of Blanche DuBois and produced commercially viable modern versions of her flouncy pastel day dresses with fitted bodices, chiffon gowns, and sheer organza wraps. But he didn't stop with the postwar Southern Belle look. Marlene Dietrich was still a strong presence—Galliano loved the vision of her smoking under a black hat veil, and he used her visage circa 1930s in sketches he did for the press kit. Another veiling influence was Edwardian women beekeepers, which one assistant remembers Harlech bringing into the mix.

Galliano also wanted to create with Crichton a series of what are known in the fashion business as "show pieces"—spectacular dresses that would look great on the runway and be perfect for fashion magazine shoots to drum up publicity but would only be available by special order. The first "show piece" he dreamed up with Crichton was what became officially known as the "shellfish dress," a spectacular voluminous skirt made of scores of layers of stiff pearl gray organza, like clamshells piled on top of one another. "He had seen a picture of all these layers of organza, and his team didn't know how to do it— they thought it might be wires or structured in some way," Crichton remembers. "And they came to me and said, 'Do you know how to do this? Can you help us work this out?' And I said, 'It's absolutely not wire, I know exactly what that is because the cutter who had taught me had worked in that fashion before.'"

Crichton made the skirt at home, and constructed a simple strapless bodice for the top. When she took it in to show Galliano, she says, "He absolutely loved it." To dress up the plain top, he added a matching organdy shawl and long satin gloves. The overall effect was classic 1950s couture beauty crossed with Cinderella romanticism. It was sublime.

THOUGH GALLIANO AND CONRAN were a couple, there was an unspoken professional competition developing between the two—the patrician Conran and the working-class upstart Galliano—and it appeared to Galliano's circle that Conran wanted to win, no matter how much pain it would cause. Conran's curiosity and frequent visits to the studio worried Piggott—and with reason. Not long before the shows, Conran talked Galliano into trading slots on the calendar. Galliano had been assigned a much better time than Conran, and more important, his slot was before Conran's. When Piggott found out that Galliano had given his show time to Conran, she flipped. Galliano explained that he thought it was harmless. Piggott said, "No, John, it's very important. Now Jasper is going before us." If Conran's clothes resembled Galliano's, Piggott feared it would appear that Galliano was copying Conran, and not vice versa.

In addition, Conran hired Galliano's deejay friend Jeremy Healy to do the music and started booking the same models as Galliano. After doing their Conran fittings, the models reported back to the Galliano camp that Conran's designs were extremely similar to Galliano's. "Some of the girls were crying, saying, 'If we had known, we wouldn't have allowed ourselves to be booked [by Conran],'" Piggott recalls.

To make matters worse, when Patrick Cox arrived backstage during the rehearsal to deliver the shoes, he happened to pick up a program and saw that, after more than a half dozen seasons of collaborating with Galliano, he was no longer credited for his work. He went over to Galliano and said, "Excuse me, but it doesn't say 'Shoes by Patrick Cox,'" like it usually did.

"People getting paid don't get credit," Galliano snipped.

Cox stood there, stunned. The amount Galliano paid him barely covered the cost of the leather, and Cox had financed the production out of his own pocket. Furious, he packed up the shoes and walked out, swearing he would never work with Galliano again.

WHEN CONRAN PRESENTED his collection in the late afternoon of Sunday, October 11, in the Marquee tent behind Olympia, many in the audience were perplexed. "Jasper Conran was known as Lady Diana's tailor," Cox says, "and suddenly he came out with all the circular cutting and everybody went, 'What?' That wasn't Jasper. It was irrelevant to his market and to what he knew how to do."

Galliano's team felt that Healy had created a far better soundtrack for Conran. Then they saw Conran's models coming off the runway in very Galliano-like clothes. "Everyone was upset, but John got into a state. Really a state," remembers one of his assistants. "It was one of those 'Oh shit' moments. Those clothes weren't Jasper, they were Jasper reinvented, and John damn well knew it."

Two hours later, Galliano presented "Blanche DuBois." As always, the crowd was a wild fashion scene with Galliano groupies in outlandish outfits. From the moment Marlon Brando's epic cry of "Stella!" blasted from the soundtrack through the tent, it was obvious that this was nothing like what Conran—or anyone else—was doing. The waistlines were way up high, at the bosom, and way down low, on the hips. There were halter top ball gowns, a few reworkings of Crichton's hitched-up skirts, and *Streetcar*-like 1940s day dresses with flouncy skirts that were feminine and flattering. Many of the outfits were dotted with origami appliqués that Galliano had St. Martins students make.

Finally came the moment for the "show pieces": three models wearing the shellfish dresses walked down the runway. "The room went silent, and we thought, 'Oh, God, everyone hates these things,'" Crichton remembers. Then the audience erupted into applause and cheering. "I was completely overwhelmed," she says. "We all were." (Today, one of Galliano's shellfish dresses is in the permanent collection of the Victoria and Albert Museum.)

The critics responded with a deluge of praise. Liz Smith of *The Times* of London declared Galliano "our undisputed star," and said that his show "provided one of those memorable moments when original design and polished creation fuse." Sarah Mower—the writer who had blasted Galliano two years earlier—wrote that the collection "proves his stature as a designer of international standing who can rival the creativity of Rei Kawakubo of Comme des Garçons, or Yohji Yamamoto."

AT THE END OF THE WEEK, the British Fashion Council held its annual gala at the grand Banqueting House of the seventeenth-century Whitehall

Palace. With the rise of British designers on the international scene, Princess Diana as their ambassadress, and the solid support of the Thatcher government, British fashion was enjoying an extraordinary success and had become the country's third-largest manufacturing industry.

Its top cheerleader, surprisingly, was the country's prime minister, Margaret Thatcher. When interviewed by the BBC World Service in 1984 about the British fashion industry, she said, "It needs to be seen to have government support. . . . It is big business. It is important to business. It has repercussions for many, many other industries and, you know, being British, we tend perhaps sometimes to think of it as a little bit, what should I say, frothy or not quite so important because it is fashion."

At the gala, Lord Young of Graffham, the secretary of state for trade and industry, presented Galliano with the British Designer of the Year award. Galliano looked like a dapper young businessman, dressed in gray trousers with a sharp crease, a well-tailored blue blazer, white shirt and burgundy red necktie with white polka dots; his hair was slicked back neatly and he smiled broadly and proudly. Ever shy in public, he kept his acceptance speech extremely brief: "Thank you to all the press and retailers for their continued support."

"BLANCHE DUBOIS" was a sales bonanza: Galliano's orders quadrupled from the previous season. Everyone was working like mad in the Shelton Street studio, processing orders, boxing clothes to send out to retailers worldwide. And the shellfish dress became the wedding dress of the season: It was even featured in a *Sunday Times* of London story about the wedding of twenty-three-year-old *Harpers & Queen* writer Raffaella Barker, who chose it after the magazine's fashion editor told her that everyone who was anyone was marrying in Galliano that season. Barker went for the complete look, down to the long satin gloves and beekeeping veil. Total charge: 2,000 pounds ($3,500).

Unfortunately, Galliano's success wasn't enough to keep Aguecheek in the black. By the end of 1987, Bertelsen had lost more than 5 million pounds ($8.75 million) in three years, and had almost 13 million pounds ($22.75 million) in liabilities, and at its best, only 11.9 million pounds ($20.82 million) in annual sales.

Several of Galliano's staff decided it was time to move on. They were replaced by underlings, most notably Steven Robinson, a twenty-year-old from

Norfolk who had arrived a couple of seasons earlier as an intern and had worked his way up to assistant.

Robinson was a sad sack of a man. Painfully shy, short and obese with thinning blond hair and a sickly complexion often riddled with acne, he camouflaged himself in faded oversized polo shirts and baggy khakis. But he was hardworking and wholly devoted to Galliano. "Steven loved John the moment they met and wanted John all to himself," says one Galliano assistant who worked in the studio at the time.

FOR HIS NEXT COLLECTION, Galliano turned to 1930s Paris—specifically *The Secret Paris of the 30's*, a book of Hungarian-born photographer Brassaï's pictures of French prostitutes, barkeeps, and café customers. Galliano adored the decadence and sensuality of that period and re-created it faithfully, down to the models' kohl-lined eyes, rosebud red lips, and slick bobs crimped with hairclips. It became known as the "Hairclips" collection.

The key look was the bias-cut dress—a slinky silhouette invented in the 1930s by French couturier Madeleine Vionnet, which Galliano adored. He actually didn't know how to construct it, so he asked Crichton to make the show samples. To get the right shape and fluidity, she used the old couture technique of draping the fabric directly on "the stand," as Stockman dummies are known in the business.

Magazine editors loved the bias-cut: it was sexy and photographed like a dream. But everyone else was up in arms over it. "The reviews were saying, 'Who could wear the bias dress? No woman can wear a bias dress!'," Steven Robinson later told me, explaining that the clingy jersey mercilessly highlighted women's lumps and bumps. What's worse, he said, "No factory would look at the production of the dresses because they said, 'You can't produce it. It's not possible.'" Fabric cut on the bias has stretch to it, which meant when it was run through machines on an assembly line, it would easily get pulled out of shape, making crooked, twisted dresses. As a result, Robinson said, "They all had to be produced in the studio."

THE STRESS OF GALLIANO'S JOB—of the nonstop creating of something wildly imaginative that would top what he had done a mere six months earlier—was starting to wear him out. To protect himself psychologically, he divided himself into two separate personalities: there was "John," his normal, grounded self who answered to corporate executives and managed the studio; and "Galliano's Girl," the creative soul who could be a drama queen. His staff so embraced the split personality that they had T-shirts made up that read "Galliano's Girl."

He also started drinking significantly more, and losing focus. His spring–summer 1990 collection, presented on Sunday, October 15, at 6:30 P.M. in the BFC tent at the Duke of York's Barracks on King's Road, mystified editors and retailers with what Bernadine Morris of *The New York Times* described as "giant caterpillar-shaped hats and diapers," and Liz Smith of *The Times* of London called, "tribal armlets clamped on to striped jackets, [and] a gleaming hammered copper breastplate worn with authentic satin boxer shorts." Peder Bertelsen left before the show was half over.

Many of Galliano's employees and friends blamed one person for the creative left turn: Steven Robinson. Though his talent was obviously inferior to Galliano's, Robinson managed to have a significant voice in the design process. What his greatest strength appeared to be, say those who worked there, was mind manipulation. More than one former member of Galliano's inner circle has described Robinson as "Machiavellian."

"Steven was not nice," a close friend of Galliano's told me. "He came in determined that if he couldn't be John, he would control John. And his methodology was to be indispensable to John."

Soon enough, Galliano became so reliant on Robinson that Robinson became "like a crutch," says an assistant. Members of the Galliano team were stunned by how Galliano—a man who was *always* and unquestionably sure of his vision and his design voice—would have days when he was incapable of making a decision without first asking Robinson for his opinion.

Robinson was the catalyst of much internal office strife as well. He focused mainly on the women—"picking them off one by one," as one put it. The only one who seemed immune was Harlech, because she spent the majority of her time in Shropshire with her family.

Galliano intimates believe that Robinson understood that Galliano's greatest weakness was alcohol and plied him with it as a way to control him. "He put a bottle of gin in front of John," one observer said. "A bottle of gin every night."

When drunk, Galliano had a habit of stripping off his clothes, all of them, no matter where he happened to be. It was, says a close friend, a way to "act off." "I've seen him walk down the street naked," the friend remembers. "He was not ashamed of his body at all. Never was."

Eventually, Galliano's friends and colleagues realized that his alcohol abuse needed to be addressed. With the support of American *Vogue*'s new editor in chief, Anna Wintour, they staged an intervention and confronted him. Since this was before rehab became fashionable, all that they could do and did was counsel Galliano and offer to help him stop—or at least curtail greatly—his drinking. But this, too, was undermined by Robinson. "Steven was smuggling John bottles of whiskey," states one of the friends. Not surprisingly, the cure didn't take.

IV

Savile Row: two words that have been synonymous with good taste, refinement, and craftsmanship for more than a century. A short street in the heart of Mayfair in central London, Savile Row is the epicenter of London's bespoke tailoring trade and has been the home of most well-known names in traditional men's clothing. Among these is Anderson & Sheppard, a favorite of such distingué gentlemen as film director John Huston, tycoon J. Paul Getty, and Tom Ford. It is best known for the fine "English drape" to its coats—a silhouette that is "roomy over the chest and shoulder blades . . . the fabric not flawlessly smooth and fitted but gently descending from the collarbone in soft vertical ripples," as author David Kamp wrote in *Anderson & Sheppard: A Style Is Born*. As former managing director

Charles Bryant explained, Anderson & Sheppard was and is the tailor for men who want "to look right without giving the appearance of having studied their clothes."

Anderson & Sheppard was not a posh establishment—nothing like a women's couture salon in Paris, for example, with velvet-covered love seats and silk taffeta curtains. You entered the multistory neo-Georgian building through a pair of substantial corner-facing doors into a mahogany-paneled front room and walked across the herringbone parquet to long cutting tables stacked high with bolts of wool, silk, cashmere, and cotton, mostly in sober tones. It was, *Vanity Fair* editor in chief Graydon Carter admits, "a dark, intimidating place."

Back in the mid-1980s, in the workshop of No. 30 toiled a round-faced teen named Lee McQueen. At sixteen and from one of London's hard East End working-class neighborhoods, McQueen was a bit more coarse than his fellow apprentices—he dressed in T-shirts and jeans, instead of shirtsleeves and trousers, and his thick Cockney accent was often hard to decipher.

Yet, as unpolished as he was, it was immediately apparent to the managers at Anderson & Sheppard that he was gifted with a needle and thread. "We taught him technique, but he had the talent in his blood," remembers John Hitchcock, who hired McQueen in 1986. "You can't teach that to anyone."

McQUEEN CAME FROM a tradition of service: his father, Ronald, and several other relatives were London cabdrivers; his mother, Joyce, at times worked as a teacher and a florist. He was born to them on St. Patrick's Day in 1969 at the Lewisham Hospital in South London, the last of six—three boys (Michael and Tony) and three girls (Janet, Tracey, and Jacqui). The McQueens lived in a simple home at 43 Shifford Path in Lewisham at the time. Soon after, they moved briefly to Burdett Road, Stepney, a working-class neighborhood in the East End, before settling in nearby Stratford in a charmless council house on Biggerstaff Road that backed up to a lot used for storing construction materials.

The East End has historically been London's toughest section of town, an urban pocket surrounding the Port of London that for centuries served as the center for immigration and manufacturing, and in turn, prostitution, organized crime, gang warfare, and acute poverty. It was where the serial killer

Jack the Ripper roamed, slaughtering and slicing up five or more women in 1888, and where Londoners gawked at Joseph Merrick, the "Elephant Man," who was thought to have been deformed by neurofibromatosis and was kept in a cage in a shop window on Whitechapel Road. Friedrich Engels simply described it as "the world's largest and most wretched working-class district."

By the time McQueen was growing up there, the East End was better, but only somewhat. The area had been devastated by the Blitz of World War II and had never really regenerated; unemployment was high and the local economy had been in a perpetual slide for three decades. Neighborhoods were this side of slums; schools were lousy and at times dangerous; households were loud and brutal.

The McQueens were relative newcomers to the East End. Ronald's father hailed from the Isle of Skye, Scotland's second-largest island; Joyce's came from the Forest of Dean, in Gloucestershire, near Wales. Both grew up in East London. Ronald was one of a dozen children, and as McQueen noted, "just trying to put food on the plate for twelve kids is not easy." McQueen said his paternal grandfather "was a drunk," and the preferred method of discipline during Ronald's childhood was often physical. "My dad was beaten a lot by his father and his mother," McQueen said. "Beaten. So was the rest of his brothers and sisters."

When Ronald Samuel McQueen met Joyce Barbara Deane, he was a truck driver's assistant who helped unload cargo and make deliveries, and she was the daughter of a warehouse worker. They married in 1953. "Money was tight in those days," their son Michael McQueen recalled. "When Dad was a lorry driver he would get up at 5:00 A.M. and arrive back at 9:00 P.M. six days a week. Mum, a teacher, did all the accounts. He was quite draconian and she was far more liberal and creative. She would sit at the kitchen table doing watercolours and researching our family history." By the time Lee McQueen was born, Joyce admitted, "There wasn't much left in the kitty."

He was a lean boy with long blond wavy locks and Caribbean blue eyes. Early on, he felt a pull toward fashion, recalling at the age of three drawing a Cinderella-like ball gown on his sister's bedroom wall—to his father's consternation. The room was eventually wallpapered, covering up the picture. Later, when McQueen asked if he could remove the wallpaper to find it, his father responded, "If you peel off the wallpaper, you can paper the whole fucking room again."

As a youngster, he attended Carpenters Primary School in Stratford. In the summer, the McQueen family vacationed at Pontins in Camber Sands, a camping resort on the coast of East Sussex known for its sand dunes. McQueen described it as "a trailer park with caravans," and it wasn't the most pleasant of holidays for him. When they arrived in Ronald's cab the first time, he recalled, "I looked out the window . . . and there were these two men with these scary masked faces on and I shit myself there and then in the cab! I literally just shit my pants!" He said on another day, "[I] was coming round the corner and seeing my two sisters getting off with two men. I thought they were getting raped and I went screaming back to my Mum and I wound up getting beat up by my two sisters!"

It was at Pontins when he was six or so, he said, that he figured out he was gay. He entered the "Prince of Pontins" competition and won. "But I wanted the boy who came second to win because I fancied him!" he said. "I just knew I had feelings for boys rather than girls." He described himself as "the pink sheep of the family."

After Carpenters, he enrolled in Rokeby Comprehensive School for Boys, a state-run institution open to all aptitudes in Stratford. Rokeby was the bad boys' school of Stratford. The Rokeby boys were known to be the savage bullies of the hood.

McQueen was miserable there. A dyslexic who appeared to also suffer from attention deficit disorder, he struggled with his studies; his report cards often had comments about his difficulty concentrating on his work. A visual learner and creative child, his best grades were in art. His relations with the other boys were just as difficult. The school, he said, "was full of nutters. I didn't learn a thing. I just drew clothes in class." This made him a target, as Galliano had been at Wilson's. The Rokeby bullies called him "queer boy" or "McQueer," which wounded him deeply. "I got the piss taken out of me for a few years," he said. "I survived, ducking and diving." One time, he didn't duck fast enough and, he said, "I had my face smashed against the railings . . . [in] a fight in the locker room." He knew his education at Rokeby was basically worthless: in the eyes of the school, he said, "you're just another East End oik going nowhere fast."

McQueen wasn't the only frustrated artist in the family. His mother, he said, went to art school in her youth, but had to abandon her dreams of becoming an artist to get a "proper" job as a social science teacher. "She was on the verge of actually becoming a separate identity to my father then all of a sudden it stopped, which was kind of sad," he said. "But that's just the way it is." His sister Jacqui enrolled in art school to study graphic arts, but she too had to quit and get herself a proper job—as a secretary. His older brother Michael was an "even better artist," McQueen said, but he wound up working as a cabdriver like their father.

His salvation was his mother, a handsome woman with the same turquoise eyes. "The East End is a matriarch society," explains an East Ender who grew up near the McQueens. "East End mothers will defend you to the death, and if you are effeminate, you will be protected." Joyce worked hard to smooth out her youngest child's rough spots, teaching him basic good manners and forbidding swearing in the house—a rule he respected without question. She may have been the only person in his life whom he completely obeyed. She also understood that her youngest boy was artistic and sensitive and needed coddling. "He was always very quiet and spent most of his time in his bedroom drawing and designing, hardly ever going out," she said.

When he did emerge, it would be to do things he really enjoyed, like going over to the house of Aunt Renée, to spend the afternoon watching videos of old Alfred Hitchcock thrillers; bird watching with the Young Ornithologists Club; taking judo classes, where he earned a brown belt; and playing rugby. He played in the forwards, and, he said, "loved getting tackled."

His favorite sport by far, however, was swimming, and he spent as much time as he could at the local pool. When he was nine, he messed up a back flip, landed face-first on the cement edge and cracked his front teeth. "That's why I've got a face like a saucepan," he later quipped. He had the teeth capped badly when he was a teen, and they became discolored and decayed. Despite the pool accident, he kept on swimming and joined a local synchronized swimming team, the lone boy among forty girls. For one of his performances, he had to wear a grass skirt. "My mum was so embarrassed," he later recalled, "she couldn't watch me." Looking back, his brother Michael now says, "I should have realized then that he was gay."

As with Galliano, there was a dark, violent side in the household. McQueen described his upbringing as "hard and homophobic," and recalled his father coming home after long nights in his cab ranting about the gays he had to drive home from the clubs. McQueen's sisters were victims of "abusive relationships," he said. He grew up witnessing it helplessly; once, he said, one sister "was nearly strangled to death. I haven't watched it on TV; I've been there."

The worst attack, however, happened to McQueen: when he was eleven a man he knew raped him. The attack didn't turn him into a homosexual—he knew by then that he was gay. But it did destroy him emotionally and psychologically. Of his rapist, McQueen said: "He fucking stole my innocence."

To cope, McQueen adopted a brutish demeanor—a real swaggering bully with a foul mouth and penchant for fighting. "There's a breaking point in everyone," he explained. At fifteen, he became a skinhead. "In my uncle's pub in Stratford, there used to be a private bar where the ICF, the Inter City Firm"—a notorious football hooligan gang—"used to go and you would see people get glassed," meaning cut on the throat by a broken glass or bottle. "I had seen all that shit go down. . . . It was like cannibalism, the way they fought. They were like fucking warriors."

At the same time, McQueen discreetly nurtured his interest in fashion. "I was the only kid [at Rokeby] who read books about dresses," he said. "I knew Giorgio Armani was a window-dresser, Ungaro was a tailor." He doodled clothing designs in his notebooks and by the time he was in his early teens he was making dresses for his sisters and advising them on what to wear. "They would call me up to their room and I'd help them pick out clothes for work," he recalled. "Just, you know, what skirt with what cardigan, but I was always trying to make them look strong and sheltered."

When he was sixteen, McQueen finally gave up at Rokeby, exiting with one O-level, in art. "I had to draw a stupid bowl of fruit," he grumbled. He continued to study art in an evening class in East Ham, and eventually earned his A-level.

Family was important to McQueen. He was especially close to his sister Janet, who was a London black cabdriver, like their father—one of the few women in the job at the time. Janet was the oldest sibling, and, according to her son Gary, she was "a bit like a second mother figure" for McQueen. She too lived in Stratford with her young family—a place, Gary recalls now, that "had a bit of a melancholy feel to it."

From time to time, when Janet was out driving her cab, McQueen would babysit her boys Paul and Gary, who were roughly eight and ten years younger than he was. "He'd bring over horror films like *An American Werewolf in London* or *Scanners*. Gore films," Gary says. "And we'd watch five or six at a time.

I used to love them. . . . Horror films work on your imagination when you are younger. It's more about being surreal, trying to get away from this miserable planet."

Gary liked to draw, an activity McQueen encouraged. Paul and Gary were also artistic subjects for McQueen. As a teen, McQueen had become interested in photography and bought a camera. One day, he dressed the boys in big over-coats, took them back behind the house in Stratford, and shot a beautiful, photojournalism-like black-and-white portrait of them with the neighboring construction site as the backdrop. "You can see the cranes in background," Gary says.

Whenever the boys started misbehaving, McQueen would bust out Bruce Lee–like kung fu moves, Gary says, and "he'd chase us around and scare us." Sometimes he'd lose his temper, and "go off on you," Gary says. "But in the next breath he'd be the nicest person. Two extremes."

To appease family pressure to learn a trade, McQueen enrolled at a local technical school, but he quickly gave it up. "Dad said I had to earn some money," he said. "I worked as a messenger during the day and in my uncle's pub at night, clearing glasses for the underworld." It seemed that McQueen would be an East End roughneck forever.

His mother wanted more for him. In 1986, she found a possibility: the two of them were watching a TV program about the lack of apprentices on Savile Row.

"Why don't you go down there, give it a go?" she asked him.

Why not? he thought.

They both realized this could be his ticket out of the East End, out of the McQueen cycle of taxi drivers, construction workers, and barkeeps, out of poverty and violence. He went to see John Hitchcock at Anderson & Shep-pard. Hitchock liked his earnestness and enthusiasm and hired him on the spot. "In a working class family in London you have to bring the money in and artistic routes were never the means to that end," McQueen later said. "But I put my foot down. . . . I thought: 'I'm not gonna do that. I'm not gonna get married, live in a two-up, two-down and be a bloody black cab driver.'"

WHEN MCQUEEN ARRIVED at No. 30 Savile Row for his first day of work, dressed in his usual baggy Levis, pullover sweater, and Doc Martens–style boots, he was given a thimble and a large pair of shears. Like the other apprentices, McQueen worked from 8:30 A.M. to 5:00 P.M. Monday through Thursday—on Fridays they were off at 4:00—and earned the starting wage of 100 pounds a week. "He left school at [a young age], same as I did," Hitchcock says. "You didn't go to college unless you were rich or very smart. You went for an apprenticeship."

McQueen's master tailor was a strict Irish Catholic from County Cork named Cornelius O'Callaghan, or Con for short. A small, slim, perfectly turned-out man with a commanding voice, Con was a legend at Anderson & Sheppard; perhaps the best tailor on staff at the time, he was assigned "special work" such as handling Prince Charles's clothes. He also taught young apprentices the craft of tailoring and was known to be a strict yet engaging instructor. The work "was like Dickens, sitting cross-legged on a bench and padding lapels and sewing all day—it was nice," McQueen later recalled. "You never met the customers. We had people down on the shop floor who did that. You was just a little mouse upstairs working away."

Under Con's thoughtful guidance, he mastered basting, pattern cutting, fabric cutting, sewing a "forward"—which is a jacket with minimal seaming, ready for a fitting—and "padding" a lapel, which Hitchcock describes as "sewing hundreds of neat stitches to give the lapel its shape. It's hard, precise work. And that's what we give to apprentices." McQueen worked diligently in his designated workstation, cutting and sewing as he listened to club music he played quietly on a small radio. "I sat for two months padding collars and two years learning how to cut a jacket," he said. Normally, it would take an apprentice three years to learn to make a forward—but McQueen mastered it in two. Con was so pleased he allowed McQueen to work on clothes of the house's top clients, including Prince Charles.

McQueen was shy and kept to himself. But after a bit, he became more self-confident and developed a nice friendship with fellow apprentice Derrick Tomlinson: They'd lunch or have tea together in the kitchen area or on occasion meet up after work for a drink at a nearby pub. "He loved to chat and talk," Tomlinson says, mostly about work and personal interests, but rarely about the future or his dreams. "He kept his cards close to his chest as to what he was going to do."

In time, however, McQueen's East End rebel side burbled forth. He later claimed to reporters that he wrote "McQueen was here" (or something more vulgar) in the linings of Prince Charles's jackets. That way, he explained, "I'd know I was always close to his heart." (Later, when the news was published, Hitchcock says, "I said to the prince's valet: 'Is there any chance we could take the suit back and check the canvas?' And we got it back and looked inside the jacket and didn't see anything. It was all make-believe.")

Worse, McQueen started not showing up for work and therefore not getting his tasks done on time. "He would sometimes disappear and that would let the customer down. 'Sorry,' we'd have to say, 'it will be another week,'" Hitchcock recalls. "Con would be annoyed because he was teaching Lee, and would have things for him to do. For Con, it was a waste of time. Certain men are reliable, but Lee wasn't one of them."

By mid-1987, after a long spate of unexpected absences, management sent someone to the McQueen home on Biggerstaff Road to find out why. McQueen explained that he had been busy taking care of his mother, who he said had been ill. "If he'd have told us [ahead of time] we would have been more understanding," Hitchcock says now. It was agreed that McQueen would leave Anderson & Sheppard. "It was a shame, really," Hitchcock concedes. "Because he was really very good."

STILL ANXIOUS TO LEARN TAILORING—as well as have a job that wasn't deep in the East End—McQueen went to work down Savile Row as a trouser cutter for Gieves & Hawkes. But he claimed he was a victim of homophobia. After an acute attack against him, he said, "I went straight to the head of Gieves & Hawkes and said the situation had to change. And it didn't, so I left"—on his twentieth birthday, as it happened. He found a new job at Bermans & Nathans, the theater costumers, as a pattern cutter. "I was interested in the technical side," he said, "learning all these old techniques, sixteenth-century pattern cutting and stuff like that." He worked on costumes for several splashy major productions, including the West End musicals *Miss Saigon* and *Les Misérables*.

As much as McQueen enjoyed learning about sixteenth-century tailoring techniques, he wasn't so keen on the work environment at Bermans. "[It was] just too camp," he said. "Too many queens for me."

But it did help him figure out his career ambition.

By the time he left Bermans, he said, "I knew I wanted to be a fashion designer."

Among the hip young talents on the British fashion scene was Koji Tatsuno, a Japanese designer who made his name in the early 1980s with an indie brand called Culture Shock, a hybrid of avant-garde Japanese and traditional British tailoring, that he ran with two friends, Yuzun Koga and Jeannie Macarthur. By the late 1980s, Tatsuno had his own business, backed by Yohji Yamamoto, with a bespoke tailoring shop on Mount Street near the Connaught Hotel. Everything was made to order on the premises by Savile Row–trained tailors, and Tatsuno personally took measurements of his customers, including Sting, David Bowie, and Paul McCartney.

One day in 1989, twenty-year-old McQueen walked into the shop, looking for a job. "I didn't care about a CV," Tatsuno says. "I thought he was quite interesting and so I took him on." McQueen started out as a pattern cutter in the basement workshop and found it simply liberating—the designs were so much more fashionable, experimental, and interesting than straitlaced Savile Row. Working at Tatsuno, McQueen said, "was the next stage for me, to move further into the designer area without losing my tailoring background."

Eventually McQueen moved upstairs and assisted the tailors at their worktable, which was in the front window of the shop, so passersby could watch them as they cut and sewed. He remained low-key and quiet, silently observing the tailors at work. "Lee was so intrigued by the savoir faire," recalls Tatsuno's then-business associate Victoria Fernandez.

London fashion in the late 1980s was churning with loads of new, young talent. There was Galliano, of course, and Flett and Conran. But there were also other more street-savvy brands, like Red or Dead, which was founded in 1982 as a stall in the Camden Market. By the late 1980s, Red or Dead was a full-fledged fashion company, with St. Martin's alum and designer John McKitterick running the studio and a show slot during London Fashion Week. To keep up with the additional work, McKitterick needed another part-time machinist. One of his assistants, who also worked at Tatsuno, suggested McQueen. "Bring him along," McKitterick said.

McKitterick was intrigued and impressed by McQueen's Savile Row experience and hired him on the spot.

McQueen took the job seriously: "He was very competent, turned up on time, didn't give me any attitude," McKitterick says. As at Anderson & Sheppard, McQueen kept to himself—he never spoke about his home life, other than how fond he was of his mother, and "that he was from a family of taxi drivers that weren't keen on him being in fashion," McKitterick says. "He was just a nice boy from the East End who wanted to get by and he came to work and wanted money. It was a survival thing."

In early 1990, McKitterick left Red or Dead to start his namesake brand and took McQueen with him. By then, McQueen had grown more interested in the fashion business and was dreaming big; at a pub in the East End where he liked to hang out and play snooker, he boasted to a barmaid: "I'm going to be a designer and I'm going to be really famous." Since he hadn't attended fashion school and only had on-the-job training, McKitterick believed the logical next step would be for McQueen to go to Italy for an apprenticeship.

As McKitterick explained to McQueen, Italy was the best place for young assistants to get a start in the fashion business and really learn how it worked on every level. "You weren't just picking up pins and going for the coffee, like you would have been had you gone to work for a London or Paris company," McKitterick recalls. "You were actually putting pen to paper and choosing colors or yarns or going to the factory. You learned about fabric." And when it came to production and distribution, Italy was the tops.

The Milanese ready-to-wear fashion business was still relatively new. Rome had long been the home for Italian couture—a tradition of dressing the Italian aristocracy in made-to-order clothes and furs that the designer Valentino and the house of Fendi maintained. Florence had been the center for leather goods manufacturing, and Gucci was still based in the region. But the north, for more than a century, had been known for manufacturing and textiles production—not fashion design. That all changed in the 1970s, with the emergence of a new generation of designers, including Giorgio Armani, Gianfranco Ferré, and Gianni Versace, who decided to be based in Milan, near the factories that would be producing their clothes.

The new Italian fashion look was a hybrid of relaxed American sportswear and impeccable Italian tailoring. It was chic and comfortable—the European equivalent of preppy—and made for a grounded counterpoint to London's eccentric designs, Paris's restrictive haute couture, and Tokyo's avant-garde deconstructionism. "Italian designers obviously prefer to be known as benevolent fashion leaders," Bernadine Morris wrote in *The New York Times* back then, "not despots" like their Paris counterparts.

Where the Italians excelled most was in business: since they had long experience in manufacturing, distribution, and marketing, they weren't afraid of rolling out diffusion lines, such as menswear, secondary and children's lines, jeans lines—all of which needed designers who could oversee everything from start to finish. "The employment opportunities were endless," McKitterick says.

He explained all of this to McQueen and gave him a list of contacts to look up. McQueen went to see his sister-in-law, who worked as a travel agent, and bought a one-way plane ticket to Milan. He landed there two days later, in the spring of 1990 with no place to stay and no job, but he had McKitterick's list, and at the top of it was the Italian ready-to-wear designer and fashion merchant Romeo Gigli, who was known for his neo-Baroque designs.

Gigli had an entirely different background from either McQueen or Galliano. A debonair aristocrat, he was raised in Faenza, a small country town near Bologna, in a regal home filled with beautiful objects and liveried staff. He was homeschooled by tutors until the age of nine and his parents taught him about art, books, and fine living.

In 1985, he showed his first collection under his own name. "His clothes have been a departure—maybe even a dissent—from the fashion braggadocio that is the norm in Milan," wrote *The New Yorker*'s Holly Brubach at the time. "From the start, it has been clear that he didn't share the same frame of reference as the other Italian designers."

Unlike his confreres, who showed at the sterile Fiera convention center, Gigli staged his shows in his modernist office at his Corso Como design and retail headquarters. To further break with tradition, he had his models walk on the floor instead of on an elevated runway; wear flats instead of heels; wear very little makeup; and never smile or twirl their skirts or play to the crowd. And at the end, when the show came to a close with Graham Nash's 1971 political anthem "Chicago (We Can Change the World)" and thunderous applause, he refused to come out and take a bow. Most of that sounds normal today; back then, it was new.

In the late 1980s, Gigli had evolved from minimalism into a style that was decidedly more rococo: a soft, slope-shouldered silhouette made of gold-shot brocades, iridescent silks, and lush velvets in spice tones with rich embroidery. He looked to the Belle Époque, to Paul Poiret, Mariano Fortuny, and even Charles Frederick Worth. Many in fashion back then saw Gigli as direct competition to John Galliano—his style was modern and romantic like Galliano's—but his company was far more streamlined and his clothes were produced and distributed by Zamasport, a major Italian clothing manufacturer. Gigli was the only person McQueen wanted to work for—and learn from.

On his first morning in Milan, he headed to Gigli's at Corso Como, 10, where he met Gigli's first assistant, a New Zealander named Lise Strathdee. Gigli was tied up in a meeting with his partner, Carla Sozzani, so Strathdee sat down with McQueen and looked at his book. As she paged through the portfolio she peppered him with questions. "He was polite, very focused and present, very real," she recalls. "And he was dead keen to work for Romeo. I was intrigued by the eclectic combination of experience: Red or Dead and Savile Row. Two different worlds."

She was most impressed by his Savile Row stretch; most fashion apprentices in Milan came directly from design schools and none of them had such rigorous training. She knew that Gigli, who incorporated classic men's tailoring in his work, would be interested in this too. She took down McQueen's contact information, and though she could tell he was disappointed, she sent him on his way.

When Gigli came out of his meeting, Strathdee told him about McQueen and suggested they meet. Gigli agreed, as long as it was right away. Strathdee ran out into Corso Como and saw McQueen heading into the Garibaldi subway station. She called out to him, and when he saw her, he broke into a big smile. They hustled up to Gigli's office.

Gigli looked thoughtfully through McQueen's portfolio and asked a few questions in his Italian-accented but very proper English. "I've been working on Savile Row, trying to understand the cut of the men's suits," McQueen responded. Gigli liked this. "I need someone to help me with that sort of work," he told McQueen. "Can you start tomorrow?"

Gigli explained to McQueen that his job would entail splitting his time between the studio in Milan and the Zamasport factory in Novara, in the foothills of the Italian Alps, to make sure that the designs were properly produced by the manufacturing team.

At the studio, McQueen watched carefully how Gigli used color and fit pieces together—in effect, his process.

"You are my master," McQueen told Gigli. "You are helping me grow in a good way."

It soon became apparent, Gigli says now, "that McQueen had a good attitude about fashion and a strong vision—he had a lot of strength."

On the days McQueen went to Novara, he commuted by train. He had to be there early—between 8:00 and 8:30 A.M.—because factory hours and schedules were highly structured. The factory was a state-of-the-art complex of several buildings protected by big electric gates. He was assigned to work with two senior pattern makers to get the samples just right. At times, he would butt heads with the old-timers, frustrated that he couldn't convey to them what needed to be done; they in turn were frustrated with his inability to understand how things were traditionally done in the factory. It didn't help that McQueen didn't speak much Italian, and the factory workers didn't speak much English.

Sometimes, he'd get lonely, longing to be back in the studio working with his fellow assistants. However, he realized that his time at the factory was invaluable: he was learning how to produce good prêt-à-porter on an industrial level, which, Strathdee says, "is an aspect of fashion at which the Italians excel—the Italian way to absolutely care for getting things exactly right." When the time would come to launch his own brand, he would know exactly what he needed to do to produce well-made clothes.

AFTER SEVERAL WEEKS, Gigli brought McQueen back to Corso Como to help in the studio. He enjoyed the homey atmosphere there. When they had to stay late to meet deadlines, Sozzani would order in huge platters of cheese, prosciutto, salads, and pastas and bottles of wine from neighborhood restaurants.

Gigli did not hover over his assistants. He would draw the collection at home, give them the sketches, come by the studio regularly to check in and answer queries, and then leave them to work on the samples on their own. "We did tedious work, like sketching and speccing, when you do technical drawings of the clothes," Carmen Artigas, an assistant from Mexico, recalls. "There was another building across the courtyard, where Romeo had seamstresses sewing on the second floor, and Lee would run over there and sew what he needed and then come back."

Gigli would review the samples and revise what needed work. "At the time I was looking for a new silhouette in men's jackets," Gigli recalls. "And I tried to cut that new shape, and it was quite difficult and McQueen helped the tailors to create it. When I studied the jacket the first time, I said, 'No, it's not correct here, you have to do something else here.' And he went back to work on it. By the third fitting for the jacket, it was still not perfect. When I opened the seams to see why it wasn't working, I saw written 'Fuck you!'" Gigli still laughs at the memory.

Throughout the process, McQueen closely observed Gigli's approach to design. He didn't necessarily care for Gigli's work in cut or in shape; Euro aristo-chic was the antithesis of McQueen's world and his evolving aesthetic. But he did grasp "something way more elusive and evocative," Strathdee says, and that was "the power of narrative. The power of archetypes."

McQueen was also studying Gigli the retailer at the Corso Como boutique: how Gigli successfully mixed other designers' work with his own baroque clothes on the shop floor. One day, Gigli received a few new pleated pieces by Japanese designer Issey Miyake and decided to hang them from the ceiling like an Alexander Calder mobile. McQueen adored the idea and helped Gigli install it. "He loved seeing these flying clothes," Gigli remembers.

With the rise of the fashion design industry, Milan became a creative center and developed a vibrant youth culture, with hip dance clubs, trendy cafés, and a social scene of interesting, artistic souls such as design assistants, stylists, editors, and fledging photographers, and the fun young models who worked for them. McQueen became friendly with assistants at other houses and often hit the town with them. One night, he invited Artigas to accompany him to a party hosted by one who worked for Versace. He and Artigas agreed to meet on a street corner and go together. It was pouring rain, so as he left the friend's apartment where he was staying, he grabbed a big antique Japanese paper parasol. Artigas was shocked when she saw him standing in the rain under the fragile, precious parasol. "It's going to get ruined!" she howled. He shrugged. "That was very Lee," she says. "Something unusually beautiful, falling apart."

McQueen had trouble finding a place to live in Milan. Eventually, Strathdee invited him to move in with her and fellow Gigli assistants Karen Brennan of Ireland and Frans Ankoné of Holland, in a nineteenth-century neoclassical apartment building on the narrow Via Ariberto. The four roomies all led their independent lives with their own friends, though, Strathdee says, "sometimes we'd all bump into each other in the kitchen, usually on a weeknight, drinking a glass of wine, chatting as we prepared our meals. Once I saw Lee at the stove cooking up some truly awful and unimaginable food combination—all I can remember is how horrified I was at the thought that someone would eat like that—and I immediately offered to make him dinner. Which he accepted. He ate like a Londoner: food as fuel. Not like an Italian."

Strathdee remembers another evening when the flatmates were in the kitchen and Ankoné asked about Milan nightlife. "Lee just blurted out all the names of the gay clubs in Milan—most I had heard of and a few that I hadn't," Strathdee says. "Frans, Karen, and I just swapped glances . . . and I thought, 'Oh, so you must be gay,' which was strange as from some prior comments Lee had made, I had got the impression that he was homophobic. I realized there was way more than met the eye with Lee—that he was quite a complex person."

One night, Strathdee came home to find McQueen curled up on her bed in the dark. "He was very upset over some argument he'd had and needed consoling," she says. "It took a while and I calmed him down, tried to make sense of the matter and sent him off to his room.

"Not long after, he packed up his stuff and moved out," she continues. "On a Sunday. He didn't say where to. In a bit of a mood. He left both the apartment front doors wide open and swinging, which was an I'm-outta-here gesture. A tad overdramatic, I thought at the time. He was so definitely able to create and command a scene just with his energy and mood."

AT THE END OF JULY, the Gigli studio prepared, like most Italian businesses back then, to shut down for the month of August for vacation. McQueen gave Artigas his mother's address and phone number in East London and told her to ring if she ever found herself in town. He surreptitiously swiped fabrics and clothes that he made from the studio. Then he went to see Gigli to officially resign. Once there, he was overcome with the emotion of leaving his Milan family. But he knew it was the right thing to do.

"I want to start my own collection and build my own style," he explained to Gigli, weeping. "You are a good teacher and I grew up a lot with you. Thank you."

Gigli never heard from him again.

WHEN MCQUEEN RETURNED TO LONDON, in August 1990, he went back to work with McKitterick as a machinist and cutter. McKitterick's designs at the time "were very sexual, with a lot of fetishism," he says. He was impressed by how much McQueen had matured in those few months in Milan and how inquisitive he had become about how fashion works.

"How do you begin a collection?" McQueen asked. "What comes first?"

"How do you get from these photographs on a wall to clothes on a rail?"

"Why do you include this and not that?"

Essentially, McKitterick says now, "Lee wanted to be taught fashion design. He wanted to learn the process of fashion." McKitterick suggested that he enroll at Central Saint Martins College of Art and Design, as the school was by then known. "I knew he didn't have academic qualifications, but it was a bit more liberal back then," McKitterick says. "You could get in on talent; it was more vocational." So he told McQueen go see Bobby Hillson, who was running the master's program.

Hillson was (and still is) a legend in London fashion. A St. Martins graduate, she worked as an illustrator throughout the 1950s and '60s for British *Vogue*, the *Sunday Times*, and the *Observer*—she attended and illustrated Coco Chanel's comeback show in 1953. In 1969, she founded a children's wear company, and in 1974, *The Times* of London named her designer of the year. She returned to St. Martins as a teacher and in the late 1970s she was asked to help create and oversee the school's fashion master's program.

One morning in September, Hillson arrived at her office and saw what she describes now as "a very unprepossessing boy" sitting out front.

"Are you waiting for me?"

"Yes," he responded.

She asked if he had an appointment with her.

"No," he responded, "but I've come to see you."

He motioned to the clothes he held over his arm.

"Well, come in. I'll give you five minutes," she said. "I really am in a rush."

As she reviewed the clothes—most from Romeo Gigli, which she immediately clocked as original samples that McQueen had pilfered—he told her about his experience.

"A tailor from Savile Row—*this* intrigued me," she says. "A tailor from Savile Row going out and not getting a job with Armani or one of the more tailoring-based designers—but with Romeo Gigli. I thought this was very odd."

Hillson was keenly interested to hear and see more.

"By the way," she asked as they were both preparing to leave. "Can you draw at all?"

"I've drawn all my life."

"Come back with some of your drawings," she told him. "I'll talk to you."

Some days later, he returned with a selection of sketches in hand.

Hillson took a look at them and was so impressed, she suggested that he skip undergraduate studies and go directly into the master's program. McQueen agreed. She apologized for not being able to offer him a scholarship—they had already been all doled out—but he assured her he would be able to raise the money for tuition.

After McQueen left, Hillson walked over to the office of Jane Rapley, then the dean of fashion and textiles.

"Jane, just to warn you, I've taken this boy," Hillson told her. "He's got none of the right qualifications but I think he's brilliant."

As it happened, after McQueen's grandfather died, his aunt, Renée Holland, came by the Biggerstaff Road home. "She saw the designs in [Lee's] room and said, 'He must go to college,'" Joyce later recalled. McQueen remembered Aunt Renée as a stylish woman and "a fantastic dresser." When she was told that he had been accepted to the fashion master's program at Central Saint Martins but couldn't pay the tuition, she immediately loaned him 4,000 pounds for the down payment.

In October, McQueen reported to Central Saint Martins's fashion department for the first day of classes. Another M.A. fashion student, Simon Ungless, a shy twenty-four-year-old from Berkshire, walked in and immediately noticed McQueen. "He looked really young—like fourteen, fifteen years old," Ungless says. "He had this curly, raver kind of hair down to his chin.

Huge bell-bottom raver jeans, all ratty, and a vintage kind of baseball jacket, and I thought, 'Well, he must be one of the teacher's kids.' I didn't consider for a minute he was another student on the program, because he just looked too young."

During the summer weeks preceding the new school year, the master's students were given an entry project to do. On the first day, they presented the projects for their fellow students to critique. "One," remembers Ungless, "was just the most horrible thing I'd ever seen. It was sort of fail. I thought: 'How did this person get into this program?'"

Hillson reviewed the project and asked the student: "Well, who's your customer?"

"*Kye-lee*," he responded in a fey, lispy voice, referring to the pop singer Kylie Minogue.

"I'm gay," Ungless says now. "But he was *really* gay. The way he said, '*Kye-lee*' . . ."

Ungless imitates it, and pauses for a moment, remembering the scene.

"I just started laughing and this young kid with the raver hair started laughing and we just couldn't stop laughing," he recalls. "Bobby asked us to leave the room because we were being so rude."

The kid introduced himself as Lee McQueen.

"And that was it," Ungless says. Instant friends.

As the pair got to know each other, they discovered they had similar working-class upbringings—though McQueen's was in the city and Ungless's in the country. Ungless earned his B.A. in fashion and textiles from the University of East London, and freelanced for a few years for companies in New York, Paris, Tokyo, and London, including for Paul Smith. He liked that McQueen also had professional experience and was especially impressed that McQueen had worked for Gigli. "I think that's why me and Lee bonded," Ungless says. "Because we weren't quite so precious in that art school way."

As with Galliano before them, the school's environment allowed each young man to emerge from his protective shell and explore fashion, the arts, and contemporary culture. "What I really liked [about Central Saint Martins] was the freedom of expression and being surrounded by like-minded people," McQueen said.

McKitterick, who had recently started teaching menswear at Central Saint Martins, was amazed by McQueen's evolution. "The change in him was remarkable—he was more grown-up and worldly," McKitterick says. "I remember meeting him in the street on his way to class and he was talking about things in a way he never had before. Like: 'I'm off to the Chapman Brothers exhibition.'"

Despite this new maturity, McQueen had a hard time fitting in at Central Saint Martins. "He hadn't been in the academic situation before, and the other students had been, and they knew how to react to critiques and those processes, and he didn't. So I think they found him annoying," McKitterick says. "He would butt in and remark on things and the students thought you shouldn't speak to a tutor that way. And he had very strong opinions that were usually very right, which got up the nose of students and tutors alike."

TO KEEP UP THE PAYMENTS during his two years at Central Saint Martins, McQueen hustled up all the side work he could. Along with working part-time at McKitterick, and making clothes for fellow students, he picked up a few other freelance gigs.

One was helping Jasper Conran produce costumes for Simon Callow's touring production of *My Fair Lady*. Among the eight hundred costumes Conran designed for the show was a suite of complicated dresses for the aristocratic ladies in the Ascot horse race scene. The gowns were so angular and unusual that Conran's chief cutter was confounded by how to cut and construct them. One of the young pattern makers on the team piped up: "We should use this boy, this Saint Martins student who's a fantastic cutter. He'll understand what we're trying to do."

Not only did McQueen manage to figure out how to cut the gowns, he actually sewed them. Conran was thrilled and utterly relieved.

McQueen's father, Ronald, was concerned about McQueen's lack of money. "There was always an atmosphere when he and Dad were together," his brother Michael says. "Lee would be at home sewing and Dad would turn round and say, 'Why don't you get yourself a proper job?'" Eventually resigned to McQueen's career choice, Ronald suggested that he make some trousers to sell at the Roman Road market in East London. McQueen was aghast: "He wanted me . . . to get a stall, a market stall! All he saw was the bad side of the situation: 'You don't have money for eighteen months!'"

Once McQueen had cash in his pocket he was hesitant to let it go—even to pay his tuition. "Jane Rapley had terrible times getting the money out of him," Hillson recalls with a laugh. Back then students could pay by the term, which was twelve weeks long. "And so about week five, I'd call him in and say 'You haven't paid, Lee, and you can't stay if you don't pay,'" Rapley says. "And he would say, 'I'm waiting for a check. Once I get it, I'll pay you.' And eventually he *would* pay. But he struggled throughout the two years he was there."

AT THE END OF their first year at Central Saint Martins, Ungless and McQueen connected on a Wednesday evening, hit a couple of bars and wound up at the club Heaven. It was the first time they had been together at a gay club. In fact, up until then, Ungless wasn't positive about McQueen's sexual orientation. "Looking at him," Ungless says now, "he would have been the last candidate for being gay. All of us gay guys had shaved hair—we had this look." And McQueen, with his long curly hair, his "angelic" face as Ungless puts it, and his tough comportment, didn't fit the form.

Ungless still remembers what McQueen was wearing that evening: a sleeveless patchwork sheepskin vest over a T-shirt. Ungless thought McQueen was going to swelter in the sheepskin, but McQueen refused to take it off, because "he was really self-conscious about his body," Ungless explains. Since McQueen refused to remove the vest, he refused to dance, "because he didn't want to sweat," he continues. But McQueen did really want to pick up a guy that night, and hit on one so provocatively—what he said was so vulgar Ungless still cannot repeat it—that the shocked fellow turned and walked away. "That's when it really hit me how gay Lee was," Ungless says. "He was good at hiding it. But that's the East End upbringing. It was really a tough place to be gay."

MCQUEEN AND UNGLESS would hang out together, in school and at Ungless's pad in Tooting Bec, South London. Much of the time, they'd gossip about people they knew, "photography, sex, music, more sex," Ungless says with a laugh. But their favorite subject was fashion, especially what was happening in Paris. They loved the work of Helmut Lang, the young Austrian who was making news with his modern minimalist clothes, and Martin Margiela, the Paris-based Belgian avant-gardist who was obsessed with anonymity and, like Kawakubo, was a leader in deconstruction. They also admired Azzedine Alaïa for "his cut and simplicity and perfect details and devoid of decorative junk," Ungless says. They'd travel together to Paris for fashion week, share a room in a youth hostel, and sneak into the shows to see what Lang, Margiela, and Alaïa were doing.

McQueen's favorite, however, was the French couturier Yves Saint Laurent—in particular his wardrobe for French actress Catherine Deneuve in *Belle de Jour*, Luis Buñuel's 1967 Surrealist gem about a frigid bourgeois housewife who works as a high-end call girl.

Saint Laurent's work from back then "is something that attracts some of us to fashion in the first place," Ungless explains. "That mythical being that is Yves Saint Laurent—what we all perceive as Rive Gauche; his women Loulou de la Falaise, Betty Catroux, Paloma Picasso, Deneuve; that lifestyle and story—it's quite addictive and so sexy. For McQueen, the perception of Saint Laurent was so much sex. Lee always would talk about Saint Laurent. I knew he wanted the Saint Laurent job someday."

There were two designers who were decidedly not creative influences on their work: Vivienne Westwood and John Galliano. Especially Galliano. He had been a regular fixture on the club and London fashion scene for so long that "he didn't hit the radar anymore," Ungless says. When teachers would say, "You draw like Galliano," Ungless and McQueen would roll their eyes and groan. In their opinion, Westwood and Galliano were not doing modern fashion. "It felt like lessons in the history of fashion," Ungless says. "What they were doing didn't seem relevant to us."

But McQueen did quietly admire Galliano's achievements.

"Galliano was always the benchmark for Lee," McKitterick says. "Galliano was the one that Lee had to be—or had to be better than."

ON A SUNDAY NIGHT in early 1992, Ungless planned to meet up with his friend the jewelry designer Shaun Leane and invited McQueen to join them. Leane was boyish, darkly handsome, and preppy—more or less the opposite of McQueen. "Lee was wearing a completely horrible sleeveless vest he had made from a Romeo Gigli fabric he had 'acquired' and a pair of Jesus sandals," Ungless remembers. Despite their differences, the threesome became fast friends, and together explored London's homosexual underground, hitting gay clubs that they might not otherwise have considered and daring each other to go to London's parks to watch men having sex.

When it came time for McQueen to start working on his degree collection, he chose an extremely dark theme: Jack the Ripper. "I had a fascination with Jack the Ripper," McQueen explained. "My mum's a genealogist and found out that one of the victims had been staying at one of my relative's inns in Whitechapel. I was ready to solve the whole bloody mystery."

McQueen also used the Marquis de Sade's famous *The 120 Days of Sodom*—an eighteenth-century tale of orgies and sexual and physical abuse at a remote French castle—as an inspiration. "That was one of our couldn't-put-it-down books," Ungless recalls. He insists that for him and McQueen, it was "really enlightening—the sex acts were things one had never imagined."

McQueen told McKitterick that he loved Pier Paolo Pasolini's film adaptation of it, *Salò, or the 120 Days of Sodom*. In Pasolini's version, four rich Italian fascist libertines during World War II kidnap eighteen teenagers—nine boys and nine girls—torture them sexually and mentally for four months, then murder them. "It is such a disturbing film," McKitterick says. No doubt McQueen's own sexual abuse as a child came into play—indeed it may have been the root of the collection. He would later say that much of his work was autobiographical.

To further explore his collection's theme, McQueen researched Victorian pornography and fetishism and the history of menswear cutting techniques, and he became obsessed "with distorting the human form with way-too-small pants and elongating the torso," Ungless says.

All of these creative threads were, in their way, a continuation of the work he did for Anderson & Sheppard (traditional British tailoring), Tatsuno (complicated construction), McKitterick (fetishism), and Gigli (nineteenth-century decadence), but synthesized by the dark, East End, former skinhead's mind. He decided to design sharply tailored clothes in rich tones and transparency. They would have historical references and lines—like traditional frock coats lined in mauve, a Victorian color for mourning—yet they would look resolutely modern. And though they were difficult in their construction—with twisted sleeves and asymmetrically pleated bodices—they could be worn with ease.

As McQueen worked on the collection, Hillson would pop in to see how he was doing. She realized he was using fabrics that he'd bought for little money from cloth merchants on Berwick Street in Soho and, she says, "He was *torturing* these fabrics—printing them, crushing them, until they were not recognizable. I said, 'You can't do that to cheap fabrics!' I unearthed fabrics that the Swiss textile companies had donated to us. I knew the only way fabrics would survive what he was putting them through would be to use good ones."

McQueen added all sorts of curious elements to his constructions. He used human hair in the linings of the tailored coats and jackets—a reference to Jack the Ripper's victims, since prostitutes in the nineteenth century often cut and sold their hair for extra money. He tore or distressed some of the pieces to imitate the tattered clothing of the prostitutes, and splashed some with red paint to invoke the brutal murders the women endured. One fabric—a rich pink satin—he printed with a large black pattern of what he wanted to be barbed wire but became long branches with thorns. The structural leitmotif of the collection was tailoring. "Working on Savile Row was about getting a basis," he said. "Before you can deconstruct a garment, you need to know how to construct one."

Like Galliano, McQueen enlisted help from classmates. A first-year textile student made the patchwork that he would use for a full circle skirt; she also created a collage made of burned magazine tear sheets that McQueen turned into a full skirt with a bustle. Ungless put together long strings of tiny red glass beads, which McQueen sandwiched between layers of black chiffon for pants, and cut and shredded pleated feathers for a sleeveless tunic, sleeveless top, and pants.

"I remember working with him on one of the jackets that had a peplum that stuck out at ninety degrees from the back—it was being held up with a string of calico," Ungless says. "An instructor asked how he planned to make it work without being tied up. He said he didn't know. The instructor claimed we were both quite mad and walked off. Of course Lee worked that shit out and the peplum did what he wanted it to do."

While reading *The Face*, McQueen discovered the work of Simon Costin, a London jewelry designer who specialized in body sculpture made of animal parts and matter. Costin learned taxidermy at the Natural History Museum from the age of eleven to sixteen. Once he finished college, he began to make necklaces and headdresses using hair, teeth, blood, semen, and bones. McQueen thought this was in perfect synergy with his collection.

He contacted Costin and asked if he could borrow some pieces for his degree show. By then, Costin was working with a gallery making multimedia installation art, but he still had some jewelry pieces in his studio. He agreed to lend McQueen seven, including a black lace necklace decorated with rabbit skulls; a jet-beaded headdress; a bird-claw brooch; and a choker with little bear paws he'd harvested from a moth-eaten taxidermy. When McQueen picked them up, Costin found him to be "a charming, rough-and-ready lad, with a raucous and irreverent sense of humor."

McQueen showed his ten-outfit collection, entitled "Jack the Ripper Stalks His Victims," to McKitterick. "I saw it on the rail," McKitterick says, "and I thought it was really very strong." When the lineup was announced, McKitterick was surprised that McQueen was not the finale; he was second to last.

The Central Saint Martins M.A. Fashion Show was scheduled during London's fall–winter 1992–93 Fashion Week in the British Fashion Council tent at the Duke of York Barracks on the morning of Monday, March 16, 1992—the day before McQueen's twenty-third birthday.

As the graduation show unfurled—twenty-three students each presenting a half dozen ensembles that they had styled themselves, to music they had chosen—it was easy to see some overarching themes: Armani's soft lines and beige-gray palette, Jil Sander's and Helmut Lang's minimalism, Yohji Yamamoto's Asian purity, Thierry Mugler's S&M leather look, and a lot of Galliano—particularly from the "Witness" collection. Some actually looked like tryouts for jobs at specific houses.

Then came McQueen's collection. In his program notes, he stated that it was "Day into evening wear . . . inspired by nineteenth-century street walkers," and gave a special thanks to his "sponsors": Renée Holland, his aunt, and Joyce Deane, his mother. To a cool house-music beat, the show opened with a high-waist, skintight pair of dark red satin peg pants with a black asymmetrical bandeau top and long ropes of tiny black beads. Next came a sheer black chiffon sleeveless shift over a black bra and black double-layer chiffon pencil skirt hemmed with goose feathers, and a Simon Costin neckpiece of black feathers and bone.

That was followed by the fashion magazine collage hoop skirt and black satin frock coat with the ducktail-like derriere, worn over a naked torso and loosely tied closed just below the breasts; a long, swishy patchwork skirt, paired with a sharply tailored satin jacket; a sleeveless blood red and black feathery tunic, worn as a microminidress with torn sheer stockings; a tailcoat made of the pink satin printed with black thorn branches, worn with a black bra top and black satin pants; a black satin tailcoat lined with red satin, worn over a naked torso with black satin tuxedo pants trimmed with sparkling red beads; a sheer black feathery sleeveless top with an open back and feathery peg trousers; a fitted, wasp-waist black coat with a 3-D peplum, over a scarlet pencil skirt sprinkled with twinkling beads; and a sheer deep red sleeveless blouse with jet bead epaulets that cascaded down the front and a pair of high-waist black satin peg pants.

There was nothing soft or mainstream commercial about the collection, though each piece could be worn easily. It was the only collection that had any hint of sensuality to it; indeed, it was very sexy and it made the girls look strong without sacrificing their femininity. Most important, there were several silhouettes that would eventually become McQueen signatures: the frock coat; the tailcoat; the sleeveless tunic minidress. Remarkably, at the age of twenty-two, Alexander McQueen had already found his voice, his line, and his vision.

V

S ince the court of Versailles, Paris has reigned as the capital of fashion. What drew and still draws designers there is the craftsmen; the
materials; the heritage; the savoir faire and the *art de vivre*. "It's the
Shangri-La of creativity," milliner Stephen Jones says.

Galliano wanted to be a part of it. "London was dead," he said. "Nothing
was happening." The recession had nearly killed London Fashion Week: retailers and editors had tighter travel budgets and often skipped London and
went straight to Paris. So Peder Bertelsen agreed to finance Galliano's first
show there. In late 1989, Galliano requested a slot on the official calendar for

the fall–winter 1990–91 season. And when the time came, he took his team's core—Deborah Bulleid, who was now officially COO; sales director Hannah Woodhouse; chief pattern cutter Bill Gaytten; Steven Robinson; and Harlech—to Paris to help him stage the show.

On Wednesday, March 14, 1990, twenty-nine-year-old Galliano made his Paris debut, in a tent in the Cour Carrée of the Louvre. His inspiration, he said, was "biker girls—modern women in complete control of their lives." It began nearly an hour late, to a thumping Healy soundtrack and with pop star Annie Lennox of the Eurythmics in the audience. There was a mix of red and silver satin princess coats with wide, cut-out collars; riding jodhpurs with waistcoats; sharply tailored cropped jackets with skinny stirrup pants; white fencing-like outfits with a reprise of the beekeeping veiling pulled tight to look like a fencing helmet; and white satin tuxedos and tailcoats. To add to the theatrics, Galliano doused the models with water—as he had in London for "Fallen Angels." When he took his bow, he was drenched too.

The press approved. Bernadine Morris called it "a credible showing . . . flinging fabric about with the audacity of the Japanese designers," and added, "His clothes were inventive enough and varied enough to hold the international audience." *Women's Wear Daily* declared that the day "belonged to John Galliano."

Paris had opened Galliano's eyes and his mind and his heart.

"I knew," he said, "I could make my dreams come true there."

JOHN FLETT'S CAREER was going far less well. Though, as Galliano pointed out, he "was a good Jewish boy—he had a passion for the business side of fashion as well as the creative," and *Details* fashion editor Bill Cunningham described him as "a big talent waiting to make his claim on the international stage," his form-fitting stretch dresses sat on store racks. In the economic recession that followed the 1987 stock market crash, few were willing to pay 500 pounds (or $830) apiece—an astounding amount at the time—for a frock by an unknown designer. In response, he upped his heroin intake.

Some of Flett's friends began to wonder if his spiral downward was rooted in a crisis of confidence creatively—that he realized he was "too much in the shadow of Galliano," Hamish Bowles says. Another friend suspects that Flett's jealousy of Galliano's success might have been eating at him. His heroin addiction was making him erratic and he began to steal from the company. When his backer Miles Gill confronted him, he fled to Paris and briefly worked for Claude Montana at Lanvin; eventually he landed a design job at Enrico Coveri in Florence.

On the evening of January 18, 1991, a few days before he was due to sign a contract to relaunch a namesake brand with a new Italian backer, Flett woke up in the middle of the night in his Florence apartment violently ill, so much so that he collapsed on the floor and lost consciousness. Flett's boyfriend Nunzio Carbone called a doctor, who believed Flett was suffering from a bout of gastrointestinal flu, gave Flett an injection, wrote a prescription for Carbone to fill, and left. Carbone went to the twenty-four-hour pharmacy, only to find it closed. When he returned to the flat, he saw his sister Marcella next to Flett, holding Flett's hand. She said: "He's dead." He was twenty-seven. The official cause of death was a heart attack.

The funeral was on a horribly cold and gloomy day in northern England. June Flett instructed invitees not to wear black. Dozens of friends attended, including Galliano, who donned a pair of Flett's gold sequin shorts in homage.

Flett's obituaries in the British papers were full of great praise. The *Telegraph* called him "one of the brightest and best designers of his generation."

Even today, friends still mourn the loss. "I think he would have gone on to do great things," Bowles says, "because he had real talent."

"John Flett is fashion's unsung unknown hero," says another longtime friend, adding, "Without John Flett, there wouldn't have been a John Galliano."

BERTELSEN WAS LOSING INTEREST in high fashion. The young Brits just weren't commercial enough and he had dropped them all except Galliano. Bertelsen's critics charged that he was only backing the designers for quick profits, and when he didn't earn them, he bailed.

Galliano felt the squeeze in early 1991. He kept nagging Bertelsen to allow him to design menswear, which he loved. Instead, Aguecheek launched Galliano Jeans and Galliano's Girl, a lower-priced, younger secondary line that was named for Galliano's alter ego. Galliano's Girl, which Galliano described as "much more accessible, younger and funkier," retailed for 30 percent less than the main collection. Its top market was Japan, followed by Italy, and then Britain. The jeans were pricey: they sold for 150 pounds back when a pair of Levi's cost 30. Galliano justified the high price by explaining, "There's an awful lot of detail. Fabric innovation, stretch and bonded fabrics, PVC."

But Galliano's Girl was a tactical mistake for the brand, made by one of Bertelsen's bad hires, an executive from a sporting goods company. And sportswear wasn't what Galliano's customers—thirty-plus, wealthy, fashion-obsessed women—wanted. They loved his bias-cut gowns and elaborate frock coats. As Robinson said, Galliano's Girl "wasn't a good direction."

The biggest blow came when Bertelsen told Galliano that he could not design, show, or produce a ready-to-wear collection for the fall–winter 1991–92 season for Fashion Week in March. Instead the company would focus on selling Galliano Jeans and Galliano's Girl. Galliano was devastated by the decision: it was the first season he did not produce a high fashion collection since his St. Martins degree show in the summer of 1985.

To calm his nerves, he began to drink excessively, again. But ever the determined soul, he continued to go to the office every day and work like a demon to make his company succeed. As when he and Brun were sliding toward bankruptcy, Galliano thought that press coverage could save him. That summer, he sat down and did a Q&A interview with his longtime friend Paul Frecker to be published in *Blitz*. (Unfortunately, the magazine folded before the piece could run, so Galliano never got that needed media bump.) During the interview, Galliano was unusually frank.

When asked if fashion was art or business, he responded, "Business. It's definitely a business. You have to sell frocks." He added that, looking back, he and his fellow St. Martins graduates who went into business "weren't prepared" to run companies. "We were creating a demand and the world's press was creating a demand with us, which we couldn't fulfill because we didn't have the necessary know-how or business acumen."

He also reflected on the demands of his work. "I'm quite obsessive . . . because I care so much, because I am so passionate about clothes." He described his job as "the daily grind, the sleepless nights, the frayed nerves," but said, "That's what I thrive on—the constant search for perfection." He said that the month leading up to a fashion show "is exhausting, it's endless," but added, "I'm quite addicted to it, I think. For a month your body's running on pure adrenaline. You just want to make these girls look as beautiful as you can."

"I worry before collections," he continued. "It's like slicing yourself open and letting the whole world see, warts and all, what you're about, what you're thinking, what your attitude to women is. You're laying yourself open to all that."

But the pace was taking its toll. "I can't think of any other trade where every six months you have to come up with completely new ideas, ideas that have to be tried and tested. That work, that dry clean, that won't shrink, that you can live in, that make you feel beautiful. I can't think of any other trade where you have to go through that."

His most gratifying moment so far, he said, was "walking into the Cour Carrée at the Louvre and seeing my name above the tent for the first time. I was very proud of that."

And his professional goal?

"I'd like to see the whole world wearing John Galliano clothes."

GALLIANO WAS DETERMINED not to miss another season, so he found a stopgap measure of sorts: Shellys, the London-based shoe company, agreed to underwrite more than half the cost of his show in Paris in October. He was greatly relieved, but there was still the matter of where to design the collection and who would pay for the materials. His friend and German sales agent Dietmar Schloten had an idea: Fayçal Amor, a Tangier-born, Paris-based fashion executive who owned and ran the successful French ready-to-wear company Plein Sud.

Galliano told Amor he was in a bind for his spring–summer 1992 show— Shellys could only pay so much—so Amor allowed him to work in the Plein Sud studio and helped out with expenses. Paris designer Azzedine Alaïa, whom Galliano met through the British retailer Joseph Ettedgui, offered half his showroom in the Marais to sell the collection to retailers; the other half would be used by Vivienne Westwood.

A FEW WEEKS LATER, on October 16, 1991, Galliano presented his spring– summer 1992 collection in the Cour Carrée tents. To Healy's music—opening with a remix of Wham!'s early eighties hit "Everything She Wants"—the models came out with their hair curled and piled up in a sort of postcoital nonchalance, their eyes darkly made up, their lips a deep plum, their cheeks dotted with beauty marks, their walk a Mae West swagger in tall, needle-heeled bedroom slippers. The first passage set the tone: the girls were dressed in white bras, panties, and girdles—and sometimes topless—sheathed in a transparent white veil. Then came the same in black, with tailcoats and sheer cropped pants and veiled silk top hats à la Dietrich.

There were sherbet-hued satin eighteenth-century jackets with explosions of ruffles on the cuffs and on the derriere, over lacy strapless bras and silver satin briefs. There were the ubiquitous bias-cut satin slip dresses topped off with gigantic frothy meringue-like picture hats, and long-sleeved black bias-cut satin gowns with Christian clerical collars—a nod to his devout Catholic upbringing perhaps—and flesh-revealing slashes across the bodices. As the music slowed down to the Sounds of Blackness's gospel meditation "The Pressure, Part 2," he sent out tailored frock coats over glistening naked torsos and cream corsets slightly torn or disheveled. It was naughty. It was modern. It was hot.

Throughout the show, the audience whistled, whooped, and cheered, and when Galliano came out to take his quick bow, in a ratty T-shirt and shorts and waving his hand in a peace sign, the place exploded in applause. "There is no reason at all for these clothes to be seen in public," wrote Bernadine Morris in *The New York Times*. "But Mr. Galliano's show, in addition to a cloying sweetness, had a kind of lunatic charm."

Cathy Horyn, the new fashion critic at *The Washington Post*, was less adulatory: "His clothes . . . are vulgar. They degrade women. . . . And yet, somehow, all this nonsense is endearing, like watching a clever child dress up in his mother's clothes and tap-dance across the living room. Maybe after all these years of watching Galliano exist on the fringe, on what appears to be a shoestring, we've learned to allow him his excesses."

THE CRITICAL PRAISE and acclaim was not enough to save Galliano's business, and in late November 1991, the inevitable became official: Bertelsen announced to the press that he was withdrawing his financial support of John Galliano. "He just wasn't selling well enough," Bertelsen said. "John's market, which is the very trendy market, is the first to leave when economic times get hard."

Aguecheek would continue to produce and sell the Galliano Jeans line, which had sales of about 100,000 pounds ($179,000) a season and was licensed with U.K.-based Tula Ltd., a company Bertelsen half owned, but Galliano's Girl would be shuttered. As with Brun, the relationship ended badly, with Galliano's archives chucked into bins and assets sold off in liquidation.

The day after the announcement, Galliano told *Women's Wear Daily*, "I think Peder and I have gone as far as we can go together." He said, "I am going to Paris this evening to begin the search for a new backer." He planned to "avoid rushing into anything," adding, "I want to make the right choice. I'm still young."

VI

One of the audience members at the Central Saint Martins M.A. Degree Fashion Show on the morning of Monday, March 16, 1992, was a small, elegant English aristocrat named Isabella Blow. An associate editor at British *Vogue*, she made it her mission to find and nurture London's fledgling fashion geniuses. "She was like a truffle hound for talent," said her friend Hamish Bowles. And for her, the Central Saint Martins degree shows were like the yearling sales for a racehorse owner: the perfect place to spot a potential star.

Habitually tardy, she arrived when the tent was full and was forced to sit on the stairs. She patiently watched nearly two dozen presentations, ranging from Armani-esque minimalism to cheerful beachwear, but nothing particularly moved her. Then McQueen's collection came out. "It was obvious from the first outfit that here was someone of enormous potential and great gifts," she later said. She was particularly taken with McQueen's precise, bold tailoring. "No one spotted it," she noted. "They kept thinking it was just blood and paint, they weren't looking at the cut!" When she got home that evening, she told her husband, Detmar Blow: "Det, his clothes move like birds. He can cut material like God."

A true English aristocrat—she was a descendant of John de Delves of Cheshire, who is said to have rescued Edward the Black Prince during the Battle of Poitiers—Isabella grew up on her family's vast estate, Doddington Park. To her chagrin, she did not live in the property's grand eighteenth-century manor, Doddington Hall, but in a smaller outbuilding—her playboy paternal grandfather Sir "Jock" Delves Broughton had squandered the family fortune. He was later acquitted of murdering his second wife's lover in Kenya—a scandal recounted in the book *White Mischief*—and eventually committed suicide at a hotel in Liverpool with an overdose of morphine.

Her paternal grandmother—Jock's first wife, Vera—was far more fun: a much-photographed society beauty, she abandoned her husband and family in 1931 to embark on life as an explorer in Africa, Southeast Asia, and the Antipodes with her lover.

Isabella embodied her grandmother's spirit, if not her looks: she was petite—five-foot-two with straight-back posture—and *jolie laide* with a long face, downturned eyes, a short chin, and narrow overbite. "My face is like a Plantagenet portrait," she once declared. She had an air of mourning about her too, rooted in a family tragedy for which she was blamed: in 1964, when she was five, her two-year-old brother drowned in a shallow garden pool, and she was the only witness. Her severe father, Sir Evelyn Delves Broughton, wedded to the English tradition of primogeniture, was inconsolable; in his mind, he no longer had an heir. Isabella and her two sisters were packed off to boarding schools; eventually, their mother moved to London and the couple divorced.

Isabella used fashion "as a protection against the world, a protection against the inadequacies, as she perceived them, of her own body and her looks," Bowles said. "Clothes were a way of refocusing attention away from those things." But in time, clothes became Isabella Blow's raison d'être: She wore them in the most incongruous ways and supported their creators in any way that she could. "Issie understood that [fashion] is very, very serious business in terms of civilization and culture," her friend the writer A. A. Gill explained. "Not everybody reads poetry or listens to music, but every single person in the world gets up in the morning and puts on something, and whether you like it or not, that's a statement about who you are."

Her gift was how naturally and easily she wore clothes: she could make even the strangest ensembles seem perfectly normal while simultaneously making herself astonishingly alluring. "Severity with a twist" is how she described her look. Often there was a bustier involved, hoisting her ample bosom up and out, and a wasp waist to accentuate it. She usually wore a skirt, since she had beautiful legs, and always—*always*—vertiginous heels, which she walked in with grace. There was also a dose of humor or wit—like the time she wore a necklace to a dinner at Princess Michael of Kent's that read "Blowjob," or when she went to Karl Lagerfeld's for dinner wearing a Givenchy rubber dress and a greasy chain, which she dragged across his Aubusson carpet. And she never ceased to surprise, like when she'd arrive for her job as Anna Wintour's assistant at *Vogue* in New York "in red chinoiserie, a Chinese dress with brocade, and black gloves above the elbow," her former *Vogue* colleague André Leon Talley remembers, or in a ball gown.

Her signature, however, was her hat. She rarely stepped out of the house without one—primarily made by a young milliner named Philip Treacy, whom she discovered while he was still a student. She met him in 1989 at the offices of *Tatler* magazine, where she worked; he had come by to pick up a hat that he had made for a shoot. He was tall and reed-thin, with the palest of complexions and a shock of red hair. He told her that he had interned for London milliner Stephen Jones, and now, at twenty-two, was completing his master's degree at the Royal College of Art as the fashion department's first millinery student.

But none of that mattered to Isabella at that moment. All she wanted to do was see what was in the box that he was carrying.

He opened it and slowly lifted out a green felt 1920s-style cloche with jagged edges, like crocodile teeth.

"I'd never seen anything like it," she later said. "It was beautifully made and an emerald green . . . no, more like grasshopper green. It was so exquisite that when we pulled it out of the box it was like we shouldn't be touching it."

A few weeks later, she rang him and asked him to design her hat for her wedding, which was a few months off, in November. She invited him to meet her at her mother-in-law's home on Elizabeth Street. Also there were Manolo Blahnik and Talley—neither of whom young Treacy had heard of. Isabella told Treacy that she was interested, as she put it, in going back to her "Mediaeval roots" for the wedding as a nod to her ancestor who saved the Black Prince.

For her dress, she explained that she had first approached John Galliano and asked him to make her something in chain mail, but for some reason, it didn't happen. So she hired a little-known designer named Nadia La Valle, who designed a long-sleeved fitted gown in purple velvet. Blahnik was going to do her shoes: gold slippers, with extra-long pointy toes.

For the hat, Treacy proposed a gold filigree crown inspired by Cecil Beaton's 1930 photograph of the British socialite Lady Diana Cooper as the Madonna. Blow knew the image, and loved the idea. "I couldn't believe that I'd hit upon the one person who didn't expect tulle and veiling and pearls for her wedding hat," Treacy said. "Issie could have had anyone in the world to make her hat. I was just a student from somewhere, but Issie didn't care. . . . For some reason she just believed in me."

When he finished his studies at the Royal College, she asked him: "Why don't you come and make hats in my house?" Treacy accepted and set up his studio in the basement on Elizabeth Street. And she took him on as if he were her charge, insisting he learn more about arts, history, style, and culture, and to break the rules, to go farther with his designs. He did, designing wonderfully imaginative *chapeaux* for her such as a giant transparent orange disc that shrouded her face; the word "Blow" spelled out in feathers hovering above her head; a miniature replica of an eighteenth-century French sailing ship in black satin with full rigging; and most famously, a lobster. She wore Treacy's hats everywhere, effortlessly—"like she was not wearing them—like they happened to be there," he said. And she helped him land a job as the milliner for Chanel in Paris.

UPON SEEING "Jack the Ripper Stalks His Victims," Isabella Blow decided that Lee Alexander McQueen was going to be her protégé. And now that she was at British *Vogue*—she joined the glossy in late 1989 as a fashion editor—

she felt she had the voice and the place to herald him as he deserved. She tracked down the number for his family home on Biggerstaff Road. McQueen's mother answered and told her that he was out of town.

When he returned, his mother said, "There's this mad lady keeps calling that's in love with your clothes."

He resisted Isabella's overtures for a while—to him, she seemed "nutty." But, he said, "[She] wouldn't stop badgering me." Finally he gave in and agreed to meet with her at Central Saint Martins.

She arrived wearing "these great collapsed black organza horns on her head," he recalled. "I just thought she was incredibly fab." She tried on a jacket and asked the price. He told her 450 pounds.

"That's a lot for a student," she responded.

Nevertheless, he stuck by his price. And she bought it.

For years, Blow claimed that she purchased the entire collection for 5,000 pounds ($9,000) and McQueen never disputed her. But Ungless says now with authority: "It wasn't the entire collection."

What is for certain is that she bought much of it and paid for it in installments. "This was, in fact, Issie's usual modus operandi," Detmar Blow later explained. "She never had enough money to buy outright the clothes, hats, or jewelry that she wanted." To get paid, McQueen would call on her at the London offices of Condé Nast, with his clothes in a plastic trash bag. Then the pair would go to a nearby cash machine, she'd withdraw what she could and hand it over to him. "Lee was always desperately trying to get money—some money—out of her," Ungless remembers.

She couldn't wait to tell Philip Treacy about her new discovery. "Philip, I've met this boy," she said, almost dreamily. As she described McQueen, and his clothes, her eyes lighting up brightly, joy beaming from her with each word, Treacy could see what was happening. "What we had was like a love affair," he says. "And now she was having a new affair."

Treacy was fine with it. After all, he made hats. He was not competing with McQueen on a creative level; only when it came to Isabella. McQueen and Treacy got on, but they weren't exactly "friends"—at least not at first. What linked them was Isabella—her support, her kindness, her profound generosity—and for this reason, they had a genuine respect for each other.

Despite Isabella's enthusiasm, McQueen kept looking for a solid job in fashion as a design assistant for an established house. He met with Alice

Smith and Cressida Pye at the employment headhunting agency Denza in London. He went to Paris hoping to land an internship with his idol, Martin Margiela. To his surprise, he scored an appointment with Margiela in person, and when they met, Margiela said he thought McQueen was too talented to work as an intern and told him to return to London and start his own company. Instead, he went to see Jean Paul Gaultier but "there was this queen at the desk who said, 'You don't have an appointment,'" he recalled. "So I said, 'Forget this,' and went back to London."

In September 1992, McQueen moved out of his parents' home and into the second bedroom of Ungless's place in Tooting Bec. They furnished it with charity store finds and family castoffs as well as two sewing machines, a few Stockman dress forms, and Ungless's drawing board. The walls were giant mood boards, tacked with pictures, swatches, press clippings, bits of yarn, and bric-a-brac that served as inspiration for their designs. The backyard became a Hazmat area where they worked "with chemicals that had terrible odors," Ungless says. "Latex and resin were the worst."

To unwind, Ungless would have a whisky. But McQueen hardly ever drank alcohol, and when he did, he was wussy about it. "Lee's tipple was cider," Ungless says. "A half pint of cider and he was anyone's. Seriously, he could not handle his booze."

They picked up work as they could, making clothes for music videos and creating textile designs that they sold to various clients in the United States and Japan. Ungless set up a second studio in an old warehouse on Tooting High Street to do printing; on Mondays, McQueen would join him there and the two would spend the day drawing and painting designs. "He would always be doing beautiful Japanese koi, carp, and fighting fish," Ungless recalls. "And one of my print agents, years and years before, said, 'You can't do fish. People won't buy fish print. They won't wear it.'" Nevertheless, Ungless put one of McQueen's fish prints in the portfolio and sent it to New York. "And it was the first thing that someone bought."

While McQueen was quietly making things in Tooting Bec, Isabella Blow was talking him up throughout fashionable central London. She even managed to wrangle a few pages in the November issue of British *Vogue* for a photo-driven article about her and Detmar at Hilles, the Blow family estate in Gloucestershire; for the pictures, Isabella would primarily be dressed in McQueen clothes and Treacy hats.

Hilles is a curious house—an Arts and Crafts manor with an Elizabethan air, designed by Detmar's grandfather, an architect named Detmar Jellings Blow, and constructed in 1914. The decor was and is rather medieval—armor, pre-Raphaelite tapestries, and august portraits of relatives and British royalty. Like the Delves Broughtons, the Blows didn't have much of their family money left, and Hilles was somewhat désusé. Once Isabella and Detmar married, Isabella buffed up the place and made it their country retreat, inviting their friends in fashion, the arts, and the aristocracy for intimate weekends or raucous themed parties, such as the Feast of Baghdad and a Beggar's Banquet. "The house had a renaissance with Issie," Detmar admitted. "[She] brought the whole place alive, opened the doors, filled it with people, the way my grandfather intended."

In the *Vogue* shoot Hilles, Isabella, and Detmar all shined on the glossy pages—as did McQueen. Isabella wore several pieces from the "Jack the Ripper" collection, including the black wool hunting jacket with the ducktail-like peplum and the thorn-printed pink satin coat, which she paired with a towering black Philip Treacy hat.

She helped another of her preferred designers, John Galliano, by wearing one of his elegant white evening suits with a long flared skirt for a photo in front of an Edward Burne-Jones tapestry. The loveliest picture of all, however, was of Detmar and Isabella together, both dressed in new McQueen: he in white trousers and shirt with a pastel pink striped waistcoat and an immense white organza ruffle ascot tumbling down the front, and she in a white gown with a somewhat sheer organza sleeveless bodice in which McQueen had slipped faux rose petals, topped off with a Treacy hat of enormous pale pink English roses.

Isabella Blow was, in essence, McQueen's Amanda Harlech: a muse, mentor, cheerleader, and walking billboard. She convinced Hamish Bowles, by then an editor at American *Vogue*, to go see McQueen in Tooting Bec. "I went to south, south, south London, it took hours to get there," Bowles recalled. "And this really terrifying creature greeted me, and he was inarticulate and abrasive and just absolutely brilliant."

Blow introduced McQueen to her longtime friend Lucy Helmore, a former model who had worked with New York photographer Robert Mapplethorpe, had recently married Roxy Music front man Bryan Ferry, and was great friends with Amanda Harlech.

One night, Lucy's new Dior coat was pinched at a party in London.

"I'm really annoyed about my stolen coat," Lucy told Isabella.

"Well, I know a student who is really talented and could make you a new one," Isabella offered.

McQueen went to Lucy's home in Kensington.

"He was this little East End boy," she recalls. She explained what the coat looked like, that it was made of red alpaca. "And he did a little sketch in a book and it looked great," she says now. He told her he didn't have any money for materials, so she wrote him a check for 300 pounds to pay for the fabric. They agreed to meet again once it was made.

When it was ready for a fitting, McQueen brought the coat to Ferry's house. She liked him: "He was very busy, rushing about," she says, "and he had a wicked sense of humor, quite bitchy but not in a nasty way. A very, very fast-moving mind—you had to be on your toes to keep up with him. . . . He was like a naughty child."

He told her stories about his apprenticeships: "When I was working at Anderson & Sheppard, I'd sew my pubes into the queen's soldiers hats," he boasted, with a laugh. He talked about his process and his inspirations, which he collected in a scrapbook. He handed it to her.

"I opened it and it was filled with pictures of napalmed children and war pictures and really horrible things," she says. "I was so flabbergasted I didn't know what to say, so I shut the book and ignored it. I just thanked him and said, 'See you when the coat's ready.'"

She later realized that he was showing her his sense of extremism—that in his realm, nothing was off limits. He reminded her of Mapplethorpe, a respected downtown Manhattan portraitist and still life photographer best known for hardcore homoerotic pictures and who died from AIDS-related complications in 1989. "They had a similar character: childish, naughty, pushing it," she says.

Through Blow, McQueen also met fashion photographer Richard Burbridge and his fiancée, Cecilia Sim, who worked for furniture designer André Dubreuil. McQueen liked that Cecilia wasn't a "fashion person," she recalls.

"We would talk about other things, like his homosexuality, his choice of career, and how incredibly supportive his mother was. He liked having someone like me around—someone who wanted to get to know him for who he was as a person."

When Burbridge and Sim decided to get married, Sim asked McQueen if he could make her wedding dress.

"Yes, of course," he responded. "Let's go to Brick Lane and buy some silk."

The pair went down to the East End of London to the Indian fabric shops and bought several yards of silk in off-white and oyster. Back at the Tooting Bec house, he draped the fabric on Sim, pinned it here and there, picked up his shears, and started cutting it directly on her.

In a couple of hours, McQueen had created a two-tone 1930s slip dress with an asymmetrical neckline. He hand-twisted one of the two straps, and there were no hooks or zippers. For Sim's wrap, he made a Gigli-like cocoon coat in two layers of pale mushroom gray tulle, in between which he slipped fabric rose petals and butterflies. McQueen made the groom's waistcoat too, and it echoed the cocoon coat, with a layer of tulle encasing rose petals and butterflies. McQueen charged the couple nothing—it was his gift to them.

Despite the freelance work and welfare checks—both Ungless and McQueen were on the dole—money was scarce. When McQueen went to see his parents at home on Biggerstaff Road, his mother recalled, "He was so broke, he couldn't afford to get the bus here from his flat. I used to pay for a taxi to pick him up and then clear out the fridge for him to take back. He would often go hungry so that he could afford to buy a piece of cloth."

When McQueen and Ungless weren't working, they were out on the town. "We kind of became inseparable," Ungless recalls—so much so that they referred to each other as "sister." McQueen and Ungless's social routine was pretty simple: "We'd probably start somewhere near Soho, like the gay bar Comptons, on Old Compton Street, do a little bit of a pub crawl," Ungless says. "Then the night would usually end in some not-so-savory place, like a club called Man Stink. Oh my God! We loved that place! The music was good and the men were hot."

EVERYONE AROUND MCQUEEN—Ungless, Blow, headhunter Alice Smith—was pushing him to start his own company. He wasn't convinced, and still wanted to land a "proper job" with a fashion brand. To pay the bills and fill his days, he made clothes and experimented with materials, shapes, and techniques. Before long, Ungless recalls, a "collection just started to take form."

Some of the designs had references to the Sandinistas in the Nicaraguan revolution in the 1970s and 1980s: McQueen collected portraits of missing/ murdered people, which Ungless printed in black and white on cheap cotton cloth that McQueen used to make a short skating-style skirt and a small vest. He also incorporated the image of Robert De Niro's character Travis Bickle in Martin Scorsese's 1976 psychological drama *Taxi Driver*—McQueen was captivated by the scene in which De Niro shaves his hair into a Mohawk. They found a poster of the scene at a store near Leicester Square, and Ungless enlarged the image and printed it onto gray taffeta, which McQueen turned into a long vest. He titled the collection "Taxi Driver," which, over the years, friends and experts have said was in tribute to his father. But Ungless disagrees: "I think it was more to do with the fact that De Niro looked incredibly fuckable."

McQueen experimented with new materials, such as latex, which he used to coat the edge of fabrics rather than sewing a traditional hem. On the backs of some of the shirts, he exposed the zippers—a technique he had reworked from what he had learned with McKitterick. He incorporated feathers that Ungless brought back from the country, sandwiching partridge plumes in between clear plastic shower curtain that he turned into a tank top and attaching pheasant tail feathers vertically to the neckline of a leather bustier to frame the face like an Elizabethan collar. "The references were diverse," Ungless admits. "But it all seemed to work together."

Most important, McQueen designed a new drop-waist silhouette for pants, something he dubbed "the Bumster" because it revealed the top crack of the bum, which he felt was "a very underexposed erogenous zone," Ungless says. Rarely in fashion does someone actually create a new line. Coco Chanel did it with her soft, corset-less silhouette in the 1920s; Christian Dior with his wasp-waisted, full-skirted New Look in 1947; Yves Saint Laurent with the Trapeze Line (known today as the A-line) in 1958; Mary Quant with the miniskirt in 1960. Most fashion designers strive their entire career to come up with something "new" and never achieve it. McQueen did it in his first collection out of school.

As the collection came together, McQueen realized he needed a name for the company. Isabella Blow long claimed that she suggested he use his middle name, Alexander, instead of his first name, Lee, because it sounded far more aristocratic and powerful—"like Alexander the Great." In fact, McQueen later said he came up with the idea of using Alexander so he could keep drawing welfare checks under the name Lee McQueen.

Next, he needed a label. He had an idea: on the patchwork dress in his degree collection, "Jack the Ripper Stalks His Victims," he had small plastic squares that contained human fluids and hair that were supposed to represent remains of the Ripper's victims. McQueen decided to use the clear plastic square as his label, and fill it with a lock of hair. The hair was a nod to several different practices. First, he said, to the Victorian period, when "prostitutes would sell their kits of hair locks, which were bought by people to give to their lovers." It also had to do with the idea of keeping a memento of someone, such as when Victorian women wore a clip of their baby's hair in a locket, or American Indian warriors scalped their conquests, or serial killers kept the hair of their victims. For his first labels, McQueen used his own hair.

To build up his reputation, and hopefully land a few sales, Blow took McQueen around London to see retailers and present his clothes. One of the first stops was Joan Burstein at Browns. "He brought in just a few pieces of the tailoring, stuffed in a bin liner" or plastic trash bag, she says. "I saw them upstairs on the rail and said, 'Let's have a look.' He was standing there, very gauche. There were some pieces that were cut superbly, and I said to Isabella: 'The boy has got real talent. Keep at him. Guide him. I can't buy this as it is now as a collection,' because it wasn't a collection. But there were pieces, and those pieces identified the sort of man he was."

LONDON FASHION WEEK WAS IN A RUT. The recession had forced buyers to cut travel and buying budgets; the Department of Trade and Industry was slashing its subsidies; and Galliano, Katharine Hamnett, Rifat Özbek, and Westwood had decamped to Milan or Paris to show. To give it a boost, in early 1993, the BFC announced that it would invite a half dozen aspiring designers to join the sixty professionals presenting their collections at the London Fashion Week trade show in March, held this time at the Ritz Hotel. To qualify, applicants had to have been in business for less than two years and submit examples of their work to be judged by members of the BFC and its press committee. McQueen made the cut.

In theory, the newcomers' showcase sounded glam and professional. In reality, at least for McQueen, it was a bit of a ramshackle circus. Since he had no money, he hung his collection on a mishmash of wire and plastic hangers. Ever the East Ender, he dressed carelessly in tattered jeans, an army surplus T-shirt, and paint-splattered boots to receive reporters and retailers. All the while, Isabella Blow trotted up and down the corridor in her stilettos, breathlessly telling everyone she saw that they *had* to see McQueen's clothes.

There were a few gems among the dozen or so pieces, such as a padded silver gray silk coatdress with a jeweled collar inspired by a Queen Anne button-back chair and made with fabric that McQueen picked up at the Berwick Street market in Soho. While beautiful from the front, the back was daring: McQueen sliced open the center seam to reveal the wearer's spine. Officially, it was known as the "Scarlet Pimpernel" coat and McQueen priced it at eight hundred pounds. *The Times* of London called it "a confection fit for an empress."

"A lot of people came by," says Cecilia Burbridge, who helped out. But McQueen wasn't always happy with their reactions or questions. "At the time, people weren't quite sure about him," she admits. "And he was quite defensive when they commented about something. He had thought so much about research—he had this whole thought process going into his work. He needed to tell people that it wasn't just something he'd knocked off but that he had a reason for what he did. He wanted people to understand that."

Lucinda Alford of the *Observer* seemed to grasp what McQueen was doing. In a review that was generously long for a newcomer, she wrote that McQueen's "first collection demonstrates his indisputable skill as a pattern cutter. . . . It contains some of the most interesting cuts around . . . [and] is meticulously executed. . . . Like Martin Margiela and John Galliano, McQueen considers his work to be more artisan than commercial; he says he is not interested in volume sales and would be happy to supply a small number of retailers."

When the exhibit came to a close, Ungless and McQueen shoved the clothes into plastic trash bags and went out to celebrate. They wound up at Man Stink and stashed the sacks of clothes out back behind the club's Dumpsters rather than pay the coat check fee. They downed a couple of sherries and danced a bit, then jumped in a cab and went home.

The next morning, over breakfast, they remembered that they had left the bags in the alley. McQueen raced over there, but they were long gone: garbage collectors had already passed by and picked everything up.

DESPITE HIS SOLID CRITICAL START, McQueen was ambivalent about continuing in fashion on his own—there was too much responsibility, not enough money, and the nagging fear of failure. The idea of securing an assistant's position with a steady paycheck still tempted him greatly. As he looked for a job, he kept making clothes and selling them as he could.

One afternoon at the Elizabeth Street house, Isabella Blow invited McQueen over and introduced him to a new junior editor at British *Vogue* named Tiina Laakkonen.

"Tiina, you have to have him make your clothes," she said. "He has to make clothes for you."

Laakkonen liked him instantly. "He was a very sweet person," she recalls. A former model from Finland who had studied fashion design in Paris and had worked as an assistant for Karl Lagerfeld at Chanel and for Lanvin, she understood McQueen's potential. "As soon as I started to see his work, I thought: 'Wow, very interesting, and really different,'" she says. "Such beautiful, exquisite, sophisticated clothes coming from someone who was pretty much the opposite—at least on the surface. I was completely blown away."

"You're going to be as big as Yves Saint Laurent," she told him.

"Oh, fuck off," he responded.

"No, really," she insisted. "You are going to be the next Saint Laurent."

Blow and Laakkonen wanted to do fittings with McQueen at *Vogue* during the day, but as Isabella later explained, "They wouldn't allow him into the *Vogue* office. His teeth looked like Stonehenge." So Blow and Laakkonen would sneak him in at lunchtime when the rest of the staff was out and meet with him in the storage closet.

Like Blow and Treacy, Laakkonen called him "Alexander"—*never* Lee. "Lee's a name for a guy from the East End," she explains. She would ask him to make her a jacket and he'd say, "Sure," but asked for eighty pounds up front in cash to buy the fabric. Always cash. Or she'd say she needed a suit, and he'd look her over and figure what sort of suit she should wear—though he wouldn't say a thing, not even what color. One time, she complained that the dress she was trying on was a bit snug in the hips, so he whipped out his shears and whacked off the bottom, turning it instantly into a top.

A week or so later, he'd return to *Vogue* at lunchtime carrying a stuffed plastic trash bag. "And what came out of those plastic bags were some of the most beautiful things I had ever seen in clothing," she says. There would be the new jacket or dress in a style and color that was an utter surprise, or something else he had cooked up that he thought might suit her.

BACK IN TOOTING BEC, McQueen had become what Ungless describes as "a little too obsessed" with recent Central Saint Martins graduate Hussein Chalayan's degree collection, "The Tangent Flows." Chalayan made several silk dresses, then buried them in his backyard for a few weeks to decay. The rotten dresses were the hit of the degree show, and as with Galliano's "Les Incroyables" collection nearly a decade earlier, Browns bought the clothes and put them in the store's windows. The press embraced the tale of the backyard interment and made much of it; Isabella Blow latched on to Chalayan as a new potential protégé, irritating McQueen that much more.

McQueen decided to take Chalayan's backyard decay idea and do it better. He draped and cut white chiffon on the stand, turning out pretty dresses that Ungless remembers were "quite romantic, actually." They bought some red clay, watered it down, dripped it all over the dresses and left them hanging in the backyard for a few weeks. The clay stained the fabric, dried, cracked, and peeled. The dresses turned out to be a sort of brick red with small chips of clay embedded in the fabric. The effect was "very *Quest for Fire*," Ungless says, referring to French director Jean-Jacques Annaud's prehistoric fantasy.

Before long, a collection started to take form. Along with *Quest for Fire*, McQueen was using Sade's *The 120 Days of Sodom* as a reference again. "I actually think of [Sade] as a great philosopher and a man of his time," he explained. "Where people found him just a pervert, I find him sort of influential in the way he provokes people's thoughts."

Vivienne Westwood once spoke about how punk was rooted in the need to "fuck everything up" and destroy in order to create something new. "The idea of destroying in order to create was very powerful to Lee," Ungless says. McQueen began to study how natural disasters such as flood, fire, and drought created virginal landscapes where new life could be born. One of his favorite sources for these stories was *National Geographic* magazine: he was obsessed with its brutal, honest images of society, nature, and mankind. He was particularly struck by an article about locusts wiping out thousands of acres of crops in Africa, leading to widespread famine.

At the same time, he had been experimenting with plastic wrap—like Saran Wrap: he used it to protect the dress forms from "wet mud, liquid latex, and whatever else we wanted to throw, drip or paint on a dress," Ungless explains. He found that the plastic wrap itself created a perfect dress; all he had to do was slice it up the back, sew in a zipper, and he was done. "It was a happy mistake," Ungless says. McQueen realized this was how he could invoke mass destruction by nature: he would cover the plastic wrap shift entirely with formaldehyde locusts, as if the locusts were devouring the person wearing the dress—the ultimate fashion victim. Ungless was tasked with sewing the insects on one by one.

McQueen and Ungless also started experimenting with latex in the backyard in Tooting Bec. One afternoon, Ungless accidentally kicked the can and knocked it over. The latex spilled onto a drain cover on their concrete patio. Jazzed by the mistake, McQueen threw a handful of glitter in it. Once the sparkly latex dried, they peeled it back, and it had the gridlike imprint of the drain cover. They decided to use it for the front of a dress.

ISABELLA BLOW, Bobby Hillson, Alice Smith, Cressida Pye, and Simon Ungless urged McQueen to stage a bona fide fashion show. He agreed, and booked the Bluebird Garage in Chelsea—an immense Art Deco building constructed by the Bluebird Motor Company in 1923 to hold three hundred cars, making it the largest garage in Europe at the time. (Today, it is one of Terence Conran's restaurants.) The show was scheduled for the afternoon of Monday, October 18. McQueen called the collection "Nihilism" because it was about anti-Romanticism.

McQueen had the models styled as modern punks, bruised and smeared with dirt, their eyes made up to look drug-addict hollow, their hair in Sid Vicious–like Mohawks tinged with red. The inspiration for them was Ika, the female character in *Quest for Fire*.

A crowd of about three hundred—some editors and a lot of CSM students—filtered into the first-floor warehouse-like room as a soundtrack of house and riot grrrl music blared on the sound system. There were a few rows of seats, with Isabella Blow and McQueen's mother front and center, but most of the audience was standing.

When the show started, about half an hour late, the models exploded with a hard attitude and stormed past the crowd as the deejay played Nirvana, L7's "Pretend We're Dead," and Cypress Hill's "I Wanna Get High," punctuated with silences. One girl pogo-danced all the way down the runway. Another model, a student from Central Saint Martins also named Lee who had a boy/girl look about him, came out bare-chested to shock guests with the gender confusion. Many of the models simply gave the crowd the finger as they walked by.

McQueen wove some Galliano-isms into the show—he played with the look of les Merveilleuses and even doused models with water to make the dresses cling to their skin as Galliano had done for "Fallen Angels." But where Galliano's interpretations of that period looked historic and costume-y, McQueen's take was defiantly modern and flagrantly sexy: sleek sleeveless ivory columns molded erotically on the breasts like S&M harnesses; cling-wrap panties; trousers sliced down the back seam to reveal the buttocks; Bumsters, which he reprised from "Taxi Driver," cut so low that the models had to shave their pubic hair backstage. One T-shirt, with his logo printed large across the breasts, had two smeared bloody handprints down the front, as if a violent murderer was leaving his mark on his latest victim.

If Galliano was a romantic, McQueen was a pornographer. The Larry Flynt of Fashion. He didn't believe in frontiers. He didn't believe anything was off-limits. Nothing was taboo. He accepted the brutality of human nature, didn't try to suppress it. He didn't want to put women on a pedestal like untouchable, unreachable goddesses. He wanted to empower them and help them use the force of their sexuality to its fullest.

"That show fucked me and everyone who saw it sideways," Ungless says.

"Wow, what have I unleashed?" Bobby Hillson thought as the audience erupted into cheers and applause.

"It was his vision and nobody else's," Hillson says now. "He took you into his world. He made you see his vision. You were in another world."

OVER THE NEXT FEW DAYS, the handful of journalists who attended the show devoted an impressive amount of time, thought, and space to McQueen, considering he was a debutant. "The last show of the season gave editors the aggressive British attitude they had been expecting," wrote *The New York Times* fashion critic Amy Spindler. "But the meanest thing about Mr. Mc-Queen's hard vision is the cuts of his Edwardian jackets. . . . [McQueen's] was a hard show to take, but at least it offered one solution to the identity crisis of London fashion."

The *Daily Telegraph*'s Kathryn Samuel thought McQueen's show "evoked repulsion and admiration in equal measure, in the Westwood and Galliano tradition."

"McQueen, who is twenty-four and from London's East End, has a view that speaks of battered women, of violent lives, of grinding daily existences offset by wild, drug-enhanced nocturnal dives into clubs where the dress code is semi-naked," Marion Hume of *The Independent* observed. "As such, his clothes probably speak with more accuracy about real life than some swoosh of an evening gown by Valentino."

The majority of the British fashion press, however, either decided not to cover the show or took nasty swipes at it. The *Evening Standard*'s David Hayes squawked that McQueen's "blood-spattered 'Carrie' dresses, savage punk hair and morning-after make-up were straight from a Hammer horror."

The retailer response was respectable: McQueen reportedly took orders for two hundred pieces from the collection. That was a fraction of what stores would buy from an established brand, but a gangbusters order for a start-up. Unfortunately McQueen didn't have a manufacturer, so none of the clothes were made and the orders were never filled.

ISABELLA BLOW WAS STILL maneuvering to get McQueen's clothes in British *Vogue*: for the December 1993 issue, she was asked by her boss, editor Alexandra Shulman, to assist celebrated American photographer Steven Meisel for his first assignment for the magazine—in particular, to help cast the models. Blow decided it could be cool to hire her beautiful young blueblood cousins and friends, most of whom had never modeled before—sort of a new version of the 1930s' Bright Young Things. Among those she roped in to posing were Plum Sykes, Honor Fraser, Louise Campbell, and Stella Tennant, who was the granddaughter of the duchess of Devonshire. Tennant arrived looking ultra goth, with jet black hair, kohl-rimmed eyes, and a gold ring pierced through her nostril. Shulman wanted her to remove it, but when Isabella explained the procedure would require a doctor, Shulman acquiesced.

For the shoot, Blow asked Meisel's stylist Joe McKenna to take a look at McQueen's clothes as possibilities for the shoot. When McQueen arrived and pulled the clothes out of his ubiquitous plastic trash bag, McKenna was aghast. "I'd come from New York, where fashion was very slick," McKenna later said. "I was expecting a rack of clothes—or at least a garment bag." Once McKenna did get a look at the clothes, he admitted: "I just didn't get it. Until we put them on Stella Tennant and then you could see that there was something going on."

"London Babes" was a huge success in the media and in fashion—kicking off the aristo model movement in fashion, and calling attention to a new hip cultural vibe in the United Kingdom. "It was the emergence of the upper classes as sexy," the British designer Antony Price later said. "Nobody had seen them as that before. [Isabella] repackaged them."

Unfortunately, "London Babes" was also the beginning of Isabella's undoing at *Vogue*. Along with the Tennant nose ring debacle, the shoot cost a fortune and Isabella had a power tussle with McKenna. Within months, she was off staff, relegated on the masthead to "contributing editor," meaning a contracted employee, occasionally engaged. She was always terrified of going broke—especially after her father died in January 1993 and left her next to nothing from the family estate. Losing her full-time job amplified those fears.

McQueen was in a far worse financial pickle, and he and Ungless were forced to give up the Tooting Bec house. He moved into a ground-floor flat that his sister Janet owned in a public housing estate in Dagenham, a suburb of East London so far-flung that he had to take a commuter train to get there. His diet consisted mainly of fast food; in fact, he'd recently lost one of his rotten front teeth while eating a Big Mac. He was self-conscious about the gap, but could do nothing about it—he was too broke to replace the tooth— and it made him look even more loutish and intimidating.

Though his mother, aunt, and sisters were solidly behind his budding fashion career, his father was still riding him to get a proper job with wages. McQueen was not convinced that he was on the right path either. Early in the New Year, he met up with his old friend John McKitterick in the East End for drinks. McQueen was feeling especially introspective and frank that evening. "I've never really wanted to be a fashion designer," he told McKitterick. "I wish I could have been something like a war photographer."

Nevertheless, fashion was the path he was on, and he decided, at least for the moment, to continue to the best of his ability. While still in Tooting Bec, he and Ungless started working on a new collection for the next round of fashion shows, in late February. As a central theme, McQueen chose "Irish folklore about banshees heard wailing when a boat sank," he said; because of this, he decided to call the collection "Banshee."

But given that this was McQueen, a collection was never simply based on a single idea; there was a cacophony of inspirations coming from all directions, usually with a tinge of perversity or dread, "because," he explained, "there are so many sides of me in conflict . . . I don't think like the average person on the street. I think quite perversely sometimes." A major theme was Buñuel's *Belle de Jour* and the concept of repression—"People who are cloistered and restricted but then all of the sudden they find a part of their life that has been closed," he said.

As weeks passed, the collection began to take form. There were molded plaster breastplates, inspired by Greek sculptures; sharply tailored black silk suits with elflike shoulders, skinny sleeves, and sliced-open armpits; and sailor-inspired jackets with flared cuffs and gold piping. There were gowns with tailored bodices, Empire waistlines, and flowing tulle ball skirts—a mix of hard and soft, constricted and flowing. Some dresses had high cliclike collars; some had Elizabethan-style scoop necklines; a few had wide cuffs and bustlines trimmed with swooping gold cord, like ecclesiastical robes.

He reprised the Bumster again—it had already become a McQueen signature after only two collections as well as a fashion trend: other designers were dropping pant waistlines down to the hip too. McQueen believed the Bumster was a hit because, he said, "It reveals the part of a man's body I really like, so I presumed that it was the same for straight men and women." For this collection, he added a new version that he called the "Cuntster": a pair of pant legs held up on the thigh with toupee tape. The Cuntster would be worn with a long tuniclike shirt that just covered the naked pelvis.

Through Isabella Blow, McQueen met a young Welshman named Julien Macdonald, who was studying fashion textiles and interning for former Mc-Queen employer Koji Tatsuno. Macdonald's specialty was knitwear, and when he met with McQueen, he showed some new knitting swatches he had created with transparent fishing line. "Lee had never seen such an unusual material used for knitting and thought it was hilarious," Macdonald recalls. "He drew up a quick sketch of the sweater"—it was a pullover turtleneck with transparent vertical panels that revealed the bosom—"and he named it 'Get Your Tits Out' whilst laughing hysterically. He loved the shock value and told me that it reminded him of a fetish outfit he had seen in a club the night before."

Macdonald took the sketch and returned to his student group house in Brighton, where he went to work on the sweater on his domestic knitting machine in his tiny bedroom. He made the neckline, shoulders, bottom, and sleeves out of mohair, Lurex, and steel wire, and then used the transparent fishing line for the breast-revealing inserts. It took a week to produce because, he says, "the fishing wire kept falling off the machine." McQueen so loved it, he asked Macdonald to do three more in different variations on the same theme.

One night, Ungless arrived at the Dagenham flat and discovered that Mc-Queen had made a stunning frock coat in black taffeta—Ungless thought it must have taken him days to create it—and he wanted Ungless to pour resin on it. Ungless resisted; he felt the coat was far too lovely to deface with resin. McQueen insisted, and Ungless hesitantly and carefully splattered a few drops on the coat.

"No!" McQueen howled. "Cover it!"

Ungless poured the resin over the shoulders and it ran slowly down the coat, hardening as it dripped. "It looked like black glass," Ungless says. "The hem and sleeves had shards of resin hanging off them. It was totally beautiful."

Since McQueen was broke, the collection and the show were underwritten by his welfare checks; cash infusions from Detmar Blow, whom McQueen referred to as his "solicitor"; and Stella beer, which one reporter described as "a much-needed sponsor." He was aware, however, that to keep going he needed retail orders and to produce clothes to fill those orders. "Last year," he said, "I wanted to give London a kick and a shout. 'Let's get on with the creativity.'

This time, there'll be more tailoring and it will be more salable. My aim is to marry Savile Row with ready-to-wear."

But his work was more than that, and he knew it. Like the frock coats, which, he explained, were "cut in a sixteenth-century method based on architecture, on a horizon point, so you get a flat surface that swings away. I mean I was a technologist before designer and a constructionist before I was a technologist. That's the way I work, it's like a jigsaw puzzle."

McQUEEN WAS ONE of twenty-nine designers showing on the official London Fashion Week calendar. He was slotted to close the week on Saturday, February 26—London Fashion Week organizers understood clearly that he was the best showman of the lot.

Isabella Blow rang all her powerful fashion friends and insisted they attend the show. "If you see only one show," she said, "it *has* to be McQueen."

Everyone who helped out—the lighting team, makeup artist, hairdresser, and the models, some of whom were posh fashion friends, and some of whom, Michael Roberts recalled, were "street people of mixed race, size, and indeterminable gender"—worked for free. McQueen particularly liked using lesbians as models, because, he explained, "If anyone's going to tell me they hate something it's going to be a lesbian. They're not going to wear anything by a man that doesn't emphasize their sexuality."

Tiina Laakkonen, who modeled in the show, remembers how ad hoc it all was: "There were no fittings. You'd just show up and he'd say, 'I want you to wear this and I want you to wear that,' and we had to wear our own shoes because he didn't have any. There was no concept of a 'show'—it was just completely raw and home-cooked." Macdonald arrived from Brighton thirty minutes before the start time with the sweaters he made. McQueen's mother Joyce was backstage, serving everyone homemade sandwiches on a tray and making cups of tea, a cigarette perpetually dangling from her lips.

McQueen instructed the makeup artist to make the models look like the Edvard Munch painting *The Scream*. "Our faces were whited out with putty-colored foundation and hollows were painted on our cheeks with brown and gray powder," said Plum Sykes, one of the "London babes" who was walking in the show. "Alexander was out to shock and disturb—which he did. All the girls in the show looked like chic but unhappy skeletons."

Hairdresser Eugene Souleiman suggested he stencil the McQueen logo on the models' hair in metallic paint. McQueen loved the idea. "It was like this fashion 'Helter Skelter' ride," Souleiman says of working for McQueen. "You were never comfortable with what you were doing, but it inspired you, that feeling of insecurity, a mix of fear and excitement. You never were really sure where it was going to go. . . . You had to be quite brave to work with him. But to be around him, you became braver."

Not many fashion players showed up. Along with Roberts and Blow, there was Manolo Blahnik, some daily newspaper writers and indie press editors, and that's about it. The rest of the crowd was made up of Central Saint Martins students and friends.

The show began in near silence, with a heavily pregnant model with a shaved head dressed in an ample black Elizabethan-like gown and the name McQUEEN stenciled in silver on the side of her scalp. McQueen based the look on Dutch master Jan van Eyck's 1434 masterpiece *The Arnolfini Portrait.* This was followed by the suite of Ancient Greece–inspired pieces made of plaster of Paris. One model wore a long white dress that had been covered with the plaster that was smashed when dried, so as she walked, the pieces clinked like a wind chime.

As the show went on, the music grew louder and harder. Isabella Blow— also with the name McQUEEN stenciled on her hair—did a turn, wearing a top decorated with broken Stella beer bottles. Plum Sykes walked down the runway twice, first in a flesh-colored sequined dress, and then a nautical-inspired minidress with huge regimental cuffs—an outfit she so loved, McQueen eventually gave it to her. Laakkonen wore the black resin and taffeta frock coat and flinched so hard at the end of the runway that the resin shattered dramatically.

The model Tizer Bailey wore the new "Cuntsters" and when she stopped to pose for photographers, she lifted her tunic, pretended to stick her finger in her vagina, then popped the finger in her mouth and walked off. The space vibrated with a female rapper snarling, "Am I a bitch? Yes! Am I a whore? No! You wanna fuck? Let's go!"

"My mum was in the front row and she thought it was shocking but she understood the meaning behind it all," McQueen said. "Usually it's black male rappers saying 'Let's fuck,' but this time it's a woman."

After the show, Michael Roberts went backstage. "Without hesitation [Isa-

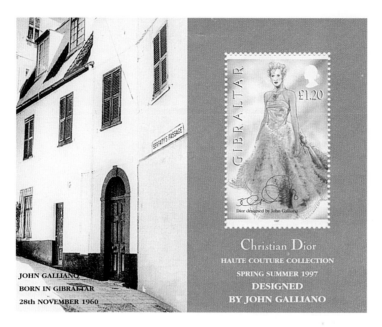

(*left*) John Galliano's childhood home on Serfaty's Passage in Gibraltar.
(*right*) One of Gibraltar's John Galliano commemorative stamps.

Wilson's Grammar School class picture, 1972. John Galliano in the front row, left.

Galliano's Central Saint Martins degree show "Les Incroyables," 1984.

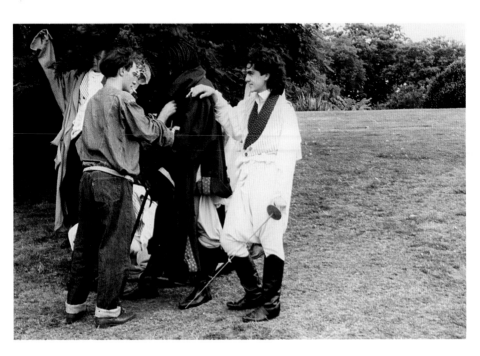

Galliano styling a photo shoot of "Les Incroyables," 1984.

John Galliano, 1986.

John Galliano modeling in "Afghanistan Repudiates Western Ideals," 1984.

(*left*) "The Ludic Game," 1985.
(*right*) John Galliano modeling "The Ludic Game," 1985.

Helena Bonham Carter modeling for
"Forgotten Innocents," 1986.

Sibylle de Saint Phalle in
"Fallen Angels," 1985.

Johann Brun.

John Galliano with Peder Bertelsen, 1988.

Stephen Jones and Steven Robinson, at Epsom School of Art and Design, 1985.

John Galliano receiving
his first British Designer
of the Year Award, 1987.

Alexander McQueen's childhood home: 11, Biggerstaff Road, Stratford, London.

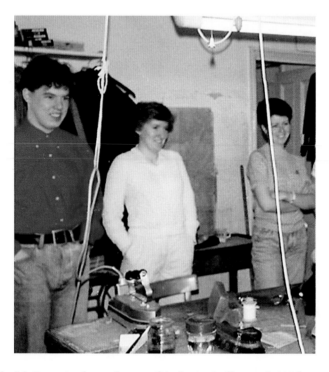

Alexander McQueen in the workroom of Anderson & Sheppard, 1986. *(Derrick Tomlinson)*

(*right*) Alexander McQueen's
Central Saint Martins degree show
"Jack The Ripper Stalks His Victims," 1992.

(*below*) Alexander McQueen at
Hilles, 1994.

(*left*) "Nihilism," S/S 1994.

(*right*) Julien Macdonald's Get Your Tits Out sweater at McQueen's "Banshee," F/W 1994–95.

(*left*) Pallet wrap dress from McQueen's "The Birds," S/S 1995.

(*right*) The Bumster from McQueen's "The Birds," S/S 1995.

McQueen's "The Highland Rape," F/W 1995–96.

(*left*) McQueen's "The Hunger," S/S 1996.
(*right*) McQueen's "Dante," F/W 1996–97.

Alexander McQueen and
Sebastian Pons, 1995.

Ruti Danan at
Hoxton Square, 1995.

(*left*) Soulika Danan in Fez, Morocco, in 1940, age eighteen.

(*center*) McQueen's "Dante" headdress, 1996.

(*right*) Skeletal reprise of "Dante" headdress for Givenchy Haute Couture, F/W 1997–98.

Debra Shaw in McQueen's "La Poupée," S/S 1997.

John Galliano, S/S 1992.

Kate Moss in Galliano's
"Princess Lucrecia," S/S 1994.

John Galliano,
Anna Wintour, and
Oscar de la Renta at the
Metropolitan Museum of
Art's Costume Institute
Gala, 1993.

John Galliano and
John Bult, 2006.

Nadja Auermann in Galliano's
São Schlumberger show, 1994.

Galliano's Pin-Up show, 1994.

bella] took me through rails of clothes, which were as different, new, and difficult to understand as those shown by the Japanese designers when they first took Paris by storm," he said. "McQueen came to say hello. He was tongue-tied and chubby, with an open, childlike face that should have been advertising baby food. He let Isabella speak for him and then he ran away."

The few reporters who did attend the show realized that they had witnessed something extremely special—and new. Mark C. O'Flaherty of *The Pink Paper* called "Banshee" "an eclectic mix of fully blown romance offset by an aggressive edge" and "the wardrobe from the best film that Derek Jarman never made." O'Flaherty especially made a point to applaud the fact that, unlike most of McQueen's peers, who "assimilate Vivienne Westwood's entire oeuvre and regurgitate," his work was 100 percent his own. McQueen "has demonstrated an individuality that by the end of this century will see him usurp Westwood as the U.K.'s greatest fashion expert."

But most of the British fashion establishment did not concur—particularly Blow's colleagues at British *Vogue,* who considered McQueen a ne'er-do-well who did not deserve any attention whatsoever. Once he wrapped up his show and sales appointments in London, he went to Paris for Fashion Week to attend a few fashion shows. After one, he hitched a ride with Blow and Laakkonen in the British *Vogue* team's van, and Laakkonen was shocked at how the whole team ignored both McQueen and Blow.

McQueen didn't help matters with his pithy or vulgar responses.

Of the increasing trend of deconstruction in fashion design, he sniffed, "I can do it because I can construct in the first place. For a lot of others, it's just a way of getting by without any talent."

He lashed out at the respected British fashion writer Colin McDowell, who had recently launched a debate in fashion circles on whether male designers could design well for women:

"What a load of cack. He's a right fucking queen. The female body is like any other body. It has lumps and bumps and you make the most of it. I make a woman look sexy and hip or chic—never dowdy."

He saved his harshest words, however, for the British press, for which he had already developed a profound loathing. One outburst in particular may have been his most honest and prescient:

"I always try to slam ideas in people's face," he told O'Flaherty. "If I get someone like Suzy Menkes in the front row, wearing her fucking Christian

Lacroix, I make sure that lady gets pissed on by one of the girls, you know what I mean? These people can make you or break you, and they love you for just a moment. I may be the name on everyone's lips at the moment, but they can kill you."

DEREK ANDERSON, head of a New York–based fashion PR company called In The Mix, invited McQueen to New York to reprise "Banshee." The timing was impeccable: American *Vogue* had just published a piece that declared, "London is hot again," with the opening paragraph dedicated to McQueen and the "Nihilism" show. "Among the Scotch tape G-strings, clear plastic shoes, silver-painted legs and spiky hair lurk ideas . . . that will eventually walk down other runways," the magazine reported. It was the major media validation that McQueen desperately needed.

During the New York trip, Anderson scored McQueen an interview with *Women's Wear Daily*—a real coup for such a young designer. Ever the mouth, McQueen spouted to the reporter what he really thought about the New York fashion industry, blasting that it consisted of "two hundred Anna Suis and that guy Todd Oldham." He also talked about how he saw his own work, describing it as "classic tailoring with a hint of perversity."

In The Mix invited the top players from New York's fashion corps to the show, including *Allure* creative director Polly Mellen, *Interview* editor in chief Ingrid Sischy, and American *Elle* fashion editor Constance White. They were knocked out by what they saw: the pregnant bride in black, and the ethereal Empire-waist gowns; the see-through tunics and Bumsters, which one fashion writer described as "cut so low that they seemed to consist of nothing but a cup and legs"; the military-trimmed frock coats and the splendidly tailored suits. For one passage, McQueen covered the model with makeup resembling bruises and wrapped her in clear packing tape and twine. "There was a gasp in the room," Anderson remembers. "Ingrid Sischy almost had a heart attack." Mellen declared: "I have seen the future of fashion, and it is Lee McQueen."

"Within days, every major editor came through to see the collection," Anderson recalls. "Anna Wintour, André Leon Talley, Hamish Bowles [all from *Vogue*], Liz Tilberis [editor of *Harper's Bazaar*], Gilles Bensimon, and Marin Hopper [of American *Elle*] all saw the collection and went crazy." The magazines called to borrow the clothes for shoots; *Elle* and *Interview* wanted to do stories devoted to McQueen.

But McQueen needed to sell clothes to stay in business—something he hadn't managed to do very well up to that point. To help, Anderson went to see sales rep Barbara Kramer, who had a top fashion showroom in New York, to see if she could carry the line or offer some advice. One of her assistants was working with a London-based Italian fashion agent named Eo Bocci, who had production deals with a few designers, including Jean Paul Gaultier and the Belgian designer Ann Demeulemeester. Anderson met with Bocci in a Soho showroom and brought along some McQueen samples to show. Bocci liked what he saw and asked if he could talk to McQueen when he returned to London.

Bocci arranged to meet McQueen at the Maison Bertaux in Soho—the same French pastry shop where McQueen had celebrated his twenty-fifth birthday. McQueen arrived with his usual plastic trash bag and set it on the floor next to him. They ordered something to drink and McQueen started talking—about his dreams, his vision, his family. "Just speaking with him—hearing his ideas—I liked him," Bocci says now. "His vision was very interesting and different from other designers I had met, and it was beautiful."

After two hours of talking, Bocci asked McQueen what was in the trash bag. He pulled out two pieces. The first was a red-and-white checked cotton shirt with a high collar and exaggerated proportions. The second was a jacket: "Ivory chiffon, transparent, double layered, Savile Row cut, perfectly executed," Bocci recalls. "Between the two transparent layers there was hair. From afar it looked like a graphic design. He told me it was his mother's hair that he had cut himself." Bocci had never seen anything like it before; he found it to be simply remarkable.

BEFORE DRAWING UP AN AGREEMENT and officially underwriting the company, Bocci wanted to see another collection and show. McQueen, however, was out of money again, so Anderson wired him some via Western Union to pay for fabrics. Isabella Blow felt that McQueen's studio in Dagenham was too far away and invited him to live at her mother-in-law's at 67 Elizabeth Street, which had been damaged by neighboring construction. Treacy relocated next door to No. 69, where his boutique remains today.

McQueen moved into the dilapidated house with his boyfriend Andrew Groves, a young fashion designer from Maidstone, Kent, who was one year older and worked under the name Jimmy Jumble. For both young men, it was their first serious relationship. They had met a few months earlier at Comptons, the Soho gay bar. A mutual friend introduced them, and Groves says, "We got drunk and we got thrown out." They took the train back to McQueen's sister's flat, and Groves says, "Before I knew it, I was his boyfriend and his machinist."

Their setup at Elizabeth Street was rough. "It was really like a squat—horrible," Groves remembers. "Lee's studio was in the basement, which was like an old farmhouse kitchen. There were some windows, so there was natural light, but there was no hot water and the electricity was on a key you had to charge up at Victoria station. On the ground floor in the front room was all these rolls of fabric, which were [Detmar's sister] Selina Blow's"—she too did fashion design—"and in the back was a small area where we put a mattress on the floor and that's where we slept." Since there was nothing to cook on, Groves says, "we went to McDonald's a lot."

"Outside there was a ping-pong table which we used as the cutting table," Groves continues. "And as you went upstairs, there were dusty old floorboards and nothing but boxes and boxes of Philip Treacy's hats." McQueen freely helped himself to Selina Blow's fabrics—just as he had at Romeo Gigli's. "But he was so respectful of Philip," Groves notes. "He didn't touch Philip's hats."

And there was Isabella Blow, arriving in full opulence and wit, chatting nonstop as McQueen worked. "She was disruptive but not in a bad way," Groves recalls. "We used to call her Lucrezia Borgia"—after the much-married illegitimate daughter of Pope Alexander VI—"and she'd come in and she was as much of a foul-mouthed fishwife as he could be. She would see what he was doing and say, 'Look at this!' and she would strip off naked and be throwing things on." And McQueen would stop and watch and be charmed and enthusiastic. "They just excited each other," Groves says.

For his fourth official collection and third show, McQueen "was feeling pressure to up the game," Anderson says. He needed to prove he could compete against the best in Paris, New York, and Milan.

The central theme—and eventually the title of the collection—was *The*

Birds, Alfred Hitchcock's spooky, stylish thriller from 1963 starring Tippi Hedren about thousands of vicious, maniacal birds that attack humans. It was one of McQueen's favorites among the Hitchcock movies that he watched as a kid at his Aunt Renée's. From a fashion aspect, he was taken with the pencil skirts that Hedren wore in the film, what he described as "a very sleek, feminine 1950s silhouette." Yet he wanted to make the look "more extreme," Ungless says. "Tippi is made vulnerable though the hobbling effect of her clothes in the movie—this beautiful, sexy woman placed into a different environment and put at extreme risk but winning in the end. All very McQueen."

A secondary theme was roadkill. The idea came from the scene in *The Birds* in which everyone is fleeing the mad flock by car. For McQueen, it was like what the locusts represented in "Nihilism": "Complete chaos and human vulnerability in the face of nature gone wrong," Ungless says. McQueen chose to interpret it as tire marks on clothes—"I thought: 'Birds, road, car tire, splat!'" he said with his goofy laugh—and he asked Ungless to design the tire track print. Since they had no money for materials, Ungless raided the fabric storage closet at Central Saint Martins, where he was teaching textile printing. McQueen also picked up "a hideous cheap black lamé fabric that we bought from the guy on Berwick Street who sold remnants from his barrow," Ungless recalls. Once the clothes were made, Ungless printed the tire tracks across seams and details, "giving a kind of run over by a steamroller look."

Last, McQueen wanted to use birds as a print theme on the fabrics. Both McQueen and Ungless had done some bird watching as kids. Ungless still had his bird book and showed it to McQueen. "I wanted hawks and crows and Lee picked garden birds—one was a Robin. I put the print together and printed it. It was awful—like a Christmas card gone wrong. Stodgy little robins and blue tits flying about didn't quite have the desired dangerous effect." Thankfully, Groves stepped in and laid out a new print of flying swallows.

Another idea for the collection came from a story that Groves told McQueen. A few years earlier, Groves had experienced a curious rendezvous in the South London suburbs with a middle-aged American man he met through a personal ad. When Groves arrived at the house, the man opened the door dressed as an American cop. He took Groves up to his attic, which was kitted out like a dungeon, with all sorts of kinky devices. "Before you know it, he'd wrapped me from head to toe in [plastic] pallet wrap," Groves says. "Obviously, I could have been chopped up and murdered, but the house and the decor/setting was so provincial that it never crossed my mind." Groves recounted the tale to McQueen, who found it fascinating and kind of wacko. Not long after, they were walking down Elizabeth Street at night when McQueen spied something on the sidewalk.

"Pallet wrap!" he cried. "Oh! Gotta make a fucking dress!"

He hauled the bolt of plastic into the house and enrobed a dummy with it, trimming with shears where needed. In no time flat, he had transformed it into a chic, transparent sleeveless shift.

"He thought it was amusing—that it was our little joke," Groves says.

Groves was astonished by how quickly and easily McQueen could create a garment from scratch. "He put a huge piece of silk on a stand, cut a neck hole out of it, wound thread all around it, poured latex on it, slash down the back for a zipper and said, 'There's one dress,'" Groves remembers. "Ideas like that were getting churned out every hour or so. Lee didn't realize what he was doing was so different."

What he did see, however, is that his career was starting to take off, and it made him more than a little nervous. In the weeks leading up to the show, he sat for an interview with *Dazed & Confused*. "All I have in my mind now is . . . the day of the show, and it's doing my head in," he said. "It's getting to the point where I'm not doing it because I enjoy it but because it's what's expected."

"Everything in my life is run by time," he continued. "I've always wanted to go to Spain, to some desolate place where there are no clocks. . . . I'd really love to sit down for a week and just tailor one beautiful jacket but now I can't 'cause I don't have the time. . . . I've got the feeling I might become a recluse one day . . . I've got the feeling I could lose my grip altogether."

WHEN IT CAME TIME to figure out where to stage the show, McQueen started looking for a suitable site; he zeroed in on Bagley's, an old warehouse in then-seedy King's Cross where he and Ungless had attended raves and which was rumored to be owned by East End mobsters. McQueen went to see the property's managers to negotiate the deal. They looked at him a bit askance when he explained he needed it for a few days for a fashion show.

McQueen talked the rate way down to somewhere around five hundred pounds, which was then the price of a pair of Bumsters. No doubt it helped that McQueen was a lifelong East Ender who claimed to have had a relative who'd worked for the Kray twins, notorious East End gangsters.

While preparing for the show, McQueen met up with Simon Costin, the jewelry and set designer, to ask if he could borrow a few pieces for "The Birds." Costin agreed, but he too had a request:

"Let me do the show set for you. It would be nice for me to do the set."

McQueen agreed.

Since they had "something like fifty pounds" for the budget and there were tire marks on the clothes, Costin says he decided to simply paint a broken white line down the dark cement floor, like a road. He put up a black backdrop and built a short tunnel for an entrance. McQueen also had Costin make a black feather neck/shoulder piece, which was placed on a gold shift like a feather dickey.

For the hair, McQueen hired the hairdresser Eugene Souleiman again and explained that he wanted a look of "destruction." Souleiman understood. He didn't propose anything based on *The Birds* star Tippi Hedren's blond upswept bouffant do—that, he says, "was a bit too obvious. Lee would have hated if I had done that." Instead, Souleiman decided to blow the models' hair sleek straight, except at the ends, which he would crimp into fluffy poufs. This would allow the hair to float cloudlike as the girls walked. The makeup, by Val Garland, was light, with pale skin and delicate orange-red lips. "We looked like dangerous angels," says Laakkonen, who was modeling in the show again for free.

The eeriest effect, however, was something McQueen had dreamed up a few weeks earlier: He wanted the models to wear opaque white contact lenses. He got the idea from young British illustrator Richard Gray, whom he and Ungless would see at London bars and clubs wearing full-eye black contact lenses. McQueen became obsessed with the look—he felt that it would remove the models' personalities and make them more clonelike—and he found an optician in London who would make them for the show. Of course, they cost a fortune, and McQueen couldn't afford it, so he called ever-supportive Anderson in New York, who wired more money.

McQueen had a new stylist on hand to help sort out the looks and dress the girls: Katy England, the British-born fashion director for *Dazed & Confused*. "I'd seen her around, at the shows in Paris, and she just had this great look about her," he said. He asked her to assist him with styling.

England helped McQueen develop the collection, bringing into the mix a few found pieces, such as leather jackets. Backstage before the show, England told her assistant Trino Verkade to go outside and fetch a wheel off her car. England covered the tire with smudge and rolled it on the girls' naked bodies, so flashes of tire marks would show from under a jacket or on an arm. "I loved the combination of the highly sexy undertone and this surreal violence, and the way the girls looked with the contact lenses, these surreal women," Laakkonen says. "But it was never at the expense of women, like: 'I'm trying to belittle women.' I never felt that Alexander made women seem like victims. I never got that vibe from him in his work."

Again, McQueen's mother, Joyce, was backstage, serving her homemade sandwiches and tea. Joyce, Groves says, was "a real East End mum, a real matriarch, white hair, formidable, scary. She was not small talk and chat. It was nothing, or 'Lee!'" McQueen was comforted by her presence there, which made it easier to work with him. "His mask would drop when his mother was around," Anderson says.

"He felt protected by her," Groves affirms.

THE SCENE OUT FRONT "was insane," remembers Kim Blake, McQueen's London PR consultant. Since there was no money, there was no security, and Blake had to work the door. "Someone found me a bucket and we turned it upside down and I stood on it so I could see what was going on," she says.

The audience consisted mainly of club kids and fashion students; there was only a handful of fashion journalists and retailers—many of whom Isabella Blow had persuaded to attend. "There was no Anna Wintour and the whole scary front row," Groves says. McQueen knew that and it hurt him deeply: "London gives me fuck all," he said of his hometown fashion establishment. "If they offered me Young Designer of the Year I'd throw a right tantrum—they haven't given me shit."

An hour and a half after the show's scheduled time, with the crowd growing visibly restless, McQueen was ready to start. The lights were turned down and the room grew silent in anticipation.

Suddenly, an alarm bell blared in the darkness, shattering the audience, and a bright spotlight shot out of the tunnel. The first model walked out in silhouette through the light, as in the climactic scene in Steven Spielberg's *Close Encounters of the Third Kind*, when the aliens descend from their spaceship. She was dressed in a long, sharply tailored Victorian-style jacket worn open over her tanned naked torso, and matching cropped Bumsters. On the back of the jacket, between the shoulder blades, was McQueen's label: the plastic two-inch-square filled with a curl of hair.

Next came a sexy 1960s-style shift, looking as if it were made from a plastic shower curtain—which some McQueen friends believe was a reference to the murder scene in Hitchcock's *Psycho*. The model's breasts were visible, as were her little-girl-style cotton briefs. Protruding from her shoulders were two chrome spikes, like a medical device. The hot lights made the models' opaque white eyes shimmer eerily.

"The girls looked like zombies!" Bocci still hoots in amazement.

"They looked like they had been attacked by birds, with those lenses in their eyes, that's for sure," Souleiman recalls. "That's what was cool about it."

As the music ramped up to a thumping techno, there was a sharp, white broad-shouldered power suit, the lapels and arms printed with tire tracks, the skirt so tight the model baby-stepped her way down the runway; a Julien Macdonald white cropped sweater with long sleeves and a plunging neckline; and a tightly tailored orange pantsuit with black flying swallows, worn by Plum Sykes. There were more sexy form-fitting shifts: in black plastic with white tire marks; in orange nylon with red tire marks; in vibrant pumpkin fishnet over matching cotton briefs; and in the found plastic pallet wrap over black high-cut panties.

By the end of the show, people were standing on their chairs, stomping. "Everyone went completely crazy," Anderson says. When McQueen came out, dressed demurely in a blue Oxford shirt and khakis, he waved to the cheering, whooping crowd, dashed over to his mother, who was sitting next to Groves in the front row, to give her a big hug, then shyly ducked backstage. McQueen later learned that his father had arrived unannounced, quietly stood in the back to watch, then left without saying a word.

In the days that followed, the reviews of "The Birds" rolled in and were, for the most part, fawning. *The New York Times*'s Amy Spindler called McQueen "easily the most talked-about designer" of the moment and proclaimed that his tailored jackets were "nothing short of perfect."

Women's Wear Daily declared that the collection was "filled with raw sex—and should help resuscitate London's reputation for street fashion." The trade added: "Thanks to Alexander McQueen, we'll be keeping an eye on our cousin's distant shores for a long time."

"'The Birds' was a big turning point," Derek Anderson says now. "It crowned Lee as *the* rising star. Before he was *a* rising star. But after 'The Birds,' he was the one to watch."

VII

G alliano needed a new backer—again. This time, he wanted someone "with a manufacturing base," he said, "who can provide me with marketing and distribution."

Most important, however, he wanted to stay in Paris—not just to show, but to live and work all year round. He loved Paris—its culture, its beauty, the savoir faire—and he found it easier to be poor there, less Covent Garden guttersnipe, more *La Bohème*. He assimilated easily with the French; he understood both their Latin temperament and their bourgeois formality; it was, in a sense, a collision of his Spanish upbringing and British grammar school education. Paris made sense to him.

He explained his predicament to Fayçal Amor, and Amor agreed to help. "I said, 'Come to Paris. Let's see what we can do. Let's find some financing. But you must do a collection. If you don't have a collection, if you miss another season, you will be forgotten.'"

Amor rented an apartment for Galliano on the rue Vieille du Temple, in the Marais, the oldest section of Paris, and offered Galliano workspace in the Plein Sud headquarters. Galliano had a small office, which he shared with Steven Robinson, who had maneuvered his way up to become first assistant. Harlech seemed not to mind. Robinson filled the creative gaps in the studio when she was home in Shropshire, and she was impressed to see how well he could keep up with Galliano's rat-a-tat idea runs: "John will say 'pearl,' and Steven will say, 'sea glass,' and they go on and on creating a picture," she said.

Amor decided to underwrite Galliano temporarily until he could find a permanent partner. The deal was announced in the fashion trades in August 1992: the Société Amor would finance Galliano's signature ready-to-wear line and the secondary line, Galliano's Girl; Bertelsen's Aguecheek would retain the license to produce Galliano Jeans.

Surprisingly, Amor discovered in his due diligence of Galliano's business affairs that he had never trademarked his name. "I said, 'John, how can you have been working ten years and never registered your name? That's incredible!'" Amor recalls. "So it was decided that I would register his name around the world—it was me who was paying—and we would hold fifty percent each."

Galliano brought over the team from London. Amor put the pattern cutter Bill Gaytten on the payroll. Harlech came to style the show, along with "a bunch of beautiful people from London—students—to help," Amor says. The collection would be called "Filibustiers," a play on a term for pirates. The story was vintage Galliano: a shipwrecked crew of beautiful giantesses attacked by marauders—the "filibustiers"—who pillage the ship's treasures. The women are saved by soldiers, who arrive dressed in Union Jack jackets and chase away the bad guys.

For the show, Galliano and Amor booked the Salle Wagram, a great rococo dance hall built in 1865. The show was scheduled for Wednesday, October 14 at 9:00 P.M., and everyone arrived at the appointed time and waited.

And waited. And waited. "One hundred and three minutes of bum fatigue and brain drain brought on by the continuous playing of the score from [Oliver Stone's film] *JFK*," *Washington Post* critic Cathy Horyn complained in her review.

Finally, at eleven, the lights went down and as the crowd whooped and cheered, the models marched out fiercely to Healy's thumping club music, their wigs made of ratty dishwater-colored hair woven into the shape of upside-down *T*s as broad as the fringed epaulettes on their deconstructed Napoleonic coats. They vamped and scowled and fanned themselves as they paraded about in filmy asymmetrical mini-nightgown dresses, and frock coats with oversized cuffs and splayed sleeves. There were dresses made of faded American flags, the train draped over a sheathed sword, and a sheer black cutaway dinner jacket had its tails suspended in midair, as if by magic. The bias-cut gowns were in layered pastel organdy, some topped off with a distressed satin corset with giant poufy mutton sleeves. It was "Les Incroyables" redux, with a decade of experience, more highly skilled seamstresses, and a bigger budget.

Then came a suite of tight, sexy cheongsams in red, black satin, and shimmering gold, set to a remix of Ryuichi Sakamoto's haunting soundtrack from *The Last Emperor*. Some were strapless with breasts popping out; some slashed suggestively across the bodice; some embroidered with dragons; all were breathtakingly sensual. This was Galliano's first major riff on the late-nineteenth-century Chinoiserie movement that he would later embrace fully.

The show was an endless parade of creative ideas, much of them deconstructed—"Admiral Nelson goes Acid House," as *Women's Wear* put it. At a time when most of fashion was steeped in minimalism in a somber palette of navy, beige, and gray, Galliano was like a lightning bolt crashing through. "It is fun to see imaginative clothes," *New York Times* critic Bernadine Morris wrote of Galliano's collection, "even when they're on the wacko side."

Despite all the good reviews and retailer orders Galliano was receiving, he and Amor were having a hard time finding him a full-time backer. To help the effort, Amor decided to teach Galliano how to become a proper Paris couturier, to give him the skills and the polish that he was lacking and backers obviously wanted to see. "The English were considered not sufficiently refined or couture-savvy or too technically skilled," Amor says. "And I explained this early on to John. 'If you come to Paris, it is to become a great couturier. You can be the couturier for Dior. But you must stop doing rags. You have to be more luxurious in your creation, not trash. You could do trash, but it has to be sophisticated trash, not just trash with students doing the cutting, like you do in London. Couture in France is a spirit, the technique of the cut, the sewing, the finish. It was a whole education. It is our know-how.'"

Amor took Galliano on a tour of his high-tech factory in Châtellerault, near Poitiers in west-central France, which Galliano compared to the mad scientist's lair in the James Bond movie *Dr. No*. "I've never seen anything like it," he said. "The machinery is extraordinary. There are sewing machines with electronic eyes that can put a zip in like a dream, like God had made it."

"I learned a lot from Fayçal," Galliano later acknowledged. "He was so practical."

Galliano didn't stage a ready-to-wear show in March 1993. His official excuse was that he hoped to show during couture week in July instead, but in reality, there simply wasn't enough money, and couture week came and went without him too. In his downtime, he began cultivating new friendships with wealthy socialites Béatrice de Rothschild and São Schlumberger, and most important, with *Vogue* editor André Leon Talley.

Talley was a fascinating and powerful figure in fashion. A fervent Francophile—a passion fed by reading *Vogue* magazine and watching Julia Child's *The French Chef* program on PBS as a youth—Talley's first job out of school was as a volunteer assistant to legendary fashion editor Diana Vreeland when she was a special consultant for the Costume Institute at the Metropolitan Museum of Art. Vreeland not only mentored Talley; she became what he describes affectionately as his "surrogate fashion mother."

In 1983, Talley was hired at American *Vogue*—first as fashion news editor, later as creative director—and during his time there, he became known for supporting young, unknown talents. He first met Galliano at a party in London back when Galliano was dating Jasper Conran. "They were both dressed as Little Lord Fauntleroys," Talley later recalled.

A few years later, Talley traveled to Wales with his then-assistant Isabella Blow to oversee an American *Vogue* shoot featuring Harlech at Glyn Cywarch. During the three-day assignment, he admired several beautiful items in Harlech's wardrobe, such as "a jacket that was structured but in black organza and see-through, and in it was silvery sparkles that moved like when a child has a toy and turns it upside down and the glitter floats," he recalls. "Remarkable." Harlech said that they were designed by Galliano.

When Galliano began to show his collections in Paris, Talley attended them, and once Galliano settled there, the pair grew from social acquaintances to good friends. "We had these Sunday afternoon video marathons," Talley remembered. "I lived in the Seventh Arrondissement, this very uptight bourgeois neighborhood, and one afternoon . . . we watched this Katharine Hepburn/Fred MacMurray film, *Alice Adams*, where Hattie McDaniel screams, 'Dinna's served.' We watched this movie three times over, sitting on the sofa while she said, 'Dinna's served. Dinna's served.' And John started screaming out the window into the courtyard, 'Dinna's served! Dinna's served!' I thought they were going to throw me out."

COME FALL, Galliano set to work on a new collection: spring–summer 1994. His inspiration came from an article about royal Russian bones being genetically linked to the duke of Edinburgh. He and Harlech dreamed up a story of a ravished Russian royal named Princess Lucrecia who flees from danger at home to Scotland. "She's got very pale skin—you can almost see the blue veins on her forehead," Galliano said of his fictional heroine. "She has badly hennaed hair and dirt under her fingernails from gardening. She's a very sensuous woman, in complete control of her own destiny."

The show would start "with the feeling of Anna Karenina escaping Russia," he explained, then switch to modern-day Scotland—a section he titled "Highland Fling"—where, he said, the princess "chances upon the dotty duke and dotty duchess. She gambles. She goes to the races. She drinks gin." Finally, he said, "she comes across her prince, falls in love and goes back to rewrite history in her bias-cut dresses."

Upon returning to Paris after the Milan fashion week, Talley went to Galliano's studio late one night to see what his friend was up to. Talley looked at Galliano's *toiles*—the muslin prototypes of the collection. Galliano and Harlech described how they envisioned the show, and Talley was bowled over.

"It was astonishing!" he cried. "I thought it was one of the most wonderful, romantic things I'd seen for a long time in fashion. So I went straight to see Anna Wintour, saying, 'This is it.' And then I went to Béatrice de

Rothschild saying, 'You've got to see it.' And then I told São Schlumberger, 'You've got to come.'"

Galliano staged the show in one of the official Fashion Week tents in the Cour Carrée du Louvre on October 8. It was funded in large part by Fayçal Amor, but socialites São Schlumberger, Dodie Rosekrans, and Lucy Boutin contributed too.

As the lights went down, one witness reported, "A shudder went through the crowd." Suddenly, the sound of howling wolves filled the immense dark space, and a model appeared from behind the backdrop in a satin corset top and an enormous hoop skirt—like those worn by the women in Jane Campion's recently released film *The Piano*—and she darted wildly down the catwalk, looking over her shoulder as if she were running for her life. She was followed by a few more models, their hair in long matted braids and curls powdered gray and mauve, their swooping ball skirts billowing as they zigzagged with terror in their eyes.

The dramatic opening was followed by a tarty parade of what had become Galliano's signature silhouettes: tightly fitted eighteenth-century jackets, this time paired with swishy, flimsy mini-kilts and ruffled bikini bottoms; slinky asymmetrical bias-cut dresses with handkerchief hems; gowns with corset tops, bosoms squeezed mercilessly. The models smoked and posed and flipped up their little mini-kilts to moon photographers with their bikini-clad derrieres. The crowd erupted into a wild applause. Nobody had ever done a show like that—in Paris, in London, anywhere. Galliano had changed the game with his baying wolves and runaway princesses.

As GALLIANO'S TEAM SOLD clothes to retailers Amor was out with Galliano trying to find a long-term backer. "We went to see everyone," Amor said. "And everyone said no. I had a meeting with Bernard Arnault and the then-president of LVMH, who wrote to me kindly saying, 'We are not interested in creators of this sort.'"

The financial stress on both men was starting to take its toll. Like Brun and Bertelsen before him, Amor had sunk a "considerable amount" of money into Galliano's company, and the returns were meager at best. "Everything was made by hand for the show and the collection," he says. "And then we had to do industrial production of those garments, which was almost impossible."

Worse, orders were not delivered to retailers on time, and as Barneys' then–women's fashion director Julie Gilhart says, that "is the kiss of death" for a designer. When a delivery is late, the retailer has less time to sell it for full price—known as "sell-through"—before the price-reduction sales season arrives. And if the retailer has to sell the clothes at a reduced price, it has a smaller budget for the next season.

As with his two previous backers, the more stressful the situation became, the more agitated and aggressive Galliano grew. He had been evicted from his Amor-rented flat "after neighbors complained about his wild partying," *Women's Wear* reported—a real feat, given Paris's strict pro-tenant laws—and was sleeping on Steven Robinson's floor. "He couldn't function, he couldn't talk," Talley remembers. "He was shaking, trembling."

"I couldn't keep it up, and I explained that to John," Amor says. "I wrote to Madame Anna Wintour, 'You know me, you know that I have a clothing line, and I support John, and I support you, but I can't keep up helping him because I can't afford it anymore, and I hope you know someone who could help.'

"She never responded to my letter," Amor says. "Never called."

Instead, Wintour invited Galliano to New York.

WINTOUR WAS AND IS fashion's kingmaker: not only can she make or break a career by choosing who appears in the editorial pages of her magazine, she advises designers on what to design and where to work and counsels company executives on who to hire. This is a power that she has cultivated on her own; until she took over the editorship of American *Vogue* in 1988, editors were editors, and they focused solely on their publications; there was still a vague separation of church and state between media and business. Anna Wintour broke down that barrier by talking to CEOs directly, acting as a consultant, matchmaker, and in designers' cases, a career counselor—and linking all of this business back to *Vogue*. "It's a very positive way of demonstrating her power," François-Henri Pinault, CEO of Kering, which owns Gucci, Stella McCartney, and Alexander McQueen, has said. "She lets you know it's not a problem if you can't do something she wants. But she makes you understand that if you could, she would be very supportive with her magazine."

Wintour achieved this in part by riding coattails and in part by hard work and unwavering determination. Journalism was in her blood. Her father, Charles Wintour, began a career as a newspaperman, eventually becoming the respected and somewhat feared editor of the British daily the *Evening Standard*; his manner with his newsroom staff could be so brusque and austere, his nickname was "Chilly Charlie."

In the mid-1960s, at fifteen years old, and with her father's help, Anna landed a job at the groundbreaking Swinging London fashion boutique Biba. Later she did the training program at Harrods and worked for an underground magazine called *Oz*. She moved into fashion journalism in the 1970s, first as an editorial assistant at *Harpers & Queen*, then as junior fashion editor at *Harper's Bazaar* in New York. In 1983, she joined American *Vogue* as creative director. When its then–editor in chief Grace Mirabella asked her what she wanted at the magazine, Wintour famously replied: "Your job." After stints as editor of British *Vogue* and *House & Garden*, Wintour had it.

Wintour's managerial approach has been known to be as frosty as her father's—she earned the nickname "Nuclear Wintour" and was deftly sent up in the novel and film *The Devil Wears Prada*. But she understood the potential of her influence at *Vogue*—she was not simply an editor, but a leading voice and force in a growing global industry.

By the end of 1993, Galliano needed that sway and she was pleased to help. She bought him a coach-class ticket to New York, put him up at the trendy, Philippe Starck–designed Royalton Hotel, and seated him at the *Vogue* table at the Costume Institute's gala opening of an exhibition dedicated to Diana Vreeland. "I felt that John was at a point at his career where he needed some exposure and to be visible, and that kind of an event was helpful for that," Wintour later told me. "It made a lot of sense from *Vogue*'s point of view. I thought he was a designer with a vision—a brilliant designer—and I was just trying to help to get him out there to be seen and meet people because he needed help financially and to get press."

Everywhere Galliano went during this New York trip, he said, "I just started telling people what my dream was—of a couture house for the future. How I want to offer a service to women . . . helping a woman get what she wants. . . . I was invited to amazing parties, and I just kept telling everyone my dream." One listener was Catie Marron, a *Vogue* contributing editor and the wife of Paine Webber chairman Donald B. Marron, at a dinner in honor of Talley at the fashionable Upper East Side bistro Mortimer's. Intrigued, Catie Marron asked Galliano to send her a video of his shows. Talley did the next day. She watched it with her husband, and he wasn't interested. But she thought that John Bult, the chairman of Paine Webber International, might be. Bult and his partner, Mark Rice, were looking for companies to invest in.

Talley sent Bult the video. He didn't know quite what to make of it—fashion was not his forte—so he gave it to Rice. After Rice watched it, he told Bult that they should go meet with Galliano in Paris. Bult's secretary rang Talley to arrange a meeting at the Hôtel Bristol, where they would be staying. When the towering Talley, the always-perspiring Steven Robinson, and the sari-clad Galliano arrived at the hotel's reception the following afternoon, the concierge rang up to Bult and Rice and announced drolly, "Your *friends* are here."

The five men sat down in the hotel's lobby lounge and Galliano explained what he wanted to do and what he needed to make it happen. Talley was eager for them to move forward on a deal of some sort. Galliano, after all, wasn't just doing great work himself; he was starting to set trends and influence fashion's top stars: both Karl Lagerfeld at Chanel and Christian Lacroix had adapted Galliano silhouettes for their haute couture shows in January.

Independently, Bult and Rice met with their Paris-based French lawyer Jean-Pierre Duclos to see what they might be able to do. About a week later, Bult and Rice returned via Concorde to Paris and invited Galliano to Duclos's office to hear their proposal. Talley accompanied Galliano, who this time was far more demurely dressed in a black T-shirt, trousers, and pea coat, and they were both extremely nervous. To their immense relief, Bult and Rice told Galliano that their investment firm, Arbela Inc., would help finance the show and, if all went well, they would all sit down afterward and discuss establishing a company. There was no contract, only a verbal agreement. Though Talley was deeply involved in making the deal happen, he did not receive a finder's fee or a percentage of the deal from Arbela for his efforts. Arbela's total investment for the show would be about $50,000—not a huge sum, especially for Galliano, who was known to burn through money easily.

Talley and Galliano went around Paris in a taxi looking at possible show venues. Then Talley remembered that São Schlumberger had an eighteenth-century mansion on the Left Bank near the Luxembourg Gardens that had long been for sale and was sitting empty—therefore, in theory, free of charge.

They invited the aging socialite to lunch at Chez Pauline and put forth their idea.

"São, there is no such thing as a free lunch," Talley said. "We have this extraordinary thing we want to do: we want to put on this fashion show in your former house, and it will really be incredible, and the world will come and it will be extraordinary and you can order all the clothes you want."

"Of course you can have my house," she responded. "All I have to do is go get a mini facelift. Just a mini facelift." And then she let out a little laugh.

GALLIANO STILL NEEDED to work with Amor to produce the collection. But Amor had reached his limit. "[Galliano] was bankrupting him," a friend says. "He just said, 'I don't want to do it.' He was out." According to an American *Vogue* spokesman, Talley and Wintour "encouraged Fayçal Amor not to block Mr. Galliano from showing one season after his prophetic Spring 1994 collection show at the Louvre." Amor acquiesced, allowing Galliano to continue to work in the studio and providing seamstresses and support staff as needed. He also counseled Galliano: "Do not give your fifty percent share of the company away. Guard your independence."

There would be only eighteen looks—about a third of what the Chambre Syndicale, the French fashion association that oversaw Fashion Week, required designers to show, but Galliano was given a pass because, as he explained, "We hadn't time to make more."

Since the budget was tight, Galliano and Robinson bought a roll of cheap black synthetic satin crepe and used both the shiny and grainy sides as contrasts. The overarching theme was Japonism, the romantic European take on traditional Japanese wear. "Nineteen-forties tailoring fused with Japanese kabuki" is how Galliano described it.

He told his investors that the collection's narrative was a continuation of Princess Lucrecia's adventures: she was returning to her house in Paris after the war, a widow; her lover had died in combat—therefore for the first look, she would be wearing a long military coat. From there, the show would be about her life as a chic night creature in 1920s Paris, with lingerie, kimonos, short furs, and diamonds. The jewelry would be on loan from Harry Winston, Fred, and René Boivin.

One afternoon at the office, Rice was looking over the budget of the show and asked Galliano: "What do you need? What do you want?" He responded, "I want my own couture house. I want to be like the house of Dior." Rice rolled his eyes. "Right. Okay. But what do you need by this Friday?"

Talley called every day from Milan, where he was covering fashion week, to go over guest lists and model choices. The early 1990s supermodels—such as Kate Moss, Naomi Campbell, Christy Turlington, and Linda Evangelista—who earned then-record fees, agreed to work for Galliano for free; they knew he couldn't afford to hire them, but they, like his staff, believed in his talent and they knew their presence would draw the attention he needed.

When Talley returned from Milan, he met up with Galliano and Robinson to do the seating for the show. Since the mansion was a labyrinth of small- and medium-size salons and hallways, the number of seats would be limited to only two hundred—a fraction of what the major designers had for their shows in the Louvre's new modern underground exhibition space, the Carrousel du Louvre. To make up for the loss, Galliano decided to stage two shows: one at nine thirty in the morning, and another at one in the afternoon.

Harlech and her team set to decorating the place. They arranged delicate gilded chairs in rows two and three deep along the walls of the oak-paneled rooms, punctuated here and there with Victorian velvet love seats and small round sofas known as bornes, to create a couture house–like setting where guests could see the clothes up close. To give it the romantic feel of a dilapidated, abandoned mansion, they put chandeliers on the floor, scattered leaves about, sprayed theatrical dust, left love letters on tables and chairs, and set up fans to blow dry ice smoke to create a hazy glow. Galliano and his assistants bought five hundred rusty keys at the Paris flea market to send with the invitations.

THE MORNING OF THE SHOWS—Saturday, March 5—Galliano's team was running about two hours late. "At 10:45 A.M. I could still spy a seamstress frantically sewing Naomi Campbell into a tiny slither of bias-cut satin backstage," wrote *The Independent*'s Marion Hume.

The guests, however, were on time. The crowd was a mix of the shiny set and the fashion crowd, including socialites São Schlumberger, Béatrice de Rothschild, Dodie Rosekrans, and Isabelle d'Ornano, Paris couturier

Emanuel Ungaro's wife, Laura, shoe designer Christian Louboutin, Anna Wintour, and Christian Dior's creative director Gianfranco Ferré. Talley helped seat all the VIPs and introduced them to Bult and Rice.

When Healy's club mix came on, they all sat up with anticipation. Out walked Carla Bruni in a voluminous black satin shoulders-baring wrap that skimmed her derriere with nothing below except Manolo Blahnik vamp heels and only a Stephen Jones sculptural black plastic ribbon hat on top. There was Nadja Auermann in a short mink-collared leather coat and a Jones black felt cloche decorated with a big floral Harry Winston diamond brooch; Helena Christensen in an ample black inside-out fur over a skintight turtleneck and long black satin skirt slip sliced to her hip; Michele Hicks in a sheer mini-kimono with a pale yellow satin, rose-embroidered obi sash around her bosom and a black garter belt with seamed black stockings; Kate Moss in a sheer pale pink mini-kimono with a black satin obi sash; Linda Evangelista in a kimono-like black satin cutaway with flared sleeves; Christy Turlington in a form-fitting pink satin strapless gown with voluminous train and a black mink wrap; Naomi Campbell in satin tap pants and a plush mink wrap. Other lesser-known models wore leather trenches, black satin pant suits, and black satin tuxedo jackets with kimono sleeves.

The makeup and hair were 1920s flapper style; the Blahnik shoes tall and strappy; the Jones hats spare and modern. Each model sashayed slowly from room to room to draw the show out a bit. In a matter of twenty minutes, all eighteen outfits had been presented. Galliano came out shyly at the end, dressed in a black T-shirt and jeans, and short hair buzzed on the side, quietly nodded to the crowd and smiled.

"Perhaps the finest hour of the weekend shows belonged to John Galliano," wrote Cathy Horyn in *The Washington Post*. "In just twenty [sic] outfits, some of which were still being finished the night before, Galliano managed to convey a wicked sense of elegance. . . . It was brilliant." London's *Sunday Times* called it "as close to perfection as it is possible to be."

They set up the showroom in the Schlumberger mansion and orders rolled in: Bergdorf Goodman, Saks Fifth Avenue, Neiman Marcus, and I. Magnin department stores in the United States; Liberty, Peter Jones, and Harrods in London; L'Eclaireur, Maria Luisa, Victoire, and Galleries Lafayette in Paris; and Cosi in Milan. Sales went so well that Bult and Rice decided to form a company, set up a studio, and organize production and distribution. They all met with Duclos to work out the details. But before the contract could be signed, Bult and Rice had to secure Galliano's brand name legally. They bought Amor's portion and paid off Galliano's outstanding debt to Amor. And Galliano sold his portion to Arbela, despite Amor's advice against it. "John gave everything to John Bult; he didn't listen to me," Amor says. "And after I gave John his fifty percent, I never saw him again."

DUCLOS DREW UP official contracts this time. The company was called John Galliano SARL, the French version of a limited partnership. Arbela owned 75 percent; Galliano 25 percent. Bult, Rice, and Galliano agreed that once Arbela recouped its investment, Galliano could own his name outright.

They hired Duclos's wife, Jacqui, an American who spoke French, as the company's *directeur general*, or president, and Galliano's friend Robert Ferrell, an American-born Paris modeling agent, as the commercial director. The Galliano's Girl line was shut down—everyone agreed that cheap Galliano was a bad idea. They found a studio/office in a humble, seventeenth-century building at the end of a cobblestone alley called the Passage du Cheval Blanc, just off the Place de la Bastille. At the time, the Bastille neighborhood was gritty—there were muggings and drug dealing, a rarity in Paris back then—but it was considered up and coming.

Bult and Rice put Galliano on a salary of about 25,000 French francs, or $4,470, a month—enough back then to live comfortably in Paris—and all his business expenses were covered.

Everyone seemed happy with the deal, even Anna Wintour. She met Bult, Rice, and Talley at the Ritz for lunch and wanted to know, like a father of the bride, what Bult and Rice's intentions were with Galliano, what their plan was, how they were going to make the company work. Once they explained everything to her, she approved and gave her blessing.

A few weeks later, Bult sat down and penned a note to Amor that read, "I want to thank you for all that you did for John."

Amor wrote back: "Good luck."

E o Bocci realized that "The Birds" was McQueen's make-or-break moment and he stepped in to help make it happen. He drew up two contracts: the first guaranteed him distribution of McQueen fashion for fifteen years; the second was a manufacturing agreement, in which he would act as the go-between, finding McQueen just the right factory to produce the clothes. "McQueen understood what I was offering in one second," Bocci says.

He signed.

McQueen kept the news of the deal to himself. "You'd think he'd say,

'Oh, I've signed this deal for three years and I get X percentage,' and so on," Andrew Groves says now. "But no. He said nothing. Just suddenly there was money."

Like Galliano, McQueen compartmentalized his life. But he didn't do it to hide his homosexuality from his family or his working-class upbringing from his fashion supporters, as Galliano had done; McQueen was openly gay and proud of his East End roots. No, his compartments were about keeping information from those who thought they were close to him to create conflict. "He was a master at setting people against each other," Ungless says. It was as if he needed to keep his combustible East End upbringing churning around him at all times; he couldn't live with peace and harmony.

Groves endured McQueen's passive-aggressive upheaval firsthand regularly. Like the afternoon on Elizabeth Street, when McQueen turned to Groves and said rather matter-of-factly:

"I have to go now to the palace. Princess Diana is doing this thing for Fashion Week."

Groves stood there, dumbfounded.

"You're only mentioning this now?" he responded. "You don't think this would be something quite exciting to talk about?"

McQueen shrugged and toddled off to Kensington Palace for the party. Without Groves.

Another day, Groves and McQueen went to a street style exhibit at the Victoria and Albert Museum to see a dress that Groves had on display. McQueen packed some things in a bag and they headed over to the museum. While Groves was in the loo, McQueen went through security; when Groves met up with him, McQueen was in a fury.

"Fucking cunt! I'm not fucking going in there!" McQueen howled. "They searched my bag and I had a dildo in it."

"What the fuck is *that* doing in your bag?" Groves gasped.

McQueen didn't explain. Instead, he shouted, "We're not going!" and they left.

When it came to socializing, McQueen either went out with Simon Ungless and Shaun Leane, or he went out with Groves and a friend named Nicholas Townsend, who performed under the drag name Trixie, or he went to Hilles with the Blows. He never mixed it up.

His evenings with Groves and Trixie were particularly wild, and often they'd wear crazy getups. For a night at Maximus on Leicester Square, McQueen and Groves stripped naked and Trixie wrapped them in gaffer tape—Groves in the form of a miniskirt and top; McQueen in a mummy-like body wrap. Both carried chains. "There was no makeup or anything," Trixie says. "They just looked like a couple of blokes in gaffer tape." On the way home, they crossed through some street fairs, and McQueen ripped the bottom off Groves. "He stood there bollocks naked in the street," Trixie remembers with a smile.

But McQueen's looks weren't always so silly. When he, Groves, and Trixie went out to Kinky Gerlinky at Leicester Square one night, he wore an ensemble that took a precise shot at John Galliano. He squeezed into a coarse wool Galliano women's suit that Isabella Blow had borrowed, put on a pair of chain sling-backs and a tricorner headpiece made of cardboard cones wrapped in raw wool like in Galliano's "Filibustiers" show. The look was astounding and biting at the same time. It was also dreadfully uncomfortable: the suit's fabric was so rough it made McQueen's nipples bleed.

"With Lee, there was no shade and nuance about anything," Groves recalls. "It was that or that."

He was a vocal atheist and unwavering antiroyalist. "He had really strong opinions about people, like Madonna," Groves says. "He didn't even know her, and if she was doing something for AIDS, he would rant, 'Oh, she doesn't give a fuck about the event or the people, she's doing it for the press and the publicity.'" And he had very high moral standards of what everyone should or shouldn't do.

Like swearing.

Over tea with Joyce and McQueen at Biggerstaff Road one afternoon, Groves said he was "pissed off" about something.

"Don't you fucking swear in front of my fucking mother!" McQueen shouted.

His most revealing outburst was about himself: One night, out of the blue, Groves says, "Lee talked to me about when he was sexually abused. He didn't say who it was other than it was someone in the family, or if it was once or more than once. He cried uncontrollably for half an hour and that was it. He never mentioned it again."

McQUEEN WAS STILL NOT fully accepted by the London fashion establishment, and Isabella Blow knew why: his social class. In New York the American press adored McQueen and his designs; they didn't care about his roots, his rough talk, or his bad manners. All that mattered to the American retailers and press was that the work was good or, in McQueen's case, excellent, and that it sold.

But the United Kingdom was and is a country ruled by a class system. Where McQueen came from—deep in the East End—most definitely mattered to the British fashion powers-that-be. They liked—they loved— Galliano because he had buffed up his accent, had the formal Spanish upbringing, and was always polite and deferential to those who held sway. McQueen had remained stubbornly working-class. He was gruff. He maintained his Cockney accent riddled with profanity. He shaved his hair into a Mohawk, had tattoos before they were fashionable, dressed in faded T-shirts and ratty jeans, and was missing a front tooth. The British fashion establishment did not like him, and quietly wished he would just disappear.

Isabella Blow had come from the upper class, and she tried to impart some of her upbringing to McQueen. She took him to art exhibitions, nice restaurants, and important events. She invited him to Hilles, where she introduced him to the aristocracy and their way of life. Once she learned of his love of bird watching, she hired someone to teach him falconry—the gentlemanly sport of hunting with a trained bird of prey. He spent weekend afternoons in the fields at Hilles, working with the majestic birds, having them land on his heavily gloved arm, as Isabella—dressed in full fashion regalia, her heels sinking into the soggy earth—watched with pride. She was trying to create a more well-rounded, less scary man—one that the British mainstream press might eventually embrace. McQueen was aware that she was playing Professor Higgins to his Eliza Doolittle; he said she was "like a disease—a terminal disease. Everything she does rubs off on you."

REALIZING THAT McQUEEN was the hottest ticket on the show calendar, the British Fashion Council invited him to show in the larger of its two offi-

cial tents on the lawn of the Natural History Museum and offered to underwrite the cost. Though the setting felt too predictable and sterile for McQueen,
a free show was a free show, and he accepted. "That's a lot of pressure for me
to pull it off in that massive tent," he admitted.

One morning, a petite Israeli woman named Ruti Danan went to the studio to see McQueen. She first discovered him during his "Taxi Driver" presentation at the Ritz and followed his career. She worked for a fashion studio
in Knightsbridge, and one of her colleagues had attended Central Saint Martins with McQueen. When Danan heard this, she asked if the girl knew how
to get in touch with him. The girl gave her the Biggerstaff Road phone number. She rang and spoke to Joyce.

"I want to work for your son," Danan told her. "Can I have his number?"

Joyce gave his address instead. When Danan got there McQueen wasn't in
yet. She decided to wait. He showed up about an hour later in a huff. "He was
really angry and nervous about his assistant, who didn't do what he wanted
her to do," Danan recalls.

He turned to Danan.

"Who the fuck are you?"

"I really want to work for you," she responded. She showed him her book.
And he liked it.

"Okay," he said to Danan, "you can stay."

He turned to his assistant:

"And you can fuck off."

McQueen was working on a new idea for a collection: designs that referenced England's many invasions of Scotland. Since his father's family had
Scottish roots, McQueen had been reading up on the Scottish upheavals and
the Clearances of the eighteenth and nineteenth centuries, when the English
forced the Highlands population to the coastal regions—sometimes
brutally—to make way for sheep farms and other agricultural projects primarily owned and run by English aristocrats. The murderous rampages,
which devastated Scotland's clans, have been described as ethnic cleansing by
some historians. "England's rape of Scotland" McQueen called it. He was fed
up with Vivienne Westwood's and John Galliano's "flamboyant Scottish
clothes," which he found to be cliché, costume-y, and having nothing to do
with either Scotland or modern dress. He was going to make clothes that

truly reflected, in his mind, the history of Scotland and he was going to do it in a way so women could wear them in contemporary everyday life. He titled it "The Highland Rape."

McQueen also used as inspiration German author Patrick Süskind's *Perfume: The Story of a Murderer*, an award-winning novel about an eighteenth-century perfume apprentice born without a body smell who stalks and murders virgins in his search of the perfect scent.

McQueen's last thread of the collection's themes came from something deeply personal: Danan says McQueen told her there was a woman in his life when he was young who was raped—and the horror of that act affected him greatly. "All of his collections are autobiographical," Danan notes.

The cornerstone fabric was the McQueen tartan—a rich red and pine green check with a thin sunshine yellow line crossing through it. Since McQueen couldn't afford to pay for it, Detmar Blow covered the cost. McQueen used the tartan to construct complicated dresses based on traditional Scottish attire, some with bustles and crinoline skirts, and modern suits with sculpted plunging necklines and Bumster pants or skirts. At every seam, no matter how complicated the cut, McQueen made sure the plaid matched perfectly.

Another essential component was lace, which McQueen bought for 1.50 pounds ($2.50) a yard from Barry's Stall, a merchant who sold fabric remnants from an old wooden cart on Berwick Street. To create different color and texture effects with the lace, McQueen sprayed it with metallic car paint. "He wanted expensive fabrics, but he couldn't afford them," Danan says. "Instead, he used really cheap fabrics and he made them look expensive. That was the magic."

McQueen loved all things William Morris, the nineteenth-century textile designer, artist, and writer who was a member of the Pre-Raphaelite Brotherhood. Isabella Blow encouraged McQueen's passion for Morris since Hilles had been designed by Detmar's grandfather, a Morris disciple. Ungless had a Morris-like print of melting flowers in his freelance portfolio that McQueen so admired and he asked if he could use it for the new collection. Ungless agreed and produced it in gold on a black background, which McQueen turned into a sleeveless fitted shift. Ungless also printed it clear on tartan, which McQueen used for a jacket and skirt.

McQueen worked with more colors than he had in the past, including royal blue, periwinkle, bronze, ivy green, and lavender. He made a mid-calf pencil Bumster skirt in lavender silk held together with gaffer tape—a nod to his crazy night out with Groves and Trixie. (He gave it to Trixie afterward.) He bleached the crotch of a pair of navy Bumsters to look like it had been ripped open during a sexual attack.

He called on Julien Macdonald to make the knitwear again. While they were discussing the collection, Macdonald remarked that McQueen had blood running down his arm. McQueen said he had accidentally sliced himself while cutting fabric. They decided to base a sweater on his wound: a long-sleeve pullover made of scarlet yarn and clear fishing line that looks like a torso ripped apart—slashes of red across a nude body—with threads dangling like dripping blood.

McQueen also enlisted several new contributors, including his friend Shaun Leane, who created jewelry accessories, such as silver chains that would be slung through the crotch. McQueen brought on Katy England's assistant Trino Verkade, a cool English redhead in her mid-twenties who had studied fashion design and marketing, to be the "accountant, press officer and personal assistant," as she described it. He hired Karen Maher, an assistant at Kim Blake's PR agency, to help with press too.

Like Galliano, McQueen was "incredibly hands-on" when it came to his brand image, Blake says. "He was in control of every aspect of the company: what the invite looked like, who could borrow the clothes, and which clothes." At times, his obsession was disruptive. "He would call up at obscure times in the night and say: 'I've just thought of something,'" Blake remembers. "And I'd say, 'Okaaaay.' But he always qualified the call. It wasn't ever for nothing."

Blake could see that McQueen was having a hard time with the British press. British *Vogue* editor Alexandra Shulman had recently dismissed McQueen's Bumsters as "all about titillation." And he had been deemed difficult because he refused to be photographed or insisted on having his face obscured—for *Sky* magazine, he wore a mask of gaffer tape, and when he appeared on *The Clothes Show*, he had his back to the camera. He explained that he did this because he was still signing for welfare and didn't want to be recognized by government officials and lose his benefits.

Then a major breakthrough came rather unexpectedly: *International Herald Tribune* fashion editor Suzy Menkes rang Kim Blake and asked her to set up an appointment to see McQueen. Blake booked a car and the two of them set off to the East End. When they got to the studio—"a horrible place," Blake remembers—McQueen politely introduced himself and he and Menkes chatted for a bit. Then he had Katy England put on a pair of Bumsters. As England modeled them, Menkes got down on her hands and knees and asked England to turn around. "Oh, okay, I see what you've done," Menkes told McQueen. Then she talked at length with him about tailoring. "After that," says Blake, "Suzy was a McQueen supporter."

The indie press was behind him too, and he was far more available to them because he knew that welfare officials most certainly didn't read them. Shortly before the show, McQueen sat down for an interview with a reporter from *The Face* at a dumpy neighborhood pub near his studio. Over a pint of beer, he opened up as he hadn't before with anyone, but if the interview was supposed to help defuse his reputation as fashion's Rottweiler, it didn't.

"I've been called 'the new Saint Laurent' by some woman at *Vogue*, but what the fuck does that mean?" he growled. "It just sounds so poncey. At the end of the day, clothes are clothes and I'm making really good ones."

He dismissed the critics who called his work "couture." He admitted that "you've got to have my technical knowledge to do what I do. . . . I am a tailor and I cut the cloth to give it real shape." But he insisted that his clothes were ready-to-wear, sniffing, "I'll leave that couture thing to John Galliano."

"THE HIGHLAND RAPE" was scheduled for March 13, 1995, in the British Fashion Council tent. The catwalk was strewn with dried thistles, heather, leaves, and moss that Verkade had rustled up from florists for free. The invitation was a color image of a five-inch brownish-yellow gash in human flesh pocked with suture scabs. The show was dedicated to Isabella Blow because, McQueen said, it was "very Issie—in a way macabre, romantic, theatrical, streetwise, and honest."

To help cover costs, he received some funding from an unlikely source: a British health association that was conducting a "Put Smoking Out of Fashion" campaign. In return for 10,000 pounds (roughly $7,000 at the time), several designers, McQueen included, agreed to create an antismoking outfit for the runway. No one at the association seemed to mind that McQueen himself was a smoker. Unfortunately, he forgot about it, and never made anything. One of his assistants realized this backstage. After a burst of "fucking hells," ranting, and accusations, McQueen came up with a solution: he smeared glue onto a pair of latex hot pants and dumped an ashtray full of butts onto it. Problem solved. (McQueen later told Ungless that Michael Jackson bought the knickers.)

While the models dressed, McQueen made changes to some of the clothes. "There were all these beautiful blue lace dresses and he was hacking at them with his shears," said his mother, Joyce, who was backstage. "And I was crying, 'No, don't spoil them.'"

The final touch was opaque contact lenses, this time in blood red. "The models looked like aliens," Danan remembers. For his preshow pep talk, McQueen told the girls: "Give the audience the finger. Be rude. Don't be afraid. Show your bum. Stick out your boobs."

The scene out front of the BFC tent was sheer pandemonium. "I had never seen so many people trying to get into a show," Ungless remembers. Kim Blake was perched on a shed trying to handle the crowd without any security or a headset or any of the perks of a professional show setup. She spotted top editors such as Hamish Bowles in the sea of bodies and pulled them in.

Inside, on each seat, there was a note in McQueen's hand that stated: "The Scottish Highlands have been of great inspiration to many designers in the past. But they have been romanticized all too often. There were swathes of tartan but only as protection against the elements. Protection proved not to be enough against the fury of soldiers, as in many places and at many times across the world."

As the soundtrack of whistling wind and clanging bells filled the tent, the models wandered out, seemingly dazed, wounded, and scared. Their hair, by Colin Roy, was a tangled mess as if it had been "brushed by the thistles that lined the runway," one observer noted, and the clothes were ripped or lopsided, like someone had tried to tear them off. Smart tailored jackets scooped low to reveal the models' naked breasts. Some dresses were made of draped sheer black chiffon or torn lace, lightly veiling the girls' nude torsos and derrieres. Leane's silver crotch chains jangled as the girls stumbled down the runway. The overall effect was disturbingly erotic.

When the show was over, Blake says, "Lee was mobbed. I mean *mobbed*."

She had to escort him to a government-sponsored party celebrating Fashion Week, both of them still in their sweaty clothes and trainers. "We looked dog rough when we got there," she remembers with a laugh. But McQueen was the man everyone wanted to see. "From then on," she says, "it was superstardom."

"THE HIGHLAND RAPE" made McQueen a superstar not because of the beauty of the clothes—though they were breathtakingly beautiful as well as truly original—but because of the violence the show evoked in name and in execution. Ungless and Laakkonen could feel the rumbling in the audience as soon as McQueen took his bow. "People were furious and shocked," Laakkonen says. "They thought he was terrible."

The New York Times's Amy Spindler seemed to understand what McQueen was trying to achieve, calling it "an obvious ploy at provocation . . . packed with restless, rousing ideas, by far the best of the London season."

But the rest of the press, for the most part, hated it. "Rape victims staggering in dresses clawed at the breast were a sick joke, as were the knitted dresses that [mass retailer Marks & Spencer] would make better for a fraction of the price," wrote the *Independent*'s Marion Hume and Tamsin Blanchard. "To admit to not liking his collection is to admit to being prudish. So, we admit it. . . . The show was an insult to women and to his talent." The *Guardian*'s Sally Brampton hissed: "It is McQueen's brand of misogynistic absurdity that gives fashion a bad name."

"People were so unintelligent they thought this was about women being raped," he said of the backlash. "Highland Rape was about England's rape of Scotland." He added that, even though the press "crucified me for it, I'm glad I did it. The British killed families, kids, children, everything. It's happened to everyone in the world—it's happening in Croatia now, it happened to gays and lesbians in World War II."

Groves saw it as yet another interpretation of McQueen's life on the runway. McQueen's work "was his story, who he was as a person," he explains. "'Jack the Ripper' was about his family, and 'Taxi Driver' was about his dad. 'Highland Rape' was about him, and that's why he was so angry at people for misreading it. It was about him."

"The Highland Rape" raised McQueen's profile phenomenally, and he was fielding offers to work as a freelance consultant for major houses, including Calvin Klein. But none of them materialized. Very little of the collection was produced and sold, too, and McQueen was so broke he stopped paying his studio rent. Eventually, the landlord changed the locks. Danan sensed that this was coming, so she rushed over and grabbed what she could carry: sketches, bolts of fabric, clothing samples. Everything else—sewing machines, worktables, dummies—was seized as payment for back rent.

McQueen and Danan walked around the East End to look for a new work/home space and found a basement flat on Hoxton Square across the street from the park. McQueen thought it could work, especially at such a cheap price, and signed on the spot. His neighbor upstairs was a Philippine-born, American-raised freelance hairdresser named Mira Chai Hyde. "He walked into our unit and said 'Hi!' and I said, 'Come in for tea,'" she recalls. When she said she did men's hair and grooming for fashion shoots and shows, he immediately asked her if she'd do his next show.

The next women's wear season—spring–summer 1996—was rapidly approaching, and McQueen was scheduled to present in the BFC tents at the National History Museum as the closing show again. For the collection's theme, he chose two spooky 1980s movies he loved: Paul Schrader's erotic thriller *Cat People*, about how the sexual urges of a young woman, played by Nastassja Kinski, transform her into a voracious black leopard; and Tony Scott's 1983 *The Hunger*, a sexy vampire movie with Catherine Deneuve, Susan Sarandon, and David Bowie.

He had Danan to assist him, but he knew he needed more hands. He rang Sebastian Pons, a young Saint Martins student from Majorca who had been one of Ungless's students and whom he had met through friends at a pub. He invited Pons over to the Hoxton studio for an interview. When Pons arrived, McQueen was fussing with a couple of Ikea boxes that contained new worktables. "Your first project is to put these two tables together, so we have a surface to work on," he told Pons.

They assembled the tables and then went to work on a new print of long branches with thorns. "He drew it on white paper," Pons says. "He really knew what he wanted—where the thorns would be." When they finished the design, McQueen told Pons: "Okay, see you tomorrow!"

As was the case with everyone else working for McQueen, Pons wasn't paid. "I never asked him for any money because I knew he didn't have any,"

Pons says. "It was not easy. But I knew I was a part of something that was going to be big—that it was going to pay off in the long term."

McQueen preferred to work at night. "It was very peaceful and quiet then," Danan says. "He didn't like many people walking in and out of the studio when he was making things." She worked closely with him, serving not only as an assistant but also as a fit model. Like Anderson and many others in McQueen's sphere, she was astonished by his prowess. "He'd sit like a little old lady, stitching. This was his therapy, the hand stitching."

Danan quickly learned some of his tricks, like stuffing clothes with horsehair to get the correct shape, or sewing weights in hems so the clothes would hang just right. He told Danan that he was concerned for his father, who had been diagnosed with cancer and was undergoing treatments, and that most everyone in his family thought he "was weird, fucked up, because they had quite ordinary day jobs."

REALIZING THAT the Italian manufacturers he had contracted for McQueen could not produce McQueen's complicated designs on a large scale, Bocci decided to find a bigger, more efficient factory. He negotiated a production and marketing agreement with M.A. Commerciale of Civitanova Marche, Italy, for the next two seasons, as well as a Japanese distribution deal with Bus Stop, a Japanese retailer that was part of the Japanese apparel giant Onward Kashiyama. This gave McQueen more freedom to create, and it brought in more international sales.

Part of the Onward Kashiyama deal required McQueen to design menswear. He came up with a look that he thought young men like himself would want to wear: well-cut flat-front trousers in leather and men's suiting fabrics; 1950s-style short-sleeved button-front shirts; tailored leather jackets; and of course, his signature Bumsters, all in keeping with *The Hunger* theme.

McQueen provided Ungless and Pons with a beautiful jersey that he sourced in Italy and they did a *dévoré* treatment on it, a "cool effect that McQueen loved, like wallpaper falling apart," Pons recalls. They printed a men's T-shirt with "rude graffiti" about fisting, Pons says, and a dress and a skirt with a gaping slash that resembled female genitalia. And they did a photographic print of a prowling leopard's face, which McQueen turned into a sexy shift.

There was a lot of sharp 1980s-style tailoring, much of it in leather, and fitted long-sleeved jersey dresses in black and in beige, which McQueen slashed this way and that. The slashes were a reference to his practice of self-harm: "Lee was very into cutting himself," Danan says. "Self-destruction," Ungless says now with sadness. "He was used to hurting himself in some way."

For one dress, McQueen wanted to make a clear corset filled with worms. "He was obsessed with death—he found it quite romantic—and was talking about worms and rotting matter all the time," Danan says. He hired a model and made the two-layer-thick transparent Perspex corset to fit her, lopsided breasts and all. He bought worms from a fishmonger and two hours before the show he covered the bottom layer of the corset with the worms, then put the top layer on—"like a sandwich," Danan says. The model wore it with a high-waist red taffeta skirt with a chain through the crotch and a fitted silver gray kimono jacket lined in matching red silk. From afar, the ensemble was chic and sexy. Once you got a closer look, however, and realized what those squiggles were, it made you squirm like the entombed worms. That, in one look, was exactly what McQueen was about: he wanted the viewer to feel uncomfortable, to question conventional beauty, to respect nature, and to be confronted by the eventuality of death.

Pons worked on a dress that was going to be made of metal wire with a matching faceless head mask by Philip Treacy—it was the first time McQueen and Treacy worked together. When Treacy came to the studio to do the fitting, McQueen suddenly realized he didn't have a model for it, and Treacy needed to fit it on the girl who was going to wear it. McQueen turned to Katy England and said, "It will have to be you." She agreed. "No one will know," she said, "because my face will be covered."

For knitwear, he called on Julien Macdonald again.

"Oh, I've got an idea," McQueen told Macdonald. "I want you to knit a sweater with my mother's dog's hair." He pulled a plastic bag out to show Macdonald the fur. "I've got this much now." He said he would keep collecting it—off the furniture, from the vacuum—and once he had enough he'd give it to Macdonald to turn into something wonderful.

Macdonald found the idea rather extreme—"That was pushing it," he says now with a laugh—but he was game.

A few weeks later, as the show approached, Macdonald asked McQueen:

"Where's the bag of dog hair?"

"I can't find it!" McQueen responded.

In truth, McQueen had given the bag of dog hair to textiles consultant Kim Hassler, who turned it into a sweater with a dreadlock-like scarf.

WHEN PR ASSISTANT KAREN MAHER started working on the show's seating plan, McQueen took a keen interest. He remembered the nasty reviews of "The Highland Rape"—the wounds still hurt—and now it was time for retribution: he stripped at least one leading London daily fashion critic of her usual front-row seat and moved her back to the dreaded third row. Some were simply scratched from the list.

The runway, this time, would be stark white—no decoration whatsoever. Eugene Souleiman did hair directly inspired by the 1980s New Romantic style in *The Hunger*: spiky Mohawks and mullets, tinged red or bleach blond. Val Garland did similarly inspired makeup: catlike eyes with sharp brows. Joyce was backstage, "with two pitchers of lemonade and cucumber sandwiches on white bread," Souleiman remembers.

For the show, McQueen decided to mix the menswear in with the women's wear. His models were a hodgepodge of professionals, non-fashion folks, and some British celebrities, such as the drum and bass artist Goldie, who was dating the Icelandic singer Björk; punk rocker Jimmy Pursey of Sham 69; and No Bra singer Susanne Oberbeck. Again McQueen instructed them to be rude to the audience—give the finger, scowl, swear—as they marched to the thumping club music punctuated with monkey howls.

Tailoring in solid black, white, navy, gunmetal gray, and brick red dominated the first half, the women wearing sharply cut jackets without shirts so they could flash their breasts and Bumsters slashed vertically to reveal their buttocks; the men wore more casual variations of the jackets, with flat-front trousers and Bumsters. The second half was more fluid and soft, with the gashed jersey dresses, floral and feather print shifts, and long pencil skirts. Some models wore nude body stockings wrapped strategically with torn lace across a breast and the pelvis and around to the derriere, where it fell to the floor like a tail. The most striking pieces were the woven metal dress and suit, worn with the faceless masks; Stella Tennant in the prowling leopard shift; and the worm-filled plastic corset ensemble. When McQueen—with a bleach blond Mohawk—came out to take his bow, he dropped his trousers and mooned the audience.

"The Hunger" was by far McQueen's most commercial and accomplished collection to date. Retailers placed 400,000 pounds in orders, putting the company in the black for the first time. The press, however, was getting tired of McQueen's bad-boy antics. "Alexander McQueen certainly generates excitement, and is indeed an extremely clever designer, yet his ideas appear too wrapped up in his angry young man pose," wrote Iain R. Webb in *The Times* of London. "In among the scary-Monster models . . . are some genuinely unique cutting skills and fresh perspective. If only it didn't hurt so much to watch."

Despite that, McQueen's design style was starting to reverb across fashion. "[McQueen] offers the kinkiest, most fetishistic clothes on any runway," *The New York Times*'s Amy Spindler noted. "But extremes are powerful, which is why so many ideas that started with Mr. McQueen have been co-opted more commercially elsewhere—from the decaying lace that he worked with again this season to his oh-so-low-riding trousers that, an inch or two less precarious, were seen all over Europe."

A few days after London Fashion Week came to a close, *Sunday Times Magazine* writer Colin McDowell penned a major piece examining the sorry state of British fashion.

"Atavism can never be a basis for creativity," he opined. "That is why, for all the success and creative acclaim they have reaped, I often wish that John Galliano and Vivienne Westwood had not decided to duck the issue of what fashion should be for the 1990s by slipping so wholeheartedly into their hazily romantic fairylands." The BFC had just given Galliano the Designer of the Year award yet again—his third—a situation McDowell felt was embarrassing and laughable.

The only British designer McDowell thought was producing modern design was twenty-six-year-old Alexander McQueen—which was a major validation for him in the British press.

"What McQueen has he shares with Man Ray and Magritte—the wit and awareness to take the present and catapult it into the future before anyone knows what he is up to. That is where his strength lies. . . . [He] understands that the new femininity is more about giving the finger than it is about mincing along in court shoes like a 1950s deb."

SHORTLY AFTER "THE HUNGER," Ungless dropped by the Hoxton Square studio and found McQueen working on a back-to-front, one-arm jacket that was nearly identical to one that another young London designer named Owen Gaster had produced a few weeks earlier. Verkade quickly pulled Ungless aside and whispered in his ear: "Please say something."

Ungless walked up to McQueen and sang: *"Anything you can do, I can do better!"*

McQueen busted out laughing.

Isabella Blow still continued to bring people around the Hoxton Square studio who she felt could give McQueen a publicity boost. One was a skinny twenty-five-year-old brunette named Annabelle Neilson, a London social butterfly who was dating the banking scion Nathaniel "Nat" Rothschild. They quickly became friends and soon she was spending a lot of time hanging out at the studio.

For a Christmas present to himself, McQueen went to the Chelsea dog center and adopted a mutt that he named Minter, after the English middleweight boxing champion Alan Minter. "The puppy would keep Lee company at night, since the studio was freezing cold," Danan says.

COME THE NEW YEAR, McQueen had to get to work on the next collection—London Fashion Week for the fall–winter 1996–97 season was coming up and fast. For it, McQueen wanted to use the photo-print process again somehow. He and Ungless talked about various subjects, when McQueen zeroed in on one that fascinated him: the work of the award-winning British photojournalist Don McCullin. He and Ungless looked through books of McCullin's war photography, and his oeuvre echoed nineteenth-century French artist Gustave Doré's haunting illustrations for Dante Alighieri's *Inferno*.

About the same time, Danan told McQueen about a choreographer friend in Israel who had created a dance based on Dante's *Inferno*. McQueen admitted that he had never read it, so she gave him a copy of the book and showed him pictures from the dance production. He was intrigued and decided to call the next collection "Dante," and use the story as a theme. With all these threads, McQueen wove together an idea "about war and peace of mind in the fourteenth, eighteenth, nineteenth and twentieth centuries," he said.

McQueen contacted McCullin's photo agency for permission and was denied. He told Ungless to use the images anyway, and Ungless printed them on T-shirts, dresses, jackets, skirts, and pants. McQueen also found a picture by the American photographer Joel-Peter Witkin of a crucified girl on a cross that he wanted to incorporate. Simon Costin had participated in a museum exhibit with Witkin in Milan, and gave McQueen the catalogue; Witkin's photos were darker than the darkest of McQueen's creations—truly transgressive. Ungless reached out to Witkin for reproduction rights, and he too refused. McQueen took the image, had a miniature version of the girl made in silver, and placed it on the brow of a black bandit mask.

McQueen's passion for photography and photojournalism was sincere, and he still spoke to Groves about his ambivalence toward fashion. "It was like he realized that he was really, really good at something but it wasn't the thing he wanted to be good at, which must have been frustrating," Groves says. "Like a concert pianist who wants to be able to play tennis. Hating the gift you've been given."

What kept McQueen at it was his desire to succeed. "Lee had the ambition to be the best designer ever," Groves explains. "He wanted to be better than anyone else—better than Galliano, better than Westwood. He was deeply competitive. That's what drove him. And it drove him to a point, I felt, that he was chasing after success for its own sake. For more success."

BOCCI TRIED TO INSTITUTE order in McQueen's business, like introducing the idea of having a show collection that was heavy on artistic one-offs and a showroom collection that was more commercial and appealing to retailers. But McQueen couldn't think that way. "It was madness," Groves says. "There was no planning, like: 'This is for the show collection and this is for the selling collection. And how many dresses do I have?'"

The collection samples would now be made at factories in Italy, and the manufacturers required sketches to make patterns. Before Bocci, "there were never sketches. It was all in Lee's head," Groves says. McQueen cut the patterns for the manufactured clothes himself. Since he couldn't afford proper pattern paper, he used newsprint; his favorite was Page Three of Rupert

Murdoch's tabloid daily *The Sun*, which features a photo of a girl posing topless. Eventually, Bocci set up a system where McQueen would provide drawings and a pattern cutter in Italy would turn them into patterns and produce samples. The problem, says Bocci, was "McQueen was not good at drawing—he would sketch a bit with a Bic on A4 paper, that's it."

To make it work, McQueen and Danan traveled to Italy once a month so McQueen could explain to the cutters what he wanted. Once the garments were made, he would do fittings at the factory. "He'd fix the samples," Danan says. "He'd put them right."

The pair learned much about the fashion industry while on these trips. "You have so many skilled people in small villages and all they do is this one thing—shoes or the bag or knitting," Danan says. "Eo knew McQueen had complicated designs so he had to find all these specialized craftsmen. And when you see what they can do for your collection, you get even more inspired."

At night, McQueen and Danan shared a bed—"He was like my brother," Danan says now. Sometimes, he would wake her in the wee hours. "Let's go walk on the beach. Let's cruise," he'd tell her. "I need to find someone."

The partnership with Bocci started out promisingly, but in short order it began to sour. McQueen couldn't bear the compromises he was forced to make to sell clothes at a retail level. "It was always like: 'This is what I'm doing, I'm an artist, and I don't want to discuss dirty things like business,'" Groves recalls. "'It's about the vision.'"

"He had a difficult time with the Italians," Danan confirms. "It was the first time he got into production and he wasn't very happy with the way they did things because they made his designs look too ordinary. He had this edge in his clothes and it took time to train them to understand his ideas and designs."

For "Dante," Kim Blake managed to land a new, generous, and rather unlikely sponsor for McQueen: American Express. It was a huge cash infusion for McQueen—not far from six figures—which meant he could afford better materials and more help. "For 'The Birds,' we had four thousand pounds and a bucket for me to stand on," Blake recalls. "The American Express deal was a complete turning point."

Joseph Corré, the son of Vivienne Westwood and Malcolm McLaren, who had recently launched a lingerie company called Agent Provocateur, provided McQueen with sparkly spandex bras and panties that shimmered gently under the lace and chiffon. Vicki Sarge of Erickson Beamon jewelry design made a bird claw neckpiece in jet and matching talon earrings. McQueen took a deer antler headdress and draped it with black lace—a look inspired by an old photograph that Danan had of her Jewish mother Soulika in a towering Spanish-like mantilla. While everything about the collection was at a higher, more professional level, Ungless felt the loss of their earlier, freer days in the backyard in Tooting Bec. Now, he says, "there was the manufacturer, and there was a team of people, and there wasn't so much time for us to really experiment like we used to."

One night at the studio when everyone was working on "Dante," Groves says, "Lee broke out some cocaine."

"What's that?" he asked pointedly.

"Oh, it's to help everyone sew," McQueen replied.

Up until then, McQueen had dabbled in social drugs, like poppers and Ecstasy. He didn't drink much—cider, sherry, or a cold beer was his usual choice—and he yelled at Ungless from time to time for overimbibing and smoking too much.

The sudden appearance of cocaine surprised not only Groves, but Ungless too, given the fact that none of them had much money. McQueen seemed to have taken a turn in his social life that no one had seen coming. It hit Ungless when he went to a party at the Battersea Power Station. "I was amazed how many people Lee suddenly knew, like everyone. Hanging out with Goldie and Björk," he says. "I was very much watching a person I did not know."

When Ungless questioned McQueen about his cocaine use, he replied that it provided relief for his recurring back troubles. "Lee had a terrible back. Always in pain," he says. "Not sure what the original injury was but hours bent over an industrial sewing machine and a pattern-cutting table made it worse. When he first started doing a little coke he told me it helped his back and made his spine feel like it was washed clean."

McQueen wanted to find an appropriate place to stage the show, something with character and history. He decided on a church because, he said, "I think religion has caused every war in the world." He zeroed in on Christ Church, Spitalfields, a then-rundown Anglican parish in the East End, which many considered the masterpiece of the eighteenth-century architect Nicholas Hawksmoor. He said his mother had discovered through her genealogy research that Christ Church was "where my ancestors were baptized in 1790 and where a lot of my relatives are buried." It also happened to be down the street from where Jack the Ripper's last known victim, Mary Jane Kelly, lived—which tied the show back to McQueen's degree collection.

For the lighting, McQueen called Simon Chaudoir, a South Londoner and longtime colleague of the show's producer, Sam Gainsbury. McQueen explained that he had been unhappy with the lighting at his previous shows and this time he wanted a soft glow. Chaudoir and his team spent a day and a half constructing a lightweight steel cross, hung seventy light bulbs from it, and suspended it from the church's beams.

The show was scheduled for Friday, March 1, at 7:00 P.M.—again, the closer for London Fashion Week. McQueen chose a Dante image for the invitations and Verkade persuaded the Liberty department store—which carried McQueen's clothes—to pay for the printing and postage. And he asked Costin to get a skeleton. Costin found a plastic one at a medical supplier and spray-painted it gold. McQueen placed it in a front-row chair, next to Britain's most esteemed fashion journalists. "Because, for him," Bocci says, "the English press was dead."

BACKSTAGE WAS A MADHOUSE, as always. One supermodel had a fit because there was no champagne. "I've worked on this six months and you're not going to fuck it up in one night!" he shouted at her. As the two sparred, the McQueen staff scraped together some cash and sent someone out into the rain to a liquor store to get her a bottle. That didn't soothe McQueen's nerves. He had a head full of cocaine, which made him strung out and paranoid.

Shortly before the show started, Isabella Blow dashed in to see McQueen. "I'm going to have a drink," she told him in her chirpy voice, her towering Philip Treacy feather hat bobbing as she spoke. "Bryan Ferry is waiting for me." McQueen wouldn't start the show until she returned, with Ferry in tow.

The makeup team, led by Val Garland, applied Shaun Leane–crafted gold thorns onto the faces of the models with eyelash glue; the effect was as if their faces were randomly pierced. The hairdresser Barnabe turned the models' hair into knotted Mohawks, some with long, twisted, ropelike braids swinging down their backs. Several had villainous silver spikes by Leane sprouting from the Mohawks—the effect was considered so treacherous to the models' well-being that McQueen had to take out special insurance.

The scene outside was, once again, a mob. "There were six hundred people trying to get in," Groves recalls. *Women's Wear Daily* described it as a "life-threatening crush." Inside, on each seat, there was a program with a sweet image of McQueen and Minter on the cover. The church was dark, except for the glow of the candles, and the explosive sound of a jet taking off filled the transept. As the lights came up, a percussive beat thumped, and out walked Honor Fraser in a long black dress cut like a priest's coat with transparent chevrons across the breasts. On her face was the black mask with the tiny silver crucified girl on her nose; on one ear dangled a black bird claw. The audience erupted into cheers.

She was followed by a suite of models wearing tailored cashmere and jersey dresses, sweaters, and pants, in charcoal gray and black, also with transparent slashes across the bodices or sleeves. The music shifted into religious choral works mixed with percussion and the sounds of helicopters and gunfire. There were fur-trimmed trenches, gold velvet tunics, camel cashmere blazers, pinstripe Bumsters, and elegant dove gray shifts and suits, some decorated with Simon Costin's feather and bone neckpieces. The menswear was simple: the models, looking like 1950s Latin gang members from *West Side Story*, came out in denim jackets and jeans splashed with bleach, well-cut black cashmere coats, flat-front trousers and Bumsters. All the models were relatively sedate for a McQueen show: there were no rude hand gestures or swearing or dazed flailing. They were in a church after all.

The strongest section, by far, was the black-and-white Don McCullin prints on fitted jackets, T-shirts, minidresses with torn hems, and a corset dress, which was worn by Annabelle Neilson. But the most beautiful were the mauve silk and lace pieces, topped with military coats with gold rope frogging. The show closed with Honor Fraser in patchwork flared jeans and a lavender and black lace corset, her waist cinched to eighteen inches. She teetered and wobbled as she slowly made her way down the runway. When McQueen came out to take his bow to a standing ovation, he received two large bouquets of flowers, which he in turn gave to his mother and to Isabella Blow.

With "Dante," McQueen seemed to have finally found the perfect balance between commerciality and showmanship—and earned kudos across the board. "Alexander McQueen went to church and became the savior of London fashion week," wrote *Women's Wear Daily*. "[He] produced the city's one true fashion happening . . . [and it] more than lived up to all the hype surrounding him."

Earlier in the week, Philip Treacy also staged a show, styled by Isabella Blow. Treacy's show also earned a standing ovation and wowed critics. But it was Amy Spindler who summed it up best: she deemed McQueen's and Treacy's presentations "the two strongest shows in London this season." Isabella Blow's nurturing of her two charges had paid off. "Our success was her success," Treacy told me.

RETAILERS LOVED "DANTE." Bocci restricted sales so that the choicest pieces were exclusive to certain accounts, including Neiman Marcus in the United States. The remaining two thirds was sold to thirty-one stores worldwide, including Bergdorf Goodman, Charivari, and Linda Dresner in New York, Maxfield in Los Angeles, Alan Bilzerian in Boston, Ultimo in Chicago, and the Isetan group in Japan. The collection reportedly raked in more than one million pounds in orders, half of which came from Japan.

McQueen's influence was evident on the runways in Paris, Milan, and New York: his torn lace dresses from "The Highland Rape" and his sharp tailoring from "The Hunger"—"the pointy lapels, the fitted waists, the long jackets," Maher says—were everywhere. "It was a much more powerful way to dress women," she says. Like Yves Saint Laurent in the 1970s, McQueen wanted to empower women with his clothes. Despite his objections, he was becoming the new Saint Laurent.

Coco Chanel liked to say: "Imitation is the highest form of flattery." McQueen did not agree. Seeing knock-offs and reinterpretations of his work by other designers and mass-market brands drove him around the bend—especially when they claimed that they did it first.

With his increased drug use, his temper was growing shorter and more explosive. A Central Saint Martins student who mocked McQueen behind his back at the Soho gay bars learned this firsthand when he ran into McQueen one night: McQueen clocked him in the face with a glass ashtray. And a few weeks after "Dante," a former assistant came by the studio to give him a birthday card.

"Fuck her," he snarled. "I don't want to see her."

"I thought: 'What's that all about?'" Groves says. "'You can't spend your whole life telling people to fuck off.'" But McQueen increasingly felt that he could.

DEREK ANDERSON DECIDED to bring the "Dante" show to New York, as he had two years earlier with "Banshee," for a reprise for the North American press who didn't cover London. McQueen didn't want to simply re-create the London show, however; he wanted to improve upon it. He asked Philip Treacy to make a hat especially for it. Treacy came up with a figure-eight shape that sat low on the head and was made of black lace. Anderson booked a disused synagogue on Norfolk Street on the Lower East Side that was now serving as the Angel Orensanz Foundation center for the arts. It was simple going: there was no heat or electricity, but it was just as spooky and gothic as Spitalfields.

For the trip, McQueen brought along an entourage: There was Trino Verkade, who had become his overall facilitator; Katy England, who would oversee styling and model casting; and Isabella Blow and Tiina Laakkonen, who were there for moral support. Isabella Blow was a constant source of comedy and consternation for Anderson's team at In The Mix—especially when it came to McQueen's increasingly passive-aggressive relationship with her. "I remember McQueen standing in Derek's office, and saying: 'Just pick up the phone and call Anna Wintour. You used to work for her. Call her!'" a staffer says. "And Isabella was crying and howling back at him: 'You have to understand, she fired me! So Anna doesn't really like me! Let me see if Lucy [Ferry] is in town and she can call.' He kept saying, 'Oh come on! Call her!' He was pacing around and she was crying."

Sometimes Isabella would arrive at the In The Mix office in a complete state. She'd stagger into the West Broadway office, dolled up from hat to heels, fall into the doorjamb, and pant: "I need water! I need water! I've been walking since Twenty-sixth Street!" Her high drama wore out the staff. "She was insufferable," recalls one, "and made you think: 'If she'd just sit still for a minute, it will all be all right.'"

McQueen indulged all his bad habits in Gotham. "He had quite an appetite for sex, and he wanted to know where all the sex clubs were in New York," remembers an In The Mix assistant. "When I told him, he said, 'Should we go tonight? Let's go tonight!'" McQueen spent most nights at leather bars until about 4:00 A.M.—"the most down and dirty places you could imagine," Anderson says—and he found a dealer to deliver cocaine and Ecstasy to him. Surprisingly, Anderson notes, McQueen's sex and drug addiction issues "never got in the way of the work. Nothing got in the way of the work. He was a perfectionist in every way."

Except when he ate. When Anna Wintour took him to lunch at Forty Four—"her de facto lunchroom at the time," Anderson says—he ordered lobster and chowed down on the pricey crustacean with his mouth open, slobbering melted butter down his chin as he told her his ambitions. Wintour was said to be appalled.

THE SHOW WAS SCHEDULED for April 2 in the evening, and McQueen had a list of orders for the In The Mix team to make it work. First, he told them to book supermodels, including Kate Moss, Jodie Kidd, Helena Christensen, and Carla Bruni—preferably for free. In addition, McQueen wanted fifteen Sikh boys in turbans to stand around the runway for "ambiance," and he didn't want to pay them either. Eventually, the In The Mix staff rustled up a half dozen Hispanic boys with tattoos. McQueen approved.

The buzz was so huge that, while New York fashion's top editors and retailers were at the Todd Oldham show in Soho, scores of club kids, students, and groupies turned out en masse without invitations, or with counterfeit ones, and tried to get in. "It was chaos," says longtime McQueen supporter and friend Cecilia Burbridge, who was then living in New York—so much so that fire marshals threatened to shut the event down and send everyone home.

Backstage was just as disorganized. There was no heat and the lighting was hardware store lanterns plugged into generators. The supermodels got dressed in their corners without dressers assisting them and there was nothing to eat—more expected perks gone astray. The press team didn't have headsets, so they were running back and forth between the riot out front and backstage, relaying updates. Someone lost the seating chart, so In The Mix staff had to sit in the front row to save seats for key editors, retailers, and VIPs. The soundtrack tape that McQueen had sent from London didn't work in the sound system. And McQueen walked around backstage, in a pullover and jeans, yelling at everyone.

When editors began to arrive from the Oldham show, the scene turned surrealistic. There was a clublike bouncer out front, with a PR assistant next to him, pointing out who was important enough to be given access. By the time Anna Wintour appeared in the wet, snowy darkness, the mob was so thick and unrelenting that she had to be hoisted over a cab and the ropes. "When Anna walked in, the entire room erupted into applause because they knew the show was going to start," Anderson says. Isabella Blow was seated with Laakkonen and Blow's friend Prince Dimitri of Yugoslavia in a small balcony above the crowd. She was wearing a bright orange plumed hat that Treacy made for her, called "The Pumpkin." From below she looked like a queen in her royal box.

Backstage, McQueen changed into a three-piece suit and put black contact lenses in his eyes. "He looked like a vampire," an assistant remembers. As the soundtrack of organ music riddled by gunfire swelled, the supermodels strutted down the candle-lined runway in the McCullin prints, the torn lace dresses, the slashed dresses, the horn headdress, and Treacy's black hat. Blond bouffant Kate Moss came out in Bumsters; Helena Christensen in a military jacket over black lace and chiffon; Honor Fraser in the lace corset. "There were more ideas on this runway than in a whole season of New York shows," Spindler wrote, "and [McQueen] brought the level of work here up a full notch. At the age of only twenty-seven, he may be the reason that the post-McQueen generation will shine a little brighter."

IN MAY, McQueen signed a much bigger production and distribution deal with Gibo, the Italian subsidiary of Onward Kashiyama. He went to Japan by himself to sign the deal: he flew economy class and stayed in an average hotel. Gibo would produce and distribute McQueen's men's and women's wear collections worldwide. The agreement was initially for two years, with an option to renew for another three years. "This is a big step for me," he said, adding, "The Japanese want me to stay in London because they recognize I'm the largest thing here. There's no use going to Paris or Milan and just being a small fish."

While all was going well with McQueen's business, his personal life was in upheaval: the relationship with Groves was unraveling. McQueen's inner circle was quietly relieved. No one liked Andrew Groves. Friends had all witnessed heated arguments and crying. "We went to see a counselor at Lee's insistence," Groves says. "And that was useless, because we were always arguing. The relationship was dysfunctional, and I think it was he who needed the help because he was bringing all that baggage from his childhood to the relationship, half of it I didn't even know." It became apparent the relationship was beyond repair.

Publically, McQueen put on a stoic face. "There's someone in the world for everyone," he told the *Guardian* newspaper. "I've just got to be a bit more patient, wait till he comes along. I don't usually go for looks that much. I have to connect mentally. Physical attraction only lasts as long as the first screw. After that you want to be able to talk."

But privately, he was devastated by the breakup. Not long after, McQueen went to Italy with Danan on a production trip. He was so depressed that he confessed to her that he was feeling suicidal.

IX

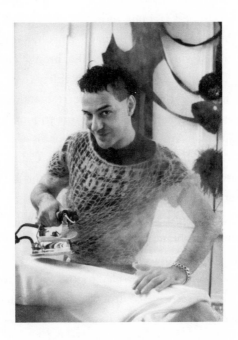

On June 21, 1994, to celebrate the first day of summer as well as the launch of his new perfume, Flower, the Paris-based Japanese fashion designer Kenzo staged a magnificent event in the heart of the city: He decorated the entire Pont Neuf, Paris's oldest bridge, with thirty-two thousand pots of colorful begonias, forty thousand ferns, and two thousand ivies. Several hundred of *le tout Paris* attended an inaugural champagne reception on the bridge at dusk, and in the middle of it, ever-jovial Richard Simonin, the French-born CEO of both Kenzo and Givenchy—two major brands in the LVMH luxury group—was beaming.

Not only was Simonin pleased with the event, which was perhaps the splashiest perfume launch Paris had ever seen. He had finally figured out how to solve a nagging issue: who to replace revered French couturier Hubert de Givenchy, who was soon retiring from the couture house he founded in 1952.

Luxury fashion was in the throes of a transformation from small, founder-run companies that catered to a niche clientele to global, publicly traded corporations headed by business tycoons with no previous link to the industry. The trailblazer of this movement was Bernard Arnault, a real estate developer from the north of France who, in the late 1980s, through clever maneuvering acquired Christian Dior, then at the nadir of its thirty-five-year existence.

From there, Arnault began to build his luxury brand group. He first secretly persuaded Patou designer Christian Lacroix to jump ship with no advance notice and launch an Arnault-backed brand of his own, leaving Patou in shambles. Arnault then acquired a majority stake in Céline, a forty-year-old conservative French women's wear brand, promising the founders they could remain. Within months they were ousted.

In 1988, he launched a hostile take-over of LVMH Moët Hennessy–Louis Vuitton, the French luxury brand group that included Louis Vuitton, Kenzo, and Givenchy. The fifteen-month-long boardroom battle—known as "The LVMH Affair"—was covered play-by-play by the French media. When Arnault finally succeeded in securing control of the group, some Vuitton family members left the company headquarters in tears.

Once Arnault had formed his group, he decided to renovate the sagging brands with younger designers, take them global and make them more "democratic" to cater to the ever-growing middle market of aspirational shoppers. It was a radical idea: until then, luxury fashion had been a gentleman's business, and even the most best-known brands such as Chanel and Yves Saint Laurent were still small and founder- or family-run. Arnault shook that all up with his far more capitalist approach to business, which he honed during a three-year stint in New York in the early 1980s. So shocked was the French establishment by his forthright manner and unwavering focus on profits that he became known in the French media as "the Wolf in cashmere."

Arnault's first major creative move came in May 1989 when he unceremoniously sacked longtime Dior couturier Marc Bohan and replaced him with Italian ready-to-wear designer Gianfranco Ferré, known as "the architect of fashion" due to his architecture degree and his strict, spare line. Ferré's mandate was to bring Dior back to its 1950s levels of success, when it was run by its namesake founder and was known as "the General Motors of Fashion." Ferré's appointment scandalized the French fashion establishment. "I am very shocked that they weren't able to find a French person for the position," said Yves Saint Laurent chairman Pierre Bergé, who was also the head of the Chambre Syndicale de la Couture Parisienne. "I don't think that opening the doors to a foreigner and an Italian is respecting the spirit of creativity in France. This makes me worry about Mr. Arnault and LVMH."

But as he had proved with his hostile takeover of LVMH, Arnault didn't care what the old French business establishment thought of his bold American-style tactics. The forty-four-year-old Ferré would push Dior directly toward a younger, more cosmopolitan demographic, which in turn would equal greater sales.

Next on Arnault's renovation hit list was Givenchy. The house had a storied past: it was founded by Count Hubert Taffin de Givenchy, the son of an old French aristocratic family who had apprenticed with Jacques Fath, Lucien Lelong, and Elsa Schiaparelli, and been mentored by Cristóbal Balenciaga, considered by many in fashion to be the greatest couturier of all time. Of Givenchy's debut, one journalist said, "These dresses remind you of that first glass of champagne," and *Harper's Bazaar* Paris correspondent Marie-Louise Bousquet declared him "the future of French Couture." Givenchy became best known for dressing Hollywood darling Audrey Hepburn for many of her roles, including for *Sabrina*, *Love in the Afternoon*, *Funny Face*, *Breakfast at Tiffany's*, *Charade*, and *Paris When It Sizzles*. Arnault wanted to get some of that sizzle back in the house, and he tasked Simonin with the assignment.

Simonin came up with a radical plan: close the couture division, which lost about twenty million euros a year, and turn the company into a French lifestyle brand that centered around ready-to-wear with a couture flair. His criteria for a designer, he said, was simple: someone who was young and relatively well known and could target the new generation of aspirational customers with excellent ready-to-wear.

Simonin went to Arnault with his new strategy, and Arnault shot it down. "And here's why," he explained. "If I say I am stopping haute couture *chez* Givenchy, I am going to have ministers and the president of the Republic calling me saying I am sacrificing the tabernacle of French luxury, the history of savoir faire. For twenty million euros a year, I can avoid their wrath. So I will avoid it."

Simonin asked French *Vogue* fashion director Jenny Capitain who she thought should take over Givenchy.

"John Galliano," she declared. "You should take a risk, and John is the one who is going to launch the revolution."

Ever since the São Schlumberger show, Galliano had dominated the fashion trades and press. New York designer Diane von Furstenberg made news by wearing a Schlumberger show gown with an obi sash to the Clintons' white tie state dinner at the White House for the emperor and empress of Japan. And Galliano received a barrage of coverage in May when he restaged the Schlumberger show in the Goodman family's long-abandoned apartment on the top floor at Bergdorf's, with diamonds provided by Van Cleef & Arpels. About 120 guests, including Bult and Rice, attended the show, followed by a champagne brunch to celebrate Galliano's opening of his in-store boutique. "John understood women and what women wanted to wear," says Dawn Mello, who was president of Bergdorf Goodman at the time. "No one else was doing what he did. It was advanced and stood out, as he did."

While in New York, Galliano sat for several interviews, including with Hal Rubenstein of *Interview* magazine. Their meet-up started out inauspiciously—he slept right through their appointed rendezvous. "John was locked up in his room for three days. He wouldn't answer his phone," Jacqui Duclos recalls. "John Bult was flipping out. I kept saying to Steven, 'This is not normal, this is not normal.' And Steven said, 'He's a genius, and geniuses are like that.'"

The next day Rubenstein rang up from the lobby of the Royalton for the rescheduled interview and Galliano was in bed again. "I've got an idea," sleepy-voiced Galliano told Rubenstein. "Why don't we do this like this, on the phone?" When Rubenstein balked, pointing out that he was already downstairs, Galliano responded, "Then come up here. We'll listen to records." Rubenstein said no, and insisted that Galliano come down to meet him as planned. "Ten minutes later," Rubenstein wrote, "across the Royalton's runway lobby, strides this elfin devil with a grin so disarming he could sell Versace used Medusas. And he knows it."

They talked about his last visit to New York, when, Rubenstein said, "you and André Leon Talley closed down Sally's II"—a major midtown drag club. Rubenstein asked if Galliano had been out the night before, figuring that it would explain his narcolepsy. "We went with Naomi and Kate [Moss]. . . . It was . . . oh, I can't tell you. You'll print it and get me in trouble." Galliano then took off his shoes and socks to show off his Jungle Red toenails. Rubenstein asked about the clash between big business and art in fashion. "But I'm not an artist," Galliano insisted. "Maybe an artist with a small *a*."

Simonin had followed the coverage and he liked Capitain's forthright suggestion. "John has the spirit of a couturier, is relatively young, is already pretty well known, and has an affirmed talent," Simonin told me back then. Most important, "he has a very modern vision, not at all archetypical haute couture." Simonin set up a series of meetings with Galliano, Robinson, and Harlech, and decided to use the upcoming show in October as a tryout for the job.

AS THE AUTUMN FASHION SHOW SEASON approached, Galliano and his team began to create the new collection. To top the Schlumberger show would not be easy. But this time he had a $200,000 budget, so he had the means to do better. Galliano planned on showing only twenty-eight outfits. "What I want is to keep it tight and focused," he explained. "All that matters to me now is my fashion. I'll work to midnight every day until everything is perfect."

His most successful collections in the past referenced the high glamour of the mid-twentieth century—and those romantic tailored looks had now become his signature. As with "Blanche DuBois," he wanted the new collection to capture "the grit and grim of a Brando movie to make the divas stronger and more feminine." He decided to use Elia Kazan's 1954 drama *On the Waterfront*, with Brando starring as a washed-up boxer turned New York longshoreman, as his inspiration. It fit in well with his penchant for using his shows as an allegory for how he perceived himself and his life. In the film, Brando's character, Terry, takes on the waterfront's corrupt bosses, and struggles between self-interest and integrity, questioning where his own as well as others' loyalties lie. By the end, Terry is the lone hero.

A bigger show required more hands, and now that Galliano had some funding, he could afford to employ a few more people. But much of the support staff was brought on simply because they were beautiful and well connected, like Harumi Klossowska de Rola, the ravishing young daughter of the artist Balthus, who was an intern, and Vanessa Bellanger, the willowy, blond Franco-American daughter of French *Vogue* publisher Gardner Bellanger, who became Robinson's assistant.

Galliano was regularly in touch with Harlech, who was in Shropshire with her family. They'd discuss ideas over the phone and from there she would develop themes and color palettes. A few weeks before the show, she'd arrive in Paris to "put it all together," Duclos recalls. "Especially decor. She had a good eye, a lot of taste, a great sense of style." Usually she stayed in what Talley described as a "dingy hotel" near the studio and during one visit she was mugged and had all her money stolen.

When in Paris, Bult and Rice met with Harlech for lunch or dinner and began to understand and appreciate her contributions and respect her talent. They were surprised when Galliano and Robinson drew up a list of who should go on the payroll and Harlech was not on it. They disagreed and offered to cover her expenses when she came to Paris. They knew that losing her would be a huge blow to the company.

Some at the studio had an inkling why Harlech was still kept at a distance: Steven Robinson. His obsession with Galliano was becoming pathological. They worked side by side during the day, and some nights he slept on Galliano's bedroom floor. "Steven was the gatekeeper—literally," says one of the team members at the time. "He was Machiavellian—a total strategist, tactician, at making things happen, getting from point A to B." Rarely did Galliano actually work directly on clothes anymore: "He would say: 'I want this, this, this,' and that was it," says a former intern. "I never saw him do any draping. . . . Steven was the one who ran everything, who was there at ten in the morning and opened the door for us."

Galliano was clueless to the hold that Robinson had on him. "John's impression was, 'I have trained Steven very well, this is what I've created,' and not the other way around," says another source. "But I think it is strange to be cut off from every other person and think you are controlling it all. It's all about access: who has access. Since Steven had access, he was controlling everything."

On October 6, 1994, Galliano dashed off to London to receive the Designer of the Year Award from the British Fashion Council at the Natural History Museum. Then he hustled back to Paris to oversee the staging of his show a week later. It was scheduled for Wednesday, October 12, in the evening, as the climax of the day's shows. Originally, Galliano had booked a garage on the rue du Faubourg Saint-Antoine near the Bastille as the venue, but due to security issues, Harlech says, "at the last moment, we had to find a new place." They went to see Studio Pin-Up, a photography complex in the fourteenth arrondissement favored by fashion photographers. Galliano loved it. "John looked at me and said, 'Transform it,'" Harlech says. "It was probably one of the most exciting but most terrifying things I've ever done."

Harlech thought about the *On the Waterfront* theme of the collection, with its working-class roots, and the downtrodden Parisian neighborhood where Pin-Up was located, and went from there. "I wanted to feel the sweat, the ethereal passion, the beauty and grandeur and nobility in the impoverished surrounds," she says. "I wanted to find ingenuity in corrugated metal walls, and we did it and it was a team effort, and John was involved at every level. It wasn't a question of him saying, 'Amanda, go and do the set.' . . . There would be points where he would come along and I would be in my T-shirt, taping things on the wall or peeling off wallpaper to make it look like I wanted and he said, 'Let's put rose petals in the bath.' That was John. It's a great gift to be able to work with somebody who can give out positive criticism without flattering you and that drives you forward. . . . He wanted more. He required a certain honesty." As a final touch, Harlech hung her lingerie on a laundry line draped across the room. "To create a mood," she said.

For the invitations, Galliano and his underlings bought eight hundred old leather-bound books at the flea market and one thousand roses at the Paris wholesalers. They pressed a rose in each book, stuck the invitation in the pages, tied each up with twine, and sent them off to their recipients.

Who would receive them, however, was a sore point at the studio. Galliano refused to invite all the staff and atelier hands who had made the clothes and realized his creative dreams. "These people worked so hard," Duclos said. "We would be working twenty-four hours a day for weeks. I had to fight with John for them to see the show."

Most hurtful, however, was Galliano's sharp tongue. He mocked Bellanger behind her back, likening her to a doting old aunt. When he was told that ever-supportive Suzy Menkes of the *International Herald Tribune* was on her way in to see him, he turned to Duclos and snipped, "Old pillow head's here," referring to Menkes' signature pompadour hairstyle. Then he walked out and embraced her like a long-lost friend. He "talked trash" about deeply supportive and powerful glossy editors too. "No one escaped him," Duclos says. "It didn't matter what level of closeness, he was always negative. As far as he was concerned he was already the best. Everybody else was a piece of shit."

THE NIGHT AIR was surprisingly warm for October. The crowd began to filter into the space and they discovered a setup like nothing fashion had ever seen before. There were deco chairs and old velvet-covered love seats curving around several tableaux: a wrought iron bed with a beefy, tattooed male model dressed only in Calvin Klein briefs spread across the sheets; an old claw-foot bathtub with a lace curtain and rose petals floating on the milky surface; antique birdcages; torn book pages lacquered onto corrugated metal siding; a dressing table with perfume bottles, brushes, and dried flowers; a buffed 1950s Oldsmobile rented from a local car museum; the clothesline with Harlech's silk lingerie pinned up.

On each seat was a small program that appeared to be penned by Harlech. Officially, the collection's tale was about a woman named Misia Diva, "an Oriental alouette, fêted by the intricacies of friendship, courtship, in the salons of oil paint, Chinese white marble dust and granite, virtuoso song and grease paint. Mandarin in Edwardian hose." In part inspired by Coco Chanel's great friend Misia Sert, the notes recounted their fictional heroine's influence on artists such as Proust, Diaghilev, Debussy, Cocteau, and Picasso and her many marriages, including to "the brooding beauty of the young boxer—the torso of Brando, the disbelief and desperation of James Dean. . . . She shattered our way of seeing. . . . She was avaricious, splendid, spendthrift but generous, a crafty brigand, a seductive cajoler, a diva who suffered every word, every stroke of the brush, every prophetic flash of the camera."

Among the audience members were Simonin, his wife, who was the fashion director of Spanish *Vogue*, and Elizabeth Kan, a young, American-born, Harvard-educated LVMH executive who was assisting Simonin with the

Givenchy recruitment. But no one noticed them. All eyes were on the celebrities and socialites, like French actress Arielle Dombasle, who lounged on the bed with the nearly naked male model. I spotted Madonna sitting on a love seat next to the photographer Steven Meisel. Waiters passed trays of champagne, which helped ease the wait, but only so long. Eventually Madonna gave up and left.

Finally, at 9:45 P.M.—a good hour and a half after the appointed time—the show began with Healy's club beat mix punctuated with lines from Brando's famous "Contender" speech from *On the Waterfront*:

"I coulda had class. I coulda been a contender. I coulda been somebody, instead of a bum, which is what I am."

The models sashayed about in full 1950s glamour, their hair in slick updos by Julien d'Ys, their makeup—all arched brows, thick eyeliner, cherry red lips—by Stéphane Marais. They flopped on the bed with the boy toy, caressed the boxer next to the bathtub, perched on the hood of the Oldsmobile, and careened and vamped in pointy-toed Manolo Blahnik stilettos like woozy girls after a long night at El Morocco.

The clothes referenced 1950s couturiers Jacques Fath and Christian Dior. The silhouette was hourglass, with tailored jackets paired with pencil skirts or long satin skirts. The fabrics were black-and-white houndstooth, silver moiré, and silky satins in black, white, and beige. There were interesting tailoring details like lapels that melted into the jackets and cascading flamenco ruffles, swaths of fabric pulled across the torso and pinned at the hip, and white leather perforated with kaleidoscope-like swirls.

Kate Moss came out in a short-sleeved white skirt suit, with a wasp waist defined with a skinny black belt; Kristen McMenamy in a long black bias slip dress flecked with sequins; Naomi Campbell in a corset top with white frill trim and a long, lean black satin skirt. The big finale look was a platinum blond Linda Evangelista in a strapless canary yellow feather-covered corset and an immense daffodil yellow tulle skirt. In twenty short minutes, the show was over. Galliano took his bow dressed in a black T-shirt with cut-off sleeves and blue leather pants. McMenamy pulled him down on the bed with the other models and they all laughed wildly.

The crowd erupted with a standing ovation and cheers. When the roar finally cooled down, guests filed out all aflutter, gasping and cooing about how beautiful it all was.

The next morning, Simonin had made up his mind:
"I'm going to do it," he told his wife.

THE NEXT FORTY-EIGHT HOURS were a whirlwind for Galliano and his team. The reviews were remarkable: Marion Hume of the *Independent* loved the "sleekly fitted pencil skirts of the kind Claudette Colbert would have worn to lunch with Clark Gable, and orientalist kimonos a latter day Gloria Swanson would wear for reclining on a chaise-longue. . . . [Those clothes] make you want to believe in romance."

Menkes called it "brilliantly crafted high-camp couture." The only problem, she noted was, "He was supposed to be showing ready-to-wear."

Retailers descended like locusts on the Passage du Cheval Blanc studio and ordered up a storm. Galliano's only serious problem was the same issue he had during the Johann Brun years: "The clothes did not fit," Bergdorf's Dawn Mello told me. As in London in the 1980s, French manufacturers could not mass-produce Galliano's intricate or bias-cut designs to spec, and everything turned out cockeyed. Customers didn't seem to mind. "The clothes were always beautifully designed and everyone loved them," Mello says. "Even though they didn't fit we would sell them because customers would have them altered."

TWO DAYS LATER, I went to see Galliano at the Passage du Cheval Blanc for a story I was writing about him for *The Washington Post*. When he finally showed up, about a half an hour after our appointed time, he seemed like he was on a different plane—though I don't know whether it was due to drugs, drink, or exhaustion mixed with euphoria.

I started by asking him if there was room in modern society for such retro glamour.

"Yeah," he responded, taking a drag from his cigarette. "There is as much room as there is for sportswear. . . . I thought there was a need to return to glamour. After deconstruction, the only way to move forward and be modern was with construction, [but] with a lightness of touch. Not heavy or constipated. By using modern fabric techniques, so you don't have to wear girdles.

"I think women, as well as men, are tired of hiding under all these shape-less clothes, and want a return to structure. The waist, the hips, the bosom," he continued. "I like to think of my clothes as sensual, rather than overt. Sensual in the way they are cut, the choice of fabrics, and the way they are molded or draped. [Sensuality] is as important as eating good food, or drink-ing a good wine, something that perhaps we are taking for granted and we aren't enjoying as much as we should."

After a bit more talk about his salon-like shows, and his new backers—"It's good to be taken seriously after so many years," he confessed—I asked if he ever feared running out of ideas.

"Uh, the end of one collection is the beginning of another," he stammered. "It's like an evolution. Just one thing leads to another. You come up with something, and that in turn becomes something else, and that's the way"—he paused for a moment—"we are."

DURING THEIR PARIS TRIPS, Bult and Rice—like Johann Brun and Peder Bertelsen before them—didn't notice Galliano's excessive partying ways. What they saw was a hardworking young professional, staying late, making sure everything got done. He might have been sweaty and shaky, but they just wrote that off as exhaustion from overwork. He was so focused and on top of everything, they thought he was simply obsessive.

Then during one visit, they were told by staff that Galliano was suffering from "exhaustion," that he was "very nervous." But, they were assured, he would be fine—he had a good doctor who looked after him and wrote pre-scriptions when needed. In fact, Galliano's partying had, in the view of his colleagues, grown into addictions, and it was starting to affect his work. He would go on benders and not show up for work or appointments. Following Pin-Up, Madonna asked to come by the Passage du Cheval Blanc to see the collection (since she hadn't stayed for the show). When she arrived, Galliano was nowhere to be found; Talley, who was there, showed her the clothes in-stead.

No one said anything. It wasn't their place. It was Robinson's job, but he didn't say anything either. It became obvious to Galliano's team that this was yet another way for Robinson to exert control over Galliano.

SIMONIN PROCEEDED WITH the negotiations to hire Galliano for Givenchy. Rice and Bult invited Simonin to meet with Galliano at the Passage du Cheval Blanc after work hours, to not attract attention.

All seemed to be going forward nicely when a major PR bomb dropped—in the literary weekly magazine *The New Yorker* of all places. For a profile on Talley, who was then *Vogue*'s creative director, the writer Hilton Als accompanied him and Galliano to the Gaiety Theatre, an all-male nude revue on West Forty-sixth Street in Manhattan. When one dancer came out in nothing but cowboy boots, Talley could hardly contain himself. "'What can one do?' he moaned. 'What can one do with such piquant insouciance?'"

"Before the end of the performance, Talley led Galliano into a room on one side of the theater, where several other men were waiting for the dancers," Als wrote. "Upon identifying André Leon Talley as 'that fashion man off the TV,' a black drag queen, who wore jeans, a cream-colored halter top, and an upswept hairdo, and sat on the lap of a bespectacled older white man, said, 'That's what I want you to make me feel like, baby, a white woman. A white woman who's getting out of your Mercedes-Benz and going into Gucci to buy me some new drawers because you wrecked them. Just fabulous.'"

LVMH executives knew that Galliano liked clubbing and partying, and who could object if he was discreet; in French culture, there is a specific delineation between private life and professional life, and privacy is seriously respected as well as protected by strict laws. But Galliano was being more than indiscreet, and some straitlaced LVMH executives felt that Simonin was out of his mind to bring such a wild and debauched deviant in to run an esteemed and elegant couture house.

Galliano's salvation? The wave of fawning stories on the Pin-Up collection that flooded the fashion press, all of which echoed what Sarah Mower—the writer who had so savaged him in 1986—wrote in *Harper's Bazaar*: "You had to be a witness. To understand what had taken place . . . to grasp the magic of the clothes, you had to be there. . . . Anyone who saw the crowd spilling out into the street or overheard the conversations in the restaurant and hotel bars after John Galliano's spring '95 show had a right to think the audience must have been drugged or intoxicated. In a way, we were."

SIMONIN WAS GETTING PRESSURE from LVMH executives not to hire Galliano. Particularly against the move was Concetta Lanciaux, the personnel chief for the group and longtime trusted Arnault lieutenant. Lanciaux prided herself on recruiting just the right candidates for jobs, and Arnault was usually happy about her suggestions. Lanciaux did her due diligence on Galliano and she did not like what she discovered. She penned a memo to Arnault and other LVMH executives formally advising them not to hire Galliano for known reasons, such as alcohol abuse and salacious public behavior. Simonin was furious. But Arnault dismissed her counsel, declaring that it was none of her business—this was Simonin's assignment.

Galliano knew that if he was to lock in the job, he had to do something particularly special for his next show. He asked his set designer Jean-Luc Ardouin to recreate an urban *La Bohème*–like winter wonderland in an old factory, replete with chimneys, skylights, weathervanes, and twenty-nine tons of fake snow. "We spent 100,000 francs to rent the snow machines," Duclos remembers with a sigh. "And it cost a *fortune* to clean up afterward."

The fictional muse was a Spanish woman named Dolores who was in love with the dashing Jaime; the invitations were her billets-doux to him on Rose of Alhambra hotel stationery, with a lock of her hair and a locket enclosed.

The clothes were supposedly from Dolores's steamer trunks: slip dresses, tailored jackets, long black frock coats, and transparent chiffon gowns dotted with flower petals, and, as the show piece, an ivory satin-backed crepe bias-cut gown inset with black georgette carnations and no visible seams or darts.

Unfortunately, after Schlumberger and Pin-Up, the show felt flat—looking back now, it is obvious that, unbeknownst to Galliano and his team, he had peaked creatively. Even then, the press and the audience sensed a dip. "If last season's show by Mr. Galliano evoked a never-ending party, this show felt as though an all-night revel had rudely met the dawn, with dead Champagne, smudged makeup and the models longing to be safely home," Amy Spindler wrote in *The New York Times*. "Somehow, the beautiful, jaded aristocrat's clothes, so triumphantly fresh last season, made the audience feel a bit jaded, too, this time."

The collection sold well, but not well enough for Bult and Rice to recoup their investment. "John Bult was not making money," Duclos says. "He was on the edge. John was spending over a million francs ($200,000) at each show. Now that's nothing. But at the time, it was a lot and I was doing what I could to control spending, but he didn't give a shit about Bult's money. Basically, he was going to do his thing. He was just like a spoiled brat."

EVENTUALLY, Arnault told Simonin: "Okay, I would like to meet John."

Simonin set up the meeting at LVMH headquarters on the Avenue Hoche.

When Galliano heard, he was "in such a state," Duclos remembers. "Robert Ferrell had to lend him a suit, because he did not have a suit. He got all spiffed up and was very anxious." Since the negotiations were still under the radar, Galliano had to be sneaked in, unseen. Simonin sent his LVMH-issued, chauffeur-driven sedan to pick up Galliano, then escorted him from the underground parking lot into an elevator directly up to Arnault's conference room. Galliano later described the arrival as "very James Bond."

Simonin quietly watched as Galliano pulled out his scrapbooks of sketches, fabric swatches, photos, and other inspirations, and made his pitch to Arnault. Galliano found Arnault to be "elegant. Restrained. Still. Very in control." Galliano, however, was so nervous he began to sweat.

The two men spoke for an hour and a half—a break of protocol for Arnault, who was known throughout LVMH for his efficient thirty-minute meetings. "[Arnault's] main concern was how would I sustain the interest," Galliano later told me. Arnault also asked Galliano if he felt that he could suppress his own distinct design voice while working on Givenchy collections—"that it would be like asking Beethoven to play Mozart," Galliano said. "Could I do it?" Galliano believed he could.

Days went by, and Simonin had no word from Arnault. Simonin kept on with his negotiations with Galliano, readying contracts. He orchestrated all sorts of benefits for LVMH: having the right of first refusal if Galliano decided to sell his company; first refusal if there were ever Galliano brand perfume or accessories licenses.

Finally, Simonin asked Arnault: "So, what do you think? The contract is ready. Do you want me to sign him?"

"Okay, fine," Arnault said. "I authorize you to sign him.

"But if there is one leak of the news before Hubert de Givenchy's last show, I will fire you."

To keep the negotiations on the down low, Simonin had only one copy of the contract, which Galliano signed two weeks before Givenchy's last show. According to LVMH sources, Galliano's annual salary was roughly 2.5 million French francs, ($500,000) and he would receive a bonus if sales of ready-to-wear excelled. He would be allowed to do haute couture as he pleased; management would set a budget and as long as he stayed within it—or didn't bypass it by very much—they would leave him alone. For ready-to-wear, however, Galliano would have to submit a creative proposal to his bosses for approval. Management would have the final say.

There was also a provision for Harlech. "We spoke about it," Simonin told me back then. "They have worked together for a long time, so we organized for her to collaborate with him at Givenchy on the general inspiration and the conception of his setting for his shows."

Once the contracts were signed, Galliano, Robinson, and Harlech set to work on the first collection, and they remained extremely discreet; no news leaked whatsoever. Or so Simonin thought. One morning, Hubert de Givenchy called, furious. John Fairchild, the publisher of *Women's Wear Daily*, had heard about the Galliano contract signing and told Givenchy.

"So, you have already decided who will replace me?" Givenchy said sharply.

"You said you wanted no word on the subject," Simonin responded. "That was the deal."

Thankfully, Arnault did not follow through with his threat—Simonin was not fired.

On the morning of Tuesday, July 11, Hubert de Givenchy presented his last couture show, in the rococo ballroom of the Grand Hôtel. The front row was a veritable who's who of fashion: Christian Lacroix, Philippe Venet, Hanae Mori, Kenzo, Jean-Louis Scherrer, Paco Rabanne, Valentino, Oscar de la Renta, Yves Saint Laurent, and Pierre Bergé. The collection was classic

Givenchy: the silhouette pure and clean, the shoulders wide—but not too—the waists pulled in gently, often with a belt or sash, the hemlines grazing just above the knee.

At the end, Givenchy walked down the runway with a bride in a bubble-gum pink ball gown, to a standing ovation. Behind him stood his sewers, fitters, and tailors in their traditional white work coats. All took a bow. "That was so touching," Pamela Harriman, then the U.S. ambassador to France and longtime Givenchy client, told me. "They all loved him so much."

Backstage, Givenchy received his friends and colleagues and all their good wishes. He was touched that so many of his peers came to bid him adieu—"Especially Saint Laurent, who has not finished his collection," Givenchy said. "To take the time to give me that salute, this is wonderful."

AN HOUR AFTER GIVENCHY took his curtain call, the Givenchy press office announced that Galliano would be taking over the creative helm of the house. Reporters and critics for the most part lauded the appointment. Talley was over the moon: "It's the biggest thing in his career so of course he's going to live up to it and make it work. He's totally able to do that job and he will do a magnificent job. I know he will," he told me. "Ten years ago, a person who looked and dressed like John Galliano could not have gotten this job. But the world has moved and moved fast, and the global marketplace is geared toward young people. It's totally right."

Not everyone in fashion was convinced that it was a judicious appointment. "He has a wonderful imagination, but I am not sure that technically he knows everything about how to make a dress," Valentino said.

"John is a genius," said Gianni Versace. "But he needs some control."

"He's a fuck really," said someone who had known Galliano well since the 1980s. "His sense of balance just goes. He loses it so totally and so publicly. I can't imagine Bernard Arnault wouldn't have some sort of intelligence to clue him in on stuff like that. John's going to require a lot of spin control."

Least impressed with the appointment was Alexander McQueen.

"Have you heard that John Galliano is going to Givenchy?" John McKitterick asked McQueen.

"It's so boring," McQueen responded. "Why does he want to go with this boring fashion house?"

A FEW DAYS LATER, I went to see Galliano at his studio in the Passage du Cheval Blanc to interview him for a *Washington Post* story I was writing about his new job.

Galliano chain-smoked Marlboros and exuded an extreme arrogance as he spoke—far more than I had ever noticed before. He told me that the official credit for anything he designed for the house would read "John Galliano for Givenchy" and that he wasn't worried one bit about the added pressure of designing six more collections a year—two couture; two pre-collection (resort and holiday); and two runway—making a total of eight. "When there's that kind of pressure on me it releases a certain energy," he said, puffing on his cigarette. "As long as we can manage it well and keep the identities of Galliano and Givenchy separate"—to have a separate image for each—"we'll be fine. It's a big house. Here [at the Galliano studio] we have six machines. There [at Givenchy] they have sixty. It's a completely different world.

"I'm going over with my creative director Amanda Harlech and my assistant Steven Robinson, [who] oversees pretty much every department," Galliano continued. "[Steven] knows how I like things run and is able to make decisions and when I walk into the showroom, there isn't an ashtray overflowing or there are certain flowers the way I like them arranged. He's really on the case and understands me."

When I told Galliano that I had just interviewed Givenchy while he was correcting a dress he had showed the day before, Galliano sniffed: "He shouldn't have sent it down" the runway.

"What is Givenchy to you?" I asked.

"A spirit and vehicle for couture," Galliano responded. "It's the true meaning of elegance and chic."

"Do you think you'll be able to please the longtime Givenchy clients?"

"I don't *intend* to please them," he said, blowing smoke into the air. "I'm not going there to please them. And probably a lot of them will move away. But I am going to bring a larger, younger clientele."

And what about the legacy and archives of the house, I wondered—did he plan to respect that?

"The period of his work which really electrifies me is the Audrey Hepburn period," he said. "Every woman I talk to wants to look like Audrey Hepburn.

That was a magical moment. And the influence from Balenciaga—the early, early things where he was trying to find that majestic line, that purity of line—there were moments where it actually worked, I thought. Take away all the big shoes and the silly hats, which were all too heavy, there was a very strong pure line there. So yeah, those are the two periods I'm really electrified by. The rest I can leave."

I asked him about his dreams:

"Now I definitely want to have John Galliano couture," he said. "I'm insatiable. How long will I stay [at Givenchy]? Who knows? Who knows what's going to happen tomorrow?"

I asked him about his partying and hedonistic reputation:

"Well, yeah, I'm young and it's all a part of where my inspiration comes from: being *alive*," he said. "Sometimes I'm sketching until five o'clock in the morning. Sometimes I'm dancing until five o'clock in the morning. It's all inspiration. It's all a part of what I do."

Last, I told him that not everyone had had the nicest things to say about him.

"I wasn't born to be loved," he replied.

X

For more than forty years, Hubert de Givenchy had run his company like a stately aristocratic home. There was a strict division between the studio—meaning Monsieur de Givenchy and his studio assistants—and the atelier, where sixty workers did the pinning, cutting, and sewing. As at all old couture houses, tradition, protocol, and respect for hierarchy reigned.

The plumber's son blew all that up. He told everyone, atelier hands included, to call him "John"—something unthinkable during Monsieur de Givenchy's era. His first day on the job, he strolled into the company canteen for lunch, which made staff mouths drop; Monsieur de Givenchy would never have considered dining with the help. "Lentils and fish and sixty people, staring at me," Galliano recalled.

Givenchy was always impeccably dressed in a suit and tie topped off by a white couture smock, his straight hair perfectly combed back. Galliano would roll into work wearing tank tops, pajama pants, and flea market finds, his hair in dreadlocks; old-time staff couldn't help but gawk, aghast. On the rare occasions when Galliano addressed the Givenchy staff in French, he shockingly used the familiar "*tu*" instead of the formal "*vous*" as Monsieur had. And when he sent clothes back to the atelier with a note that read "Tighter, smaller, tighter, smaller, tighter, smaller," the seamstresses were "bowled over," a witness recalled.

"They were a little bit scared of John with his crazy hair, Amanda the English aristocrat, and Steven, the big fat guy who was in control of the world," Robinson's assistant Vanessa Bellanger recalled with a laugh.

"There were a lot of people who were very destabilized," a Givenchy assistant says. "The patterns and silhouettes were completely different. Monsieur de Givenchy's silhouettes were for middle-aged women and had big, gold buttons. John's silhouettes were lean, with skinny sleeves, rounded shoulders, and very discreet closures. Hubert de Givenchy was a man from the north of France, with a very sober style. John's was Mediterranean: warm, colorful, and sexy. Hot. The old ladies who worked there for a long time were perturbed."

But the younger staff was quietly relieved by his "revolution at the château" as one described it. "John was fantastic. Really a breath of fresh air." He brought on all of his favorite helpers from the London days, including Vicki Sarge to do jewelry, Stephen Jones for hats, and Sibylle de Saint Phalle to help with press, and they were all agog over the luxury of Givenchy: the gifted seamstresses, an endless supply of fabrics and notions, "this big white studio overlooking the Avenue George V," Bellanger said. "It was like Christmas had come early."

Galliano was more succinct: "My springtime has come."

DESPITE ALL THE BUILT-IN STABILITY that Galliano had in his life now—the solid backing of the John Galliano brand at the Passage du Cheval Blanc, the steady salary at Givenchy, the car and driver to ferry him back and forth between the two companies, the loads of support staff—he was careening wildly.

As before, his finances were a disaster. Duclos suggested he put away some money so he could pay his taxes later in the year, but that flew right over his head. "He had a banker who was pretty nice with him when he wasn't overdrawn," Duclos says. "But John was *always* overdrawn."

He was partying in excess: at times, while out on the town, he would "go berserk," said an associate, and "might not come in for a day." When he did show up, he could be moody and temperamental. He fell out with his master draper, Bruno Barbier, and Barbier left the company. Jenny Osterhoudt, who was so devoted to the Galliano cause that she even did his laundry for him, couldn't hack the abuse anymore—the "slave" treatment as Duclos described it—and quit in tears. "They weren't appreciated and they weren't being paid enough and suddenly he made it and they still weren't being appreciated or being paid enough," says a former intern. "He started believing the myth."

During the pre-Givenchy era, Harlech explained, "we all worked for John because we loved John and loved the work and it inspired our lives. But once there were big salaries and who gets jobs and who doesn't and who gets clothes and who doesn't, there is resentment. I remember there was a time when how many hours you worked didn't matter and nobody complained and when the show was over there was this joy and disbelief. 'We did it.'"

Those days, it now appeared, were over.

Galliano's vanity had soared too. He spent afternoons at the day spa getting massaged and waxed, and had Duclos paint his toenails red. "He was obsessed with what people thought or said of him," Duclos recalls. "He liked nothing better than being photographed—he had English photographer Lord Snowden do portraits of him at the studio. It was like working for the Sun King."

FOR HIS FIRST GIVENCHY SHOW and his first true couture collection, Galliano decided to play it safe. He dug around in the archives and pinpointed a few things that were house signatures: a white shirt with ruffled, flamenco dancer–like sleeves known as the Bettina blouse; full-skirted ball gowns; bows. As Lagerfeld had done with Chanel, Galliano wanted to take these house "codes" as they are known in the fashion business and build the collection around them. He had discreet guidance from the Givenchy atelier heads Colette Maciet, who was in charge of *flou*, or soft fabrics, and had worked for Coco Chanel, and Monsieur Kemal, who oversaw tailoring and had been trained by Balenciaga. Galliano had great respect for them and referred to them as "living history."

Though he had waged a revolution those first few months at Givenchy, by the time the collection was ready for fittings, he had learned very well and took advantage of all the old-school protocol of directing rather than doing. "No drawing, no cutting or pinning or sewing," says a former Givenchy staffer. "I never saw John even with a pin. *Never*. He would tell everyone what to do. He had great taste, but he never used his hands. Steven was the one who made things happen."

For the show, Galliano wanted a dose of his now-signature theatrics, though not too much—he didn't want to overdo it for his couture debut. Instead of showing in the rococo ballroom of the elegant Grand Hôtel in central Paris, as most of Paris's couturiers did back then, Galliano booked a vast room at the Stade de France, the new eighty-thousand-seat stadium located in the poverty-stricken northern Paris suburb of Saint-Denis. The Chambre Syndicale de la Haute Couture, which was in charge of the official show calendar, scheduled Givenchy for late Sunday afternoon, which infuriated Arnault, because it would not get coverage on the much-watched Sunday evening French network news.

Usually, the run-up to a show is a busy time. To add to the crunch, Galliano not only had to design the spring–summer 1996 haute couture collection; he also had to produce the 190-piece fall–winter 1996–97 "pre-collection," the more commercial ready-to-wear collection that retailers would review and order while in Paris for couture week in January. Galliano and his team had two short, breakneck months to do it all.

On a cold January afternoon, more than nine hundred reporters, retailers, and wealthy society mavens arrived—primarily by limo or taxi—in downtrodden Saint-Denis and took their seats in the cavernous bowels of the stadium. The front row had a plethora of boldfaced names: along with Richard Simonin and Bernard Arnault there were the actresses Joan Collins and Marisa Berenson, the granddaughter of Elsa Schiaparelli; Paloma Picasso, the daughter of Pablo; Malcolm McLaren and Tina Turner, as well as the designers Azzedine Alaïa, Kenzo, Gianfranco Ferré, Inès de La Fressange, and Gianni Versace. It was quite a different lineup from Monsieur de Givenchy's old money clientele.

Backstage the scene was beautiful chaos, with assistants buzzing about and the models done up in full Galliano glory. Many of the seamstresses who were on hand were in tears. "Everyone has been using techniques that they haven't used in thirty-five years," Galliano told me. "It's like suddenly they've come alive. They said, 'It's the first time we were pushed to do these things.'"

The show started only half an hour late and opened with a "Princess and the Pea" tableau: two models in immense seventeenth-century-style taffeta gowns, sitting on a pile of mattresses, playing with ribbons and ropes of pearls. There were only fifty looks altogether: slim Saint Laurent–style tuxedos, kimono-like opera coats, burnished orange and red sari-like sheaths, day dresses dotted with bows, and duchess satin ball gowns with laced corset bodices and twelve-foot trains.

It all seemed lost in the vast space and the opposite of what couture should be: one-of-a-kind fashion presented in an intimate setting so guests can see up close the superb craftsmanship, as Galliano had so perfectly done with the Schlumberger show. Now he had money and endless support and he went huge—too huge—and the show was deemed a failure. The applause was muted. Versace frowned. McLaren told me he found the opening tableau "a bit schmaltzy" and the collection "very English and slightly kitschy." Joan Collins said sarcastically: "There are great individual pieces—especially if you are going to play Auntie Mame." Of the India-style gowns, *Time* magazine snipped, "Does one go to Paris for a sari?"

Menkes called it "a fashion moment that missed," adding, "the show did not propel haute couture into the next millennium or define a new image for the house." Galliano champion Sally Brampton of *The Guardian* jabbed that at times it was "like gazing at the pages of a history book."

There were two in the house, however, who loved it.

"It's fantastic," Arnault declared after the show. "Fabulous. Is it a good investment? We'll see in some years."

"I said I was expecting a renewal," Simonin said. "The renewal is on. I'm quite sure it is a good investment, but it will take time. It's always a long story."

THE ONLY DESIGNER who had mastered designing at several houses at once was the indefatigable Karl Lagerfeld, who over the years, while working at Chanel, had served as artistic director of Chloé and his own brand in Paris and consulted at Fendi in Rome. *Women's Wear Daily* referred to him as the "Kaiser of Fashion." Could Galliano measure up to Kaiser Karl? Would the Givenchy and Galliano shows both be as elaborate as the usual Galliano presentation? Could he design enough fabulous frocks to make two successful collections simultaneously? Would Galliano look like Galliano and Givenchy look like Givenchy?

Harlech was sure he could pull it off. "We realized that John needs to work on two collections," she said. "It's not that he can do two collections—he *needs* two. For all of his ideas to be articulated, explored and resolved, he needs more than one collection. Before, everything had been squashed into too small a vehicle."

Harlech could see, however, that the ready-to-wear design process at Givenchy was not smoothed out yet—particularly when it came to her role. "There was decision making going on that seemed to negate my position because [the executives] would employ an ad agency to come up with a concept, e.g. girls on a catwalk, and John would say, 'No, over my dead body' and 'That is not what this collection is about.' And they would say: 'This has to appeal to Miss Middle America' and 'This is ad-driven' and art people being run by executives in suits. I stood up at a meeting and said, 'You employed John Galliano for his vision. You have to listen to what he's saying and what he wants.' They were quite difficult times. There was a struggle."

Thankfully, there was still the John Galliano brand at the Passage du Cheval Blanc, where Galliano had total freedom and needed Harlech without question. For that show, a couple of days after Givenchy, Harlech recalled, "John walked into the studio and said, 'Indians—Native Americans.'" Just like *Buffalo Bill's Wild West Show* at Disneyland Paris. Harlech instinctively knew what he meant. "Yes, yes, yes!" she wailed.

As Galliano had become more comfortable in his new job at Givenchy, his addiction issues resurfaced. "I saw John in really a state of falling-down drunk," a studio assistant remembers. "He would take anything he could find—anti-inflammatories, codeine—and mix it with alcohol. He did whatever he could to get a buzz." According to a Givenchy source, two weeks before the March ready-to-wear show, Galliano went AWOL. Givenchy executives turned a blind eye and Robinson stepped in to make sure everything got done in time.

But Robinson too was showing his true nature. Givenchy staffers were shocked at his brutish manner and by how his dark energy poisoned the studio atmosphere. "Steven was very mean," remembers one assistant.

The Galliano show was staged on a Thursday night in an indoor equestrian ring in the Bois de Boulogne, a large park on the western edge of Paris. Galliano said his muse was "a proper little squaw on her podium straightening her seams." Harlech described it as "Cherokee babes."

To set the mood, the sandy riding ring was decorated with a large tepee, bales of hay, an old car tagged with American Indian icons, rusty oil drums, a vintage refrigerator, overstuffed chairs and sofas—like a flea market version of Ralph Lauren's western vision. "Was there a Sonia Delaunay rug on the dirt?" asked Spindler in *The New York Times*. "Did a man on horseback in a football jersey ride through the room? Was everyone in the fashion industry there? Could that possibly have been Liza Minnelli in the front row?" The answer to all was: yes.

The models were supposed to be a mix of Hopi Indians, the duchess of Windsor, and Natalie Wood in the John Ford western *The Searchers*. They came out with war paint on their faces and wearing Navajo-style blanket coats over tailored tartan trousers; fringed suede flapper dresses embroidered with tiny beads; and Wallis Simpson–like peplum suits with pencil skirts. At the end, Galliano and Harlech ran along the catwalk, yelping like Tiger Lily and Peter Pan.

Women's Wear said: "This collection was elaborate, rich, imaginative and romantic in the way we sometimes forget fashion should be—at least on occasion." *The Guardian's* Susannah Frankel called it "the week's most accomplished show so far."

But who would ever wear these clothes?

Galliano's shows had become fashion's equivalent of a "tent pole"—the megaproductions that Hollywood studios put out each summer and Christmas, like superhero movies, that "hold up" or underwrite the rest of the slate with big box office profits and all tie-in merchandise. Arnault adopted that business model for Givenchy—except that the tie-in merchandise was handbags, lipstick, sunglasses, and perfume. Menkes advised Bult and Rice to do the same: "The Paine Webber Inc. investors had better sign some product licenses or find a fragrance partner to capitalize on Galliano's soaring, romantic imagination," she wrote.

Two days later, on March 16, 1996, Galliano mounted his Givenchy women's wear show, at a television studio in the far-flung suburb of La Plaine Saint-Denis. His theme for this collection was Spain—specifically the mid-century era that Hemingway romanticized; the star bullfighters Dominguín and El Cordobés; the Iberian culture of his mother's youth and his upbringing. I went backstage before the show and found it was littered with empty magnums of Pommery champagne—curiously one of the few major brands not owned by LVMH. Simonin told me that the sales for the pre-collection were double the previous season and the number of retailers in the United States had tripled. Forty-five minutes after the official show time, the models were dressed and everything was ready to go.

But Galliano wouldn't start the show.

When Simonin asked what the holdup was, Galliano responded:

"Karl Lagerfeld was forty-five minutes late. So I will be an hour and a half late."

Simonin tried to talk Galliano into starting, but he refused. Not yet six months into the job, and only one failed couture show under his belt, and he was already behaving like a full-blown diva.

When the show finally did begin, Jeremy Healy opened it with an excerpt from the film soundtrack of *My Fair Lady* of Audrey Hepburn carefully enunciating: "The rain in Spain stays mainly in the plain." It was a nice nod to Hubert de Givenchy's long relationship with Hepburn, but *My Fair Lady* was one of the few movies from her golden era for which he did not design her wardrobe.

For day, Galliano sent out handsome gray matador suits with gold epaulets; white ruffle Bettina blouses; high-waist tuxedo pants; strapless gray flannel jumpsuits; and ornate capes. For evening, there was a flurry of pastel chiffon cocktail dresses with silver-dollar-size polka dots; and his signature bias-cut gowns, this time in red chiffon. The models had slick ponytails and clean, dramatic 1950s makeup with thin, arched eyebrows and bloodred lipstick. Healy played a cut from Madonna's *Evita* soundtrack, months before its official release; Galliano had an inside track since he was making some of Madonna's costumes for the movie.

As with his eponymous show, the press found the Givenchy show to be, as one reporter called it, "triumphant." Janie Samet of *Le Figaro* declared: "It's a win!"

Menkes said the clothes were "fresh, youthful and wearable," adding, "This Galliano-Givenchy marriage, if not made in heaven, might become a fruitful partnership."

Retailers placed a record number of orders. Saks Fifth Avenue in New York announced it would be the first to sell the collection in the United States, dedicating five hundred square feet of retail space and window displays to it. "The collection will be played up big," Saks president Rose Marie Bravo said.

GALLIANO WAS GETTING increasingly demanding and fussy with Givenchy staff—the Spanish politesse was giving way to the Bad Boy nastiness—and used his seemingly close relationship with Arnault as a blackmailing tool. "If you don't do what I want, I'll take the phone and call Bernard," he'd threaten.

In May 1996, Galliano was invited by the queen of England to attend a state dinner at Buckingham Palace for President Jacques Chirac of France. He traveled to London on the same Eurostar as Chirac and checked into a hotel rather than stay with his family in Peckham. The night of the event, he didn't show up—and he didn't call the palace to alert the protocol office that he wouldn't be attending.

When the news broke in the French press, Galliano's official reason was that he was confined to his hotel bed with a migraine. Lady Harlech was trotted out to convey his mea culpas. "John feels absolutely awful," she said. "He was so looking forward to meeting the Queen."

Galliano later confessed the truth to *The New York Times*. "I had a panic attack," he said. "I got completely dressed—oh, I wish you could have seen it, the jacket was so fierce, and there was lots of jewelry—and then had a serious panic attack. I thought, 'My God, John, you're going to the Queen's for dinner. What are you going to say?'" He did eventually write to the Queen to apologize.

Arnault didn't seem to mind the faux pas too much. In mid-June, just two weeks before the next Givenchy couture show, he called Simonin for an unscheduled meeting at the Avenue Hoche headquarters. When Simonin arrived, Arnault surprised him with congratulations on the success of the Galliano appointment.

"You insisted and you were right," Arnault said.

Simonin couldn't believe what he was hearing. In his five years with the group, he had never received one compliment—plenty of yelling, scolding, blaming, but no pats on the back. He was overcome with suspicion.

"Mr. Arnault, what is this meeting really about?" he asked.

"John Galliano walks on water," Arnault said. "He is too good for Givenchy. I am putting him at Dior."

Arnault had been thinking about replacing Ferré at Dior for some time. The company under Ferré had grown tired and boring and sales were not up to Arnault's hopes. The following February, the house would be celebrating its fiftieth anniversary; to mark the occasion, the Metropolitan Museum of Art's Costume Institute was going to mount a major Dior retrospective. Galliano, in Arnault's opinion, was the sort of "romantic" who could steer Dior creatively into a new era, and his media-hyped shows would help turn the company into a powerhouse global brand.

Simonin was floored.

"If you do this, Givenchy will not survive," he shot back. "Or if it does, and you pour money into it, it will take ten years to get it back to where it is now."

"No, no," said Arnault. "It will be fine."

Simonin called his old friend and mentor François Baufumé, the CEO of Christian Dior.

"Why did you steal Galliano from me without giving me any warning?"

"It wasn't my idea," Baufumé responded firmly. "John was not my choice, I assure you."

WHEN ARNAULT INVITED GALLIANO to LVMH headquarters to offer him the Dior job, Galliano says, "My hair was all matted, [and] I had the wrong color toenail polish on." Nevertheless, he was thrilled and accepted without hesitation.

Galliano confided the news to Robinson. But he didn't immediately tell Harlech or Saint Phalle.

"I didn't know anything about it until we were in New York [for a Givenchy event]" several weeks later, Harlech told me. They were riding through Manhattan in a stretch limo when Galliano suddenly burst forth with the news:

"I've got it!"

"Got what?" she responded.

"I've got *it*!"

"Got *what*?!"

"I've got Dior!"

"Oh my God!" she squealed. "I'm so happy for you! That's your dream!"

Harlech's life, however, was spinning uncontrollably downward. For a couple of years, her marriage had been on tentative ground, especially after her husband was arrested in Shropshire late one night for drunk driving and possession of cannabis and a semiautomatic rifle without a proper license. The final blow came when her eight-year-old daughter asked her why another woman was sleeping in Daddy's bed. "I didn't want to get divorced," she later said. "But at the point where your children are part of it, you have to do something."

Galliano had no patience or mercy for Harlech's troubles. He told Duclos at the Passage du Cheval Blanc: "You know how women are. She's crazy and she's so nasty and so demanding."

From the negotiations going on between Galliano and Dior, it became clear to Harlech that she might not have a job there—a job she desperately needed now that she would be a financially strapped divorced mother of two young children.

Harlech confessed her fears to Talley. "Amanda was getting treated like she was nobody," Talley says. "It just sounded horrific. I said, 'You've got to be kidding me.' Because I've seen her organic moment—her picking up the shards of glass, putting them in a box to send to Paris, and writing the narrative for John to do a show. I've seen her sitting in the fittings; even with Steven, she still held her own."

"I thought, 'Well, this cannot be. I've got to do something now to help Amanda. She's got to survive,'" Talley continues. "She's got two children, a divorce, and bills to pay.'"

During the couture shows in July, Talley asked Karl Lagerfeld to invite Harlech to the Chanel show. Lagerfeld agreed. Afterward, Talley took Harlech backstage to see Lagerfeld. She was dressed in a "simple little black thing," Talley said. Lagerfeld was charmed by her.

"Go to the couture salon and order anything you like," he told her, and snapped his fingers.

"Oh, no, I can't," she responded.

"Just go," he insisted. "Take André with you. Get whatever you want."

Harlech took up the invitation and selected a long black wool coat that went to the floor.

Meanwhile, the fashion press corps had a new sport: "Arnault-watching," as Spindler dubbed it in *The New York Times*. The news had finally broken that Ferré was out at Dior—and there were loads of rumors as to who would replace him. Westwood's name came up; so did Gaultier, Lacroix, and Marc Jacobs. Arnault fueled the debate by telling Menkes that he hadn't yet found a successor and was "thinking very hard about" whom to hire.

To gauge what was the truth, fashion reporters took to observing him carefully in the front row of his brands' shows and at LVMH-sponsored events. He stood for Lacroix's three ovations. To the fashion pack, this was surely a sign that Lacroix was a serious contender for the Dior job. At the Givenchy show at the Stade de France on a miserable rainy day, Arnault beamed. But he didn't let on to anyone that this would be Galliano's last couture show for the house or that he'd already been hired to take over Dior.

FOLLOWING HIS ENORMOUS SUCCESS with "Dante"—both in London and in New York—Alexander McQueen's studio and his life underwent a major reshuffle. After two years of hard work for very little pay, Ruti Danan decided it was time to move on. To fill the void, Ungless suggested one of his second-year students at Central Saint Martins, a quietly efficient and eager blonde named Sarah Heard from Macclesfield, Cheshire. Heard had been brought up in a far more middle-class and provincial environment than McQueen. She was one of five children, her father an accountant, her mother a music teacher. She attended Central Saint Martins, where she had Ungless as a professor in print textiles.

"I had so many students who would come to me, all the time, and ask,

'Can you get me an internship at McQueen?' They'd see Lee and me wandering around Soho, and they'd kind of try to get in our field of vision—'Hi! Hi!'—and I'd resist," Ungless says. "But when Sarah came to me and asked—I had seen her level of commitment, she just did the work. So I said to Lee: 'You know, there's this girl who's really quite brilliant,' and he asked to see her."

During Heard's interview at the Hoxton Square studio, McQueen asked her: "Do you believe in UFOs?" Verkade wanted to know if she could do denim production. "I did not have a clue!" Heard later admitted. She fudged it and was hired.

When Heard got back to Central Saint Martins, Ungless sat her down for a serious heart-to-heart talk. He had heard all the intern horror stories—the ones that made students run out the Hoxton studio door—and he wanted her to understand what she might be in for.

"Look," he told her, "you could be washing up a shitty dildo."

"It's fine," she insisted. "I really want to work with him."

McQueen took good care of her. "He taught me how to cut an S-bend in chiffon and how to put in a zip, which I didn't know how to do," she said. "[And] he would talk about Romeo Gigli a lot."

Ungless knew that with Heard on the team McQueen was in good hands—such good hands, in fact, that he decided it might be time to explore other professional options. He was invited by Gladys Perint Palmer, executive director of fashion at the Academy of Art University in San Francisco, to teach for the summer. McQueen was unhappy at the thought of Ungless's moving halfway around the world. But Ungless insisted it was only for a few months.

As the summer went on, McQueen's suicidal funk began to dissipate—primarily thanks to a new beau, a twenty-five-year-old Scot named Murray Arthur. They met at a party in the East End in mid-July: Arthur had too much to drink and vomited, McQueen heard him and said, "Are you all right?" From that inauspicious start, a love affair began.

Almost immediately after meeting McQueen, Arthur moved into the Hoxton Square flat and began working at the studio, eventually overseeing staff administration and accounting. McQueen needed to have his boyfriends nearby all the time.

McQueen's relationship with Arthur was particularly gentle and kind. "Murray is epileptic," he explained. "So I care for him an awful lot. I'm there when he has his fits in the morning. I hold him still so to stop him from shaking until he goes white, and I stroke his head. I'm there to bring him back out of it. No other queen in the world would, I don't think."

McQueen adored Arthur—described him as "very intelligent and analytical"—and believed the union would be for life. McQueen took Arthur for weekends at Hilles with the Blows. He regarded Hilles as his place "to get away"—he had his own room and he truly exhaled there.

Later that summer, Arthur invited McQueen to Aberdeen, Scotland, to meet his family. It was McQueen's first trip to his ancestors' homeland. "It was unreal because I stepped off the plane and I just felt like I belonged there," he said. "I felt like I've lived there all my life."

AT THE END OF JULY 1996, just before Givenchy closed for August vacation break, Simonin handed over the president's job to a forty-year-old French executive named Georges Spitzer, so he could focus solely on Kenzo. All summer long, LVMH had held a sort of open call to replace Galliano at Givenchy. But no one seemed right.

Upon the return from the summer break, Spitzer took up the hunt again—this time in London. "For one and a half years, people have said to me: 'Keep your eye on McQueen,'" Spitzer told me. On a Monday morning shortly before McQueen's show, Spitzer rang McQueen at the Hoxton Square flat. McQueen was asleep in bed with Arthur when the call came in.

"When I contacted him, he was surprised," Spitzer said.

"I thought they wanted me to do handbags or something," McQueen told me.

When Spitzer indicated that they wanted to talk to him about becoming the creative director of Givenchy, McQueen couldn't believe his ears.

He thanked Spitzer for the offer, said he'd think about it, and hung up.

RUMORS STILL FLEW ABOUT the fashion business as to what LVMH was up to—and Galliano helped string them along. He went to New York in early September to personally introduce his Givenchy collection at Saks Fifth Avenue. "With a deep tan, a chestful of gold chains, a bandanna on his head, loose plaid pants, painted toenails and a sheer white shirt, Galliano literally stops traffic as he crosses the street outside his Upper East Side hotel," *Women's Wear* observed.

During the interview, they talked of the recent renovations of the Givenchy boutique in Paris to his specs and of his habit of getting professional pedicures complete with vibrant polish. "If you're going to get to know your customer, you have to know what she does," Galliano explained without irony.

Then the *Women's Wear* reporter brought up Arnault's designer musical chairs, putting forth the latest buzz: that Galliano was going to Dior.

"I'm very busy right now working on future collections for Givenchy," he said with a poker face. "To do Dior as well isn't humanly possible."

McQueen focused on his upcoming spring–summer 1997 women's wear show, "La Poupée," based on 1930s German artist Hans Bellmer's disturbing photographs of dismembered pubescent dolls. The show was staged in the majestic Deco-design Royal Horticultural Hall near Victoria train station.

Once again, to make it happen, McQueen called Simon Costin. "Lee had all these pictures of [artist Richard Wilson's] installation at the Saatchi gallery," Costin says. "It was an elongated triangular space, like a waist-high tank, with a passage that you walked into and it was filled with black sump oil. Because the concrete floor had no vibrations, it was perfectly still and looked like an enormous piece of black glass. Lee said, 'How can we do something like that?'"

Costin went to see the show venue to do a test: he took a black tray, filled it with water he fetched in the loo, and "jumped up and down to see how solid the floors were," he says with a laugh. The water didn't ripple. "I thought we could probably get away with it," he says.

He had an enormous shallow tank constructed out of plastic—about one hundred fifty feet long, twenty feet wide, and two feet high. To make the models' entrance more dramatic, McQueen and Costin decided to have a small stage at the foot of the runway with a dozen steps down to the tank. McQueen's team roped in Tanqueray Gin as a sponsor to help cover costs.

For head decoration, McQueen enlisted Welsh sculptor Dai Rees, a former Saint Martins and Royal College of Art student who, in the mid-nineties, began sculpting cagelike headpieces out of what he calls "denuded quills"—goose feathers stripped down to the quill—that he found at a lake in north London.

A friend suggested he show the denuded quill cages to a fashion stylist, so he took them to Katy England at *Dazed & Confused*. She found them to be quite interesting and sent him to see McQueen. When Rees arrived at the Hoxton studio, Isabella Blow was there too. "I opened the box and showed him the pieces and he and Isabella absolutely loved them," Rees recalls. "They both tried them on in front of a huge mirror."

"Can you make more?" McQueen asked Rees.

"Yes, of course."

"Have you worked with leather?"

"No, I have not."

"Have a play around and see what you can do," McQueen said. He commissioned fifteen pieces.

Rees created several cages, including one gilded in silver, one painted red with silver glitter, and another covered in coffee grounds "to look like rust," he says. He also made several leather pieces—neck collars, headpieces, and chinstraps like wrestlers wear—and decorated them with bare, colored quills. When finished, they were, Rees admits, "rather aggressive." McQueen was pleased with the final result. "What set Lee apart from other designers at the time," Rees says now, "is that he had a good eye for finding accessory designers who were on the edge of fashion. They didn't come from a normal trajectory of fashion."

The most subversive piece in "La Poupée" was one McQueen commissioned Leane to make: a square metal frame with manacles on each corner that attached to a model's upper arms and thighs, effectively shackling her into a square form. McQueen asked the African American model Debra Shaw if she would open the show wearing the frame.

"Well," she responded, "what is the history behind it? Is it a reference to slavery?"

"No, God," he insisted.

He told her about Bellmer: how he came up with the doll project in part as a response to German fascism and its obsession with control and perfection; that his work was subsequently labeled by the Nazis as "degenerate"; and that he was forced to flee to Paris, where he was embraced by the Surrealists. The frame, McQueen said, was a commentary on all of that: constraint, Aryan beauty, Surrealism, and what he saw as the fascist dictates of fashion—the rules of taste and what was acceptable set by a group of people he deemed bourgeois and boring.

At the time, the Milan-based brand Prada was a domineering force in fashion. Its silhouette and overall style—designed by the company founder's Milanese Brahmin granddaughter Miuccia Prada—has often been deemed "fascist" by observers because of its chic uniform-like nature. Everything McQueen did in fashion was in direct conflict with all that Prada embodied and promoted. Beauty, in his eyes, had nothing to do with "appropriate."

Shaw listened to McQueen's explanation of Bellmer and the Surrealists and had a good think about it. She knew that if the frame were about slavery, the shackles would have been around the ankles and wrists, not the thighs and biceps, and attached to chains, not a frame. She found McQueen's setup more artistic than domineering.

"All right," she said, "let's do it."

When she tried the piece on, she says now, "I felt like my body was in a picture frame." She did not feel fettered like a slave. "I'm proud of my heritage and my race," she insists, "and I would never do anything that would be humiliating."

The day of the show, Costin spent five hours filling the shallow plastic tank with black water. The lighting man Simon Chaudoir bounced lights off broken mirrors hidden behind screens so there was a ripple effect across the ceiling of the hall. "The water was pitch still when people came in and so they believed it was a big Plexiglas runway, which is what Lee wanted," Costin says. The show was held up because Victoria and David Beckham were running late. Finally, McQueen blasted, "I'm not fucking waiting for them" and started. When the first model came down the stairs, stepped into the runway and it rippled, the audience gasped.

The models sloshed through the black pool in clear plastic platform shoes so it appeared that they nearly floated across it. There were smart white suits and jumpsuits with plunging décolleté and backs; watery blue shifts; asymmetrical sheer dresses over bikini bottoms; shimmery flapper dresses with long fringe swishing at the knee. Many of the models wore Dai Rees's quill

204 | DANA THOMAS

creations—several encircled the head like hockey masks; one resembled a wrestler's helmet with the quills shooting from the chinstrap like a Fu Manchu beard.

At the halfway mark, Shaw came out wearing a black fishnet flapper dress and the frame. As she worked her way to the entrance, she suddenly realized she would have to go down the steps. "I took my time, thinking, 'I can't be fearful, I just have to do it,'" she says. "The minute I got down the last stair, the audience went, 'Yay!' and started clapping. But then I thought: 'How do I get off the runway?' It's not like you can turn and walk off. So at the last minute, I shuffled my feet and slid off like a crab."

When she returned backstage she asked to have the frame removed. "I can't do that again for the finale!" she told McQueen firmly.

He understood.

For the climax, a model came out wearing only neon pink brocade trousers, her head and naked torso enveloped by an angular cage filled with butterflies—a piece created by Costin's brother Anthony, who is a sculptor. McQueen described it as a "kind of cocoon . . . made of steel rods . . . in the form of a three-dimensional star . . . covered in this glass fabric so you could see through it. . . . This girl was inside it, but we had all these butterflies flying around her. . . . She was picking them out of the air and they were landing on her hand. . . . It was just about the girl's own environment. . . . I was thinking about the new millennium in the future, thinking you would carry around with you your home like a snail would. It was really beautiful. It threw a lot of people completely sideways."

But it was Shaw's frame that caused the uproar, with charges that McQueen exploited a black woman, shackling her like a slave.

Despite the curious accessories, the clothes were pretty and rather conventional—at least for McQueen. "It's about refining the Alexander McQueen label into a salable commodity," he explained. "I'm not trying so much to do marvels in unwearability. . . . This season is all about smoothing down the edges."

LVMH continued to chase after McQueen—they even sent him champagne and caviar in an effort to seduce him. There was a reason for their urgency to find a designer for Givenchy, and it wasn't just Galliano's looming departure for Dior. LVMH's sales figures in the fashion sector were discouraging and perfume sales for Christian Dior, Givenchy, and Kenzo were collapsing: a mere 70 million French francs ($13.7 million) for the first half of 1996, less than one fourth its 380 million French francs ($75 million) in sales for the same period a year earlier.

McQueen wasn't sure what to make of LVMH's wooing. "Lee was ringing and telling us everything, and we were just like, 'Can you believe it? Lee? Givenchy?'" Bobby Hillson recalls. "You know, how proper Givenchy was and his really wild shows in London—he thought that it was such a giggle. I don't think he was desperate to go to Givenchy; he just couldn't believe they asked him, the wild boy of British fashion. They took John but John was nothing compared to McQueen."

McQueen told his mother about the Givenchy recruitment and she was astonished—from her point of view, it was like "a fairy tale." But he wasn't so sure. "I was grateful for the offer, but it was something I could take or leave," he said. "I don't think fashion is a very stable career. You can't count on it for years. You can be as quickly dropped as you're quickly picked up."

Once the two sides were talking, and stories were leaking in the British and fashion press that he had the job, McQueen still wasn't convinced he wanted it. "They haven't made up their mind, nor have I," he said as he prepared for his own show in London. When asked if he could handle designing ten collections a year—what would be required of him if he took on Givenchy while keeping up his own line, he said, "I can't imagine anyone doing that. My first concern has to be McQueen. Givenchy would be a lot of money, but I'm not really into that. Plus, Paris does nothing for me."

"If I take the job on," he continued, "I see it as a completely separate entity from the rest of what is going on in Paris. If Givenchy employs me, they are employing Alexander McQueen. At the end of the day, I will be truthful to myself."

"Basically," he concluded, "all these big companies don't care about you as a person. You're only a commodity and a product to them and only as good as your last collection."

GALLIANO HIRED Carla Bruni's boyfriend, a French attorney named Arno Klarsfeld, to handle his Dior contract. Klarsfeld, son of the French Nazi hunters Beate and Serge Klarsfeld, had made a name for himself by assisting in the successful prosecution of Nazi war criminals Klaus Barbie and Maurice

Papon. Though contracts weren't his usual bailiwick, Klarsfeld was pleased to help out. "John was nice and it wasn't that much trouble," Klarsfeld says. "And he expressed great admiration for my father, which I liked."

Harlech's situation, however, was still not sorted out—primarily because Robinson was in charge of negotiating her contract with Dior executives. The Old Galliano Guard, the ones who had been by his side in London all those years, understood what was happening: Robinson was trying to finally rid himself of Harlech, as he had everyone else, so he could have Galliano all to himself. "Amanda—who had been there since the beginning, who was key, key, *key*," said one. "How could anybody be so foolish as to get rid of Amanda?"

Bernard Arnault and François Baufumé asked her to come in for a meeting. "They tried to hustle me into signing a contract," she says. "It was a very serious and binding contract: if you go to the United [Arab] Emirates you will be paid for two days, and you'll be allowed so much off the price of items in the boutique. It was a very rigid contract."

Furthermore, the salary was pitifully low. As Harlech said, "I thought it was missing a zero."

"It was missing several zeros," says a Harlech confidant who was privy to the negotiations.

"I had two children, my marriage was breaking up, and I needed security," Harlech says. "I don't think the Dior people understood that. It was really frightening. A friend of mine who works in opera said, 'Why don't you use my lawyer?' I had never had a lawyer in my life. He said, 'Let's ask them [for] what you really want.'"

Harlech sent Dior her financial requirements. "They thought that was a typing error," she told me. They said no, and Galliano said nothing.

PARIS FASHION WEEK had never been so newsworthy. On Tuesday, October 7, Gianfranco Ferré presented his last Dior show ever, with a ready-to-wear collection of skinny pants with bustier tops, bejeweled cocktail dresses, and backless evening gowns.

Galliano put on a gypsy circus show, à la Ava Gardner in *The Barefoot Contessa*, for his namesake brand at a dilapidated wine warehouse in eastern Paris. The scene out front was a zoo, with hordes of groupies trying to push their way through the entrance on a cold, dark autumn night. Anna Wintour arrived wearing a Bordeaux leather coat with a fur collar that Galliano had an assistant make for her at the last minute and give to her as a thank-you gift for all of her support. Unbeknownst to the crowd, Baufumé and his number two, Sidney Toledano, slid discreetly into the show.

Inside, as always, the set, designed by Jean-Luc Ardouin, was full-on theatrical with bonfires, tightrope walkers, acrobats, and gypsy accordion players. The theme and decor carried on into the clothes, with gypsy-inspired embroidered suits and ruffled skirts, frilly floral chiffon dresses, and fringed shawls. It was beautiful and fun, but as Suzy Menkes pointed out, it felt like Galliano "always turns the same trick"—an elaborate set and the most ravishing models in one-off show pieces that no one would ever wear.

For his last Givenchy show, at the Espace Auteuil in the sixteenth arrondissement, he referenced Jane Austen's nineteenth-century heroines, the Ottoman Empire, and the French Foreign Legion. None of that had anything to do with the history or "codes" of the house of Givenchy, but he didn't care—he was out of there and did as he pleased. Not surprisingly, it was deemed an utter failure.

That same morning, Amanda Harlech made a noted appearance at Chanel, thanks to Talley. Distraught by her situation at Dior, Talley rang Lagerfeld again and said: "You know, it just cannot possibly be. Amanda is being treated badly, and this has got to change. I just cannot let this happen to her because she is so wonderful."

"Darling, darling, darling, take her to the boutique, dress her, and bring her to the show," Lagerfeld said.

Talley called Harlech and told her to get herself ready. She grabbed a Stephen Jones hat and a pair of Manolo Blahnik heels. Talley picked her up in a *Vogue* car and whisked her to the Chanel boutique on the rue Cambon. They dashed in, selected a gray skirt suit with jeweled buttons, and were back in the car in fifteen minutes. Off to the show they went, and Harlech was seated in the front row, looking smashing in Chanel. The fashion elite took notice.

After the show, Talley and Harlech went backstage to congratulate Lagerfeld. When Lagerfeld spotted Harlech, he took her aside and quietly invited her to come work with him. Then he told her loudly, for the hovering journalists to hear, "If they don't give you what you want at Dior, I've got a great job for you."

Their encounter was duly reported the next morning in the press.

McQueen's uncertainty about the Givenchy job dominated the trades daily. During the negotiations, LVMH offered to buy McQueen's business; he turned them down flat. "The example of what happened to Hubert de Givenchy was enough for me," he said.

On Tuesday, October 7, he decided he didn't want the job either. But by the next morning, he had changed his mind again, and traveled to Paris. The contract signing was scheduled for the following day, Thursday, October 9— less than a week before LVMH said it would make the official announcement. For moral support, McQueen asked Isabella Blow to come along, just as Treacy had her accompany him to his first meeting with Chanel. "We needed her," Treacy said. She wasn't just a cheerleader. She comforted them, kept their anxiety at bay.

Of course, Isabella had to have the right hat to wear. She went to Treacy and asked him for something special. He gave her a scarlet red bowler from the collection, trimmed with matching osprey plumes: a strong hat for an important occasion.

For the meeting, Arnault, Spitzer, and their men were reserved and elegant in their conservative gray suits and polished shoes—a stark contrast to Blow's scarlet chapeau and McQueen's rambunctious comportment. McQueen was particularly surprised by Arnault's slim, towering stature and understated elegance. "I expected to find a big fat man with a cigar," McQueen said. "It made me feel like I'd just come out of an asylum, he was so serene and quiet."

Despite Arnault's calming energy, McQueen stood up more than once and shouted obscenities.

"Look," McQueen's lawyer said, trying to calm his client down, "they're the cart, and you're the only horse who can pull it."

"I'm not their fucking *horse*!" McQueen exploded. He turned to Arnault. "I don't fucking need you!" he blasted.

Then he stormed out of the room.

On the way out, he told the executives in graphic terms that he needed to go to the loo.

Eventually he returned, and he signed. McQueen was apprehensive about taking the Givenchy job—his contract was only for two years and reportedly for a salary of about $160,000 a year. It was a long way from the $1 million a year that Galliano would reportedly earn at Dior, but McQueen seemed fine with that. "Money's never been a big object," he said. "I mean I like to live comfortably," he admitted, but as he had long proved, it wasn't his raison d'être.

Givenchy executives knew that McQueen was exactly what they were looking for. "He is an emerging talent—an undeniable and evident talent— yet he's not too established, so he can grow with the house," Spitzer told me at the time.

McQueen's reaction?

"Givenchy is fucking lucky to have me."

IN THE MID-1990S, luxury fashion experienced a seismic shift from the business of creation to the business of hype. Wearable fashion had become an afterthought. Media coverage was what counted—and not simply on the fashion pages. News stories of takeovers and boardroom battles, profiles of savvy CEOs and designers, business stories about profits and soaring sales dominated front pages, weekly magazine covers, and television news, creating a tsunami of hype to sell big-profit items such as perfume and accessories to middle-market consumers.

It peaked on October 14, 1996, when LVMH officially announced that Galliano would be taking over Dior and McQueen would go to Givenchy. This was the dawn of the megagrowth era for luxury fashion, and with the help of Galliano and McQueen, Bernard Arnault would lead the way.

"[Arnault] is most concerned about the media attention," Talley told *The New York Times* at the time. "It's the perfume bottle and the handbag"— which had the highest retail mark-up—"and how to keep the attention there. It's about a marketing strategy. . . . It's all about the media hype. He could have taken the Princess of Wales as the designer, and he would have been very happy."

Predictably, the French establishment complained about the appointments, the press griping that Arnault hired Bad Boy Brits instead of French designers as heads of two of Paris's elite couture houses, and industry players grousing how hype had ultimately trumped clothes. "The shows have become too much," Yves Saint Laurent whined. "They are killing fashion."

Bernard Arnault sloughed off the criticism. "I chose English designers because in France we don't have the same level of creativity," he said frankly.

"We don't produce designers of that caliber . . . the modernity, the creativity, the good taste."

The British, however, were thrilled with the news. The BFC finally gave McQueen the Designer of the Year award. London seemed so hip that a *Newsweek* cover story declared it "the coolest city on the planet." Even British prime minister John Major of the Conservative Party jumped on the bandwagon: during his speech to the Lord Mayor's Banquet at Guildhall on November 11, 1996, he noted among Britain's recent achievements: "Our country has taken over the fashion catwalks of Paris."

"Did he say that?" McQueen squawked when he heard. "So fucking typical of government! They do nothing to help you when you're trying to do something, then take credit when you're a success! Fuck off!"

McQUEEN DECIDED TO BRING Katy England and Sebastian Pons to Givenchy, but he made no provisions whatsoever for Isabella Blow. She had championed him for years, she had suffered from serious financial troubles ever since her father had disinherited her, she'd held his hand through the negotiations, and she was—at least she thought she was—his best friend. She believed, as Harlech had with Galliano, that McQueen would create a consulting position for her at Givenchy. She wanted the job, she needed the job, and many, many people—friends, colleagues alike—felt she deserved the job.

Instead, McQueen turned away from her and left her out in the cold. "She's a patron," he said, brutally. "There is no way that she could be my muse. She is an enthusiast. She loves loads of designers. Anyway, if you give one persona of what clothes should look like, you limit yourself."

She could assume part of the blame. Though usually quite forthright, she didn't directly broach the subject with McQueen. "She was never one to ask outright for a job, or for money," Treacy says. "But she hoped he would bring her with him. She *hoped*."

To say she was upset is an understatement.

"Devastated" is how she described it.

"She was heartbroken," Julien Macdonald confirms. "She's spent all her life promoting Lee, buying his clothes, giving him money, and then basically, he just kicked her to the floor. He finally had money and had an opportunity to give her something back . . . but he didn't want her."

"I think the problem was that Isabella was like a butterfly," Macdonald continues. "She'd go around and fly on somebody, spend time with them, you know, introduce them to the world, and then she'd find somebody else. Lee always wanted her to himself. So they had this kind of love-hate relationship— this really bonkers relationship. She really loved him. Oh, she would have done anything for him."

ONCE PARIS FASHION WEEK had wrapped up, Harlech returned to her home in Shropshire to figure out what to do next and she invited Talley to join her. She was utterly confused: she loved Galliano, but she was still being wooed by Lagerfeld. A week after the shows, she was invited to a dinner party at Lagerfeld's Left Bank *hôtel particulier*. She arrived wearing a Galliano chiffon gown, and seemed, as one observer noted, "that she was torn between two lovers." Lagerfeld didn't let that deter him from his quest. "I consider Amanda one of the chicest women of the nineties," he said. "I like her as a personality, the way she looks at things, her brightness—everything."

She confided her disbelief and confusion to Talley as well as to other friends and confidants, including her childhood chum Jasper Conran and Anna Wintour. Everyone told her to consider herself and her children. "I had nothing," she said. Desperate, she rang up Galliano and cried, "Don't do this to me! I really need to be financially independent now!"

Talley was stunned that Galliano didn't fight to keep Harlech. "John could have taken the reins and said, 'Look, look, she's got to come with me,'" he says. "That's what was shocking: that he didn't."

Harlech's close friends counseled her on her negotiations with Chanel, suggesting that, along with a salary and travel expenses, she ask for a permanent suite at the Ritz, which is across the street from Chanel headquarters and where Coco Chanel had lived and died.

After a week of going back and forth with Chanel, a contract came through on Harlech's fax machine. It was generous and included the Ritz suite.

"Look," Lagerfeld told her, "get Dior to take you seriously. I'd love you to work for me, but you have a very special relationship with John, and I respect that. This is what Chanel would offer you. Take this contract to Dior and say, 'Match this.'"

She did. "And they rang back and said: 'Is this a joke?'" she recalled.

Harlech still couldn't accept that her time with Galliano was truly over. She told Talley she wanted to wait a year before joining Chanel—as if, like a knight, Galliano might escape Robinson's grip and triumphantly return to carry her off to Dior headquarters at 30 Avenue Montaigne. Talley was incredulous. "Nobody's going to wait around for a year," he told her. "They're giving you a job. You've got to go now!"

The last week of November, Harlech traveled to Paris and signed the contract at Lagerfeld's home. "I didn't want to take her from John because I like John," he said. "But I had the impression LVMH didn't take care of her, so she was free."

When the news broke, *Women's Wear Daily* declared that Harlech's move to Chanel "may be the biggest defection in Paris since Rudolf Nureyev leapt to freedom at Orly [airport]" in 1961.

But Galliano saw her departure "as a betrayal," Harlech said.

"We could have worked it out," Galliano later told me. "Mr. Arnault was more than prepared to work it out . . . [but] there was this fast buck coming at Amanda and she went for it."

XI

McQueen's workload tripled: he now had to design ten collections a year—six at Givenchy (two pre-collections, two runway women's wear, and two couture each year) and four at McQueen in London (two menswear and two women's wear); stage six shows annually; and commute from London to Paris. He only took the job, he said, because "I decided to sink that big money into my own company, to take on more staff. The Givenchy position gave me both credibility and the funding I needed."

As soon as McQueen got some cash in the bank, he decided it was time to take care of himself, as well as those he loved. He paid back Aunt Renée the money he borrowed for his tuition for Central Saint Martins. He had his teeth fixed. He bought himself a television, and a home in Islington to put it in. "It's the house I've been waiting for all my life," he said. He told his parents that he wanted to buy them a house too—in a nicer neighborhood, or maybe even in the countryside. Joyce was resistant. "We've lived here so long and know everybody round here," she said. "It's nice to walk down to the market and have someone call out: 'I saw [your son Lee] in the paper again!'"

McQueen was pleased with how his parents had finally accepted what he was doing. "[My father] shows me great respect now," he said. "I just wish I'd had that support in the beginning. Because I prefer people to be with me, like my aunt was, one hundred percent of the way."

Givenchy executives found McQueen an apartment to live in on the rue de Béarn in the Marais, just a few blocks from Galliano's home. The flat was 70 square meters (about 750 square feet), a three-floor walk-up, and pretty beat-up. "Appalling" is how one Givenchy assistant remembers it now. And he was expected to share it with his team from London. McQueen had the master bedroom, his Givenchy studio assistant Catherine Brickhill had the second bedroom, and Sebastian Pons had the third. When Katy England came over from London, Pons gave up his room for her and slept on the sofa. Costin often crashed there too.

The setup was far more collegiate than corporate. "Sometimes in the evening, he would collapse on the sofa and watch TV," Pons says. "The next morning, there would be Häagen-Dazs ice cream containers filled with cigarette butts. Gross! Used tissues. The mess, the mess! And his clothes were always wrinkled and messy, or they smelled of mildew." But as in Milan during his Gigli days, McQueen was happy in his group-house arrangement. "He liked to have people around him," Pons says. "We didn't socialize with anybody else. It was just us, together."

At Givenchy, McQueen oversaw a support staff of sixty. Some had come on with Galliano and decided to stay. One was Saint Phalle—like Harlech, Galliano left her behind. "He didn't offer," she later told me. "He never said: 'Come to Dior.'"

He set immediately to work on the couture collection, which was to be shown in mid-January. For it, McQueen wanted to jettison everything that Galliano had done—after all, Galliano's work at Givenchy was deeply Galliano and had very little to do with the history of the house. Instead, Mc-

Queen decided to use all white—like a clean canvas—and accent it with the gold of the company's Greek-style *G* logo. "He wanted to go back to the simplicity of Givenchy—the structure and the purity," Pons explains.

The unifying theme would be ancient Greek mythology—another reference to the logo—specifically Jason and the Argonauts, the tale of a mythical hero and his quest to find the Golden Fleece, the gold-haired wool of a winged ram that symbolizes authority and kingship. He titled the collection "The Search for the Golden Fleece."

In the old days, Monsieur de Givenchy would draw the collection on white paper with felt-tip markers and then send the *croquis* to the atelier to have the *toiles* made up. This was how most classical couturiers still worked— Lagerfeld, Lacroix, Valentino, and Saint Laurent included. But McQueen's hand wasn't very good and he preferred to work on the stand. Because of that, he was able to create extremely complex designs. But pretty soon he had a communication breakdown with the Givenchy hands. "When I sent the designs to the atelier staff they freaked out and said it was too complicated," he recalled. "I said, 'This is couture, darling, you've got to be able to do it.'"

Some of the staff were taken aback by McQueen's lack of manners. Not only was he not using the formal "*vous*" with them, as Monsieur de Givenchy had, he wasn't even trying to speak French. "It was destabilizing," remembers Maria Herrera, who had stayed on as director of publicity for Givenchy. But he surprised the old-timers with his passionate hands-on approach and won their hearts when he moved a sewing machine next to his desk so he could work on garments directly. "He was a polyvalent," Herrera says. "He could sew. He went on his hands and knees to do a hem. He seduced everyone with his talent and personality."

"At first we weren't sure [about McQueen]," atelier head Catherine Delondre, a thirty-four-year Givenchy veteran, admitted in those early days. "But then when we saw the things coming out of the atelier, we thought, *This is real couture.*" She added: "He is a true technician."

The admiration was mutual. "We're all lucky this is still around," McQueen said. "All these people in the atelier should be cherished."

DURING HIS FIRST DAYS at Dior in October 1996, John Galliano greeted each of the seven hundred staff, one by one. "They had to fill the grand hall

three times so that I could meet them all," he said. He assured them that together they would produce clothes that the world would want to wear.

Like McQueen, Galliano had his work cut out for him. Dior was in sorry
shape. Sales were a middling 156 million euros in 1995 and 187 million euros
in 1996, for fashion and accessories. "There were only ten Dior stores at the
time," Stephen Jones remembers. "Licenses were the key. There were Dior rice
cookers in Japan."

To tackle this assignment, Galliano and Robinson thought it best to learn
all that they could about Dior the man and the brand. In late October, they
went to see Soizic Pfaff, head of the house's archives, which were located
around the corner at 18 bis, rue Jean Goujon. The archive room was long and
dark—to protect the materials from sunlight—and jammed full of items.
There was an enormous closet filled with old Dior clothes, some originals
donated by clients or purchased at vintage stores or at auction, and some
newer reproductions based on sketches. There were shelves overflowing with
books containing drawings, fabric swatches, photographs, client records—
essentially, the history of the house.

Dior was founded after World War II by a young, corpulent dandy
from Normandy named Christian Dior, who, like Galliano, worshipped his
mother and romanticized the Belle Époque of the early twentieth century.
Dior came from a good family with a big house full of staff who taught him
how to sew. Upon graduating from the École des Sciences Politiques, he
mixed in the 1920s Paris art scene with musicians Erik Satie and Francis
Poulenc and artists Salvador Dalí, Max Jacob, and Joan Miró, and with his
generous allowance, he acquired a substantial art collection and opened a
gallery.

Shortly after Hitler invaded Poland, Dior was drafted into the French military and spent most of the early part of World War II digging ditches in the
south of France. He was demobilized after the French armistice and in 1942,
went to work as an assistant for couturier Lucien Lelong, who had remained
in business and served as the head of the couture fashion association during
the occupation. Lelong believed it was better to save jobs and preserve French
pride than it was to capitulate.

Once the war was over, Dior decided it was time to strike out on his own.
He partnered with Marcel Boussac, France's largest textile manufacturer, and
opened his own couture house in 1947. Dior wasn't the most obvious candi-

date to head a fashion house. Though Lelong declared that he had "great talent," he was, as American *Vogue* editor Bettina Ballard recalled, "a pink-cheeked man with an air of baby plumpness still about him and an almost desperate shyness." Just like McQueen—though with substantially better manners. And in a business where giant personalities like Coco Chanel and Elsa Schiaparelli had long reigned, Dior's timidity and roly-poly physique would no doubt play against him.

Somehow he managed to conquer the shyness—at least enough to design and produce a collection that he would show to the public. For his creative inspiration, he looked to the corseted Belle Époque wardrobe of his beloved mother and came up with modern versions of that hourglass silhouette. "The styles [of the Occupation] were incredibly hideous and I couldn't wait to do something better," he explained. "I revived the rip bosom, the wasp waist and the soft shoulders"—words that Galliano repeated almost verbatim about his own work nearly fifty years later—"and molded them to the natural curves of the feminine body. It was a nostalgic voyage back to elegance."

On a cold winter's morning in February 1947, some one hundred journalists, retailers, and fur-clad socialites filed into Dior's new headquarters at 30, Avenue Montaigne, walked up the grand staircase and took their seats on delicate chairs and love seats that lined the pearl gray and white salon. The room was filled with fragrant bouquets of blue delphinium, pink sweet pea, and lily of the valley—Dior's lucky flower. The show started precisely on time with swanlike mannequins gliding through rooms as an announcer called the name and number of each of the 150 outfits.

There was Bar, an ivory shantung peplum jacket over a full, pleated skirt made of ten yards of black wool, sewed by a young unknown Dior assistant named Pierre Cardin. There was Chérie, a navy blue taffeta cocktail dress with a round-bosomed bodice and a knife-pleated circular skirt made of thirteen-and-a-half yards of fabric cinched into the tiny waist. There was Passe-Partout, a navy wool crepe suit with a collarless jacket and slim skirt; Africain, a leopard-print muslin gown; and Corolle, a black wool afternoon dress with five large buttons down the front and a full pleated skirt.

As was convention then, the frothy pageant went on for more than two hours, and when it was finished, the crowd cheered and shouted "Bravo!" *Vogue*'s Bettina Ballard described Dior as "a Napoleon, an Alexander the Great, a Caesar of the couture." *Harper's Bazaar* editor in chief Carmel Snow declared Dior's sculpted silhouette a refreshing "New Look" after decades of soft, straight lines and the war's dour suits, and the moniker stuck.

Dior's opulent designs were a welcome relief after the war years of deprivation and suffering. France—indeed, all of Europe—was ready to dress up and go out on the town again. Embracing the gaiety and frivolousness of the Belle Époque also allowed the French to erase the unpleasantness of collaboration, at least on a social and shallow level.

Dior and Boussac steered the company into an unparalleled success: two years after its debut, the house of Dior accounted for 75 percent of French fashion exports and 5 percent of *all* French exports. They came up with the idea of partnering with other businesses to sell Dior-branded items—the first was Dior hosiery—and by 1951, Dior had licenses for handbags, men's shirts, gloves, scarves, hats, knitwear, sportswear, lingerie, and eyeglasses. *Time* put the still-portly designer on its cover; he was awarded the Légion d'Honneur and, according to a Gallup poll, he was one of the five most famous people in the world.

In mid-October 1957, Dior decided to take a cure, ostensibly to lose weight, at a spa in Montecatini, Italy. Ten days into his stay, after a postdinner canasta game, he dropped dead of a heart attack. He was fifty-two, and his company was only ten years old.

He was succeeded by his chief assistant, Yves Saint Laurent, a skinny twenty-one-year-old Frenchman raised in Oran, Algeria. Saint Laurent wowed the fashion crowd too with his first collection for Dior: the centerpiece was the "Trapeze," a stiff A-line silhouette that stood away from the body. "My dear," cried one guest to another, "France is saved." The *Los Angeles Times*'s fashion editor Marylou Luther wrote: "The king is dead. Long live the king!"

Two years later, Saint Laurent was drafted to fight in France's war with Algeria, but after nineteen days in boot camp, he suffered a nervous breakdown and was sent to a hospital mental ward in Paris. He was replaced at Dior by fellow French couturier Marc Bohan. In 1961, Saint Laurent founded his own house with Pierre Bergé, and Bohan remained the designer for Christian Dior, dressing first ladies and aristocrats in tasteful, pretty frocks, until 1989, when he was unceremoniously sacked by Arnault and supplanted with Gianfranco Ferré. And now Ferré had been dumped by Arnault and replaced by the younger, trendier Galliano.

GALLIANO SPENT THE ENTIRE WEEK poring through the archives, went back on the weekend for more, and took books and videos of past shows home with him. "He was so excited," Pfaff said. "He wanted to see everything. Old newspaper cuttings, press books, and all the little details." Most important were the *Livres de Fabrications*—or fabrication books—for 1947 and 1948, which detailed how the iconic clothes for those collections were made. After reading about the ensembles, Galliano was able to study several of the actual garments. Not all the gems were there, however; many were at the Costume Institute at the Metropolitan Museum of Art, being readied for an upcoming retrospective.

Galliano also dove into *Les Signes de Reconnaissance de la Maison Christian Dior*, a voluminous diarylike tome put together by the house that serves as an owner's manual of sorts. In it, he came across a remarkable photograph by Cecil Beaton of a chic middle-aged Romanian named Germaine "Mitzah" Bricard, wearing a leopard skin coat over a black dress, a leopard-print turban with a black fishnet veil, and a diamond bracelet and pearls. Mitzah was "one of those increasingly rare people who make elegance their sole raison d'être," Dior said.

The more Galliano and Robinson learned about her, the more they swooned. Mitzah had an impressive string of lovers, including a Russian prince who draped her in pearls. She tied a scarf around her wrist to hide a scar from a suicide attempt. She denounced socialites as cheap, sniffing: "They'll go to bed for a café crème." She dispensed advice to women: "When a man wants to send you flowers, always say, 'My florist is Cartier.'" She served as Dior's muse and aide-de-camp.

Galliano and Robinson agreed: Mitzah would be their Dior woman too. They began to build the collection around her, and added other influences, including Christian Dior the man; portraits by Belle Époque painter Giovanni Boldini; and the Masai tribe of Kenya and Tanzania. The Masai idea was pure Galliano: he saw an iconic Dior illustration by famed fashion illustrator René Gruau of a woman's elegant hand caressing a leopard paw and said, "That led me to Africa and the Masai. Upon studying pictures of the tribe, and of how proud they looked, we thought, 'Oh my god! La Belle Epoque—the silhouettes are the same!'" He and Robinson worked closely together throughout November, turning their ideas into clothes.

———

Not surprisingly, when Arnault decided to move Galliano to Dior, he also wanted to buy Galliano's label—just as he had tried to buy McQueen. The John Galliano company was doing well at the time: John Bult and Mark Rice had nursed it to the point that it was ready to move into licensing of brand extensions such as eyewear and perfumes, and ready-to-wear sales were thriving, particularly in the United States, its number-one market.

Nevertheless, the company had cost them a fortune—during their three years of backing Galliano, they had invested close to $5 million when all counted—and it had been an emotional roller-coaster ride. The ups and downs in fashion, particularly of a rising star, are relentless. They accepted Arnault's offer and sold the majority—62.5 percent—to Christian Dior Couture. They held on to 12.5 percent and the remaining 25 percent belonged to Galliano. As minority shareholders, Bult and Rice left the management of the company to Arnault's lieutenants. Arnault immediately named Dior chief François Baufumé as head of the Galliano brand as well, and together they hired Valérie Hermann, a savvy young French executive formerly of Jacques Fath, as managing director to run Galliano on a day-to-day basis.

A few years later, Bult and Rice would sell the remainder to Arnault, and eventually, Galliano did too.

McQueen returned to London whenever he could—he didn't like Paris, or the French, and couldn't bear what he saw as the ludicrous lifestyle and work of luxury fashion's top players. "No, no respect at all," he said when asked what he thought of their designs. "What, putting a bit of chainmail in a load of different bright colors? No, no, no. I've seen these people in the flesh now at a *Vogue* party in New York and it's like Michael Jackson's *Thriller*. These old and decrepit people who've lived it up and didn't know when to stop. All these zombies dancing round."

Of Armani, McQueen said: "He's close to dead. I mean, no one wants to wear a floppy suit in a nice wool—the man was a bloody window dresser. What does he know?" He didn't think much of Versace either. "I don't see the relevance of [Armani and Versace] put together," he snarled. "Actually, they should have amalgamated and sort of formed one company out of both. If you can imagine the rhinestones on one of them deconstructed suits."

Several of McQueen's confreres whacked him back.

Yves Saint Laurent called him a "talentless upstart."

Vivienne Westwood declared McQueen's "only usefulness is a measure of zero talent."

There was another reason McQueen preferred to be in London than Paris: he had a lover on the side named Archie Reed. Like McQueen, Reed was from the East End. They first met back in Stratford when they were kids—Reed was nine and McQueen was a fifteen-year-old bussing tables at a local pub called Reflections. "He looked so shy and nervous," Reed recalls. "We called him 'The Fly' because he used to buzz around."

They reconnected in 1996 at a bar called The End on Tottenham Road. Reed, the son of a former fashion model and a retailer, was a fair-skinned, fair-haired pretty boy, lean and handsome, with rich blue eyes. "We went to his home and stayed up all night, cuddling and smoking weed. I knew immediately that we were soul mates," Reed recalls. "He kicked me out in the morning as Stella McCartney was coming round. It was then I realized he was a big deal." Though Reed was married at the time—to a singer named Alexis Reed—she didn't seem to mind his carrying on with McQueen.

Murray Arthur, however, was unaware.

With McQueen often in Paris, the London staff's responsibilities evolved. Verkade became a gatekeeper and personal assistant. "She was the wall between Alexander and us," Pons says. "We didn't like her so much." Pons became McQueen's first assistant in Paris as well as London. A young staffer named Amie Witton handled press in London while Saint Phalle oversaw it at Givenchy. England shuttled between both studios. Heard helped with the licenses in Japan and answered to Verkade. Though Isabella Blow had been officially jettisoned, she was still flitting around McQueen, calling him, seeing him, inviting him to Hilles. "She forgave everything," Michael Roberts says.

By early December, McQueen was conducting fittings for his Givenchy couture collection in Paris. Some weeks beforehand, he called Philip Treacy to ask if he would design the hats for the show. They spoke about references and themes, and then, unlike Galliano with Stephen Jones, McQueen left Treacy alone to work. He trusted Treacy implicitly.

That's not to say that McQueen didn't come up with his own ideas. One was based on the curly horns of Isabella Blow's rare sheep at Hilles. Isabella agreed and helped to make it happen: on a winter Monday morning, she returned from Hilles to London, went directly to Treacy's headquarters, walked into his office with a big plastic bag, hauled out a freshly harvested rack, and dropped them—splat!—on his worktable, bits of flesh and blood still dripping from the base. "Here are your horns," she said, and let out a hearty laugh.

A few days before the show, Treacy loaded the hats on the Eurostar and took them to Givenchy. When it came time to unwrap and present them, McQueen made everyone come around and keep quiet. Treacy slowly opened each box and revealed its contents. The group remained silent except for proper compliments. McQueen called the ritual "the unveiling of the hats."

For the hair, England brought in highly regarded French hairdresser Nicolas Jurnjack. McQueen explained to him the collection: "Women warriors," Jurnjack recalls. "He wanted to tell a sort of mythology, and he didn't give me any precise ideas. He simply asked, 'What would you do?' I was surprised because I was prepared for: 'Do this and that.' He said, 'Every model has her style, and you must tailor the hair to each girl and her personality. I do not want thirty of the same'"—which was the norm in fashion at the time. "'Now you work for McQueen and we speak about individuality.'"

Jurnjack rented a big studio in Belleville, in northern Paris, to have the space to work on the wigs, and hired ten assistants to help. All the while, he never heard a word from McQueen or England. Then one day, they came by the studio to see what he had designed. "Lee looked at the pieces and he put his hand in his pocket, he pulled out two hundred or three hundred in cash, and said, 'Stop. Take a break. It's sublime. Go out and celebrate.'"

ON DECEMBER 9, Princess Diana flew by Concorde from London to New York to attend the opening gala for the Christian Dior exhibit at the Metropolitan Museum of Art's Costume Institute. The event, with a dinner for nine hundred at $1,000 apiece, followed by a dance party for two thousand at $150 apiece, was hosted by *Harper's Bazaar* editor in chief Liz Tilberis and Dior owner Bernard Arnault and served as the big annual fund-raiser for the institute.

Diana was not only the guest of honor for the Met gala; she was the first official client for John Galliano at Christian Dior. He designed her evening gown: a midnight blue bias-cut slip dress trimmed with black lace. Galliano and his team traveled to London three times to conduct fittings on the princess at Kensington Palace. She added one of her preferred pieces of jewelry: a pearl choker inset with a large sapphire brooch that had belonged to Queen Elizabeth the Queen Mother.

During the cocktail reception and dinner, in a hall decorated with five thousand white roses and ten thousand lilies of the valley, the princess charmed the VIPs, which included former top model Iman, French actresses Isabelle Adjani and Emmanuelle Béart, socialites Bianca Jagger and Ivana Trump, and *Vogue* editor Anna Wintour, as well as Bernard and Hélène Arnault, Galliano, and Ferré. By the time the dance party came around, however, jet lag had kicked in and she was running out of gas. She was whisked out of the fete to her waiting car without working the room and was ferried back to her suite at the Carlyle Hotel. "I paid all this money to be near a bunch of nobodies," screeched one appalled socialite after Diana pulled her French exit. The headline in the *Daily Star* the next morning read: "I'M OUT THE DIOR."

Some wondered if she fled because she was embarrassed by how she looked: The dress had been deemed a dud. Many fashion critics found that it looked more like a limp, run-of-the-mill slip than a one-of-a-kind haute couture creation made for a princess. The British press was aghast that the mother of their future king was, as *The Guardian*'s Louisa Young wrote, "wandering around the Costume Institute Ball . . . in her nightie."

The *Daily Mail* concurred: "The problem, and there is no delicate way of saying this, is . . . she wasn't wearing a bra. . . . A woman with Diana's figure needs more support. And it's an inescapable fact that the slip dress looks best on those hardly out of their teens."

BY MID-DECEMBER, McQueen was in good enough shape on the couture collection to start working on the Givenchy fall–winter women's pre-collection to be presented and sold to retailers during couture week in January, and the runway collection that would be presented during Paris Fashion Week in March. He also had his namesake line to design, scheduled for London Fashion Week in late February. That equaled four collections and three full-on McQueen shows in six weeks. As British writer Lynn Barber pointed out at the time, it was "a staggering workload for someone who just three years ago was on the dole."

McQueen planned on spending Christmas on Biggerstaff Road, and his family told him to bring Arthur too. Despite quietly carrying on with Reed on the side, McQueen and Arthur had grown close—so close that Arthur had McQueen's logo tattooed on his arm. McQueen had pressured Arthur into doing it and later felt so guilty he showed up with a bottle of Cristal champagne as an apology gift.

Over at Dior, Galliano and Robinson worked straight through the holidays. On Christmas Day, they took the day off and decided to make a turkey dinner. Problem was they forgot to turn on the oven. "It was awful," Robinson said. "We were so tired we just ordered pizza."

Despite the heavy schedule, Galliano was taking better care of himself and exercising regularly. He hired a personal trainer—"the one who gives Tina Turner her beautiful legs!" he boasted—and had a workout schedule that included squash and jogging in the Luxembourg Gardens. "While I run, I think of nothing but breathing," he said. "It's like a meditation; my spirit is empty and after I'm overflowing with energy."

In early January, he met with makeup artist Stéphane Marais to discuss the look for the show and they came up with an angel/devil theme. Robinson worked with the models who came in for fittings to make sure they could do a proper hooker walk. This may have been couture—the ultimate in elegance and refinement—but Galliano and Robinson still wanted the women to come across as tarted-up whores.

For the hair, Galliano enlisted top stylist Odile Gilbert. She came to Dior in early January to discuss different ideas with Galliano, and then about a week before the show they did fittings to figure out which styles best suited each outfit and model. Most were wigs, which she had made from real hair and had dyed to her specifications.

As fittings went on, Galliano stood back and told everyone what to do; unlike McQueen, he didn't crawl about the floor with needle and thread or scissors in hand to fix the dresses himself. "His great skill, apart from his imagination, is in encouraging and enthusing. It's always, 'Why can't we? *Why* can't we do it?'" said his longtime assistant Bill Gaytten.

In the weeks leading up to the couture shows, Galliano and Robinson invited McQueen and England out to dinner, "to welcome him to Paris," Galliano said. "It was great fun. Like a Saint Martins reunion."

He was less pleasant with Harlech: though she tried to keep in touch and remain friendly, he didn't return her phone calls.

FOR MORE THAN A CENTURY, for a week each winter and summer, Paris has become the world's epicenter of glamour: society's most high-profile mavens or wealthiest spouses and mistresses join the usual fashion tribe of press and retailers for a short week of shows, parties, and dinners. The clothes on display are haute couture: made-to-measure creations constructed of the finest fabrics and embellished with the most rarefied details and embroideries. In couture, there are no cost restraints, no ideas too wild. It is collected like fine wine and exotic cars, displayed in museums alongside art's greatest masterpieces, studied by subsequent generations who want to understand construction and craft. It is true luxury.

In January 1997, couture week was on the cusp of a major change: Bernard Arnault planned to turn it into fashion's greatest tool for publicity and branding. Since the early 1990s, when fashion discovered the power of celebrities wearing their clothes to the Academy Awards, there had been a handful of couture designers—most notably Gianni Versace and Valentino—who catered to them: inviting them to shows, dressing them for red carpet events, featuring them in ads.

But Arnault, with his two new young, headline-generating hires, planned to maximize the hype. His PR teams would invite the richest and most famous, dress them in clothes from the latest collection, have them arrive late to make a grand entrance witnessed by all, seat them next to him front row, center, and encourage reporters and paparazzi to interview and photograph them. He too would welcome interviews before the show and use the opportunity to praise his charges and comment about business, so the stories would cross over to the financial and even news pages. Couture would no longer be about selling one-of-a-kind clothes to the elite; it would be used as a platform to reach out to a broader customer base—the middle market—who would buy perfumes, lipsticks, scarves, handbags, and other logo-covered accessories that were mass-produced and had a substantial profit markup. (At the time, handbags retailed for an average twelve times their production cost; today it's far more.)

The ever-prickly French press adored Galliano. Like with the British media, he was good at schmoozing and wooing them, and he charmed reporters with his basic French and flamboyant style. McQueen, however, was, in their view, too low class to deserve such a haughty position at an esteemed French house, and they let him know it rather viciously in their pre-show coverage. The newsweekly *L'Express* said that he "looked like he escaped from a Stephen Frears movie to parachute into the Givenchy ateliers." Another weekly, *Le Nouvel Observateur*, wrote: "The clothes he wears . . . the slightly soiled shirt open at the neck; the chic way he carries a can of beer; and that haircut *'très football-club de Liverpool.'* Compared with him, an audience of AC/DC heavy-metal fans would win prizes for couture." Even the ever-polite Janie Samet of *Le Figaro* noted that McQueen was "clean" when she visited him at Givenchy, as if this were a surprise. But she couldn't manage to spell his name right, referring to him as "Mac Queen."

Arnault didn't mind. He was a firm believer that there was no such thing as bad PR. And he liked the idea of the media pitting Galliano and McQueen against one another.

FIRST UP WAS McQUEEN at Givenchy. The show was scheduled for Sunday, January 19, in the sumptuous early-nineteenth-century main hall of the École des Beaux-Arts on the Left Bank. "Bloody hell, this is enormous," Chaudoir, the lighting man, exclaimed when he saw it during their pre-show site visit. Since show producer Sam Gainsbury stipulated that it not "look like a commercial fashion show," Chaudoir proposed to use huge film lights—twenty-four kilowatts each—all around the room. With them, he says, "You get a gorgeous soft highlight."

For the soundtrack, McQueen told Gainsbury's husband, the deejay John Gosling, that he wanted the 1978 disco hit "Take That to the Bank" by Shalamar, which Chaudoir found "very funny." He also explained that the opera diva Maria Callas was another inspiration, since she had been the lover of the Greek shipping titan Aristotle Onassis and starred in Pasolini's 1969 film version of Euripides's *Medea*. In Greek mythology, the hero Jason was married to the sorceress Medea. Gosling suggested sampling some of Callas's great arias in the music mix—and McQueen agreed. After the site meeting, they went back to Givenchy, where Chaudoir says McQueen "was working with the old ladies with white coats, he with his skinhead cut and his jeans hanging around his ass."

As McQueen and his team worked on the collection, it became apparent to the assistants that he was relying too much on his poor man's way of making clothes rather than taking full advantage of the ateliers and Paris artisans. "Some of the clothes were dodgy," Pons says now. "Couture is about the details, and some details can kill a dress. There was a bustier dress with ivy coming out, and it was plastic ivy with gold spray paint. I said, 'Lee, this is horrible, you cannot put plastic with spray paint on couture. This should have been three days of embroidery at Lesage, or a jewelry piece, or nothing. But not plastic with spray paint on a couture dress. That's just not possible.'" McQueen simply shrugged. "People aren't going to get wonderful things overnight," he said. "I don't expect everyone to love what I do right away."

As guests arrived, including the designer Azzedine Alaïa, the New York socialite Anne Bass, and the German fashion photographer Peter Lindbergh, they spotted the male model Marcus Schenkenberg, dressed like Icarus with big wings, perched above. Isabella Blow took her seat in the front row, wearing a lavender and black lace outfit from the "Dante" collection and a big black Treacy saucer hat. She did not help out; she was simply a guest. McQueen's mother, Joyce, was there too, but without her husband, Ronald. She explained that he had been undergoing chemotherapy treatments for cancer and was too tired to travel.

The show started about an hour late. After the first look came out—Jodie Kidd wearing a gold-embroidered white opera coat over a gold lace catsuit—one French fashion writer leaned over to her friend and quietly gasped: "*Oo-la-la*. If he continues with that kind of styling, he'll lose them."

He did, and he did. Kidd was followed by Naomi Campbell in a gold satin bustier minidress knotted at the waist and Treacy's big gold horns on her head; Eva Herzigová in a white corset swimsuit with gold stud trim down the side seams and gold wings over her ears; Debra Shaw in a corseted long-sleeved white dress with amply padded shoulders and a gold lace facemask; Stella Tennant in a sharply tailored white suit, the rib sections and mid-back cut out to bare the torso; and Helena Christensen in a short white tulle ribbon dress with a long draped train. One model had an oversized gold nose ring dangling from her nostrils, like the sort bulls wear. The clothes felt Mugler in their cut, and Gaultier in their kitsch. What they did not feel was couture, or Givenchy.

After each model walked by, Isabella Blow clapped enthusiastically. But, as Hilton Als noted in *The New Yorker*: "The ladies of couture did not; they were taken aback, it seemed, by the sheer excess of youthful vitality and confusion parading before them in outrageous clothing. The distinctly *now* was clearly passing them by."

That evening, Lord Rothermere, the young heir to the Associated Newspapers company (*Daily Mail, Evening Standard*), and his wife, Lady Rothermere, hosted a celebratory dinner for McQueen at their Paris home. Among the guests around the long, grand dining table were Murray Arthur, McQueen's mother, Joyce, and Aunt Renée, and the actor Rupert Everett. McQueen was in a somewhat foul mood—he sensed that the show was not well received.

The next morning, his fears were confirmed.

"This was an extravaganza of white and golden excess," wrote *Women's Wear*. "Overwrought showmanship can reek of an amateur act, and that's just what happened here."

The New York Times's Spindler felt that it was purposely vulgar: "McQueen gilded one model's nipple that protruded from a striped sailor shirt. He did his buttocks-baring trick at the back of one dress, with a screen of openwork lace shielding little. . . . This was basically a pretty hostile collection from a gifted designer who seems in conflict about his role in the Givenchy studio."

McQueen's debut may have been way off the mark, but it wasn't the high crime that the fashion media made it out to be. "Of course I make mistakes. I'm human. If I didn't make mistakes, I'd never learn," he said. "You can only go forward by making mistakes. I'm twenty-seven, not fifty-seven. I'm not Givenchy. I'm Alexander McQueen."

GALLIANO'S FIRST DIOR SHOW was scheduled for Monday, January 20, at 3:30 in the afternoon. Originally Galliano had hoped to stage it at the Dior headquarters. "John always wanted to do it in the salons," like in the old days,

Steven Robinson told me. But the number of invitees—twelve hundred—made that impossible.

Dior executives and the studio team finally decided to hold it in the Grand Hôtel—not just in the ballroom, like most designers, but throughout the entire ground floor except for the lobby and restaurant. A team of 146 workers spent thirty-six hours replicating the salons of 30, Avenue Montaigne: they built faux walls with eight hundred meters of gray fabric and white molding; installed urns filled with four thousand soft pink roses; set up nearly eight hundred chairs, two rows deep, sandwiched between the hotel's Empire-style tufted sofas; and reconstructed the legendary Dior curved staircase where old-time VIPs such as Marlene Dietrich used to perch like sharp-eyed falcons to watch the show.

The backstage area was decorated with posters of Belle Époque illustrations and venerable fashion photographer Irving Penn's pictures of model Lisa Fonssagrives wearing rooster hats. "To instill the mood," Robinson told me loudly over pounding disco music.

There were fifty models, each with a personal dresser and one outfit to wear; sixteen hairdressers under the command of Odile Gilbert; and fifteen makeup artists working with Stéphane Marais. In the next room, clothing racks held the looks—New Look–inspired houndstooth suits; Masai-inspired gowns; the wedding dress, made of layers and layers of ruffled off-white and tea rose tulle. Dior seamstresses sat quietly next to the racks, sewing beaded African collars with threadlike wire.

The models were installed at the makeup and coiffeur stations, smoking and chatting as assistants applied magenta sequin eye shadow and attached hair weaves. Robinson walked up to the model Crystelle and gave her a book of Boldini paintings. "This is her character," he explained to me, opening the book to a specific page. "She wants to practice her poses." As he carried on his rounds, he instructed an assistant: "Make sure there is plenty of champagne—champagne at every exit—for the girls. I know someone is going to forget that, and that's the most important."

At 2:00 P.M., Galliano blew in, dressed in a made-to-measure Prince of Wales plaid suit and an oversized fedora over a black bandana. This was his chic new look: "When I'm at Dior, I dress Dior," he explained. He had another new accessory too: a bevy of bodyguards.

He walked through the makeup and hair stations, kissed several of the models, and gushed how beautiful they were. Then, after speaking briefly with Robinson, he sat down at a table in the makeshift lunchroom and poured himself a Heineken. "I slept some last night," he told me, "but not much. I kept waking up, thinking."

At 3:00 P.M., champagne was served. Several of the dolled-up models sat on the floor, drinking and smoking as their boyfriends snapped pictures. One girl fussed with her towering Blahnik strappy boots and asked worriedly: "They aren't going to fall off, are they?"

"It took thirty minutes just to get into the corset, with the atelier making sure we didn't pass out," Debra Shaw told me. "In a corset, you can't breathe. That, and with the Masai necklace on—it was really, really a challenge."

Galliano briefly disappeared, only to reemerge wearing a double-breasted black suit with no shirt and a large pearl drop earring swinging from his left lobe. He drifted from room to room, surveying. He looked at one dressed model, grinned broadly, and ran his tongue across his teeth.

Out front, the guests began to arrive, a good many in full-length mink and sable coats, and took their seats. The front row was a who's who of fashion and France: French first lady Bernadette Chirac; actresses Emmanuelle Béart, Charlotte Rampling, Dayle Haddon, and Marisa Berenson; couture-buying socialites Nan Kempner, Susan Gutfreund, São Schlumberger, Deeda Blair, and Mouna Ayoub; French minister wives Lise Toubon and Isabelle Juppé; former French president Georges Pompidou's widow, Claude; and designers Narciso Rodriguez, Azzedine Alaïa, Jean Paul Gaultier, and Marc Jacobs, who had dressed decidedly un-couture in a purple pullover, black jeans, and dirty white tennis shoes. Waiters in waistcoats offered flutes of champagne from silver trays.

In his program notes, Galliano stated: "the spirit is one of change." He wasn't kidding. When the show finally started, well after its appointed time, the models drifted gracefully along the rambling runway in a dramatic parade of tailored gray suits with flared miniskirts; Prince of Wales plaid pantsuits with frayed edges; bias-cut lace slip dresses; white leather minidresses and jackets cut like lace; Edwardian gowns with corseted waists and Masai-inspired beading and headdresses; nude fabric sheaths covered in colorful beaded designs that looked like tattoos; slinky satin cheongsams in acrid colors with floral; and ball gowns with skirts made of hundreds of meters of pastel tulle. The models were beautiful—most with long, straight hair and bangs (wigs) and china doll makeup and topped off with Jones's trilbys or berets. They pranced like deer in their Manolo Blahnik stilettos. It was over in a half hour.

Fashion had never seen such opulence, extravagance, or boldness of presentation and design. It was obvious that money was no object—that Galliano had no constraints creatively or financially. The result was couture on steroids and it left guests gasping and reeling.

"I was sitting in a row with Madame Chirac and Madame Pompidou and they looked like they had been hit in the face with a cold dead fish," Nan Kempner told me. "They couldn't believe what they were looking at: this conservative house where they've all bought their clothes for years. How much was there that Madame Chirac or Madame Pompidou could wear? Mr. Arnault looked a little knocked out too. I don't think he knew what he had gotten himself into."

As the crowd erupted in applause, Galliano took his curtain call, surrounded by his Masai and China Girl models and looking natty in his gentleman's suit and a jaunty black fedora. It was as if he was trying to show that with his big new job he had finally grown up.

"*Quelle* extravagance! *Quel succès fou!*" trumpeted *Women's Wear Daily*. *International Herald Tribune*'s Suzy Menkes called it "divine madness," and wrote, "Surely Galliano's sixteen-year career has been a dress rehearsal for this sublime moment?"

The day after the show, Dior's couture department was so overwhelmed with client appointments that its *directrice* Caroline Grouvel had to use her office for fittings too. Many of the orders were for ball gowns, often in white for weddings. But I heard a quiet rumbling among the loyal couture crowd too—whispered criticisms that Galliano's Dior designs were more like theater costumes than clothes and that Arnault's business model of using couture to drum up publicity was leaving them out in the cold without a coat. Arnault was nonplussed. In response, he liked to quote Christian Dior, who fifty years earlier said: "I don't care about what the critics say as long as it is on the front page."

AT THE END OF FEBRUARY, just five weeks after McQueen's Givenchy couture fiasco—which by then he had agreed was "crap"—it was time for him to present his namesake collection in London. He titled the show "It's a Jungle Out There."

McQueen came up with the idea while viewing a television documentary on Thomson's gazelles. "I watched those gazelles getting munched by lions and hyenas and said, 'That's me!' Someone's chasing me all the time, and if I'm caught, they'll pull me down. Fashion is a jungle full of nasty, bitchy hyenas."

With the help of his show producers Sam Gainsbury and Anna Whiting, McQueen chose an old Victorian outdoor fruit and vegetable market known as the Borough Market in Southeast London as the venue. It was a beat-up macadam spread tucked under elevated train tracks near London Bridge. "The Borough Market was really rough then," says Simon Costin, who was hired to do the set. "Now it's lovely, with cafés and Whole Foods, but then it was rough."

Costin went to see McQueen at the Hoxton studio to talk about the collection and show. "His mood boards were covered with blow-ups of images from *National Geographic* of gazelles being torn apart by tigers or lions," Costin says. "The savagery of the natural world." McQueen was also "talking about car crashes," he remembers. Costin mentioned the car accident scene in Irvin Kershner's spooky 1978 thriller *Eyes of Laura Mars*, and proposed to use derelict cars as set decor. "Yes, yes!" McQueen said.

Costin then suggested they wall in the space with huge sheets of corrugated metal punctured with holes, as if it had been blasted by machine-gun fire. Costin got the idea from the dramatic closing scene of Arthur Penn's classic *Bonnie and Clyde*, when the bank-robbing duo was mowed down by law officers in a hail of bullets. McQueen had never seen the film, so Costin showed it to him. "Oh yeah!" McQueen exclaimed after he viewed it. "Let's do that!" McQueen also said he liked the malevolent urban atmosphere of Uli Edel's 1989 violent drama *Last Exit to Brooklyn*.

McQueen called Simon Chaudoir for lighting and sound. "He told me how he wanted the audience lit, with a degradation of lighting like fabric dyeing," Chaudoir remembers. "And he said he wanted the sound of African animals at night." Costin and Chaudoir had to pull it all together quickly on a slim budget, as usual for McQueen: $100,000 for everything. "It was *just* the tipping point where we had sort of enough money to do it, but not quite enough," Costin says. Gainsbury's team of one hundred helpers constructed the set, installing bleachers, heaters, the corrugated metal walls, and a bunch of bashed-up cars.

McQueen asked Jurnjack to do the hair again. "We met in his showroom, and it was only him, alone, and he showed me animal skins—fox, yak—and said, 'Make me something sick,'" Jurnjack says. "He talked about all that is animalistic: the lion, the boar, the hyena. Everyone had teeth. It was aggressive."

Three days before the show, McQueen received writer Rob Tannenbaum of *Details* magazine at the studio to preview the collection. The place smelled of animal carcasses, bleach, and cigarette smoke. Katy England, dressed in a sleeveless AC/DC T-shirt, was busily styling the one hundred looks for the show. McQueen told Tannenbaum that he'd been "up all night taking stimulants." He showed off one outfit made of boar skin. Tannenbaum thought he said "foreskin."

"No!" he howled, but added, "I *have* worked in foreskin before." And he let out his manic cackle.

He grabbed another outfit—a cowhide dress that had blond human hair sewed into it. As he fondled the hair, he deadpanned: "This is an assistant who didn't work out."

The menswear had all arrived from the factories in Italy as expected, but the women's wear samples got stuck in customs at Heathrow. The clothes were supposed to come in on Tuesday evening—forty-eight hours before the show—but then officials told the McQueen team that the delivery wouldn't be made until the following day. McQueen couldn't wait that long. He shouted at England to drive to the airport immediately and she burst out in tears. She left at 10:30 P.M. with her boyfriend, and they sat at Heathrow for hours—"like waiting in a hospital emergency room," she said. Finally, at 2:00 A.M., they got the shipment, and got back to the studio at 4:30 A.M.

At noon, after working for nearly twenty-four hours straight, McQueen went to take a nap. When he returned later in the day, he gave England an apology gift—a small diamond, which he admitted to an onlooker "cost me four hundred quid." She forgave him. "I'm the hardest person to get along with," McQueen admitted. "I have mood swings."

Jurnjack arrived from Paris on the Eurostar a day before the show with trunks full of hairpieces. "I put everything I could find on the hair," he says.

"And the more animalistic and wild I went, the crazier happy Lee got." The makeup artist Topolino created a feral animal look for the women. Mira Chai Hyde oversaw the men's grooming; she and England agreed that the men would have nail polish and "bruisy eyeliner," England said.

The show was once again the last of London Fashion Week: on Thursday, February 27, at 8:15 P.M. McQueen dedicated it to "Mum and Dad." The crush out front was like I had never seen at a fashion show—not even a Galliano show. The crowd was a strange mix of fashion folk, students, groupies, and hooligans, and everyone pushing and shoving toward the narrow opening in the metal barriers.

The Harrods team was so put off by it that they bailed and went home. Those who did manage to squeeze through took their seats on cold benches next to Joan Collins, Oasis's Liam and Noel Gallagher, and a slew of pierced, pot-smoking punks. Some of the youths were throwing back shots of free tequila that were handed out at the entrance; others were sucking down bottles of beer they'd brought along. To set the mood, there was the soundtrack of African birds chirping and crickets cricking punctuated from time to time with a train thundering overhead.

I still remember when I arrived at the venue in the damp darkness: the lighting was eerie, with red spots revolving about, and there was a pungent aroma of rotting produce. I sensed the uneasy energy, as if at any moment a riot could erupt.

"There was a very edgy feeling to that show," Costin confirms.

"There was quite an ugly atmosphere," Chaudoir remembers. "Definitely more tension."

Backstage, McQueen was in a rage. At five minutes past nine, Naomi Campbell—who back then had a well-earned rep as modeling's greatest diva—still hadn't showed up. "She kept calling to say, 'I'm on my way, I'm on my way,'" said a model who overheard the conversations backstage. Finally, McQueen was so fed up he gave Campbell's clothes to another model and yelled loud enough for everyone to hear: "Naomi is cancelled!"

When Campbell finally arrived, McQueen told her, "Fuck you! You're too late."

Other models quietly approved. "Everybody else was kissing her butt," one remembers. "But he fired her, right there. I thought, 'Bravo! I love you for that.'"

The sound team unleashed a rattling mix of club music, including Prodigy's "Firestarter." Stella Tennant walked out in the opening look: a glove-tight, long-sleeved black vinyl dress with vinelike cutouts down the front.

Suddenly everything went dark and silent.

It was Chaudoir's worst nightmare.

"The power tripped out," he says now.

Backstage McQueen went nuts, shouting and ranting.

Out front, the nightmare turned even more sinister.

The hundred or so kids who hadn't managed to get into the show earlier surged past security and barriers and stormed the set. They rushed about like panicked animals, rashly searching for places to sit. In the free-for-all, someone kicked over a flaming grease pot and a car caught on fire just a few feet from me. The burning car looked cool in the night—some guests thought it was a part of the show—but I was starting to worry that it might actually blow up.

"Someone is going to get killed," a McQueen assistant said anxiously.

"My heart just stopped," Costin recalls.

One of Chaudoir's crew leapt down from the sound booth, ran backstage, grabbed a fire extinguisher, hustled out to the runway, jumped up on the car and, with a blast of chemicals, put out the flames. The crowd erupted into cheers, the lights and music came back on, and the show continued.

The girls looked fierce, with their wildly teased hair, little cat ears poking through, as they marched down the cement floor in vertiginous *bottines*. There were more shiny black vinyl dresses and trenches, shredded buttery suede shifts and tunics, and precisely tailored suits and coats in men's fabrics, like dove gray wool or pinstripe. The dresses often had cutouts of leaves or tiger stripes and asymmetrical hems; some outfits had reptile heads or tails or animal horns sprouting this way or that. Debra Shaw wore a butterscotch leather jacket with curly horns erupting from the shoulders, and bleach-splashed blue jeans; it became the signature look of the collection.

Dressed in a blue pullover, jeans, and running shoes, McQueen took his bow surrounded by his models as Chaudoir's team played Kool & the Gang's "Jungle Boogie." The crowd went *wild* for him—cheering, whistling, stomping, shouting, *howling*.

McQueen is "fashion's closest thing to a rock star," *The New York Times*'s Spindler wrote. "He isn't just part of the London scene; he is the scene." The show, which she likened to *The Island of Dr. Moreau*, was his "declaration that he will not be fashion's victim. No matter what happens at Givenchy, he will survive the jungle in his own house, where he is unmatched for talent, bravado, ideas and cutting skill."

WHEN I ARRIVED at the Givenchy headquarters on the Avenue George V a few days later for a *Newsweek International* cover story I was writing, Saint Phalle walked me to the studio to meet McQueen. He was pale and pudgy, dressed in a faded navy Adidas T-shirt, baggy jeans, and Nike American football shoes.

"This is my office," he said as he stood up from Mr. Givenchy's former desk overlooking Avenue George V. "Nice, eh?"

I immediately noticed the white Formica desktop was covered with bits of hair. Then I took a longer look at McQueen: he had a newly shorn Mohawk.

"I love to do things spontaneously," he cracked.

We all laughed.

I asked him what he thought about the house when they offered him the job. "I didn't know much," he admitted. "Of course, I knew about Audrey Hepburn and Jackie O., but not the house. It was quite twee—it was in the background, you wouldn't notice it. I knew it existed, but it wasn't any great shakes in relation to the 1990s. John turned that around—he gave it a blast of fresh air."

He said that the upcoming Givenchy women's runway collection was sparked by *Wigstock*, a documentary about the annual Greenwich Village drag queen music festival, and Russ Meyer's low-budget sexploitation films like *Faster, Pussycat! Kill! Kill!* "That kind of kitsch," he explained. "A full figure to look at, a complete attitude. Those women took their men, chewed them up and spit them out. Some people say I'm a misogynist. But it's not true. Opposite. I'm trying to promote women as the leaders. I saw how hard it was for my mum to take care of us, and I try to promote the respect and strength of women. Women have been on the opposing end of society and we are trying to make that change. Like the predator and the victim, and urban decay."

He stopped for a moment to reflect on his monologue.

"I'm a big mouth because I don't want to become a part of the fashion clique," he admitted. "I don't like the falseness of the fashion industry. And that gives me power to do what I want."

I asked him what the differences were between Givenchy and McQueen.

"People who go to Givenchy want to know that when they buy a suit it is the perfect suit. They don't want the attitude. Givenchy doesn't come with attitude. It comes with finesse."

The McQueen label, on the other hand "is about drugs, sex, and rock and roll," he said. "The soufflé mix that makes London rise." He chuckled at that one.

He told me that his McQueen brand was selling "quite well—fifty shops worldwide, 1.5 million pounds ($2.4 million) in sales turnover. But Givenchy gives me financial security."

That said, he wanted to make sure I understood something deeply important to him: "I never intended to be a multimillionaire. If I wanted to be a millionaire, I would have done more commercial clothes. I would have moved to New York and showed there."

Last, I asked him about his contentious relationship with the press and with his most ardent critics.

"I only get in trouble because I'm honest," he insisted. "But some people can't take it. It's like Hitler and the Holocaust. He destroyed millions of people because he didn't understand. That's what a lot of people have done to me, because they can't understand what I do."

XII

The next ten days were a whirlwind for Galliano and McQueen. It was Paris Fashion Week and both were being watched closely by the fashion tribe to see if they could keep up with their seemingly relentless new assignments. First was Galliano's maiden Dior women's ready-to-wear show, which was held at the Musée Guimet, France's museum for Asian art. For it, he channeled Chinese opium dens, with Anna May Wong–like models sashaying to Healy's club mix in slinky silk cheongsams, wasp-waist suits with swishy skirts, and his signature slip gowns. Throughout the show, the soundtrack was punctuated with a recording of 1950s movie siren Jayne Mansfield breathlessly uttering phrases like: "I would say I do have expensive taste" and "I like the Tiffany's of everything." When Galliano stepped out at the end to rapt applause, he was dressed in a suit and top hat and looked, Spindler said, "like a dignified couturier." It was obvious by this show that Galliano's heart was at Dior.

Two days later, it was just as obvious that, like an old lover replaced by a new one, Galliano had lost interest in his signature label. To keep up what had become expected theatrics, he chose a bankable dramatic theme: Cleopatra, specifically the 1917 Hollywood silent movie starring Theda Bara. He staged "The Return of Cleopatra" on the evening of Thursday, March 13, at the Musée National des Monuments Français in the Palais de Chaillot in Paris, and the set by Jean-Luc Ardouin was appropriately decadent and outlandish, with fallen monuments, hieroglyphics, graffiti-covered obelisks, piles of sand, and a sphinx.

Galliano's mythical muse for the collection was a wayward schoolgirl who loved the English 1970s punk rock band Siouxsie and the Banshees and old Cleopatra movies. Not surprisingly, much of it was absurd, like strappy beaded slave getups that barely covered the essentials, sculpted gold Egyptian headgear, and a gold lamé gown with molded scepter-holding hands across the breasts. Some outfits were so closely "inspired" by Bara's original costumes that Galliano was treading dangerously close to charges of plagiarism.

Robinson readily admitted to me that Galliano did not have the passion or hunger for innovation that McQueen had: "John likes to create images and he likes to technically work everything out rather than invent a new pleat," he said.

But the failure of this collection was worse than not exploring or pushing design further. "It increasingly feels as if Mr. Galliano is just adding gewgaws to what's already in the collection," Spindler snipped. "And it isn't going to do him any good that Alexander McQueen, his counterpart at Givenchy, is leaping forward every season at his own house, not only taking on a new subject each time but also experimenting."

McQueen knew what Spindler meant. "It's kind of a dangerous situation with John," he told *The New Yorker* in a profile published that week. "Because John is totally Frenchified now."

"'Frenchified,'" Spindler mused. "He might as well have said 'calcified.'"

AND THEN it was McQueen's turn.

Barely two weeks after the landmark "It's a Jungle Out There," McQueen had to put on his first Givenchy women's wear show. He chose to stage it at the Halles aux Chevaux, an old horse slaughterhouse on the edge of Paris, where cobblestone floors slanted toward drains for the flow of animal blood. No doubt there was some underlying meaning in his location choice.

Simon Ungless flew in to help out. "When I arrived in Paris, Lee was chain smoking, which was odd, had bottles of vodka in the freezer, which was even odder, and spent a great deal of time arranging coke deliveries," he remembers.

Cocaine is a rocking stimulant, and that helped McQueen keep up with his rapidly more demanding schedule. He increased his consumption during the weeks leading up to a show—bingeing like a college coed on speed during finals week. "He took coke like vitamin C," recalls an assistant. Then, to come off the high and get some sleep, he'd take Valium. One time, his flatmates couldn't wake him up. "He'd taken a massive amount and we thought he was dead," one recalls. "He was blue."

McQueen bragged about his drug use to reporters on the record, as if it gave him street cred—the East End thug mouthing off about how wasted he could get and still be fine. "[When] I get tired, I do what everyone else in the entertainment business does to keep going," he told a reporter for *Details* magazine, who assumed he meant snort cocaine. "You know what I mean, I'm not going to put it on paper for you. Sex, drugs and rock 'n' roll is what it is for me."

At Givenchy, fittings were, like at every traditional French couture house, very formal: whenever McQueen wanted to change something on the outfit he was reviewing, he had to tell the atelier head, who would mark the adjustments and then call the *petites mains* who would whisk the garment back to the atelier to be altered. This strict chain of command frustrated McQueen terribly. "Lee wanted to do it himself—he was so hands-on. He wanted none of that," Ungless says. But that was protocol and McQueen had to respect it—at least for the moment. "I'm not good at playing the star designer," he admitted. "Breaking down this rigid hierarchy and working as a team is the only way to go into the twenty-first century."

More disturbing, Ungless found, was the obvious disconnect between Givenchy executives and McQueen. "It was like when you are with an alcoholic parent and you don't know what's going to happen next," he says. "The bosses didn't know what they wanted and there was so much kept secret. There were so many parts of the company that Lee couldn't go into. He was deeply not happy with how things were there."

All of these unacknowledged conflicts became very apparent the day of the show. Saint Phalle arrived at the venue dressed in clothes from Galliano's last Givenchy collection rather than new McQueen-designed Givenchy ready-to-wear, which infuriated Ungless. "It was such a slap in the face," he says.

Jurnjack was doing the coiffures again, what he described as "umbrella hair": immense dome-shaped wigs cropped at the shoulder. "Someone came to see me backstage from Givenchy and said, 'Nicolas, you have to calm down the hair.' Because, you know, they had to sell the clothes. That's the way it is. I went to McQueen and Katy, and I said, 'Should I calm the hair on certain girls?' And he said, 'It's out of the question. Out of the question. They go out like they are.' Katy came backstage to make sure that I didn't make a concession on the look."

As show time approached, the drugs came out of hiding. "There were cocaine lines on the makeup tables backstage," remembers one observer. "It was for everyone: the models, McQueen, the stylists, everyone. Sibylle was trying to keep the photographers from coming back because she didn't want them to see it or photograph it." After that, McQueen was told: "You can do whatever you want, but not in front of the press."

When Naomi Campbell showed up—two hours early this time—there was more drama. Earlier that week, she and Kate Moss went to Givenchy to try on the clothes they would wear in the show. "They weren't friends with Lee then and they treated him like a piece of shit," Ungless remembers.

McQueen was still upset with Campbell for the "Jungle" debacle, and her behavior during the fittings made him angrier. He decided to exact his revenge on her at the show. When she went to her corner to get dressed, there were different clothes on her rack.

"These are not my looks!" she screeched.

"Yes, they are," McQueen replied pointedly.

"He had changed them *all*," Ungless says now, laughing at the memory.

When it came time for her turn to walk the runway, McQueen saw that she was dawdling backstage. "Lee went up and pushed her out because she was late for her exit," Ungless recalls. "It was brilliant."

MOST SHOWS ARE a straightforward parade of clothes on beautiful, thin women. Sometimes the models stop and pose. Sometimes they twirl. Up until the 1970s, couturiers staged their shows in their house salons in reverent silence except for the announcement of the number and name of the look and an occasional smattering of applause. When the ready-to-wear designers joined the fray in the 1970s, the Paris shows moved to tents in the Louvre's Cour Carrée. The statuesque star models of the era—Iman, Jerry Hall, Dalma, Pat Cleveland—livened up the process by swishing down the catwalks to disco. But it was still a parade of prettiness—until Westwood, Galliano, and McQueen came along. Westwood dressed up the models like pirates. Galliano told his girls to playact as romantic heroines. McQueen made them march like warriors and stagger like rape victims.

And for his Givenchy ready-to-wear debut for more than twelve hundred invitees, McQueen added another new element to the presentation: porn. The cobblestone walkway in the slaughterhouse was punctuated with old Art Deco iron-cast streetlights, and McQueen instructed the models—including Moss, Bruni, and Campbell—to work those poles like cavorting go-go dancers. It was quite a shock for the old-time Givenchy clients.

The clothes were a mix of tidy tailoring, such as smart gray flannel suits and Audrey Hepburn–like sleeveless shifts, and tawdry party wear, like leopard-print catsuits and tight black vinyl dresses—those Russ Meyer girls with their bountiful bosoms bursting forth. The soundtrack, again, was a message, no doubt directed to Galliano: Sparks's "This Town Ain't Big Enough for Both of Us." At the end of the show, a Mohawked McQueen, dressed in a dark suit with a geranium pink shirt, took his bow with bawdy, busty French actress Béatrice Dalle erupting from a shiny black dress.

The show, says an assistant, "was a backlash. He wanted to kill the bourgeois out of Givenchy. He wanted to make the old clients wince."

He did.

"It takes a certain nerve to face an audience that panned your work two months earlier. But Mr. McQueen has that particular nerve," *The New York Times*'s Spindler wrote. "McQueen has matured so much in that short space of time . . . [and] with his new Mohawk, [he] looked, deservedly, more than a little proud when he took his bow."

"What the herd loves about McQueen (his newness) is what they also hate (his bad taste)," American *Vogue*'s Katherine Betts smartly surmised. "He may be tacky, but McQueen's not afraid to break out of the pack. I say God bless him. At least he's not cloning."

NOW THAT MCQUEEN HAD MONEY, he could afford a better studio: he found one on Rivington Street, in Shoreditch, with two big rooms—one for sewing, the other for administration—tucked under the rooftops, with loads of windows and natural light. There was also a potential major change in staff: Sarah Heard was finally graduating from Central Saint Martins and talking about enrolling in the master's degree for fine art at Ruskin College in Oxford. McQueen would have been lost without her. Happily, she decided to stay on, which freed him up to work on independent projects, such as overseeing the cover design of Björk's new album, *Homogenic*.

People who had known McQueen for a while were surprised by how much he had grown up in such a short time, as if he had evolved from a shy, twitchy kid to a self-assured young man overnight. Lise Strathdee, his former boss at Gigli, ran into him coming off the Eurostar in London. As they stood in the taxi line together, she recalls, "He was all shoptalk. I could tell even though he was moaning and groaning about dramas he was having with the pleating at the [Givenchy] atelier that he was in his element and loved it."

Another former colleague saw him in the street in London one day and says: "McQueen had an open shirt, a shaved head, false teeth and had a Vuitton bag. I thought, 'Oh my God, he's polished himself up.'"

SHORTLY AFTER THE COUTURE SHOWS, the actress Nicole Kidman spoke with Dior to see if the house could dress her for the Academy Awards ceremony, which was on March 24 at the Shrine Auditorium in Los Angeles. She would be accompanying her then-husband Tom Cruise, who was nominated for Best Actor for his role in *Jerry Maguire*. Her career was still very much on the ascendancy—the twenty-nine-year-old's most recent performance, as Isabel Archer in director Jane Campion's *The Portrait of a Lady*, had finally brought her stardom. But she hadn't quite made Hollywood's A-list, and she knew that the right look on the Oscars red carpet and the publicity it would generate would bump her up there.

Kidman became a Galliano client when he was on the Passage du Cheval Blanc, not long after the São Schlumberger show. "I would trust him to send me something even if I hadn't seen it, and know it would be great," she told me back then. "I just love to wear his clothes. You feel so wonderful in them."

In the winter of 1997, Kidman and Cruise were living in London, where they were starring in Stanley Kubrick's last picture, the sexual thriller *Eyes Wide Shut*. In February, she traveled to Paris for the day to review the Dior couture collection. She selected Absinthe, the slim chartreuse satin column with mink-trimmed side slits and a chenille mesh back. It was a bold move; everyone else at the time was wearing pastels and primary colors on the red carpet. But Galliano applauded the choice, knowing that green on redheads was always a winning look.

There was one hitch: the first one to order it, the New York socialite Anne Bass, had to approve the sale as well as Kidman being the first to wear it publicly. Dior contacted Bass in Aspen, where she was skiing, and she said yes. A team of Dior atelier assistants traveled twice to London for fittings.

When Kidman stepped onto the red carpet wearing that vibrant green, she later admitted she felt a "little over the top." But she glowed as she walked through the sea of black tie and demure dresses, most everyone immediately agreeing she looked like a million bucks. "I couldn't believe that dress," she later told me. "It was just one of those things that you feel so honored just to even be able to wear it." Kidman in the chartreuse Dior still makes lists of top ten best Oscar looks and solidified Galliano as a world-class—and famous—designer.

DESPITE HIS IMMENSE SUCCESS and the unquestioned support he had from Arnault, LVMH, and the media, Galliano was still up to his bad behavior and hijinks. The night after his show in March, he blew off attending Anna Wintour's *Vogue* dinner at the Chez Georges restaurant—a move so insulting that *Women's Wear Daily* wrote up the incident, calling him fashion's "perpetual no-show." However, later that night, *Women's Wear* reported that he was at Les Bains Douches nightclub—"trying to hide behind a mop of micro-braid hair extensions on his way in."

Now that he was a big deal designer, he decided he needed a swankier home. He called Duclos, since she had found and helped him negotiate his last rental. "Jacqui, I really want a bigger apartment now," he told her. "You know my taste, please help me find something." His only specification: he wanted to be in the Marais, the oldest section of Paris with small cobblestone streets and sixteenth-century buildings and the gay quarter of the city, like Soho in London, with a plethora of LGBT bars and nightclubs. Duclos found what she describes as "a perfect apartment" on rue de la Perle, right behind the Musée Picasso. It was on the first floor, 140 square meters, with two reception rooms and a big chandelier. And she negotiated him a bang-up deal, even getting the realtor commission waived. When he went to sign the papers, the notary remarked: "I have never seen anybody do a deal like this."

Once he moved in, he turned his back on Duclos. "I never even got a thank-you note," Duclos says. "Nothing."

Sometime afterward, she decided to write to Galliano to, as the French say, *vider son sac*, or empty her bag—meaning clear her conscience. She addressed point by point his rude behavior and his disregard of his staff and supporters. She concluded: "John, I really wish you lots of luck in the future. But I do believe what goes around comes around. And one day you are going to pay."

GIVENCHY READY-TO-WEAR director Leslie Johnsen was horrified to see McQueen's living conditions in Paris. He was, after all, the creative director of an haute couture fashion house. "You are paying a lot for him to do the work. Support him properly," she told Givenchy and LVMH executives. She lobbied to get McQueen a better place, and eventually LVMH brass relented: he moved around the corner to a handsome two-bedroom flat in a seventeenth-century *hôtel particulier*, or city mansion, on the rue du Braque—a block and a half from Galliano's new digs. "It was amazing," Johnsen remembers, "with a cobblestone courtyard and crooked stairs." Johnsen also arranged to have McQueen picked up every morning by a car and driver, like all other top LVMH executives and Galliano. "Maybe I spoiled him," she says. "But he deserved it."

When McQueen was in Paris, he would rise early, have breakfast of a

Debra Shaw in John Galliano's first Christian Dior show: the "Masai" collection, Haute Couture, S/S 1997.

"Masai" ball gown from Dior Haute Couture, S/S 1997.

Alexander McQueen and models from "It's a Jungle Out There" for *Newsweek International*'s cover, 1997.

Alexander McQueen and Béatrice Dalle at Givenchy Prêt-à-Porter, F/W 1997–98.

(*left*) Naomi Campbell in McQueen's first Givenchy show, wearing Philip Treacy's golden sheep horn hat, Haute Couture, S/S 2007.

(*right*) McQueen's "VOSS" collection, S/S 2001.

Shalom Harlow spray-painted by robots in McQueen's "No. 13," S/S 1999.

Milla Jovovich at the premiere of *The Fifth Element* at the Cannes Film Festival in May 1997, wearing Galliano's Cleopatra gown from Dior Prêt-à-Porter, F/W 1997–98.

Nicole Kidman at the 69th Academy Awards in March 1997, wearing a silk chartreuse gown from Galliano's Dior "Masai" collection.

Courtney Love at the Golden Globes in January 2000, wearing a gown from Galliano's "Hobo" collection, Dior Haute Couture, S/S 2000.

John Galliano's
"Filibustiers," S/S 1993.

McQueen's "Dance of the Twisted Bull,"
S/S 2002.

(*left*) David Bowie in concert wearing McQueen's Union Jack frock coat, 1997.
(*right*) Kate Moss wearing Galliano's Union Jack jacket, S/S 1993.
(*below*) McQueen's "What A Merry-Go-Round," F/W 2001–02.

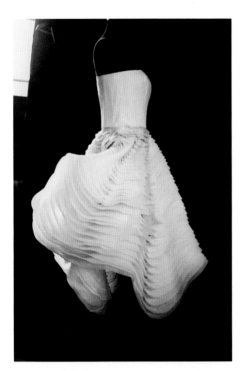

(*left*) Galliano's shellfish dress, 1987. (*right*) McQueen's "Irere," S/S 2003.

McQueen's "Widows of Culloden," F/W 2006–07.

McQueen's "Widows of Culloden,"
F/W 2006–07.

Kate Moss hologram in McQueen's
"Widows of Culloden,"
F/W 2006–07.

John Galliano; Liz Tilberis; Princess Diana, wearing Galliano's first official design for Christian Dior; Hélène Arnault; and Bernard Arnault at the Metropolitan Museum of Art's Costume Institute Gala, December 1996.

(*left*) Alexander McQueen receives the honor of Commander of the Most Excellent Order of the British Empire from Queen Elizabeth II, October 2003.

(*right*) Alexander McQueen and Isabella Blow, 2005.

Alexander and Joyce McQueen, 2004.

McQueen at Isabella Blow's funeral, May 2007.

Galliano at Steven Robinson's funeral, April 2007.

(*left*) McQueen and Treacy's "La Dame Bleue," S/S 2008.
(*right*) Alexander McQueen and Philip Treacy at "La Dame Bleue," S/S 2008.

McQueen's "The Girl Who Lived
in the Tree," F/W 2008–09.

McQueen's "The Horn of Plenty,"
F/W 2009–10.

McQueen's "Plato's Atlantis," S/S 2010.

McQueen's last collection, "Angels and Demons," F/W 2010–11.

Tom Ford, Alexander McQueen, and Annabelle Neilson at Harry's Bar in London, February 2010.

John Galliano and
Grace Coddington, 2013.

croissant, cigarette, and coffee, and head to work. He'd arrive at the Givenchy studio dressed in a cotton check shirt and low-slung baggy jeans belted loosely, his boxer shorts rising above the waistline—a look that definitely raised eyebrows among the old-time staff. He'd be grouchy, but he'd be ready, and he earned everyone's respect in the studio and the atelier with his work ethic: "He was like a Mack truck," Johnsen remembers. "I have never met anyone so brilliantly focused." McQueen liked to play club or soul music as he worked—he loved Mary J. Blige—and often broke into a little dance. "We'd laugh," Johnsen says warmly. "We'd laugh so hard." At the end of the day, he'd head back to the Marais with his assistants and have a drink at one of the bars in the quartier. "This image of the Bad Boy was so false," recalls a Givenchy assistant. "He was really kind and soft hearted. John was not kind—people had contempt for John. He never invited anyone out for a drink. Alexander—yes, all the time."

The one place McQueen wasn't winning hearts at Givenchy was in the executive suite. There was an increasingly relentless tug-of-war between McQueen and the ever-conservative French managers: They hired him for his creativity, his pomposity, and his talent, yet they couldn't understand him and tried to rein him in whenever possible. "The suits wanted him to be controlled," remembers an assistant. "We found fantastic stuff from Mr. Givenchy's archives that could have been mined amazingly, but they never wanted us to take risks."

McQueen also had no patience for the schmoozing and folderol that came with the job. "When he didn't want to be somewhere, he wouldn't go," Johnsen remembers. "He stood up the most important people in the business." He didn't show up for meetings with Suzy Menkes. He blew off a breakfast meeting with Anna Wintour in New York. Another day in New York, Johnsen says, "I had to drag him out of bed for an interview with [CNN's then-style reporter] Elsa Klensch. And I won't tell you who he was in bed with."

"Alexander had periods where he was really difficult," an assistant confirms. "He was young and his success came fast—faster than John's—and he had a really hard time digesting it all."

FRANÇOIS BAUFUMÉ and Valérie Hermann had great ambition for the Galliano brand and put a new business plan in motion. In May, Galliano moved out of the Passage du Cheval Blanc, his work home for the last three years, and into an old doll factory on the rue d'Avron in the northeastern reaches of Paris. Finally, Galliano and his team had space and natural light; airy conference rooms; well-appointed offices; a proper atelier; a state-of-the-art computer system; even a small garden out front with a charming cobblestone walk. But with the new digs came a new protocol and formality: no one had the right to walk into Galliano's office or studio without a scheduled appointment, even to ask a quick question or get a swatch or embroidery approved. "We had no more contact with John," an assistant recalls.

Following the advice of Bergdorf Goodman executive vice president Joseph Boitano, Galliano's brand would now have, in addition to the women's runway collection, a twice-a-year pre-collection. "To build a business, you must have those interim collections to keep the merchandise fresh and the floor exciting," Boitano explained.

Baufumé and Hermann planned to increase focus on the U.S. market—which already accounted for 35 percent of sales—by taking the pre-collection to New York so more retailers could see and buy it, and redesigning the Galliano shop at Bergdorf Goodman. They wanted to push growth in Asia beyond the brand's primary market in Hong Kong and were looking to hire a rep in Japan to help make that happen. They also wanted to develop the brand's accessories business, in particular handbags—a product sector that is easy to produce, easy to sell, and has a substantial mark-up—and eventually roll out independent boutiques.

Much was afoot at Dior too. Arnault decided it was time for his dearest brand to get a major facelift—not just on the runway, but in every aspect of the company. He instructed Baufumé to cut the number of Dior's licenses, from the rice cookers in Japan to the middle-market women's suits designed, produced, and sold in the United States by Jones Apparel Group. "At the moment, we're redefining the Dior image," Galliano explained. "It is difficult. Some things over the years haven't quite come up to the standard, so we are remaking that, more in keeping with a unified relation."

Arnault also decided it was time to revisit Dior's retail model—in particular, the flagship store's decor—so it would be stylistically in alignment with Galliano's modern romantic clothes. Since its opening in 1947, the Dior boutique on the ground floor of 30, Avenue Montaigne had been a symbol of understated elegance, with its demure gray-and-white palette and prim sales-women—and the satellite stores around the world echoed that look and service. Arnault was tired of all that bourgeois haughtiness. He wanted Dior to glisten, to ooze excess, and attract the sort of new-money customer who never looked at price tags.

He called Peter Marino, a New York–based American architect known for a sleek, opulent decor, to overhaul the Paris flagship store. Marino was a favorite of the fashion set. A graduate of Cornell, in the 1970s he became a regular at Andy Warhol's Factory, and eventually redesigned it as well as Warhol's uptown townhouse. In the early 1990s, Marino made his name in retail with the design of Barney's new uptown outpost—an over-the-top project that reportedly cost well over $150 million and contributed to the company's bankruptcy.

Marino proposed attacking the space like Baron Haussmann's nineteenth-century redesign of Paris—effectively reconfiguring the entire floor plan inside the façade. "Dior was an icon," Marino said. "And I had an image in my head of how it should look." He suggested a soaring rotunda for the entrance, walls of giant movie screens playing highlights of Dior shows, new broad hallways and light-filled sales spaces, and a mix of neo–Louis XVI and rococo Louis XV decor made of the most luxurious of materials possible. Arnault approved wholeheartedly.

In May, McQueen and his Givenchy team traveled to Tokyo to restage the ready-to-wear show for eighteen hundred guests. The Japanese were luxury's most important market sector at the time, accounting for up to 50 percent of sales for some brands. However, it was the first time a major international luxury brand staged such a major fashion event in Japan.

McQueen arrived with an entourage of thirty—including Arthur, England, and Brickhill; Jurnjack; and models Carla Bruni and Helena Christensen—and took up an entire floor at the new Park Hyatt, a hotel later made famous in Sofia Coppola's film *Lost In Translation*. Saori Masuda, Givenchy head of PR in Japan at the time, lined up several interviews with Japanese media for McQueen. "He was always late," she says, which in Japanese culture is seen as a profound lack of respect. He went to see Rei Kawakubo at the Comme des Garçons headquarters, and he was late for that too. But he loved

Tokyo—the culture, the architecture, and the fashion. One day he went shopping in trendy Harajuku and a bunch of stylish youths followed him like groupies. "They went wild for him," Jurnjack says. "He was a god to them."

AFTER YEARS OF STEEP DECLINE and predictions in the press by critics and fashion players alike that haute couture was on the verge of extinction, it appeared in July 1997 to not only be alive, but vibrantly so. More celebrities traveled to Paris for the couture shows that month than had in ages; a new, younger clientele suddenly emerged and made the front row sexy again; and the media coverage surged. According to the Chambre Syndicale de la Haute Couture, press accreditation increased by 15 percent in a year; this season there were 920 journalists from 43 countries; 200 photographers; and 60 television reporters. "Even the most ardent doubters have come to agree—couture is a gold mine," *Women's Wear* reported. "Not in terms of dresses sold—which for most houses is very few—but in terms of publicity and buzz." Arnault's purposeful shift from hoity-toity fashion to hype had worked.

The star attractions were Galliano and McQueen, of course—the "two impertinent roast beefs," as *Le Figaro* derisively called them. They were showmen, and everyone wanted to see what they were going to do next.

But they weren't the only big draws that season. Karl Lagerfeld, with Amanda Harlech at his side, seemed revitalized. Gianni Versace, who had just returned from several months of sick leave reportedly to battle ear cancer, put on one of the house's finest shows in years. Even classicist Valentino had embraced the new hype model—at least for couture. "We really don't care about selling [couture] dresses," Valentino CEO Giancarlo Giammetti said. "Any dresses we produce are at a loss to the house. The classic couture customer is not daring enough, and if you play it safe, there's no buzz." Jean Paul Gaultier president Donald Potard explained it all in plain dollars and cents: a couture show cost $1 million to produce but with all the new television and print coverage it generated about $25 million worth of advertising. "Even if I sold zero dresses, I won," he said.

Some of the old school lashed out at the hype. Saint Laurent scoffed that Galliano's and McQueen's first couture shows were "ridiculous spectacle which would be better placed on a concert stage." His business partner Pierre Bergé preached that couture was "a question of integrity and honesty . . .

words that Mr. Arnault does not know," and added: "They are going to kill couture."

Baufumé brushed off the bluster. "Certain of our fashion colleagues say we've ruined couture, but that seems to me to be greatly exaggerated," he responded. "Galliano attracted the youngest clients, the most happening ones. Some people want a sleek, fast racecar. Others choose a reliable model."

MCQUEEN WAS FEELING far more confident about his work at the couture house now after six months on the job. He understood all that seamstresses could do, which allowed him to unleash his vast knowledge and creativity. "Everything was in his head," Pons says. "He could describe a geisha outfit and name every piece of the kimono, or he would say, 'Let's do a Jacques Fath here, or a Madame Grès detail here.' I thought: 'This guy knows it *all*.' [And] he could twist it all around and make it his own."

For the show—fall–winter 1997–98 haute couture—McQueen had a few ideas he wanted to bat around with his favorite collaborator, Simon Costin—mainly tribal influences, which he was studying, and how couture's "refined cutting techniques [could be combined] with something that is tied together and made of organic matter or animal matter or leaves," Costin explains.

Costin liked it, but he says, "by that point I found it easier to spin a little story to have something for me to hang the design of the set on." He came up with a tale of a doctor who traveled the world collecting beautiful women, shipped them back to his Paris laboratory, and spliced them together.

Then Costin asked himself:

"What would the doctor do with the [body] leftovers? Feed them to the birds!"

Since McQueen loved birds and Costin had worked on "The Birds" collection, it made sense to bring birds back as a reference. After looking at several possible show locations, they zeroed in on the grand hall of the Paris Descartes University, a medical school on the Left Bank. Costin suggested they have a big cage of ravens and blackbirds as part of the set. McQueen approved. They titled it: "Eclect Dissect."

For the hair, McQueen called on Jurnjack and for hats, Treacy. He explained that there would be fifty outfits worn by fifty models—there would be no changes backstage—and each would have a distinct look. Some would wear hats, but most would have elaborate, sculpted hair. "Alexander said: 'Take no prisoners,'" Jurnjack recalls. "'Do pieces for museums. Imagine them in the Louvre. The Met. This time you massacre.'"

Jurnjack dreamed up all sorts of wild concepts. "We did birdcages in hair," he recalls. "Falcons. Dracula. An orange Inca coiffure." There were giant fur-covered discs hovering over ears. Football-size black mussel shells sprouting from temples. Black hair sculpted like shiny gift ribbons. Golden braids swooped up into towering beehives. Wispy bouffants the size of a beach ball. "We went so far," he says. "Certain pieces took ten days to create."

During the days that led up to the show, everything came together almost seamlessly. Shaun Leane delivered long silver claws he designed for Debra Shaw and other models to wear. Everyone discovered during "the unveiling of the hats" the beauty that Treacy had created, such as crowns of pheasant tail feathers shooting up into the air and a birdcage chapeau with a live bird in it. McQueen asked Mira Chai Hyde to cut a mammoth, shaggy, knee-length horsehair coat into shape. (Think *The Addams Family*'s Cousin Itt as a coat.) "I spent three days working on it," she recalls. "It was an interesting blend of high-end couture and punk."

For the set, Costin played with various romantic gothic inspirations such as *The Cabinet of Dr. Caligari* (again) and Mary Shelley's *Frankenstein*. He strung up red curtains as a backdrop and threw down oriental carpets and tiger skin rugs on the floor for the runway. He finished it all off with a giant birdcage and brought in several large crows from the countryside to put in it. Honor Fraser would walk with a hooded falcon on her gloved arm—a nod to Blow and Hilles. "It's all romantic, poetic and decadent, with the eeriness of a Goya painting," McQueen explained during a preview of the collection for *Women's Wear*. "In terms of showmanship, strength and unpredictability, they haven't seen anything yet."

Everything seemed somewhat under control and ready.

Then, twenty-four hours before the show, all hell broke loose. The *Sunday Times* of London published a story claiming that McQueen was using real "human teeth, and other body parts" in the collection. *Women's Wear* further reported that to avoid police confiscating the clothes for testing, McQueen "shuttled them to a clandestine location, just the way the Pentagon used to shuttle bombs during the Cold War." The house denied it all, claiming every-thing in question was made in resin in the Avenue George V ateliers. "It's a lie from beginning to end," Spitzer said.

Just before the show began, another major drama erupted: Suzy Menkes found herself sitting close to the raven cage and let it be known to Givenchy staff that she did not like birds and needed to be moved. The staff, sensing her fear, changed her seat without question.

Isabella blew in wearing one of the skintight black vinyl dresses from Mc-Queen's first Givenchy ready-to-wear collection, a bird hat, and a heavy, greasy chain, which she dragged across the set's Persian carpets. She explained that the chain represented "the burden woman carried though her life."

The clothes were, like the story of the show, a splicing together of the Best of McQueen, but made with the finest fabrics and craftsmanship instead of with remnants from a barrow covered with car paint and held together with duct tape. There were "Highland Rape" fitted tartan suits with plunging necklines; "The Birds" pencil skirts in leather with cut-outs of the flying spar-rows; a "Jack the Ripper" sheer black top draped with thin ropes of jet beads; an "It's a Jungle Out There"–like leather dress with a red feather neckline and bird skulls on the shoulders; Ruti Danan's mother's black lace mantilla from "Dante," this time held up by a skeletal hand; even a reinterpretation of the cocoon coats McQueen used to make for Romeo Gigli.

There were also glorious reinterpretations of the best of fashion: a Saint Laurent–like trench in a black crocodile so light it appeared nearly translu-cent; a tomato red Dior New Look–style coatdress with a belted waist, and long full skirt; Galliano's Schlumberger show geisha robes tailored and em-broidered so beautifully they were like fashion fantasies of Japanese perfec-tion; and a Galliano signature bias-cut navy gown with a shooting star across the bodice. As Simon Ungless once sang to McQueen: "Anything you can do, I can do better."

"McQueen left his audience . . . breathless . . . woozy, gasping for air," Spindler wrote. "His show was in turns so fabulous, so odd, so overwrought, so painstakingly created that it inspired awe as much as fear. . . . What was astounding was the absolute masterpieces of technique he created, upping the ante with every single outfit. It was like being force-fed a four-star, twelve-course dinner with the chef watching every bite."

Galliano concurred. Sometime after the show, he rang up Jurnjack and they talked about McQueen and "Eclect Dissect."

"I think it was really impressive," Galliano said. "He's pulled ahead."

THE NEXT DAY, Galliano staged his Dior couture show in the lush eighteenth-century botanical gardens of the Parc de Bagatelle on the western edge of Paris for one thousand guests. To create the ambiance he wanted, he hired Michael Howells, a British-born, London-based film production designer, and explained that the show was a tribute to Christian Dior's passion for gardening. For six days, Howells and his team busily constructed a temporary greenhouse in the gardens and filled it with crystal chandeliers festooned with satin ribbons; rose petals and white feathers on the ground; and a *Sleeping Beauty*–like bed made of moss with topiary bedposts, surrounded by lilies, peacocks, statues and vases, blue butterflies, and six thousand roses. One section was decorated with poppies. "John came down and saw all the poppies and said, 'Oh, I love this! I want some of those for the dresses!' So we had to pull them out and send them back to the house so they could be stitched onto the hem of a dress."

Galliano explained before the show that this collection was based on Mata Hari "and all her guises." Yes, yet another historical femme fatale. "Incredibly international, she was born in Holland, married an Indian prince, lived in Bali and danced amongst literary circles," he gushed, adding with all seriousness that the clothes would have "that feeling of espionage."

The day of the show, Paris was blisteringly hot. "We had a couple of models faint from the heat," Howells remembers. Some of the old guard skipped the show—most notably Galliano's longtime champion São Schlumberger, who was still miffed about what she considered rude treatment at his Dior debut at the Grand Hôtel in January. "It was so uncomfortable," she said. "We waited more than an hour, and I was seated in half a chair."

But as Baufumé boasted, there was a host of new potential clients, who were all mingling as if they were at a cocktail party for the rich, beautiful, and famous. Many sported smart straw panama hats that Dior gave out as protection from the roasting afternoon sun. Lucy Ferry was there with her husband, Bryan Ferry, who said he came along to see the "theater" of the show. Steven Spielberg's wife, the actress Kate Capshaw, attended with her girlfriend and fellow actress Rita Wilson (Mrs. Tom Hanks). English pop star Phil Collins sat in the front row "with my lady" Orianne Cevey, who, he explained, was interested in fashion. (She is now a jewelry designer.) He added that it was his first fashion show. Demi Moore, a fashion maven at the time, chatted with *Harper's Bazaar* editor Liz Tilberis.

When the show finally began, the models swanned through like Belle Époque clichés. There were grandes dames in Edwardian tweed suits with tight corsetlike waists and lean, floor-sweeping skirts. There were Klimt heroines in sheer gowns with shimmery geometric beading and Toulouse-Lautrec prostitutes in mini pouf skirts and black stretch boots held up by garters. Some models came out in Ndebele tribal cloaks and tall silver coiled collars—the sort that elongates the neck like a giraffe's and seems dreadfully uncomfortable. The "show piece"—because Galliano *always* had to have a show piece—was a body-hugging dress of one thousand pieces sewed together to look like a peacock tattoo with dragonfly wings on the shoulder. Galliano took his bow wearing a white three-piece suit without a shirt and a drop earring dangling from his left lobe.

Women's Wear decried it "disarmingly beautiful." Spindler proclaimed that Galliano "has earned his spot among the great couturiers."

The problem was, as *Le Figaro*'s Janie Samet pointed out in her review the following morning: "This fashion from turn-of-the-last-century does not correspond with the end of ours." Galliano was yet again wholly out of touch with modern women and contemporary life. His clothes were magnificent reproductions of chic ensembles of another era—an era of corsets and coquetry—and while they looked gorgeous on those pin-thin twenty-year-olds on the runway, they looked ridiculous on mature women in the street or at a party or even on a red carpet.

A WEEK AFTER the couture shows wrapped up, Gianni Versace was murdered in front of his Miami home. After a weeklong manhunt, the suspect—a California-born spree killer named Andrew Cunanan—was found shot dead on a boat in a marina in what police stated was a suicide. His connection to Versace was loose—they reportedly met briefly at a reception in San Francisco in 1990. But, it appeared to investigators, Cunanan—a lying, drug-addled gigolo—was obsessed with celebrity, and in particular with Gianni

Versace, a famous, self-made, jet-set, gay multimillionaire. This was the life Cunanan wanted but could not attain.

Versace was the first designer targeted because he was a fashion icon. The fashion community was simultaneously on high alert and in mourning. Versace had been targeted by a psychopath because of his fame. No longer were designers simply creative sorts who made clothes; they were international celebrities who made headlines and attracted stalkers, or worse. Arnault and his tycoon confreres had succeeded: luxury fashion had become a global industry, for better and for worse.

Just over a month later, a sedan carrying Princess Diana and her playboy companion, Dodi Fayed, crashed while speeding away from paparazzi in Paris; Fayed was killed instantly and Diana died at a hospital a few hours later. Though he was an ardent antiroyalist and had only met Diana at official receptions, McQueen confessed: "I was devastated by the news on Sunday. She was a light through stormy clouds . . . an inspiration . . . the only British royal I would like to have dressed."

For Galliano, the loss was more personal. He had become friendly with the princess since designing her gown for the Met gala eight months earlier and was invited to the funeral at Westminster Abbey. "She had a gorgeous sense of irony," he lamented, "and was always one of the girls."

WITHIN WEEKS, the European show cycle was once again in full swing and the big story in the fashion press that season was the neck-and-neck race between Galliano and McQueen for creative superiority. When asked how he felt about the competition, Galliano responded dismissively: "I don't really think about it."

McQueen, however, was becoming obsessed with Galliano. He felt his Givenchy job was the couture equivalent of a hand-me-down; he was still having to beg Givenchy executives for financing to do what he wanted. "Not having the same budgets as Galliano [had at Dior]—that was always a bugbear," Costin says. "Dior was through the roof. The Dior shows—you could not get more overblown. Lee was always mouthing off about [it]. There was always a rant. That was a daily occurrence."

"Alexander couldn't understand why John could have so much money to do what he wanted and he couldn't," says a Givenchy staffer. "I'd have to go see the boss and say: 'McQueen wants this. We need more.' We always needed more."

"Alexander had far greater talent than John," says another former Givenchy assistant. "He invented things and made them himself. John had plenty of books and pictures to nourish him, then Steven would design. John had this talent to create a story or to be a director. But couturier?"

Yet Galliano received all the praise, the major money, the unquestioned support from Arnault and his men—and this ate at McQueen. "He was so competitive with John," says Michael Roberts. "You couldn't mention John around him. If you wore something of John's when you saw him, he would freak out."

To make matters worse, there were rumors that McQueen was about to be fired from Givenchy. "Everyone at the London shows seems to have a story about how Bernard Arnault . . . is soliciting advice on whether to keep [McQueen]," Spindler reported in *The New York Times*. McQueen slapped the stories down—"I have a two-year contract," he said—and focused instead on his upcoming London show. For it, he was pondering the notion of yin-yang, the Chinese philosophy of how contrary forces like dark and light and life and death are complementary and interdependent. For McQueen, it was a commentary on his situation with Givenchy and his signature brand and his life in Paris and in London.

To help him realize his vision, he called Simon Costin. McQueen explained that the first half of the collection would be sexually charged designs in dark tones—as he usually did for McQueen; the second half would be all white, tailored and chic, like his work for Givenchy. As he saw it, the two companies had "two different types of clients," he said. "One is a prim, proper, Parisian lady; the other is a mental case"—and the dichotomy was starting to pull him apart.

To further evoke the contrast, Costin says, McQueen "wanted the catwalk or the environment to change color, so it would be a white runway for a black collection, and then there would be a break, and somehow everything would turn black and the collection would be white."

As with "La Poupée," McQueen asked Costin to incorporate water in the show somehow. Costin knew someone at Imperial Chemical Industries (ICI) who could supply Perspex made to measure. Costin designed a low catwalk made up of sixteen clear covered tanks that could be filled with water. He proposed that for the first half of the show, the tanks be under-lit by fluorescents, provided by Simon Chaudoir, so they would appear stark white; for the second half of the show, the water would be pumped full of black ink until the tanks appeared black. The only hitch would be the time it took for the water to turn black.

"How would you feel if there would be no fashion for five or six minutes, while the catwalk becomes a piece of installation in its own right?" Costin asked McQueen. "You would sit and slowly watch these black clouds drift into the water."

"Yeah," McQueen replied. "Let's do it."

In addition to the black walkway for the second half, McQueen wanted gold rain to fall on the models. He had decided to call the show "The Golden Shower," a reference to the sexual act of urinating on a partner, though McQueen surely had other underlying meanings to it too, like how he believed Arnault was pissing on him, or what he wanted to do to Givenchy, Arnault, and Paris. He chose Ann Peebles's original version of "I Can't Stand the Rain" as the soundtrack's centerpiece.

Costin and Chaudoir proposed installing a sprinkler system the length of the runway and Chaudoir could hit the spray of water with a golden light so it looked like gold rain. And they could do the whole thing for about $125,000—far less than a Galliano show in Paris.

McQueen was pleased. But McQueen's sponsors at American Express, which had contributed 30,000 pounds ($50,000) to the show budget, were not: when they learned the title of the show, they balked. McQueen rechristened it "Untitled."

He staged it in an old bus depot near Victoria Station and more than two thousand people attended, including pop star Janet Jackson, who had become a McQueen devotee. The show began with rolls of thunder and cracks of lightning flashing around the room. The models walked down the white runway in sheer black shirts and sheaths, string-draped halters, shimmering fringe skirts, and bondage-strap bodysuits. The tailoring, much of it in cowhide or reptile skin, was scalpel-sharp, tight, and innovative. Most interesting was how McQueen had reworked the Bumster, attaching it with a zipper to a long shirt, effectively inventing a sexy new jumpsuit. He also took the lacelike leather that Galliano showed in his first Dior couture collection and reinterpreted it into far more sensual black minidresses and trenches. He accessorized many of the looks with disfiguring silver mouth braces designed by Shaun Leane—an unsettling touch that reinforced the underlying S&M theme.

The standout showpiece was a Leane-designed silver ribcage with a curled dog tail, which the model wore like a corset over a black Lurex cocktail shift. It was the first time McQueen had asked Leane to do a large piece. "He said: 'Well, Shaun, if you can make it small, you can make it big. It's just as simple as that,'" Leane recalled. It took three months to create and he used a human skeleton to cast it.

Halfway through, the show came to an abrupt silent stop. The menacing notes of the *Jaws* theme—*dah-dun, dah-dun*—eerily echoed in the hall as clouds of ink slowly turned the watery runway black. The crowd erupted into applause and cheers. Then the golden rain began to fall as Peebles's voice wailed "I Can't Stand the Rain." The models splashed their way down the runway, all dressed in white suits and shifts, many sheer and clinging to their naked breasts as their mascara ran down their cheeks. McQueen had taken Galliano's "Fallen Angels" effect, perfected it, and made it his own.

The reviews were astounding, most echoing what Spindler wrote in *The New York Times*: "The age of churlishness, it seems, is over. Mr. Arnault can take back his Givenchy job, but he can't take back the wealth of experience Mr. McQueen has gained from time spent in the couture ateliers. Every minute of it was visible on the runway, where he proved he has built a solid, bankable, grown-up house of his own, with his own name on the door."

Sadly, though the show had been a masterful collaboration, Costin decided his time with McQueen had come to an end. "I didn't find it enjoyable anymore," Costin says now. "It had become a job." He also saw how McQueen was becoming more temperamentally explosive—firing assistants on a whim. "I'd come into the office and say, 'Where's so-and-so?' 'Gone!' 'And so-and-so?' 'Gone!' It was only a matter of time before I would be booted out too. So I left."

TWO WEEKS LATER was Paris Fashion Week, and despite the high-profile debuts of Donatella Versace in Milan and Stella McCartney at Chloé, the biggest draws were still Galliano and McQueen.

Galliano kicked it off on Tuesday, October 14, at 2:30 in the afternoon, with his new Dior women's wear show. To stage it, he took over two massive rooms at the Louvre's underground convention center and had workers spend three and a half days turning the space into a romantic, nineteenth-century-style boudoir in Dior's signature colors of gray and white. The front row was filled with its requisite middle-aged socialites, wearing conservative suits, teased blond hair, and sweet perfume. But there was a host of new young customers and celebrities, including Nicole Kidman, who came in from London, where she was still filming *Eyes Wide Shut*.

The clothes were once again an epic Edwardian-Deco fantasy, with models dressed in long bias-cut skirts sliced up the leg to reveal silk tap pants; figure-hugging gowns made of burgundy toile de Jouy—as if the mistress of the house had gone all Scarlett O'Hara and used the curtains to make her dress; a handsome Marlene Dietrich–like tuxedo suit with a long vented skirt over sexy black lace thigh-high boots; and sheer fringed flapper dresses, all accented with feathers and Masai-style chokers. "John Galliano had his big chance Tuesday to get his incandescent romanticism out of the boudoir and into Dior ready-to-wear—and he fluffed it," Menkes wrote. "But what a glorious fluff."

That evening, Kidman was the celebrity guest of honor at the inauguration of the refurbished flagship store on Avenue Montaigne. French first lady Bernadette Chirac cut the silk rope (rather than ribbon) with a pair of Monsieur Dior's shears in front of several hundred champagne-swilling guests. The store sparkled literally, thanks to the crushed mother-of-pearl mixed in the plasterwork, and was a dizzying mélange of riches and glitz. The renovation reportedly cost more than $15 million. Outwardly, Arnault appeared unruffled. "The client must dive into the universe of Dior," he reasoned, describing the decor as "both elegant and amusing." Marino assured reporters that it was well worth the investment. "People always make money off me," he bragged.

MCQUEEN AND GALLIANO were both named Designer of the Year by the British Fashion Council at the close of the fashion season. It was Galliano's fourth win, and McQueen's second. Galliano didn't attend the event in London—the second time he blew off a prize ceremony in two months; he also didn't go to New York in September to receive the Fashion Group International's annual "star" award.

But McQueen went to the BFC gala to collect the accolade, and proudly so. In his remarks, McQueen thanked Isabella Blow, and his mother, and chided Galliano for not making an effort to be there. He spoke lovingly of London—his East End upbringing, his education at Saint Martins—and stated that, unlike for Galliano, it truly was his home and his source of inspiration.

Isabella was thrilled with his win—despite his betrayal of her, she was flourishing, in large part because of her long, dedicated support of him. "His success has been really great for my reputation," she had recently admitted. "If that hadn't happened, I would have just been an eccentric and gone down the drain."

A few weeks later, McQueen was invited to appear on the Charlie Rose talk show, which was filming a program in London, at Wintour's suggestion. "Charlie trusts Anna," executive producer Yvette Vega says, "and we thought he could be an exciting get—a young designer with huge talent."

McQueen arrived at the Bloomberg studio where the show was being taped with two assistants and was dressed neatly in a beige blazer and ivory shirt, his hair cropped short and properly groomed. During the twenty-minute interview, he came across as a sweet, boyish fellow, slightly nervous and genuinely earnest.

Rose asked McQueen about what he believed he brought to fashion:

"I live in the center of London. I'm surrounded by . . . the real London, the club scene, the homelessness—the things that other designers don't really want to see," he replied. "My influences are different. I'm more, I suppose, honest and direct about the things that I care about in the world, because even though I work in fashion it's not really, you know, I still have to, you know, look at what else is going on in the world, and some of that comes into my work."

Rose: "So, we see more of a sense of the street from you than Lagerfeld and people like that?"

McQueen: "Yeah, well, my level, where I've got such a young clientele that really wants honesty in their fashion. I do, not so much shock tactics, but I do like to expose what's going on in the outside world to the fashion world, which doesn't always go down well. But then, people can either take it or leave it. I can't really twist their arm to buy it."

Rose: "What's the difference, as you would characterize it, between you and Galliano?"

McQueen: "John's more fluid and romantic. He has a great vision for romanticizing his ideal woman. . . . I really care about a woman's independence. . . . When she walks into the room, I don't like her to look so naïve and so fragile. I like her to look stronger—that if a man goes up to her, he's got to have real balls to go up to her. I don't like her to look like she can be taken advantage of."

In closing, Rose asked McQueen: "Looking back at twenty-eight, do you regret any of it? Would you do any of it—"

"Oh, I couldn't go through this again," McQueen answered, laughing. "I could never go through this again. No. Once is enough."

BY EARLY DECEMBER, McQueen was exhausted and strung out. He rang Ungless in San Francisco and asked if he could come visit for the Christmas holidays. Throughout the fall, Ungless had heard disconcerting stories from friends that McQueen's drug use was accelerating—that it had, in fact, become a habit. Ungless was trying to live a more balanced life in the Bay Area. He told McQueen that he was welcome as long as there was no cocaine. McQueen insisted that he had stopped taking all drugs.

When McQueen arrived, he was wound up tight as a top. "He couldn't sit still one minute," Ungless recalls. They went shopping in downtown San Francisco and McQueen spent a fortune at Ralph Lauren and Hermès. When they went out in the evening, he wouldn't stay at a bar for more than a couple of minutes. "We went everywhere—on and on," Ungless says. "It was insane." McQueen respected Ungless's requirement that he not do cocaine; instead he tried crystal meth, which made him sick.

Finally, Ungless whisked McQueen out of the city for Christmas in the countryside. They stayed in a cabin in the redwood forest, and drove out to Bodega Bay, where Hitchcock filmed *The Birds*. They went to see some of the buildings used as sets, such as the schoolhouse, and had Christmas dinner at The Inn at the Tides restaurant, which looks out over the stretch of water that Tippi Hedren crossed by boat in the movie. It should have been a relaxing day, but McQueen was on his cell phone much of the time arguing with Murray Arthur in the United Kingdom. Once his issues with Arthur were somewhat resolved, McQueen exhaled. The pair drove farther north and investigated coastal Native American cultures—"sweat lodges, reservations, and all that," Ungless says. "We had quite an amazing trip."

At the close of what had been a rather monumental year, McQueen was now rested and rejuvenated, and Ungless sent him back to Europe with the hope that the New Year would be a healthier, saner one.

XIII

alliano had at Dior all that he had dreamed during those long years in London and the Bastille. The fame—so much of it that his home country of Gibraltar honored him with a series of stamps commemorating his first Dior collection. The wealth—which he spent easily on things such as antiques and art for his rue de la Perle flat. He had a personal trainer who came by every morning to take him for a run through city parks or to the gym. He had specific nutrition regimes—organic; macrobiotic; special powdered food—that were far healthier than his days of bacon sandwiches and McDonald's. He cut his booze consumption way back; his spokesman back then said that he was actually off alcohol completely, though friends and colleagues contradict that statement now. In any case, he was fit, his mind was sharp, and he looked great.

Most important, he could do what he wanted creatively and Bernard Arnault never questioned any of it. "How many bastions of art are left where an artist is given *carte blanche*?" Arnault's fashion adviser, Katell le Bourhis, boasted at the time.

McQueen's relationship with Arnault was more prickly than Galliano's, and it caused him great anxiety and despair. McQueen was like the shy little brother, forever trying to impress the domineering father, but it was a pointless exercise because Arnault's favorite son was unquestionably Galliano.

Galliano was given utter freedom; McQueen still had restrictive budgets. Galliano regularly talked with Arnault about the creative direction at Dior; McQueen got very little face time with the big boss. When they would meet at the LVMH headquarters on Avenue Hoche, it was usually to discuss finances—or, from McQueen's point of view, the lack thereof. On occasion McQueen and Arnault would have lunch or dinner—with Saint Phalle, Murray Arthur, and Hélène Arnault in tow. Though Arnault could speak English, he would stick to French and have Saint Phalle translate, reinforcing the wall between the two men. The subject was invariably business.

Before the shows, Arnault would sometimes visit the Givenchy showroom and McQueen would nervously explain the collection to him. "If Arnault said, 'Add more colors,' then that's what we had to do," a former Givenchy assistant recalls. Arnault rarely attended Givenchy shows; at Dior, he was always front and center, with France's first lady usually seated next to him. That stung McQueen.

And yet, McQueen kept at it, as if he wanted to prove to the rest of the fashion world that he was superior to Galliano.

NEVER WERE Galliano's and McQueen's creative differences more apparent than during couture week in January 1998. Because both men had been pushing the limits of couture—making it richer, sexier, and more imaginative than it ever had been—their confreres had to keep up or get out. Most kept up, and couture had come back to life. There were "lots of women you've never heard of, whose husbands have made $50 million or so in the last year," one house's couture *directrice* said. Couture was a pulsating, fabulous embodiment of late-1990s excess.

Valentino, who had just sold his company to Holding di Partecipazioni Industriali (HdP), an Italian conglomerate controlled by the Fiat group, for $300 million, staged his show in his glorious new Paris headquarters: an eighteenth-century *hôtel particulier* across the Place Vendôme from the Ritz. And though he was well into his sixties and had been at this for almost forty years, his collection of lean 1920s-style cocktail dresses, pretty suits trimmed with glass bead fringe, and floral print gowns overlaid with tulle were some of the most young and lovely clothes I'd ever seen him show.

Karl Lagerfeld's collection for Chanel was equally breathtaking: black satin day dresses with soft cardigans, satin jackets over jersey skirts, and geometric beaded skirts, presented in the couture salons of the company's rue Cambon headquarters. The models descended the famous mirrored staircase where Mademoiselle used to discreetly perch to watch her own shows. Some elegantly smoked cigarettes in slim holders as they made their way past the guests seated on prim gold chairs in the plush beige rooms; some were draped in jewels; some had their faces veiled in black netting, "like glamorous young widows who had just inherited a ton of money," quipped *Vanity Fair* writer Dominick Dunne, who was there to cover couture week.

For his Dior show, Galliano wanted to make the most of his carte blanche—even more than he had with his Masai collection at the Grand Hôtel or his Edwardian extravaganza at the Bagatelle gardens. He decided that he would put on the grandest show *ever*.

In an effort to replicate the magic that he and Harlech once had together, he searched for a Belle Époque muse who would embody all that he was and adored. He found Marchesa Luisa Casati, an early twentieth-century European eccentric and great beauty who had been painted by Boldini, photographed by Beaton and Man Ray, dressed by Poiret and Fortuny, and adored by Nijinsky. Casati walked her pet cheetahs on diamond-inlaid leashes, wore serpents as necklaces, and had gilded, naked servants. She lost her pet boa constrictor at the Ritz. She lived in Venice (in what is now the Guggenheim museum), Capri (in the Villa San Michele), Rome, Paris, and London. "She would give a ball and then, to pay for it, sell her house," Galliano gushed. "We love that!" He and Robinson decided to re-create one of her famously lavish parties for the show, with the models serving as "gorgeous, salacious creatures who've been dancing for three days," he said.

And the whole thing would be set in the entrance and salons of the Palais Garnier, Paris's baroque opera house, done up extravagantly by Michael Howells. To create the sort of barn-burner Galliano wanted, Howells looked to fabulously flamboyant films such as British director Ken Russell's 1977 movie *Valentino*, with Rudolf Nureyev as the silent film star, and Franco Zeffirelli's *La Traviata* for inspiration. Instead of lining a runway with seating, he chose to install clusters of sofas and tables with chairs, so invitees would truly feel like they were at a party rather than a fashion show. He draped the tables with rabbit fur printed with zebra stripes, "so when you sat there, you would caress it," he says. He ordered twenty thousand Charles de Gaulle roses—"they're this beautiful pale mauve, they look like a rose in moonlight," he swoons—and brought in florists from England to arrange them. All the sets were built in England too, then shipped to Paris. "John always wanted to maintain this sort of Englishness" at Dior, Howells explains. The French could be "uptight," as he politely puts it, and Galliano "wanted a sort of romanticism" that he felt was uniquely English.

Remarkably, Howells says, "I never had a sense of budget." Dior reportedly paid $150,000 to rent the hall, and the show itself was said to have cost $2 million. That would make it, at the time, the most expensive Paris Fashion Week show on record.

AS GUESTS ARRIVED AT the theater on Monday, January 19, at 2:30 P.M., they were greeted and entertained by a cast of characters that included a pirouetting Nijinsky imitator dressed in one of the dancer's original costumes; a turbaned and bejeweled sultan; sailors and military officers; and matadors with swirling capes. Candles were burned down low; the Charles de Gaulle roses were full-blown and slightly faded; garlands of lavender were draped here and there; the rabbit tablecloths were petted.

Isabella Blow walked in wearing a crab claw hat with white veiling. Bernard Arnault was seated at Table Sixty-three, with Madame Pompidou to his right and his wife to his left. Squeezed between the women were the French actress Sophie Marceau; French politician wives Lise Toubon, Marie-Josèphe Balladur, and Cécilia Sarkozy; Paris socialite Bethy Lagardère, the Brazilian-born wife of media titan Jean-Luc Lagardère; and Nazik Hariri, the striking raven-haired wife of Lebanese prime minister Rafik Hariri. Behind Arnault sat a bodyguard.

Guests were served LVMH-owned champagne and delicate *macarons* as they waited for the show to start.

"It's a happening," said São Schlumberger, who was back in the audience.

Finally, a full hour late, the models came out one by one, posed at the top of the grand staircase, and then with the help of a costumed male escort, made their way tentatively down the marble steps in towering heels, swooshing their skirts or trailing their trains dramatically behind—just as Galliano had personally coached them to do. There were forty models and each had a character with a story. For Debra Shaw, Galliano explained: "You are super rich and you're having an affair with the chauffeur," which made her laugh. And each model had one outfit, such as a richly embroidered floor-length kimono; a harlequin ballerina dress; or a pyramid coat painted with roses and trimmed in mink. There were ball gowns with immense hoop skirts; a Poiret-like Scheherazade cocoon coat in bronze and burnt orange flecked with gems; sequin-strewn bias-cut gowns in dusty rose silk and silver satin; *Titanic*-like Edwardian suits with ample wraps; sable and mink; bustles and trains.

After forty minutes of this exquisite parade of luxurious excess, Galliano came out and took his bow with a model on each arm. He was dressed as a 1920s-style Cuban dancer, his mustache pencil-slim and his hair sculpted into a sleek Marcel Wave.

At that moment, thousands of paper butterflies rained down from the rafters onto the audience.

"For sheer theatrical thrills . . . no one came within a mile of Dior," Dunne declared. "[Galliano] has a vivid sense of what he wants to project, and he has made the spectacle his territory. For him, no fantasy is impossible."

But, as *Women's Wear* posited, some in the audience felt the clothes were "a museum-quality exhibit." And the trade scolded Galliano for not being able to "create a modern image for the house."

_____

GALLIANO MAY HAVE WOWED everyone with his splashy $2 million opera production, but McQueen wowed them with his clothes—beautiful, wearable clothes. Arnault must have heard from the Givenchy executive suite that this show was worth watching in person: he and his wife decided to make the trek to the Grande Arche in La Défense, the modern business district west of Paris where McQueen was staging the show, and were seated in the front row among the socialites, celebrities, and royalty.

Obviously transformed by his trip to Japan the previous spring, McQueen embraced the Zen culture of the country, both stylistically and meditatively. In an expansive room under the arch, the models serenely walked through a Japanese pebble garden, with bonsai-like trees, shallow pools with floating water lilies, and a cascade. The clothes were in soft hues such as pastel pink and pistachio green, with sleek tailoring, lean dresses, and his signature cowl necklines. He worked the Japonism theme with kimono coats, koi prints, peacock embroidery, and origami pleating, and added witty Asian-inspired touches, such as a glass bowl handbag containing a goldfish and clear acrylic shoe heels that encased butterflies he bought at the Paris taxidermist Deyrolle. "One could hear murmurs of approval from the audience," Dunne noted.

McQueen took his bow dressed in a tailcoat, with his Givenchy head tailor and chief seamstress on each arm.

"He's changed," observed a longtime McQueen follower at the time. "Alexander is much less angry than before."

The clients were over the moon. "There's a new erogenous zone in fashion," purred New York socialite Audrey Gruss.

"[The customer is] difficult to understand at the beginning," McQueen admitted, "especially if you don't come from that world."

But he was determined to figure it out. As the program noted, the show was "Dedicated to the Client."

MCQUEEN WAS INCREASINGLY FOCUSING on the growth of his own business. He renewed his contract with his Florence-based manufacturer Gibo—this time for five years, since, as Verkade explained, "Gibo is able to do [McQueen's] complicated pattern cutting" at a reasonable cost, which kept McQueen's clothes "competitively priced" at the retail level. McQueen would have his samples produced at the factory in Italy and regularly went there to conduct fittings.

At the same time, he was working on his new namesake collection, to be presented a short month after the Givenchy couture show. The theme this season was Joan of Arc. Again McQueen was the closing show for London Fashion Week, which, in large part due to his success, was flourishing: a record forty-five designers were showing that season, and retailers and editors were now making London a requisite stop on the European fashion show circuit. Bergdorf's was sending thirteen buyers from New York, including Dawn Mello. "The smart hotels are full and the best restaurants are booked solid," wrote Sally Brampton in *The Times* of London. "Britannia, it seems, is still cool."

Like the previous season, McQueen staged the show at the old bus depot in Victoria—this time on Friday, February 25—and he had the same sort of one-hundred-foot-long clear plastic runway, but covered in black ash instead of filled with water. In the front row was one of Hollywood's brightest stars, Kate Winslet, who was nominated for the Best Actress Academy Award for her performance in *Titanic*. She revealed to reporters at the show that she'd be wearing a McQueen gown on Oscar night a few weeks later.

The show opened with the sound of crackling fire, and in the darkness, swinging overhead lamps lit the space with beams of lava-red light. Out walked a model against the black backdrop in a see-through silver chain mail minidress with a plunging cowl back. It was devastatingly sexy, but the model looked like a walking cadaver: pale, with red eyes—the colored lenses were back—and thin blond braids draped across her face like rope.

She was followed by similar-looking models in beautifully tailored maxicoats, razor sharp suits and languid gowns in black, steel gray, and blood red, and frock coats and shifts with the photo printing process that he and Ungless had developed for "Dante." This time the images were of Victorian children—no worries of copyright issues there. The evening wear was a suite of red and black dresses, in lace or glass beads that shimmered in light. For the finale, McQueen sent out a muscular girl in a sleeveless red sequined flapper dress with long fringe and matching faceless gimp hood, and she dramatically cavorted in a ring of flames shooting up from the floor.

McQueen came bounding down the runway at the end, dressed in a big white sweatshirt and baggy jeans and holding Katy England's hand; she carried an enormous bouquet of red roses in her other arm. The crowd leapt to its feet in applause as he bowed to England and planted a big smooch on her lips. Because of the pyrotechnics, he said, "It was fucking the most expensive show I ever did." But he was pleased with the result. "It's kind of good," he concluded.

While the show itself was dark and somewhat frightening—and extremely reminiscent of his Saint Martins "Jack the Ripper" degree collection six years earlier—the clothes were handsome, sensual, and absolutely wearable. Enviable even. You wanted all of them in your closet. Despite having one fourth the staff in London that he had at Givenchy in Paris, McQueen had found his rhythm with his company and he had a solid design identity. His work was approaching flawless.

THE LUXURY FASHION GAME had changed; the new business model was not only working, it was ruling. The big guns of fashion—the household name brands—were growing exponentially. Ralph Lauren was doing $6 billion in retail sales annually; Calvin Klein, $4.4 billion; Giorgio Armani, $2 billion; Gucci was closing rapidly in on $1 billion. Fashion had evolved in less than a decade into a global corporate industry. And the new generation of designers understood they had to accept it or find a new career. "If you're going into the fashion business today and want to be successful, you have to have money behind you," French fashion consultant Jean-Jacques Picart explained to *Vogue*'s Katherine Betts. "It's not just about talent anymore. Ten years ago you had to have an idea; today it's not enough. If you want to be global and have a viable business, you have to marry yourself to a group. If at the end of this century you're not associated with money, then you don't have a future."

Galliano was the leader of that new business model. He continued to make headlines with a completely off-the-wall women's wear show for Dior—thus fulfilling his mandate from Arnault, who was convinced that press, good or bad, equaled sales.

Yet, all the perks, security, and posh existence that he had always craved and Dior provided had cut him off from modern life and society. He didn't know how to send an e-mail, or take money from a cash machine, or write a check. He didn't drive, and never took the Métro or any sort of public transportation; instead, he was ferried about the city in a chauffeured sedan. He'd spend his mornings nursing a hangover or working out, and would roll into the office at noon, where Robinson would make sure fittings were ready for him to review. His show designs got weirder with each season, as did his VIP demands such as fad dietary restrictions. And no one in his sphere challenged him on any of it. "John was surrounded by sycophants who couldn't give him a reality check," says a longtime friend. "But that's what happens to superstars: You have no one to tell you that asking for a room full of puppies to hug is not a reasonable request or to have bowls full of M&M's with all the green ones taken out. That kind of level of insanity where nobody says, 'Oh, for God's sake, do you really need to have someone do that for you to make you feel worthy?'"

The only person who tried to exact some sort of authority over Galliano was Dior president François Baufumé, and he failed miserably. He was known as a manager with a temper—"a shouter" a staff member remembers—and his greatest enmity was toward Galliano. "He didn't like John or the stories of John and drugs and drinking," a Dior executive confirms. "He liked to control his designers." He'd shout, he'd try to impose order, he'd try all sorts of tactics to get Galliano under his thumb. "But," as the Dior executive explains, "you couldn't control John in that manner."

Instead, Galliano rebelled even more. At one show Baufumé noticed that Galliano wasn't backstage. He had staff call Galliano at home and on his cell, and there was no answer. Finally, it was ascertained that Galliano was still in bed. "Baufumé got in his Dior sedan and had his chauffeur drive him to Galliano's flat in the Marais," says an LVMH executive who was privy to the incident. "Baufumé went in, roused Galliano, put him in the car and drove him to the show." Galliano made his curtain call. But Baufumé was livid.

Finally, on March 13, 1998, fifty-three-year-old François Baufumé announced what *Women's Wear* described as his "retirement" from Dior. "The clash between him and John was just too much," a Dior colleague said. Arnault understood this, and, as *Women's Wear* put it, he "carefully mapped out" Baufumé's departure and succession. The company said he would be replaced by his forty-six-year-old deputy general managers, Sidney Toledano, who joined Dior in 1994 to run the leather goods division and orchestrated the momentously successful launch of the Lady Dior handbag.

Toledano was born in Casablanca to a conservative Jewish family whose ancestors had fled Spain during the inquisition of 1492. His father, Boris, was in the paper business and later became the official leader of the Jewish community of Casablanca. His mother was among the Atlantic port's most ravishing women. Toledano studied applied mathematics at the École Centrale Paris, one of the best engineering schools in France, and later partnered with a Moroccan friend who owned Kickers, a French shoe and street-wear brand. In 1984, he went to Lancel, the leather goods company, where he rose to CEO and led a revitalization of the brand. It was there that he caught the eye of Arnault.

Within days of that news, LVMH staged its annual press conference to announce its 1997 results—a must-attend affair in Paris for financial analysts as well as fashion and business reporters, particularly this year, since many believed LVMH had been hammered by the Asian economic crisis. LVMH counted immensely on sales in the Pacific Rim, especially with its recent acquisitions of Duty Free Shops (DFS) and the cosmetics chain Sephora. In fact, Arnault assured the four hundred attendees that the damage wasn't too bad. The group's overall sales for 1997 were up a staggering 54 percent to $8.018 billion—thanks primarily to DFS and Sephora. But fashion and accessories increased a respectable 15 percent to $2.012 billion. "I remain persuaded that our presence in that market is invaluable," Arnault read from his prepared statement, "and that the desire to consume our products is absolutely intact."

Other expansion plans were announced, including DFS's development of a new shopping mall concept called "gallerias" that would group all the luxury brands in one setting; the rollout of fifteen new Sephora outlets in the United States; and a shiny twenty-three-story office tower, designed by Pritzker Prize–winning French architect Christian de Portzamparc that was under construction on East Fifty-seventh Street and would serve as LVMH's U.S. headquarters.

Arnault's surprisingly good news won over that tough-minded audience; his closing remarks were repeatedly interrupted by applause.

MCQUEEN WAS IN A FUNK. He and Murray Arthur had broken up for good, after nearly two years together. Though McQueen was Arthur's first love and Arthur adored him, he couldn't take McQueen's erratic mood swings and temper. "The relationship wasn't working anymore," says an observer. Curiously, Arthur never learned about McQueen's lover on the side, Archie Reed.

To lift his spirits, McQueen dreamed up a romantic fantasy for his Givenchy couture show and chose to set it in Paris's beautiful Cirque d'Hiver, a baroque indoor arena inaugurated by Emperor Napoleon III in 1852. The central character for the collection's story was the Russian Grand Duchess Anastasia, who, according to lore, was thought to have escaped when her family, the ruling monarchy the Romanovs, was executed by firing squad during the Bolshevik Revolution. (Her remains were later found in Russia, proving she did perish with her family.) In McQueen's version of the tale, Anastasia was found hiding in the Amazon jungle.

He opened the show on Sunday, July 19, with a Lady Godiva–like creature on the back of a handsome white steed and dressed only in long blond tresses and garlands of orchids. She was followed by models wearing what *Women's Wear* called "the most beautiful coats and suits imaginable"; a soft ruffle dress draped over a glistening beaded sheath; a sparkling baby doll dress under a canary yellow fur coat; and the wedding dress inspired by *The Bride of Frankenstein*. They were deadly chic clothes yet commercial, meaning clients could imagine ordering and wearing them. And more than one guest—including me—caught a whiff of Galliano references.

Though he kept it quiet, McQueen did admire Galliano's work—or at least what he *thought* was Galliano's work, in particular the famed shellfish dress from the "Blanche DuBois" collection in 1987 that Galliano had dreamed up and Karen Crichton had actually executed. "That skirt drove Lee crazy," Sebastian Pons recalls. "He couldn't work out how it was technically conceived. That skirt. That skirt! Lee had so many copies and photographs of that skirt. He would study it."

Women's Wear adored everything about the show: "The talent, the creativity and the dramatic energy all came together in the fabulous collection everyone has been waiting for [McQueen] to do."

Anna Wintour apparently agreed. Discreetly, she ordered two items for her personal wardrobe: a pink and black fox fur-trimmed tailored day jacket and a sleeveless burgundy velvet full-length gown with hand-painted flowers. This was a long way from her not even attending his shows in London and being aghast by his rabid devouring of lobster for lunch. Wintour didn't buy much couture—but she was buying Givenchy by McQueen.

If the March show in London was nearly flawless, this one went all the way. There was an unspoken understanding among those who attended McQueen's shows back then that we were witnessing a once-a-generation talent maturing into something remarkable right before our eyes. The word "artist" is thrown about recklessly in fashion, but here it felt apt. This kid, not yet thirty, wasn't just making clothes. Nor, like Galliano, was he making costumes. He was using fabrics and embellishments to create something that took our breath away, the perfect meeting of color, perspective, texture, and shape—something truly sculptural—that happened to be worn. McQueen was indeed an artist, a natural-born one with a clear and informed vision, and his work now was bordering on genius.

FOR HIS DIOR COUTURE SHOW that season—fall–winter 1998–99—Galliano, in his increasingly megalomaniac way, wanted to outdo the opera extravaganza of six months earlier. Surprisingly, Toledano did not balk.

Galliano and Toledano had settled into a good working relationship together at Dior—at least from the studio's standpoint. "One of Mr. Toledano's immense strengths is that he would just let John be free—completely free," recalls a Dior assistant. "He was very respectful of John's creations. . . . You had to be pretty ballsy to let him do it, and not criticize him, and stick behind him. John and Mr. Toledano had formal times, they had informal times, but at the end of the day they were very tight. They had a mutual respect."

About a month before the show, Michael Howells traveled to Paris for his set decor meeting with Galliano. "My brief was 'Elizabeth I meets Pocahontas on holiday.' It's like, '*Okay, John*. Okay, thanks, I'll get back to you.'"

Then, Howells says, he remembered a postcard he once saw "of a train in Paris that had arrived at the station and it overshot the platform and had gone through the back of the station and fallen down into the street." The image, well known in France, is of a crash in 1895 at the Gare de Paris-Montparnasse (then known as the Gare de l'Ouest). Though the crash was dramatic, only five people were seriously injured and there were no fatalities.

"Actually, John," Howells said, "wouldn't it be great to do the show in a train station and do it on the train, because it's July, it's the big weekend when everybody gets on the trains and leaves Paris. Let's try to do it at a train station."

Galliano approved wholeheartedly.

Howells feared it might be a tall order to pull off in less than four weeks, but he says, "The French are really behind fashion. They understand." Howells secured permission to close down three platforms in the Gare d'Austerlitz train station, and he found a functioning steam engine from 1912 in the South of France, which he had brought up to Paris.

Howells and Galliano planned to turn part of the train station into a romanticized Moroccan medina—like the Hollywood version of Tangier during Galliano's youth—with palm trees, piles of vintage trunks, white desert tents, and Saharan sand. The trunks came from the archives of Dior's sister brand Louis Vuitton; for the desert, Howells sourced three tons of tangerine-hued sand, which was used to cover the station's cement platforms. It felt very much like the opening setting of Paul Bowles's 1949 novel *The Sheltering Sky*.

The other half of the set was supposed to be an Edwardian railroad station that, for some reason, would be attacked by American Indians. There was also a whoosh of jungle and of Mexican references thrown in—Galliano was grafting previous show ideas into the current season, as he did back in the eighties, when he carried the *Witness* aesthetic through several collections. During a preview visit with *Women's Wear*, Galliano explained that the collection was "traveling through geographical and historical boundaries."

The day of the show—Monday, July 20, at 2:30 P.M.—the weather was extraordinarily hot. Hotter than hot. One-hundred-and-ten-degrees hot in that Saharan train station. Waiters dressed in white linen suits and fezzes served cold Veuve Clicquot champagne, Pimm's Cups, mint tea, and Turkish delight on brass trays. To further set the mood, there were baskets of dates and dried figs and trays of spices. The vintage trunks bore tags with famous names such as Bing Crosby, Cleopatra, and Brad Pitt.

Dolled-up haute couture clients, celebrities, and retailers, including Jocelyn Wildenstein, Mouna Ayoub, Betsy Bloomingdale, best-selling novelist Danielle Steel, and Miss Japan, sat on rattan chairs and wooden benches, fanning themselves. The standing-room crowd was relegated to antique train cars on the other platforms and were hanging out the windows like subcontinent travelers hoping for a breeze. As with every Galliano show, everyone waited and waited and waited, getting drunk on bubbly and wilting in the heat.

We were suddenly told to get to our seats because the show was about to begin. The massive black steam engine—labeled the *Diorient Express*—roared into the station, tearing through an immense orange paper curtain. Pocahontas was strapped to the front of it, and a tribe of Indian warriors from Disneyland Paris—*Buffalo Bill's Wild West Show* again—came rampaging through, hootin' and hollerin', tomahawks a-swingin', and arrows a-flyin'. The crowd erupted into cheers simply for the mad audacity of it all.

Then came the clothes. The models poured off the train to Jeremy Healy's club mix of George Michael, the Talking Heads, Indian sitars, and Native American chanting and worked their way around the souk and the Edwardian station settings dressed in gigantic Indian blanket swing coats and ponchos trimmed in suede fringe and fur; Pocahontas buckskin minidresses; autumnal-colored Tudor-style tunic minidresses with mutton sleeves and worn with matching thigh-high boots and short brocade capes; Thunderbird print skinny pantsuits with Indian beaded neck pieces; austere long black velvet "missionary" coat dresses with high cleric collars; silk taffeta corseted Renaissance gowns with pleated bubble skirts and heaving bosoms. There were only thirty-three looks in all—even though, according to couture's governing body, there should have been a minimum of fifty—and when it was all over, the models mounted back on the train and it pulled out of the station, whistle blowing.

"Whoa there! Stop!" howled the *International Herald Tribune*'s Suzy Menkes in the next day's paper. "Haven't we been here before with Galliano—delirious mixes of place and time that make his shows into magnificent but essentially ridiculous time-travel costume parties?"

"Season after season, [Galliano] faces a singular criticism: Where are the clothes?" *Women's Wear* opined. "You know, John, the real clothes, the buy 'em, hang 'em, wear 'em clothes?"

"It was an embarrassment of riches," Talley told me. "You just wanted to run."

XIV

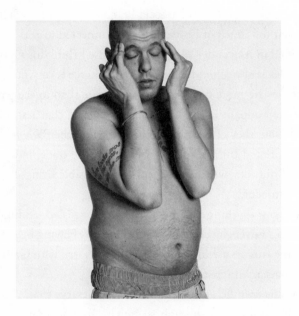

T he train wreck—that's what Galliano's "Diorient Express" show was
    dubbed by many who had witnessed it.

    And it seemed to have one major casualty: John Galliano himself.

By early September, rumors were whirling about the fashion community
that Arnault was considering not renewing Galliano's contract at Christian
Dior and moving his new favored son, Alexander McQueen, to 30, Avenue
Montaigne.

Galliano was costing Dior a fortune—his shows had already easily run $5
million that year—and retail sales were not keeping up. His productions had

grown so complex and so overwrought that the clothes felt like an after-thought. Yes, Arnault wanted Galliano to generate publicity to sell profit-generating perfumes and handbags and lipsticks by the millions, but not at the sacrifice of fashion sales. After all, Dior was a fashion house first and foremost; it had made its reputation from day one with fabulous clothes.

And Galliano wasn't simply losing support with the press and retailers; even his esteemed competitors were questioning his creative judgment. "John Galliano was very successful at a certain point because he was *not* minimal," said the queen of minimalism Miuccia Prada. "But I think Galliano's weakness . . . is that too much of his work is not connected to real life. I am much more interested in Alexander McQueen, because I think his vision is contemporary. His idea is also about fantasy—which I agree is very important now—but his fantasies are more connected to the future than to the past."

Rumors are rampant in fashion—it is one of the chattiest, cattiest industries around—but they often have merit, especially when *Women's Wear* prints them, and it printed this one. That meant that the trade had a solid source. And not only did they write about Galliano's possible firing, they asked McQueen for comment.

"I don't know anything about it," McQueen insisted, adding that he had just renewed his Givenchy contract for three years. Having been the subject of similar sacking rumors a year earlier, he commiserated with Galliano, describing the whispers as "disgusting."

"John's under so much pressure. He doesn't deserve that," McQueen said. "The poor bloke must go through so much. To read that must be demoralizing."

AFTER HIS TRIP TO NEW YORK, McQueen focused on his show, his thirteenth, which he titled "No. 13" and staged at the Victoria bus depot on Sunday, September 27. He explained that the basis of the show was the Arts and Crafts movement mixed "with the hard edge of technology of fabrics . . . there's more of a couture feeling to it that I learned from Givenchy."

That translated into a beautiful juxtaposition of hard and soft, organic and constructed. The models casually strolled out onto a bleached wood floor with windswept hair and natural makeup and dressed in soft Bumsters, suede halter tops, lace high-necked blouses, asymmetrical chiffon cocktail dresses, raffia boleros, and wooden fan skirts. The palette was stark and elegant: black, white, ivory, sandy beige, dove gray, and silver. The clothes were sculptural and filmy, formal and casual.

It was McQueen's closing tableau, however, that astonished the audience with its pure poetry: the model Shalom Harlow, wearing a simple strapless white bouffant dress and a leather belt around the bust, spun around like a music box ballerina on a turntable in the floor as two cavorting robotic arms sprayed her with black and yellow paint. With it, McQueen had crossed the frontier of fashion into performance art, and he executed it perfectly, transporting the audience with him. "The sheer volume of ideas and their fine execution—with hardly a mishit—was breathtaking," Menkes wrote. "And put in the context of McQueen's other commitments at Givenchy, it shows him, at only twenty-nine, in a commanding fashion role."

OVER IN PARIS, Galliano's job did appear to be in peril—or at least he was given a stern warning. The morning after the Gare d'Austerlitz show, which reportedly cost $2 million and lasted ten minutes, Arnault told Toledano: "You have to change that."

And he did not keep his disdain to himself. "LVMH chief Bernard Arnault put his foot down," *Women's Wear* reported.

Toledano told Galliano that the fashion shows would now be staged at the Avenue Montaigne headquarters and be smaller and more restrained than before, with a focus on clothes. Specifically: commercial, wearable clothes.

"Despite what people think, Galliano has never had a blank check," he explained to *Women's Wear*—either dismissing or oblivious to what Arnault's fashion adviser, Katell le Bourhis, had told *Vanity Fair* six months earlier about Galliano's "carte blanche."

Galliano weighed in too: "I understand that sometimes the point of my collections has gotten lost by those who do not have a degree in Gallianoism," he explained somewhat defiantly. "This time, the way we are showing it is the way it will work."

But quietly, Galliano was furious about having his wings clipped and responded by doing a Dior collection of Communist-themed clothes: pleated silk tunics; military pants; Mao jackets; Russian Constructivist print gowns in military colors, such as olive green and brown; armbands; and Red Army caps. The silhouettes were simple, as requested by the executive suite—even a bit boring.

For his own brand, he staged a "Galliano-ism" show at a gallery. For it, he cooked up a story of a theater performance by a fictional Eastern European prince—curious, given his habit of using himself as the centerpiece character of his shows. To the soundtrack from *Titanic*, out came the models in 1930s-style diaphanous pastel bias-cut gowns, floral-embroidered lace dresses, lean skirted suits with wasp waists. "All very light and fluid," I wrote at the time. It seemed then that at the John Galliano brand, where he had more restraint imposed by stricter budgets, he actually excelled. It was also obvious that, while he loved Dior, Galliano was indeed *his* house. "These clothes do not fit into the modern world of offices, subways, taxis and business meetings," conceded *The Washington Post*'s Robin Givhan, "but how sad it would be if there was no place for such magical garments."

What was evident from those two shows was that Galliano had finally realized that his arrangement with Arnault was, as Menkes noted, a "Faustian pact."

Dior "requires him to be reasonable and realistic," she wrote, but in return, he was allowed "to soar like a free spirit" at his own company. Or at least so it appeared.

McQueen had a Faustian pact too, but he seemed to be managing it better. Perhaps it was because he had all those frustrating budget constraints. Or maybe, given his upbringing in the East End, he didn't scare so easily. What was certain was that he had found a balance between creative and commercial that captured the spirit of Givenchy.

WHILE OVERSEEING THE MANY BRANDS he already owned, Arnault was still in full acquisition mode, and he had one major brand in his sights: Gucci.

The Florence-based leather goods company was *the* success story in fashion in the 1990s. Founded by a leather craftsman named Guccio Gucci in 1921, it had been run well by two successive generations for more than fifty years. But when Guccio Gucci's playboy grandson Maurizio took over, it all went awry. Sales plummeted, expenses skyrocketed, and family infighting escalated until finally, in 1988, Maurizio was forced to sell the company to Investcorp, a Bahrain-based finance firm.

Investcorp in turn hired a Harvard-educated southern Italian lawyer named Domenico De Sole to run the company, and a young, unknown Texan named Tom Ford to design the ready-to-wear. In less than five years, the pair—known in the biz as Dom and Tom—steered the company from near bankruptcy to one of the most robust brands in the fashion industry. But since it was a publicly traded company, it was also vulnerable to a hostile takeover. "We were just sitting there, waiting," Ford later said. "It was so frustrating."

De Sole and Ford's fears became a reality in early January 1999, when LVMH announced it had quietly acquired more than 5 percent of Gucci's common stock. LVMH insisted that intentions were "friendly"—that this was a "passive" acquisition. Yet, knowing how Arnault operated, De Sole was skeptical—and worried.

De Sole's intuition was right. Arnault continued to acquire Gucci's stock—including a 9.5 percent stake from Prada's Patrizio Bertelli—in what appeared to be "a creeping takeover," as a gradual acquisition of a controlling stake is known in the financial business. "I was ready to retire," De Sole told author Sara Gay Forden for her book *The House of Gucci*. "But I wasn't going to let anybody push me out."

ALL THE BUSINESS INTRIGUE pulled the spotlight even stronger onto the spring–summer 1999 couture shows that month; everyone—it seemed, was Arnault-watching again. And thanks to the Internet bubble, the U.S. real estate boom, and the European Union's thriving economy—buoyed by its new currency the euro, which had just been introduced on January 1—the couture shows that season had a distinct feel of new money about them. The old guard clientele had nearly disappeared in the three years since Galliano triggered the revolution, replaced by young women who had married up; young wives of Middle Eastern oil barons; young girlfriends of new dot-com millionaires; even the daughters of arms dealers, who, despite the provenance of their fortunes, were quite welcome. "We're not the foreign office," cracked Dior spokesman Bernard Danillon.

For the second season in a row, Galliano had to stage the Dior show in-house, and to accommodate everyone who wanted to attend, he held about a half dozen presentations, back-to-back all day long, with no more than sixty guests at each show. The dove-gray salons were decorated with big bouquets of white calla lilies in white vases, white columns, white plaster cherubs, and one live cherub: a male model in white makeup and a diaper, sitting on a mantelpiece. Galliano came out before each to greet VIPs and introduce the collection, which was in homage to the 1920s Surrealism art movement.

Instead of a runway, Galliano had a backdrop of seamless white paper torn open like a Surrealist version of a woman's vulva. The models' look was rooted in his 1980s London work—with their charcoaled eyes, Marcel Wave hair and berets, they greatly recalled the old "Hairclips" show. Galliano recycled many of his now-signature silhouettes, but reworked them using the Surrealists' distortion techniques, producing black, white, and Prince of Wales 1930s-style pantsuits with backward jackets or pulled askew so the collar opened over the shoulder and buttons ran down the side of the torso. One long day dress had a train held up by hand with a purse handle; a chiffon sequined blouse was missing a sleeve.

Adapting Surrealism to fashion wasn't an original idea: Elsa Schiaparelli worked it with Jean Cocteau back in the 1930s when it was new and thriving and Saint Laurent revisited it expertly in 1980. But Galliano's Surrealist clothes were handsome, clever, and exquisitely executed—and apart from what anyone else was doing. It was obvious that Arnault and Toledano were right to force him to stop pouring his creativity into the show production and to turn back to clothing design. And clients and reporters alike appreciated seeing couture up-close again to admire the expert craftsmanship. "It wasn't about bells and whistles and extravagance," Bergdorf Goodman's then–fashion director James Aguiar recalls. "It was actually demure and quiet."

DESPITE THE INCREASED MORAL SUPPORT he received from Arnault, McQueen was still having a terrible time getting the budget he felt he needed to do what he wanted at Givenchy. Arnault's tighter purse strings were legitimate from a business standpoint: though on the wane, the Asian economic crisis was still reverberating throughout the luxury industry. And though the press loved what McQueen was doing at Givenchy, nobody was buying it. "He put on those incredible shows but they didn't sell clothes," says a Givenchy assistant at the time. The ready-to-wear was selling "well under a hundred units per style," a knowledgeable Givenchy source told me.

As a result, LVMH bean counters were making dramatic cuts in the fashion division. When longtime seamstresses retired they were not replaced, and ready-to-wear samples were being outsourced to lower-cost independent seamstresses around Paris on a per diem basis. McQueen was saddened by the change: he loved working with the seamstresses directly and the only time he could now was for couture. Soon couture became all he really cared about at Givenchy.

To achieve what he wanted for his show that January—known as the "Villager" collection, because it was based on characters in a French village—he needed a bigger budget. And he knew now that yelling, fussing, and pouting had zero impact on LVMH executives. So he came up with a new approach: he went to Spitzer's office with the model Esther Cañadas dressed in a nun's habit. She peeled off the robes, revealing a skimpy red sequin minidress, and perched provocatively on Spitzer's desk as McQueen asked for more money. He got it.

The "Villager" show was not the success the last few Givenchy shows had been. Though expertly executed, it was too theatrical and the press backlash to it was harsh. "Oh no! Not those history-mad Brits sending out costumes!" Menkes wailed. "No one needs a suit looped from one-thousand meters of multicolored ribbons."

The news that dominated fashion as well as business pages was the War of the Handbags, as Arnault's creeping takeover of Gucci was now known. On January 25, LVMH announced that it had raised its ownership of Gucci stock to 34.4 percent, for about $1.44 billion. LVMH said it expected to name at least one and preferably two or three directors to the Gucci board, and hoped to keep on both De Sole and Ford in their current roles. Ford had made it publicly known that he had no desire to work for Arnault.

ON FEBRUARY 18, Gucci struck back: it created an employee stock ownership plan—an ESOP—which granted Gucci employees options to buy a total of 37 million new common shares. About 20 million of the options were exercised within the day, which diluted LVMH's stake to roughly 25 percent.

Arnault and his righthand man, Pierre Godé, were unusually caught off guard; neither executive knew what an ESOP even was. They soon found out, and filed suit against Gucci in the Netherlands, where Gucci was incorporated and also listed on the stock market, to block the move. An Amsterdam court ruled quickly to freeze both LVMH's Gucci shares and the ESOP and told both sides to settle the situation through negotiations.

Instead, unflattering stories about Gucci hit the papers, and De Sole and Ford believed Arnault was waging a dirty tricks–like campaign against them—so much so that De Sole had Gucci's offices regularly swept for listening devices and Ford spied what he thought was a private investigator in front of his Paris apartment building. The papers reported that Gucci had a secret weapon to stave off LVMH, known as the Dom-Tom Bomb: De Sole's and Ford's contracts contained clauses that allowed them to leave Gucci if the company changed owners. Without Ford at the creative helm, it was widely believed at the time, Gucci was worthless. Resolute, De Sole continued to look for someone to step in as Gucci's savior.

MCQUEEN SPENT MOST of February in London, preparing his new collection and show, which was inspired by Stanley Kubrick's terrifying film adaptation of Stephen King's horror novel *The Shining*. The idea, McQueen said, was to capture "the sense of isolation and obscurity" of the story. He titled the show "The Overlook," after the hotel where it is set. The invitation quoted the film's most memorable line, typed repeatedly by the lead character after he has cracked up: "All work and no play makes Jack a dull boy."

He staged the show in a big garage near Victoria Station. Inside he had his production team build a giant Plexiglas cube that housed a winter wonderland of birch trees, snowdrifts, and an icy pond, like a square, life-size snow globe. Sounds of howling wind and baying wolves echoed in the cold, cavernous space as guests took their seats around the exterior of the cube. McQueen's front row was impressive: along with his staunch fan Kate Winslet—who had recently married in a McQueen gown—there were actresses Helen Mirren and Cate Blanchett; members of the British pop group Massive Attack; and the singer Grace Jones.

The clothes were properly wintry: various shades of gray, taupe, brown, and silver; thick jersey and wool; puffy coats; Icelandic sportswear. Continuing *The Shining* references, McQueen had a set of redheaded twin girls—representing the story's murdered Grady sisters—walk hand-in-hand, dressed in 1970s-style slate gray jersey jumpers over pale gray blouses. There was a remarkable piece by Shaun Leane: an aluminum coil corset with short sleeves and high neck, inspired by the neckpieces worn by South Africa's Ndebele. It had been fitted to a cast of the model's body and required a screwdriver to put on and take off. Another gem was a below-the-knee silver and gray crinoline Petrouschka skirt—New Look in its shape—made of cut metal decorated with silver arabesques.

For the close of the show, McQueen had planned to have a winter tableau, with ice skaters and snow. But backstage, the snow machine pipe broke and snow was going everywhere except out front on the models. McQueen's tall, strong friend Miguel Adrover, in town to help, grabbed hold of the disconnected pipe, wedged it where it needed to go, and out shot the snow.

As McQueen took his bow to Frank Sinatra's "Come Fly with Me," the crowd leapt to its feet for a standing ovation—a rarity in fashion—and both McQueen's mother, Joyce, and Saks fashion director Nicole Fischelis were so overcome, they wept. The unexpected outpouring of emotion was because guests felt "that the designer was giving the best of himself," Menkes wrote. She called the show "a mix of poetry, showmanship and imagination" and believed it "confirmed [McQueen] as a major international talent."

Blanchett so loved it that a few days later, she and her stylist Jessica Paster met with McQueen at the Covent Garden Hotel on Monmouth Street to ask him if he'd design her Oscar gown—she was nominated for Best Actress for her role in *Elizabeth*. Landing a Best Actress nominee was a publicity windfall for a designer: her appearance on the Academy Awards red carpet could generate millions of dollars worth of publicity and global recognition. Blanchett explained what she had in mind and McQueen pulled out a paper and pen and sketched something for her right there on the spot. "It was strapless, light blue, fitted and beautiful—with some Asian motif on the bottom," Paster recalled. Blanchett said she'd have to think about it.

GALLIANO—oblivious to McQueen's effort to dress Blanchett for the Oscars—told his production designer Michael Howells that he would love to create something for the Australian beauty. As it happened, Howells had worked with Blanchett on Oliver Parker's film adaptation of Oscar Wilde's *An Ideal Husband* a year earlier. Howells knew that if Galliano tried, even with Dior, to go through Blanchett's official channels of agents and publicists and managers, he'd get nowhere—at least not in time for the awards, which were a mere three weeks off. "Why don't we do it the old-fashioned way, over a bowl of spaghetti?" Howells suggested.

He pulled together all the important players—Galliano, Steven Robinson, Mesh Chhibber, Paster, Blanchett, and Blanchett's husband, the Australian-born playwright and director Andrew Upton—for supper at his Notting Hill home. After dinner, they all moved to the salon, where Galliano, Blanchett, and Paster powwowed on the sofa about the perfect gown. Blanchett again described what she wanted—"She was so precise," Galliano says—and together they came up with a periwinkle silk knit sheath with a sheer back embroidered with flowers and hummingbirds. "It was her idea to put the embroidery on the back," Galliano later said, "and she was right."

Blanchett's people informed McQueen that she wouldn't need a dress from him after all. He instead landed a commission, through Givenchy, from another Best Actress nominee, *Titanic*'s Kate Winslet. Blanchett did not win the Oscar—she lost to Gwyneth Paltrow, who won for *Shakespeare in Love*—but her Dior gown made critics and viewers swoon. The "most fantastic Oscar dress ever," *Women's Wear* declared. Unfortunately, Winslet's Guinevere-like emerald green satin Givenchy gown with gold embroidered garlands and dragonflies was trashed by fashion critics and contributed to her landing on Mr. Blackwell's worst-dressed list later that year.

McQueen wholly embraced the notion that the fall–winter 1999–2000 collection would be the first clothing season of the new century: he opened his Givenchy show at the Carrousel du Louvre in March 1999 with a laser show on the mirrored silver runway, and followed it with a parade of dresses, coats, and suits decorated with sci-fi doodads like reflective tape, computerized Swarovski studs, and wiring that looked like circuit boards. For the climax, there was a pair of models wearing transparent plastic body casts wired with blinking lights so they looked like couture robots. Menkes found it "dizzying" and *Women's Wear* called it "sensory overload." "It's very hard to spit out a collection every four months," a former Givenchy assistant told me. "That's why there was a lot of smoke and mirrors on the catwalk."

A few days later, on the morning of Friday, March 19, as cameras flashed, De Sole and Ford stepped behind a podium in a Paris conference hall and announced that Gucci had found a white knight: François Pinault (pronounced "pee-no"), a financier who had built his family's lumber company into a global conglomerate called Pinault Printemps Redoute SA (PPR). He was among the wealthiest men in France.

PPR agreed to invest $2.9 billion in Gucci—which equaled 40 percent of the brand and shrank LVMH's stake to 22 percent. Together they would create a new company called Gucci Group that would acquire and develop luxury brands—in other words, compete directly with LVMH rather than be a part of it. To make the project more lucrative, that same day, PPR paid $1 billion for Sanofi Beauté, a French beauty conglomerate that owned such top brands as Yves Saint Laurent cosmetics and perfumes. As it happened, Arnault had tried to buy Sanofi Beauté in December, but after several weeks of haggling, he gave up, declaring it was too expensive. He was expected to bid again—but PPR beat him to it.

LVMH's response: a full takeover bid for Gucci—for $81 a share, $6 more than what Pinault had paid, which valued the company at an astounding $8 billion. Furthermore, Arnault dismissed the Sanofi deal, saying PPR had paid too much, and he filed another lawsuit against Gucci, this time to cancel the PPR deal and replace Gucci's board with an independent overseer. "Arnault is defending his monopoly," De Sole told me. "He is the only big luxury group in the industry actively buying companies. The Gucci Group would be a competitor."

The following week, a Dutch court ruled that Gucci had to consider LVMH's takeover deal without interference from PPR, but it refused to appoint an independent overseer for the board. The court also upheld PPR's stake in Gucci. Both sides claimed victory. De Sole and Ford added that if LVMH did take over Gucci, they would both leave the company. Some weeks later, the Gucci shareholders made their decision: they chose PPR.

McQUEEN WENT LESS AND LESS to Paris. He was supposed to be there once a week, but, as one assistant remembers, "we'd wait for him to arrive and he wouldn't have gotten on the plane." The team would then have to go to London, "lugging suitcases of fabrics that he wouldn't look at," the assistant explains. Or they would have to go to London and force him to get on the plane to Paris. "He preferred flying because it suited his attention span better," the assistant says. On one trip, McQueen had a paranoia panic attack.

"He was convinced that there were LVMH assassins on the plane," the assistant recalls. "I thought he was joking, but he wasn't. He thought someone was going to kill him and he ran off the plane in London. It was a bad sign."

When he did make it to Paris, he would spend a lot of time exploring the city. He'd hit the Porte de Clignancourt flea market to buy antiques for his home in Islington, and spend afternoons walking around the Père Lachaise Cemetery, an immense, woody graveyard on the northeast side of the city where such illustrious souls as Frédéric Chopin, Oscar Wilde, the Doors singer Jim Morrison, and Hans Bellmer—of McQueen's "La Poupée" show— are buried. McQueen so loved Père Lachaise that he staged a fashion shoot there; the theme was "beautiful death." But those trips became increasingly infrequent. "There were times we didn't see McQueen for a month or two," says a Givenchy assistant. "He didn't like Paris—he didn't feel comfortable there, he didn't know anyone."

In fact, he wasn't feeling very comfortable just about everywhere. With all his success, McQueen was increasingly ill at ease. One night that spring he took Archie Reed to a dinner for a dozen hosted by Madonna for Elton John in the bar area of Blakes Hotel in London. Among the guests was Gucci designer Tom Ford. McQueen arrived in good form, and Ford enjoyed speaking with him—it was the first occasion they had spent time together.

But in no time flat, McQueen was "smashed," Ford remembers. "He couldn't even make a sentence. He was so drunk he took potatoes and started throwing them at Madonna at the other end of the table. Madonna was wearing a Chinese wig and embroidered pants from my [spring–summer 1999] collection, and [McQueen] was flinging food at her." Ford quickly understood why: "He was nervous and he was acting out like a kid. I think he felt very uncomfortable."

Another source of McQueen's anxiety was his corpulence. "His weight was always a thing that he hated," recalls Julien Macdonald. "He'd balloon up; sometimes you'd see him and he'd be massive, as fat as a bus. He'd eat, and obviously the drinking and the drugs—a very problematic soul when it came to that. He was never really pleased with his physical appearance."

"He had this obsession to get skinny," Pons remembers. At first, he tried with diet and exercise, but he couldn't keep the new routine up. "Lee was not patient with a lot of things," Pons says. "He would get tired and bored."

Finally, when McQueen hit the birthday milestone of thirty in March, he decided something radical needed to be done about his weight: liposuction. Though he knew it was an extremely painful procedure, he felt, because of his job, he had no other choice. "It was quick and I didn't have time for anything else between collections," he explained. He wanted to keep it on the Q.T. But word got out about it among the ever-gossipy fashion set, and their words were unkind at best.

Sadly, the surgery didn't produce the miracles he had hoped for and he ballooned right back up. "Liposuction is crap," he said. "It doesn't work for men. It sucks up all the fat cells, but then they just get bigger." He went back on a diet, tried exercising again, and amped up his use of cocaine.

And he worked like a fiend. Several of his friends and assistants told me that McQueen was so driven because he was terrified of "the dip": the moment when he believed creators had reached their career pinnacle and started sliding downward. "He knew that success was going to take so much effort to maintain that one day he would be like every other famous artist and have a dip in popularity," an assistant says. "That scared him, the fear of going out of fashion."

XV

G alliano had more to worry about than going out of fashion. The rumor that he was about to get sacked was still churning. But Sidney Toledano denied it vehemently. In fact, he insisted that Galliano's appointment was an unmitigated business success at Dior. "Contrary to what people think, the sales took off quickly—as early as the first few collections," he told me. "Our prêt-à-porter sales [at Dior] were strong last year both in Europe and in the United States in our boutiques, and multibrands— independently owned shops that carry several different labels—increased their orders by nearly 40 percent. Some practically doubled their orders."

Bernard Arnault was equally supportive of Galliano. While he conceded that "the Diorient Express collection was a little over the top," and cautioned

Galliano "that too much creative proliferation, even in couture, can be interpreted badly," he told me that all publicity it generated contributed to the exponential growth of the company. "In 1990, Dior had six boutiques," he said. "Today there are seventy-eight and in the coming months we will have one hundred." Dior, he concluded, "is on the offensive thanks to the talent of John Galliano, and women's wear has become one of the pillars of the redeployment of the brand."

The John Galliano brand was thriving too. Under Valérie Hermann's command, one of the line's greatest nagging issues—fit—had finally been solved. "The clothes are so well made now that you have a sense of almost a couture quality—the way the linings are made and the way the buttons are sewed on," Bergdorf's then-president Dawn Mello confirmed. "It's not inexpensive, but it looks and feels on the body like a *very* expensive outfit."

And the clothes were commercial enough to sell in volume. "There were fashion companies back then—and still today—where you'd see clothes on the runway and there would be nothing like those clothes in the showroom," says writer Katie Weisman, who was *Women's Wear*'s fashion business reporter in Paris at the time. "But in the Galliano showroom, you'd see an easier piece to wear in the same fabric as a show piece, or you'd see a calmer, less-exaggerated cut of the look, and I'd think: 'I get it. I see how this dress came from that dress.' Valérie was an excellent merchant for John." And sales figures reflected the change.

Galliano the man, however, was not doing as well. He was living in a bubble, inaccessible to even his closest friends and longtime colleagues. And nearly everyone agreed that the reason for this was Steven Robinson. So tight was their relationship that Robinson lived for a while at Galliano's home on rue de la Perle. "Steven had a bed, a metal rack with polo shirts and sneakers, a teddy bear on the bed, and that's it," says a former Dior assistant who had visited the apartment.

Robinson was a cocaine addict too—which added to his paranoia. At Dior, he'd regularly go in the toilet across the hall from the studio, be heard "sniffing away and come out rubbing his nose," says another Dior assistant.

Even Talley didn't make it through the Robinson-imposed barricade; in the two years since Galliano had taken over Dior, they hadn't had dinner together once. "The Dior house is like an iron wall," Talley told me, describing Robinson as "The Mrs. Danvers of *Rebecca*. Steven calls the shots." Jacqui

Duclos said, "I don't think there is another person in Paris as smart and clever as Steven—except Arnault."

IN APRIL, I met up with Galliano and his spokesman, Mesh Chhibber, for lunch at Le Quincy, a bistro behind the Gare de Lyon where Galliano had dined regularly since his days at Fayçal Amor's studio nearby. He was delivered in his Dior-issued black Renault sedan by his dashing chauffeur, Eric, and was early—a first in our five-year-long professional relationship. He was tan and rested, having just returned from a weeklong vacation in the Turks and Caicos Islands where he said he spent his time reading and doing yoga— "for the first time," he said enthusiastically. "Now I'm hooked." His hair was Rapunzel gold in a straight blunt cut to the shoulder, like a Park Avenue trophy wife's.

Le Quincy's owner, Michel Bosshard, ribbed him for having put on weight—his once-protruding cheekbones were now fleshy and his biceps were thick and beefy. "I'm lifting weights," he explained as he sucked on a Marlboro that he had pulled out of a polished antique silver cigarette case and lit with his shiny Cartier lighter. He conspicuously did not touch the glass of sparkling white wine that Bosshard had served him.

"You have given up drinking, haven't you?" I asked.

"Yeah," he responded.

"When was that?"

"Can't remember."

We then moved to the business at hand:

"You are getting pummeled by the critics," I said. "But the numbers aren't showing it."

"I know," Galliano replied. "I was thinking about it on holiday. What do I do? Everything is going so well. Dior has turned around completely. The haute couture has never sold as much as it's selling, not even when Mr. Dior was there. And there we are, taking a good old pummeling. At the end of the day, clients from the street are walking into the store and buying the clothes. . . . And [retailers] are being incredibly supportive. . . . I am just very grateful that buyers [don't] take the reviews too seriously. It has not affected their buying power. The autumn–winter shows as compared to last winter increased 40 percent at Galliano. Dior increased 20 percent."

"But are you increasing from nothing to something?"

"When I got to Dior, it was pretty much nothing," he said. "Galliano in the last year and a half has shown an increase of 137 percent."

I then brought up what a public relations disaster the "Diorient Express" show had been.

"Not everyone necessarily understood what I was trying to do," Galliano countered.

"What *were* you trying to do?"

"It was a way to show these fantastic embroideries," he explained. "Everything was handmade and experimental [and] pre-collections and prêt-à-porter and lingerie and perfume spin off from that . . . All the knitwear and the slashed suede you saw at Dior [ready-to-wear] was directly inspired from there. It does filter through. It inspires the house, which is why I am there."

I asked what the budget was for the train show.

"You know, I have always come under the budget."

I asked again.

"I can't talk about budgets," he responded. "It came in under the budget."

"There was a lot of talk last summer after the 'Diorent Express' that you were told to cool it a bit, that it had been a bit too extravagant."

"The perception was wrong. The following show [Surrealism] was much more intimate."

"Suzy [Menkes] was really tough on that show too, saying it had been done before and better," I pointed out.

"I think Suzy is morally bankrupt in those reviews," Galliano said. "I am quite an easy target and I was warned about that before I joined Dior—that I would have to live with my critics. I am kind of immune to it."

I told him a lot of his critics claimed he did nothing more than recycle other designers' ideas.

"Well, I am inspired by all things, I am always using them as a springboard for the future. You have to do that. . . . I love going to the V&A and looking at how things are put together or going to the manufacturer to see how fabric is woven. It's really inspiring to crank up some of those old machines and suddenly produce fabric that hasn't been seen since the eighteenth century. I get bumps from it. It's never a rehash because I am a person of my time and my generation. . . . I mean anyone who wears my clothes knows that they are not just a rehash."

We spoke more about Dior and John Galliano and how he split his time between the two brands. "Sometimes, I do Dior at Galliano and sometimes I do Galliano at Dior," he admitted. And then he circled around again to his "pummeling" in the press. "I rely more on the facts, the sales," he said. "If the collections weren't selling, I would be worried, but I am not."

"So what is your relationship with Amanda [Harlech] now?"

"Well, it's a little sad. I mean of course, if I see her in public or at events, we talk and chat but we don't ring each other. I think she feels more comfortable that way and I understand that too. I miss her. . . . But I also realized that you have to let this butterfly fly."

"And how do you get on with Mr. Arnault?"

"He has a creative voice. He often tells me what the reviews of the shows are going to be like before they come out. He kind of sat me down and explained what was good about the collection, what was missing. . . . He's very interested in the products we are working on: the collections, the fabrics, the sketches, the concepts, the research from A to Z. He's very honest and up front with me. He speaks impeccable English. He is very kind because he tries to conduct creative conversations with me in English. And warm. With anyone as passionate as we both are about design, there is a warm conversation."

Shortly after our lunch, Dior announced that Galliano had signed a new contract for three years. Among the new provisions were that he would now be responsible for the house image and advertising campaigns as well as design shoe and accessory collections. "The windows, the ads—I will be able to control everything," he said proudly. No other details were made public.

NOT ONLY WAS DIOR fully behind Galliano, the house announced that the fall–winter 1999–2000 couture show in July would be staged at the Palace of Versailles. "It is Dior. It is the collection for the next millennium, it will be a second wind for the house," Toledano explained. "But let's get it straight. We are not showing in the Hall of Mirrors and we don't want the Sun King aspect." Instead, the show would be in the Orangerie, the magisterial conservatory constructed to house the palace's citrus and palm trees in the winter, followed by a party for one thousand in the formal André Le Nôtre–designed gardens. "So much for restraint," cracked *Women's Wear.*

Versailles—if only the Orangerie—perfectly illustrated the lavish celebration of excess that couture week had become. This season, there were fifteen hundred photographers and television reporters covering the shows, including Talley, who was there with a camera crew for *Paris Fashion Collections*, a one-hour special to air on ABC. Hip-hop star Puff Daddy attended most of the shows as well as a rocking party at the Man Ray restaurant/club, where Madonna danced to her own hits.

In the elaborate carved limestone and glass Orangerie, there was a 450-foot-long catwalk covered with squishy cushions that looked like water-bed pillows. Above the runway entrance hung a giant CD in lights. The theme was the new hit sci-fi movie *The Matrix* mixed with the eighteenth-century British portraitist Thomas Gainsborough and 1970s punk. The silhouette was a continuation of what Galliano had started six months earlier with the Surrealism collection, deconstructing traditional clothes and reassembling them higgledy-piggledy. The colors were predominently Day-Glo, much of the collection was decorated with parachute straps and D-rings. There was little applause during the show and only a polite clapping at the end as Galliano walked down the runway to an excerpt from *The Matrix* soundtrack, dressed in black combat pants, T-shirt, beret, and aviator sunglasses.

Bernard Arnault told me he loved it. He was about the only one.

"The designer who can make such magical and lyrical dresses went and blew it. Completely blew it—with a self-indulgent romp through *Matrix* meets *Mad Max* territory," Menkes wrote. "The show masqueraded as a millennial moment . . . [but] it was more of a megalomaniac moment. For everything about the show . . . seemed outsize and quite unhinged."

"Ludicrous," declared *The New York Times*'s Cathy Horyn.

"It's for the media," Arnault told Menkes. "That's the purpose of all this."

But given the extravagance and vulgarity that Galliano sent down the runway, Horyn wrote, "One would have to wonder whether Mr. Arnault had made a deal with the devil."

MCQUEEN DID EXACTLY the opposite in terms of presentation for Givenchy: instead of hiring models, he showed his designs on Lucite mannequins that rose through trapdoors in the catwalk and rotated slowly on circular wooden discs to a techno soundtrack. The collection, presented at the Studio de Boulogne on July 18, was based on the early nineteenth-century masterpiece *The Execution of Lady Jane Grey* by French painter Paul Delaroche of the beheading in 1554 of the Nine Days' Queen, which hangs in the National Gallery of London. He expressed it in beautifully tailored suits and dresses made of rich, luxurious materials, such as mink and silk organza, with historical design references like gold brocade, delicate bead embroidery, and Tudor-style roses.

"McQueen is to be applauded for his fearlessness in trying something new," *Women's Wear* said. The problem was that it felt like a museum presentation rather than a fashion show, and as Menkes pointed out, "modern clothes express themselves in movement." While McQueen showed off his masterful technique, which is what couture is about, this collection felt as lifeless as the mannequins that wore it.

IN AUGUST, Georges Spitzer left Givenchy and was replaced by Marianne Tesler, a French executive who had previously worked as controller for Whirlpool in the United States and CEO of Nike France. Tesler was pretty and friendly, and thought she could apply all that she had learned in her career to make Givenchy a more efficient and profitable company.

Some of her reforms, such as merging the main and secondary ready-to-wear lines to make one cohesive design message and reestablishing a design link between haute couture and ready-to-wear, were quickly embraced. Others, like telling everyone to call her "Marianne," rather than "Madame Tesler," were decidedly rejected.

As Tesler soon discovered, McQueen's drug habit was out of hand. When he was in Paris, she'd take him to dinner and never know what he was on. He'd go to the restroom and snort cocaine and return to the table out of his mind. At work, he was utterly uncontrollable. Tesler and her executive team tried to confiscate his stash. They would tell the studio staff: "Do not give Lee any more drugs." Yet, he always managed to get more. "He was off his head," recalls a former collaborator. McQueen knew that drugs affected his work—"it makes it more erratic," he admitted—but it didn't dissuade him from taking them.

His life in London was just as erratic. In the eighteen months since he and Murray Arthur had broken up, he had gone out with a plumber, a fashion editor, a college student from San Francisco, and he kept things going with

Archie Reed. He moved repeatedly, as if every time he broke up with someone, he needed to start afresh.

"That was a mad period," said another staffer. "I thought it would kill Lee."

To add to the chaos, McQueen decided to show his namesake collection in New York during its fashion week in early September—a good ten days before his usual London slot. That meant when everyone returned from summer break it was crunch time. McQueen was heaped with criticism in the British press for the move.

He didn't care. He liked New York and he was keen to show there, even if it was the most commercial of the major fashion capitals and the birthplace of sportswear—America's far more casual sort of ready-to-wear, which was the antithesis of McQueen's Savile Row training and design aesthetic. He asked to stage the show *on* the Brooklyn Bridge, but the New York Police Department said no, due to health and safety issues. He settled for a big room on Pier 94 on West Side Highway instead. The show was scheduled for Thursday night, September 16, in the thick of Fashion Week, and would be partially funded by American Express and De Beers.

As it happened, a hurricane named Floyd was working its way up the eastern seaboard and was forecast to hit Manhattan with sixty-mile-an-hour winds on Thursday evening. Mayor Rudy Giuliani appeared on television to urge New Yorkers with nonessential jobs to stay at home. Several designers canceled their shows, but not McQueen. The storm "will add atmosphere," his New York publicist Pierre Rougier insisted.

McQueen explained that the collection was inspired by music he heard in a Turkish cabdriver's taxi; he titled it "Eye" and said it was in protest of the repression of Islamic women.

Though he had planned it before he knew Floyd would be drowning the city, he had the models walk through a shallow pool of water—the water apparently representing Arab nations' crude oil. "There's something perversely audacious about expensive clothes being traipsed through water," jabbed *Women's Wear*.

The clothes were hard and strong: Bumsters slit up the thighs; arabesque embroidered frock coats; sports jerseys printed with crescent moons and stars; Everlast-like boxing shorts with McQueen's name in Arabic on the waistband; S&M-style bondage outfits accessorized with jangly coins, studs, and face masks. To close, a series of dancers, suspended on wires, glided above a spread of metal spikes that had risen up through the water. The first, a woman dressed in a black burqa, sat in the lotus position. The next few ran through the air. A couple more flinched as if jolted by electric shocks. *The New York Times*'s Horyn deemed the tableau "art for fashion's sake."

When McQueen came out for his bow, he dropped trou to reveal stars-and-stripes boxer shorts. "The clothes didn't break new ground, though one has to marvel at the constant audacity of his vision," Horyn wrote. *Women's Wear* concluded the show was "the defiant self-indulgence of a major talent intent on leaving his audience talking."

WHILE BERNARD ARNAULT'S DESIGNERS were dominating the fashion pages, he was still making headlines on the business pages. In recent months, LVMH had picked up a slew of brands—including the American cosmetics companies Hard Candy and Bliss; the champagne house Krug; the British shirt maker Thomas Pink; and the Swiss watchmaker Tag Heuer—and it was about to close deals for the French jeweler Chaumet and the Swiss watch firm Ebel (from Investcorp) and the two-hundred-year-old British auction house Phillips.

Arnault's biggest move came in mid-October, when LVMH joined forces with Prada to buy Fendi, a seventy-five-year-old Roman fashion house owned by five aging sisters. Gucci's De Sole had persuaded four out of five of the Fendi sisters to sell to Gucci Group and thought he could get the fifth to agree. But the LVMH-Prada partnership swooped in and closed the deal with an offer of $545 million for 51 percent of the company. Revenge, even a small dose of it, was sweet.

A few weeks later, Gucci announced that, in a $1 billion deal, it would take over Yves Saint Laurent's ready-to-wear business Rive Gauche, leaving the designer and his business partner Pierre Bergé in control of the house's $5 million couture business. The Saint Laurent deal, which included the beauty and perfume division that PPR acquired with the Sanofi Beauté purchase in March, would allow Gucci Group to have a second major brand—and one of Paris fashion's great gems—in its stable. Tom Ford planned to take over as creative director for Saint Laurent—replacing its current designer, Alber Elbaz—while continuing his design duties at Gucci.

In less than a year, the luxury fashion business had morphed from a slew of independent and family-owned companies to a handful of corporate groups run by business tycoons. The evolution had been slow in coming, with Arnault methodically building up LVMH. But in short order it had become an intense Monopoly game. Talk was of profit margins and shareholders instead of hemlines and inspirations. The business model was evolving at lightning speed, and the shift was away from fashion and toward finance. Luxury was not only going global; it was going mega.

In early December, Bernard Arnault and his crew of designers and executives traveled to New York for the opening of the new LVMH tower on East Fifty-seventh Street. The *New Yorker* architecture critic Paul Goldberger called it "a stunning, lyrical building, a sculpture in glass which manages to be at once exuberantly iconoclastic and perfectly appropriate for the proper, ordered streets of the midtown Manhattan grid."

The skyscraper would serve as the new home for Dior and LVMH's U.S. operations as well as a Dior flagship store. The previous year, LVMH racked up $7.3 billion in sales worldwide—the majority in North America. Arnault's personal wealth grew concurrently, to an estimated $6 billion, making him the fifth-richest person in France.

XVI

Every morning at dawn, Galliano's trainer would knock on his door on rue de la Perle to take him running. They'd work their way through the narrow streets of the Marais to the Seine, descend a ramp to the centuries-old quays and continue along the waterfront past *les clochards*—the city's homeless—who took refuge under the many old limestone bridges. Galliano found the down-and-out state of these "tramps," as he called them—dressed in rags, surrounded by their last possessions, and wrapped in newspapers for warmth—"romantic," and decided while panting past them that he would base his upcoming Dior haute couture collection on their look.

Back at the office, Galliano and Robinson researched the subject of homelessness on an aesthetic level, and learned about the Rag Balls of the 1930s, when socialites dressed up as hobos in shredded gowns made by the couture house Worth. They also studied mid-century American photographer Diane Arbus's pictures of the mentally ill—whom Galliano said he loved for their "beauty and naiveté"—and studied the dark, twisted paintings of Austrian Expressionist Egon Schiele. As he was wont to do, Galliano spun all of it together.

On a cold January afternoon, the fashion set, including Bianca Jagger, the French actress Arielle Dombasle, the designer Azzedine Alaïa, and Hélène Arnault, arrived at the Petit Palais museum and took their seats around a stark white runway. To Madonna's new cover of "American Pie," a model walked out dressed in a pair of overalls made of newsprint fabric. The newsprint was a collage of Suzy Menkes's stories in the *International Herald Tribune*—a move that felt much more like a diss than a tribute. The model was followed by others in torn fishermen's sweaters, shredded skirts marked with cigarette burns, ragged chiffon gowns over more newsprint, and hole-ridden baggy pants. Everything was constructed askew again and accessorized with belts decorated with dangling knickknacks and found objects—just as Harlech had done for Galliano's "The Ludic Game" and "Forgotten Innocents" shows fifteen years earlier.

After that came a suite of white gowns all askew, some made of medical bandages; a ballerina on pointe with an explosion of flesh-peach tulle tutu; and a pink-and-gray corset gown with a big Mad Hatter hat. I suddenly realized that the bandages and corsets were actually straitjackets and the models were supposed to be asylum patients. How did Galliano ever believe it would be socially or morally okay to make $100,000 dresses inspired by the homeless and mentally ill? After the show, he told me that he wanted to prove that "a tiara made of candy wrappers is as valuable as a tiara made of diamonds."

"John Galliano has more guts than the local butcher," declared *Women's Wear* and applauded him for creating "magic" on the runway.

Not everyone agreed. The French media denounced the show as socially insensitive. Protesters with placards and megaphones picketed Dior's Avenue

Montaigne headquarters. "The fact that this is a matter of life and death seems lost on Galliano and his Eurotrash following," said Mary Brosnahan, executive director of the Coalition for the Homeless, in *The New York Times*. Arnold Cohen, president and CEO of the Partnership for the Homeless in New York, condemned Galliano for the "trivializing of homelessness." He added: "I doubt that Galliano's intent was to raise social consciousness."

Galliano scoffed at the polemic, calling his critics "bourgeois people, condescending and smug." Arnault told the French daily *Le Figaro* that he thought the show was "the strongest presentation since John started at Dior," and said that Galliano "had transcended his status as a couturier, and had shown that he was a veritable artist. A gust of genius blew through the room."

Then the Pulitzer Prize–winning *New York Times* op-ed columnist Maureen Dowd got hold of the story. She penned a damning column about the show and gave Galliano the space to respond to his critics. He was, as she noted, still quite "unapologetic." Indeed, he seemed proud to have sparked the controversy.

"It's the most spoken-about topic at dinner parties in Paris," he boasted. "One can't go into a restaurant without hearing fantastic young ladies talking about the fraying of tulle of the Christian Dior show. The critics have a slightly bigoted view. One is allowed to have women mincing about in high heels and combat trousers and a scarf around their head, inspired by the war in Bosnia. One is allowed to be inspired by India, even though there is enormous poverty there. One is allowed to be inspired by Africa, even though the Masai tribe is a disappearing race. One is allowed to have bohemian chic inspired by Gypsies even though we all know now where Gypsies are coming from.

"I don't get why, just because this is on their own doorstep, it's any different. Because they don't want to know about these people?

"Children are brought up to watch *Lady and the Tramp* and Charlie Chaplin and *The Little Rascals*. I didn't set out to make a political statement. I am a dressmaker. But jogging around the Seine has thrown Paris into a whole different light for me. I call it the Wet World. There are shades of Tennessee Williams and Marlon Brando.

"Some of these people are like impresarios, their coats worn over their shoulders and their hats worn at a certain angle. It's fantastic."

The controversy grew until finally several dozen homeless activists bearing signs that read "CYNICISM ISN'T COOL!" and chanting "Respect the homeless!" stormed Dior's Avenue Montaigne flagship store. Terrified shoppers inside ran for the doors. One protester was injured. Dior was forced to close the store for two hours as riot police restored calm, and Dior reportedly invited several protesters inside to discuss the situation. "They offered us money," claimed one trash-bag-clad demonstrator. "But we want their apology in the press."

They got it: the Dior press office issued a release in which Galliano stated: "In no way did I mean it to be offensive to anyone."

McQUEEN WAS MAKING his own news at Givenchy, but it wasn't about the clothes on the runway. Most everyone agreed that the collection of handsome tailoring in his usual palette of gray and mauve was rather boring—at least for him. What set folks chattering was Menkes's scoop that McQueen might leave Givenchy ready-to-wear duties to someone else and only design the house's haute couture collections. "Nobody told me about it," Arnault responded when asked.

What everyone who covered McQueen had begun to notice was how he had grown up during his time at Givenchy: in a mere two years, he had evolved from the mouthy East End punk to a serious young man. He was spending a lot of time at the McQueen shop on Conduit Street that Onward Kashiyama had recently opened, noting who was there and what they were buying. He was eating healthily, and with the help of diet pills called Chitosan that he bought at Harrods, he had lost twenty pounds. He was fit and tan, having spent his Christmas holidays in the Maldives, scuba diving. "He is, as the French say, considerably more *bien dans sa peau* than in the days when he stomped sulkily down the catwalks," noted *The Times* of London's Lisa Armstrong. He sported a new tattoo as well, a line lifted from Shakespeare's *A Midsummer Night's Dream*, wrapped in flowing script around his bicep: "Love looks not with the eyes / But with the mind."

"I'm just a romantic really," he said with a laugh.

Indeed he was. And after a spate of quick romances, he found his new love in early 2000, in a gay bar in North London. George Forsyth was slender and lissome, with closely cropped brown hair and an intense regard. A self-described "North London Jew," he came from a good family—his mother was a magistrate; his father, a respected architect who codesigned the Museum of

Scotland in Edinburgh and the Millennium wing of the National Gallery of Ireland—and he worked in television and video production. He was equally smitten with the East Ender "Lee." "I'd no idea who he was," Forsyth said. "It was only the next day my mates told me he was Alexander McQueen. I'd never heard of him, I had to ask my mum who he was." He soon found out firsthand: "I remember walking up the road [for a *Vogue* event] and seeing all these flashes of the paparazzi cameras and this huge crowd of people . . . shouting 'Alexander! Alexander!'" he said. "That's when it really hit me how well known he was. Until then I'd only met Lee, but there he was Alexander McQueen."

McQUEEN RETURNED TO LONDON to present his fall–winter 2000–2001 show; he hadn't been thrilled with how he or his show had been received in New York and announced he wouldn't be showing there again anytime soon. "Fuck 'em," he barked. "England is where it's at. It's where all the most creative, cutting-edge people are. It'll always be my home."

His theme this season was the beauty, mystery, and mysticism of nature. He titled the collection "Eshu," after the deity of travel and fortune and personification of death for the Yorùbá tribe of West Africa. Tribalism had long been a favorite McQueen theme—"the way they dress, the rituals of how they dress," he said—and he felt studying it helped him "push the silhouette" of modern Western attire.

McQueen staged the show in the Gainsborough Studios in the East End, where Hitchcock had filmed several of his early thrillers. Out front a gaggle of animal rights protesters were taunting guests as they arrived, and since the McQueen team had reportedly received a bomb threat, there were security guards patrolling the venue and inspecting handbags at the entrance. American *Vogue* said the scene "resembled a Tel Aviv airport."

Inside, the set was simple: a runway blanketed with jagged pieces of broken slate. The show opened with a model done up like Eshu in a Victorian ivory dress smeared with dried red clay (a technique from McQueen's Tooting Bec days), an African mask, and a lion's mane–like wig, walking gingerly down the stone-strewn runway to African drumming and techno beats. She was followed by models with shimmering gold-powdered hair (a nod to the source of West Africa's riches), simple makeup, and dressed in ladylike skirt suits with square shoulders, cropped sleeves, and zipper fronts; denim Bumsters with cool shredded crop tops; a handsome putty-colored shearling coat over matching full pants; and a perforated butterscotch leather ball gown cut away to reveal the skirt's metal crinoline underneath. For one particularly beautiful showpiece, McQueen revived another early career idea: the plaster cast torso. This time he attached it to a knee-length skirt that resembled giant, overblown roses. *The New York Times*'s Ginia Bellafante felt that the look "achieved the status of art."

There were other ensembles and accessories that were particularly savage, like the Shaun Leane–designed silver mouthpiece, inspired by a Yorùbá totem, that stretched a model's lips from the bridge of her nose to the tip of her chin. "Some in the audience turned their heads, unable to look," Bellafante noted, adding, "All the discomfort Mr. McQueen was so desperately trying to create almost eclipsed the exceptional in his show."

SHORTLY AFTER the fall–winter show season was over, Sebastian Pons told McQueen that he was leaving the team to join designer Miguel Adrover's company in New York.

Though only twenty-seven, Pons had served as McQueen's right hand for several years by then, including the four at Givenchy. But he was ready for a change. "I loved Lee a lot, but I was chained to his life and his world and it got to be too much," he says. "I was run down and needed fresh air." McQueen was furious at what he saw as a defection—so upset, in fact, he stopped speaking to Pons. Just like that. He promoted Sarah Heard, who had been overseeing licenses and denim, to replace Pons. It was a big jump, but McQueen felt comfortable with and had confidence in her.

IN EARLY JUNE, McQueen and Galliano were among the many boldfaced names who attended a poolside dinner party that Italian *Vogue* editor in chief Franca Sozzani threw for photographer Helmut Newton at Monaco's Monte Carlo Beach Hotel. "Fashion, music, sports, Hollywood," said Stella McCartney, while surveying the eclectic crowd that included Sargent and Eunice Kennedy Shriver, Sylvester Stallone, Venus and Serena Williams, Karl Lagerfeld, and Jon Bon Jovi. "We're all part of the same big blob." As everyone danced to deejay Boy George's club mix, Galliano jumped fully clothed off the diving board into the huge pool and splashed around the floating candles.

McQueen had more serious things on his mind. He sought out Domenico De Sole, whom he'd never met, and struck up a conversation. He then called over a photographer to have their picture taken together. De Sole asked McQueen what he was going to do with the photo.

"I want to send it to Arnault," McQueen replied.

"This is my kind of guy," De Sole thought to himself.

For the four years that McQueen had been at Givenchy, he said that Arnault and his men "had been hounding me about buying McQueen." He always turned them down. "I didn't like the way LVMH ran Givenchy, so I wasn't going to let them into my company."

But he did admire how De Sole ran Gucci.

What came next—or so went the story that Isabella Blow put forth and McQueen never contradicted—was that Isabella said she found herself sitting next to Tom Ford at dinner in London and suggested that he take a look at the Alexander McQueen company for a Gucci Group acquisition. Ford now says that this oft-repeated tale is "totally wrong. Isabella Blow didn't have anything to do with the deal. When we made our deal with François Pinault and he gave us $3 billion, I was put in charge of finding the brands that we wanted to potentially invest in and bring them to the board," Ford told me. "So I looked around at other designers that I respected and whose work I didn't think would conflict with Gucci and Yves Saint Laurent. One I was drawn to was Alexander McQueen. I think of myself as a commercial designer. But Lee was an artist—the commerciality came second. What he cared about was the show and the impact that it made.

"I picked up the phone and called Lee. We went to dinner at the Ivy in London and I said, 'We want to invest in you.'"

McQueen was intrigued and said he would give it a think.

While conducting fittings in mid-June for his couture collection, he told one of his assistants about the conversation and that he was going to meet with De Sole. "He was very excited," the assistant says.

But McQueen was not well, mentally or physically. "There were a lot of bad hangover days, missing his plane," the assistant admits now. "He had us ask our doctor for pethidine"—an opioid analgesic similar to opium—"but the doctor refused to give him a prescription."

IT WAS A BULLISH TIME for Dior: the house announced that sales were up 42 percent during the first six months of the year, to $127 million, thanks to a surge in leather goods and accessories sales. The company planned to open an additional fourteen stores by the end of the year, bringing the count to just over one hundred worldwide, which would no doubt boost second-half year sales. In fact, LVMH was booming: the group's sales increased 40 percent to $4.8 billion in the first six months of 2000.

In mid-July, it was couture season again—fall–winter 2000–2001—and Galliano, fresh off the homeless controversy, decided it was time to go for all-out shock. That was, after all, his mandate from Arnault. Once, when Arnault thought a collection was too sedate, he ordered Galliano up to his Dior office and said: "Where is the madness?"

"So now Monsieur Arnault and I joke about the 10 percent madness," Galliano said. "It has to be there."

"What I like is to feel the emotion," Arnault said. "I understand [John's] way of thinking, which is, 'I'm not going to make a presentation to show the products that you can find in the showroom.' So really, you are shocked by what you see and I like it, I must say. And I agree even more when I see the sales results."

Arnault applauded Galliano's proposal to name Dior's new lipstick "Addict" and he approved of Galliano's new collection theme: sadomasochism. Shock made headlines, and headlines triggered explosive sales—and that was Arnault's top priority. He was playing both a short game and a long game: he wanted to be super rich now, but he also wanted to turn Dior into a powerful global luxury brand that would reign for decades to come, like Chanel and Louis Vuitton had for most of the twentieth century. Galliano said that he and Robinson came up with the S&M idea after reading correspondences between Sigmund Freud and Carl Jung. But given a story I had recently heard from a reliable source about Robinson's being found by the housekeeper hog-tied on the floor and dressed in women's lingerie, I wondered if there wasn't a bit of first person thrown in there too.

The sumptuous main hall at the École des Beaux-Arts on Saturday afternoon, July 8, was lit a fiery red and sounds of cracking whips, panting, and moaning echoed against its vaulted ceiling. The show opened with what

Vogue described as "a Felliniesque wedding processional" with the proper clothes cut askew again, but it quickly devolved into something darker and kinkier: models wearing red duct tape over their mouths, gold handcuff bracelets, and dog collars—there was even a nun with her hands tied behind her back. One outfit, of a military officer, was originally accessorized with a Nazi SS cap; when Toledano saw it during the rehearsal, he asked Galliano to remove it from the show. Galliano complied. The press reaction was brutal: "How can women be expected to embrace clothes, however beautifully done, that symbolize their degradation?" Menkes asked. "To make light of bondage straps just because they are executed with such a light hand?"

IN AUGUST, MCQUEEN MARRIED Forsyth in Ibiza, a Spanish island known for its twenty-four-hour outdoor nightclubs. McQueen had proposed to Forsyth during a fun dinner with Annabelle Neilson and Kate Moss—who had become a good McQueen friend—at the Groucho Club in Soho a few weeks earlier.

"I'll organize it," Neilson offered. "I'll be your bridesmaid, Lee."

"I'll be yours, George," Moss said.

"We thought it would be something small, a blessing in some derelict church or something," Forsyth said. "It didn't turn out that way."

On the night of the wedding, Neilson had booked two chauffeured Bentleys—one for McQueen and Neilson, the other for Forsyth and Moss—to ferry them from their rented luxury villa through the town of San Antonio to the port, where they boarded a three-story yacht reportedly owned by the prince of Gambia that a McQueen friend had chartered. British tourists shouted: "It's Kate Moss! It's Kate Moss!"

A crew of McQueen's famous friends, including Jude Law and his then-wife Sadie Frost, music producer Nellee Hooper, the model Karen Mulder, Patsy Kensit, and Noel and Meg Gallagher, were all on board to celebrate. "There were no family," Forsyth said. "It was all party people." The vows were performed at midnight by "some weird New Age priest who spoke very bad English," Forsyth recalled, since McQueen was an atheist. They exchanged diamond-encrusted wedding bands that Shaun Leane had made, each engraved "George & Lee." The union was not legally recognized, but McQueen and Forsyth didn't care: they *felt* married. Once the ceremony was complete, the boat sailed out to sea, and they kicked off the party, with "20,000 pounds [worth] of champagne . . . [and] lobster," Forsyth said. "Lee and I went down to the front, under the moonlight. It was a perfect night."

Galliano too had found love: Alexis Roche, a pretty, blue-eyed young Frenchman who worked as a stylist. They met in 1999, but because Galliano still compartmentalized his life when it came to his love life and his family, Roche remained in the shadows. It was Galliano's first serious relationship in almost a decade—since he and Conran had split up. Roche moved into the rue de la Perle apartment and joined Dior, dressing celebrities.

THE MARKETING SIDE OF GIVENCHY continued to undermine McQueen. "I'd design, they'd change the whole thing, and then the press would give me the flak for it," he later said. "I was never given that chance."

Finally, McQueen decided he'd suffered enough. He called Tom Ford, who set up an appointment for him with De Sole. McQueen liked what he heard and began talking seriously with Gucci Group. He also put in motion his exit strategy from Givenchy. He gave up his flat in the Marais and started staying in a suite at the Four Seasons George V, just up the street from the office. All his expenses were covered by Givenchy.

In September, he put together a collection in London that he called "my best yet." He titled it "VOSS" after a Norwegian town known for bird watching, and explained that it was "about nature and the elements. I wanted to get away from gemstones and all that glitz." The starting point came when he and Forsyth were walking along a beach in Suffolk and came across a pile of razor clam shells. As when he and Groves found the pallet wrap in Elizabeth Street, McQueen's creative mind popped at the sight: *Gotta make a fucking dress!* He collected hundreds of the finger-shaped shells, brought them back to London, designed a long sleeveless column and covered it entirely with them, like fringe. That led to the use of other sorts of shells, as well as sea pearls and feathers.

Another aha moment came when he was in the Porte de Clignancourt flea market and found a nineteenth-century Japanese screen made of embroidered silk. He bought it and had it shipped back to London, where he and Sarah Heard delicately sliced off the fragile fabric. They fused it to a stronger cotton, which McQueen then hand-sewed into a Korean-shaped kimono to be worn over a full skirt covered with flat black oyster shells. The ensemble would be topped off with a Shaun Leane neckpiece of silver branches decorated with gray Tahitian pearls. Because of all the craftsmanship, "VOSS" was going to be a particularly costly collection; again, American Express helped to cover expenses.

The last major influence was photographer Joel-Peter Witkin's spooky 1983 picture *Sanitarium,* of a voluptuous naked woman wearing a head mask with Mercury-like wings on her ears, reclining in a classical pose and breathing through a glass tube attached to the mouth of a monkey strung up on the backdrop wall. By then, McQueen owned seven Witkins—one was a birthday gift from Elton John and David Furnish.

"VOSS" was scheduled for September 26 at the Victoria bus depot again. Guests were seated around a giant mirrored cube, forcing them to look at themselves; it was a deeply uncomfortable moment. The show got off to a late start because Gwyneth Paltrow was stuck in traffic. McQueen said the show wouldn't begin until she arrived.

Not all celebrities were so lucky—or respected—chez McQueen. Victoria Beckham, who was still known then as Posh Spice, apparently asked to attend McQueen's show and he turned her down. "Fucking right," he said. "At the end of the day, it's about my clothes and the hard work that everyone backstage puts into it, not about the tosser sitting in the front row lapping it up. And that's why I didn't let Posh Spice come to it. . . . The stars you see at my shows, be it Gwyneth Paltrow, be it anyone else, are there because I've got a connection with them . . . [I design for] intelligent women."

Galliano didn't have the same take on the Beckhams: "Posh and Becks, they're the gods," he said.

Once Paltrow was safely in her seat, the hall went dark and the mirrored cube came to light, revealing a room with one-way mirrored and padded walls and white tile floors, like that of a psychiatric ward; the audience could see in, like voyeurs, but the models would only be able to see their reflections. In the middle sat a big box with rust-stained walls. The show opened with Kate Moss, her head wrapped in white gauze bandages by the hairdresser Guido Palau as if she had just undergone brain surgery, her makeup, by Val Garland, stark and pallid. She was dressed in a shell pink chiffon tunic and skirt draped with swaths of jagged ruffles and she stumbled around the room and felt her way along the mirrors, as if trying to figure out how to escape; it was a disturbing setup.

Moss was followed by models similarly wrapped with head bandages and flailing about. "You're in a lunatic asylum," he told them before the show. "I need you to go mental, have a nervous breakdown, die, and then come back to life. And, if you can, do that in three minutes." They did, while each dressed in an exquisite and wholly individual outfit. One wore a long jade green ostrich plume skirt and almond green chiffon top, with taxidermy hawks attached to her head and shoulders that bobbed as she walked, recalling Hitchcock's *The Birds* again. Another came out in a long black skirt covered with shiny black mussel shells, which she ripped off and smashed on the floor in a mad dance. There was Erin O'Connor in the razor clam shell sheath, which she too destroyed, per McQueen's instructions. "The shells had outlived their usefulness on the beach, so we put them to another use on a dress," he explained. "Then Erin came out and trashed the dress, so their usefulness was over once again. Kind of like fashion, really."

Karen Elson wore the Japanese screen kimono and black oyster shell skirt; another model was dressed in a gray Japanese kimono with elaborate floral and bird embroidery and a matching rectangle box hat trimmed with swaying kelly green amaranth. There was an engraved red Venetian glass corset, worn with a black pencil skirt. And for the closing look, a sleeveless gown with a bodice made of bloodred stained glass microscope slides and a skirt of red and black ostrich plumes. The dress simultaneously clinked and floated as the model moved. Sandwiched between the show pieces were some remarkably handsome and wearable clothes, such as a sea green jersey halter dress; a perfect black shift with matching trench; and smartly tailored tuxedos in black and in white.

For the finale—because now there was always a finale—the lights went down, and in the darkness, the sides of the box in the center of the room fell open revealing transgressive writer Michelle Olley, plump and naked and lounging on an antique chaise longue, as in Witkin's photo. She too wore a winged head mask and was breathing through a glass tube and was enveloped by a cloud of fluttering moths. The audience exploded in cheers and applause. "So beautiful! So elegant!" Isabella cried. "Fucking hell!"

"It's to do with the politics of the world—the way life is—and what is beauty," McQueen told Menkes backstage. "I suppose I have the vision of an artist."

Most everyone there agreed. Horyn called McQueen "a great designer who is not only making beautiful clothes, but also responding, like an artist, to the horror and insanity in contemporary culture."

MCQUEEN'S CONTRACT at Givenchy was LVMH's standard agreement—"airtight," recalls a player involved with the negotiations—and it was going to take a lot of maneuvering to extricate him from it. But Betsy Pearce, a no-nonsense American lawyer who specialized in representing fashion designers, and the legal team at Gucci Group were up to the challenge. To avoid McQueen's being seen entering and exiting Gucci Group headquarters, he met with De Sole and the lawyers in a back room of Brown's Hotel in Mayfair. It all went relatively easily on the Gucci side, because McQueen insisted, "I don't care about the money. I just care about my freedom."

The strain of maintaining secrecy, however, was starting to weigh heavily on him. Already the fame he now had gave him panic attacks; he was unable to handle all this on top of it and wanted to sign as soon as possible. During the entire final week of negotiations in London—the last week of November 2000—he dodged Tesler's phone calls. On Friday, December 1, he was supposed to have dinner with Tesler and Yves Carcelle, head of LVMH's fashion division, in London. He suspected they were going to offer to buy the McQueen company again. Instead of confronting them and saying no, he had his assistant cancel on his behalf, and he went home, watched television, and had "mad sex" with Forsyth.

The next afternoon—Saturday, December 2—he took a taxi with Forsyth and McQueen brand spokeswoman Amie Witton to the Gucci Group headquarters on Grafton Street to sign the contract. But he was so nervous, he refused to get out of the cab. It took an hour to lure him out and up to the fourth-floor offices.

Once the deal was done, they toasted it with mineral water and Coca-Cola, since, as De Sole pointed out, they were working. McQueen and his crew then went to Maison Bertaux in Soho to celebrate. Later that night, he dined with Pearce, ordered a mound of caviar and gobbled it down with a spoon.

On Monday morning, Gucci Group issued a press release announcing that it had acquired 51 percent of the Alexander McQueen company, Bluebird—named for the garage where he had staged his first show, "Nihilism"—for an undisclosed amount. The deal was reportedly for $25 million—therefore valuing the company for two and a half times its annual revenue—and McQueen would maintain creative control. "This was a real windfall for a guy, this fee," said one of the negotiators. "An astronomical fee."

Among the deal points: Gucci would manufacture both McQueen's women's wear and menswear at its factory in Italy—which, as it happened, was the old Zamasport factory where he used to work for Gigli; the company would close the Conduit Street store and open three new ones—on Bond Street in London, in Aoyama in Tokyo, and in the Meatpacking District of Manhattan; there would be a rollout of perfumes and eyewear; McQueen would stage his shows in Paris; and he would launch a bespoke tailoring line for men and couture for women. "I don't think Arnault would have ever given me that," he said, "because he hadn't given John [Galliano] it."

Gucci stated that "this relationship will become exclusive upon the expiry in October 2001 of [McQueen's] other current creative responsibilities"—namely his Givenchy contract. A Gucci spokesman pointedly added: "We did not do this [deal] because of LVMH. It's part of our long-term strategy to acquire brands in the luxury market."

"The one thing that is important is that Alexander must have his creative independence," De Sole said. "Does he really have the power and the talent to turn the Alexander McQueen label into a global brand? I think he does. Otherwise I could not have done the deal."

According to a Givenchy source, Arnault was "blindsided" by the announcement. "Carcelle kept making appointments with Alexander to talk about this rumor of defecting and Alexander kept breaking them," a Givenchy staffer told me. "And Marianne Tesler kept saying, 'Lee would never do that.' She fucked up badly and so did Yves."

LVMH responded with its own press release, which stated that, since it did not own a piece of McQueen's brand as it did with John Galliano's, Michael Kors's, and Marc Jacobs's companies, it was only "normal that Mr. McQueen should seek financing for his tiny business." Arnault said he didn't mind that McQueen was leaving. "He's always complaining about something," Arnault reportedly said, adding that LVMH hadn't fired McQueen "because we're polite."

When the news was announced, McQueen was in Paris, as was Isabella Blow, and the pair met up at the Hôtel Costes to celebrate. It was a bittersweet moment for Isabella: while she was thrilled for her friend, she was heartbroken once again. Yes, she was still fashion director for the *Sunday Times Magazine*, and flourishing there creatively, with forty fashion shoots a year, but she and Detmar weren't earning enough to keep themselves and Hilles afloat. She had hoped that with the new Gucci deal, McQueen would finally thank her for all of those years of support with a job, or a consultancy gig, or a bonus. "Isabella had expected to be a part of the deal going into Gucci," says a source privy to the negotiations. "She expected to be—*a lot*." She confided her frustrations to her friend British socialite Daphne Guinness. "She was upset," Guinness confirmed. "Once the deals started happening, she fell by the wayside. Everybody else got contracts, and she got a free dress."

WITH THE GUCCI MONEY, McQueen bought a new home in Essex for his parents and a Georgian house on Victoria Park in East London for himself, where he and Forsyth planned to raise a family. "I want to have a kid and believe I should be able to have a kid," he said.

He also went on a major spending spree. When he and Forsyth were in New York, they spent the day shopping and came home with two Warhols that cost 125,000 pounds apiece. He bought one of the huge Swarovski chandeliers he saw in the Four Seasons George V lobby for 30,000 pounds—just so he could use the crystals to decorate his Christmas tree back home in London. One night he booked a private jet to fly with Forsyth to Spain for cocktails, Paris for dinner, and Amsterdam for clubbing.

While watching a television show about Kenya that Christmas, McQueen turned to Forsyth and said, "Fancy going to Africa?" Forty-eight hours later, they were flying alone to Nairobi in the upstairs first-class section of a 747— McQueen had purchased all the seats so they could have the cabin to themselves. After a few days in Kenya, McQueen grew bored, so he chartered a private jet and flew the two of them to Naomi Campbell's villa in Cape Town to ring in the New Year with a clan of fashion folk.

IN THE NEW YEAR, McQueen had to return to Paris to put together his couture collection. Tesler had agreed to let McQueen go before the end of his contract in October, but insisted that he do the fall–winter 2001–2002 couture and ready-to-wear collections—thereby giving her time to find his replacement. McQueen was furious—he desperately wanted to go home to London and start the new chapter of his life. And Tesler was still upset that he had defected—betraying her, in essence.

"He hated it there so much," remembers an observer at the time. "And he hated them. Any chance he got just to stick a finger in the eye of Arnault, that's what he did." During an interview with the *Observer*, he described his time at Givenchy as "worse than being a gladiator." When no one was around, he pilfered bolts of expensive cloth and leather for his studio in London. While staying at the George V—still on Givenchy's dime—he swiped all the towels, sheets, bathrobes, and bath products in his suite. "He would order caviar room service and then put a cigarette out in it," an observer says. "He would take everything out of the minibar and give it to us to take home. He cleaned the place out each time he was there."

McQueen based his new couture collection on his trip to Kenya with Forsyth, and he was planning to do a lavish show at the Palais Omnisports de Paris-Bercy stadium as his couture swan song. But at the last minute, Tesler canceled the show and announced there would only be a presentation for clients in-house, with no press or photographers present. Officially, Tesler said the cancellation was because the seamstresses were on strike over the new government-imposed thirty-five-hour workweek, and there were not enough completed outfits for a show. But a Givenchy source told me then that the directive came from "way high above, higher than Tesler, to punish McQueen" for his defection to Gucci Group.

Reporters gathered in front of Givenchy's Avenue George V entrance and questioned clients as they exited about what they saw and loved. The mood was "very subdued and very lovely," one said. Models walked through two rooms to a classical music score, and there were approximately three dozen looks, which clients described to me as "unwearable," "unthinkable," and "unbelievably beautiful." Among the favorites: a long fringed bustier dress in chestnut-colored leather; a draped tan cashmere smocked jumpsuit embroidered with glass and wooden beads; a long red satin and white georgette bias striped gown with beaded peonies; and an asymmetrical gown in perforated snakeskin trimmed with faux tortoiseshell rings. And the accessories were monumental, like a pavé diamond collar held by eagle claws from each shoulder. At first, McQueen refused to take a bow, but the audience gave him a standing ovation and cheered. Finally, he emerged hand in hand with the heads of the ateliers. "It was so moving, beautiful, and humble," an observer said. Even Tesler wept. McQueen skipped back and thanked everyone backstage. Minutes later I spotted him and Forsyth speeding off in a taxi.

In the midst of the shows, LVMH reported that sales in 1999 had exploded. Louis Vuitton, the group's cash cow, experienced a "spectacular" fourth quarter, with sales jumping an astounding 45 percent, the operating profits rising more than 20 percent. Though LVMH did not state what Vuitton's annual sales actually were, analysts estimated them to be $1.8 billion. Overall, the group's revenues for 1999 rose 23 percent to $8.58 billion—an impressive turnaround from 1998, when they fell 5.4 percent to $6.9 billion.

MCQUEEN RETURNED TO LONDON to receive the British Designer of the Year award—his third—from Prince Charles. During his acceptance speech, he railed against the lack of British institutional support for local fashion, pointing out that it was an Italian company that came to his rescue. The next day, he put on his namesake label show. He titled it "What a Merry-Go-Round"—he actually had an antique carousel for the set—and it seemed like a pointed sendup of both Galliano and LVMH. In front of an audience that included McQueen's new boss Domenico De Sole, the show opened with the voice of the fiendish child catcher from the movie *Chitty Chitty Bang Bang* offering free candy and ice cream to village children so he could capture them and lock them in the dungeon of the evil Baron Bomburst's castle. The allusion to Arnault was clear.

Some of the models wore tricorner wigs like those Galliano used for his swashbuckling "Filibustiers" 1993 show, which McQueen had already mocked back then with his drag look at Kinky Gerlinky. Other models had Marcel Wave hair like Galliano had been favoring recently for his shows and himself. Their makeup was either 1930s-style, with red button lips—another Galliano staple—or clown faces in greasepaint. Some of the clothes were decidedly McQueen, like the dragon-embroidered kimono or the peacock leather miniskirt.

But much was a riff on Galliano signatures such as sheer lace slip dresses, biker jackets, French military coats, and decorative sashes, which McQueen showed to the haunting soundtrack of the horror picture *Rosemary's Baby*. One model, in a very Galliano-looking black bias-cut gown and stiletto pumps, came out with the gold skeleton from the "Dante" show holding her ankle and she dragged it across the floor as she walked. For the closing, models dressed as clowns and wearing very Galliano-like chiffon gowns, rode the carousel to the strains of Julie Andrews singing, "A spoonful of sugar helps the medicine go down" from *Mary Poppins*. "There were a lot of metaphors for my life in that show," McQueen admitted. "Some of it is fun and some is dark and sinister."

XVII

On November 27, 2001, the day before his forty-first birthday, Galliano went to Buckingham Palace to receive the Commander of the Order of the British Empire (CBE) from Queen Elizabeth II. For his investiture, Galliano wore a traditional morning suit by Brioni without a shirt; his hair was long and blond. He claimed to be "surprised" by the decoration—especially given that he had stood up the queen at a state dinner not five years before. "It's one of the greatest honors I've ever had," he said. "I'm very proud."

About six weeks later, he rang André Leon Talley, who was in Paris for the couture collections, and asked him to come by the Dior studio for a preview of the collection. Talley was touched by the call—though still friendly, they didn't see each other much anymore, due to Galliano's hectic schedule and Steven Robinson's control. "I want you to come see my clothes," Galliano insisted.

That Saturday evening, two days before Galliano's couture show, Talley went to 30, Avenue Montaigne and met with Galliano in the studio. "I have something for you," Galliano told Talley, and he went into his office and came out with a small box.

"This belongs to you," Galliano said.

Talley opened the box. Inside was Galliano's CBE decoration. He was speechless.

"He could have given it to his mother," Talley says now, his eyes welling up with tears as he recalls the moment. "But he gave it to me."

"If you ever want it back, you can have it," Talley told Galliano. "You can always take it back." Galliano assured him it was fine. Talley keeps it in a safe in New York. "I thought it was the greatest gesture he could have ever done."

GALLIANO THEN KICKED OFF an extraordinary year of wild shows and publicity events, exotic travel and nonstop store openings. While the rest of the luxury industry—Gucci Group included—was recalibrating their five-year plans to reflect new realities such as post-9/11 gloom, the war in Afghanistan, and the obviously impending one in Iraq, Dior thrived like it hadn't since the 1950s under Monsieur Dior's helm. It seemed that all that Arnault, Toledano, and Galliano had put in motion since Galliano's arrival at Dior in 1997—the new image; the publicity push; the store renovations and expansions; the development of new lines and perfumes—had finally come together gloriously and everything was selling spectacularly well. And Galliano's job appeared to be relatively secure.

For his collections, he was still stirring unrelated ideas together like a sorcerer conjuring magical potions in a cauldron. In one show he referenced Rajasthan gypsies, Wall Street bankers, Arab nomads, Tibetan folklorists; for another, he used the images of 1960s South African photographer Bobson Sukhdeo Mohanlall, who shot portraits of fellow black Africans in traditional as well as modern dress, then added Elvis impersonators and cowboys; for another, at the Centre Pompidou museum, he sent out two nearly naked Japanese Kodo drummers to pound out a beat while models marched down the runway as Eskimos, drum majorettes, and circus ribbon dancers. "Galliano slayed his audience with invention, humor and skill," *Women's Wear* applauded. "It was a tour de force of bravado and, more importantly, beauty."

To ratchet up the hype, Galliano always had star-stuffed front rows. At Dior, along with the usual French political wives there was pop singer Gwen Stefani (who had recently asked him to design her wedding dress); actresses Laura Dern, Penélope Cruz, Christina Ricci, Claire Danes, Rosanna Arquette, and Bette Midler; and rocker Lenny Kravitz.

In October, 2002, Galliano and Dior threw an insane party to celebrate the launch of Dior's new Addict perfume at the legendary Paris cabaret Le Lido. Instead of enlisting the troupe's famed feathered and spangled showgirls to stage their classic, kitschy revue, Galliano had gold-painted pole dancers gyrating to throbbing club music. He arrived by parachuting into the audience with superstar model Gisele Bündchen dressed like Botticelli's *Venus* on his arm. "I've learned that I can trust [John]," Toledano said. "So far he has been right for the advertising, for the shows and for the products."

In 2002, sales for Christian Dior Couture, the fashion and accessories arm of the company, reportedly rose 41 percent, to $535.6 million, and profits were $36 million, a substantial increase from 2001. Dior executives projected that they would double sales to $1 billion by 2006—in four years.

The John Galliano brand was an equal, if far smaller, success. The shows were just as outrageous, like the one where models with faces painted Krishna blue "stormed the runway, wearing jackets as big as zeppelins, clouds of roiling frills, layers of chiffon trimmed in marabou or beautiful chiffon sari dresses that wrapped their way up and around elaborate headdresses and hairdos built around party balloons," *Women's Wear* reported. A Galliano flagship store in Paris was in the planning. And sales for the brand were growing steadily: in 2002, they totaled $29.7 million and were expected to grow another 25 percent in 2003.

WHILE GALLIANO FLOURISHED, McQueen kicked off the new Gucci Group chapter in his life somewhat more conservatively. It started out roughly: in the summer of 2001, he and Forsyth broke up. "Lee was so successful," Forsyth explained, "and I couldn't keep up." McQueen called the separation "painful" and refused to speak to Forsyth for eighteen months. "Lee was very upset," Archie Reed confirms, "but their split made us closer."

On the business side, changes were going far more smoothly, thanks to Gucci Group's might. The McQueen company moved into three-story headquarters, at 10 Amwell Street in the East End, and he had a new CEO, Sue Whiteley, a former buying director for the London department store Harvey Nichols. There was a plan to roll out fifteen new McQueen stores in five years, but McQueen said "that seemed too fast to me [and] Gucci agreed." They dialed it back to less than half a dozen, starting a new London store to replace the small Onward Kashiyama–backed one on Conduit Street. "You know, with me it's more than the money," McQueen said. "I've fought hard to build the McQueen name." He said he wanted it to grow slowly, "to have longevity."

Retailers instantly noticed a major improvement not only in quality but also in wearability of McQueen's clothes. "It was like 'Whoa!'" recalls Julie Gilhart, who was then Barneys' women's fashion director. "One sample after another, each very salable and very sexy. It wasn't watered down for commerciality. It was totally on point. I called New York and talked to the budget and planners and said, 'We need a lot more money for this collection. It's really important.' I think we tripled our budget. I remember thinking, 'Oh my god, it's so amazing. We are going to sell a lot of this.'"

McQueen got on splendidly with Domenico De Sole—a huge change after his four-year tug-of-war with Arnault and his LVMH executives. "I actually have a much more personal relationship with Domenico," McQueen said. "I really appreciate him and respect him as a person—he believes in me and my vision. He doesn't see me as just promoting the Gucci Group, he sees me as promoting McQueen. . . . Gucci is putting a lot into [my company]. It makes me believe in fashion again."

He looked svelte and well. He claimed it was due to yoga, power walking to meetings, and his diet pills. But he was also still doing vast amounts of drugs. "He was spending 600 pounds a night," Reed says. "He had five dealers. Myself and others would try to delete their numbers, but he always found another." On occasion, he would overdose, but he was always treated in time. Gucci Group executives now say they had no idea about McQueen's drug abuse back then. Then-PPR chairman Serge Weinberg adds, "How much is it legitimate for a corporate structure to enter into those personal matters?"

McQueen was resolutely single, dating all sorts of men, including Reed, who split his time between his home and McQueen's. There was also a Welsh-born aspiring designer whom McQueen would regularly hook up with at Soho bars like Shadow Lounge. They'd go back to McQueen's most recent home, near Finsbury Park in Islington, for a night's assignation. "It was like having dates with Elvis," the designer says, "because McQueen was some-one who was completely unobtainable. He was someone I watched for years and years and years, and then we ended up having very interesting en-counters."

They would do Ecstasy or ketamine, known as "Special K"—the horse tranquilizer that the designer said "makes you numb but sort of horny." One night, when they walked into McQueen's bedroom, the designer noticed a video camera on a tripod.

"You're not going to film it," he said.

"No, no, that's the last thing I want," McQueen responded. "This is purely for me to check that I'm not raped again."

"I wouldn't do that!" the designer insisted.

"No, not you," McQueen assured him. "I was raped by a ghost when I was little. I'm going to film while we are sleeping."

First thing the next morning, McQueen watched the video at fast speed, verified that he hadn't been raped by a ghost, deleted the film, and set the camera back up for the next night. This happened a few times, the designer said. As soon as they were dressed, he'd kick his lover out. "He made me breakfast once," the designer said. But usually "he couldn't wait to get rid of me."

"I'm enjoying life," McQueen said. "I know what I want out of relation-ships, and I'm much more secure in my own mind than I ever was before."

When not in London, McQueen was in Milan at the Gucci Group show-room, Novara at the former Zamasport factory, or Paris for sourcing trips or to stage his shows. McQueen chose to show his collection in Paris, because there was a bigger audience and more media coverage than in London. That meant fashion's two great showmen were pitted against each other during Paris Fashion Week twice a year. Galliano feigned to not care; he worked with blinders on and claimed to not know what his confreres were up to.

McQueen, however, took the challenge to heart, and would either try to outdo or to skewer Galliano whenever he could. For his spring–summer 2002 women's wear show, in October 2001, McQueen put on a Spanish-themed show called "The Dance of the Twisted Bull," which was a direct hit at Galliano. Against a backdrop of a film of a swishing matador's cape and a snorting bull, models came out dressed in high-waist matador pants, jet-beaded boleros, and swinging 1950s dresses, as Galliano had done during his brief tenure at Givenchy. The most poignant look was a model dressed in a red polka-dotted Galliano-style señorita dress, speared through the torso.

For his spring–summer 2003 collection "Irere," in October 2002, McQueen used as his primary inspiration Roland Joffé's 1986 film *The Mission*, a historical drama about a Spanish Jesuit priest (played by Jeremy Irons) who tries to protect a South American indigenous tribe from capture by Portuguese slave traders. One of the grand ball gowns was made of ivory organza with a shredded asymmetrical top and thick waves of ruffles to the floor: it is a masterful reinterpretation of Galliano's shellfish dress—the one that McQueen had obsessed over for years—and it was far more beautiful and elegant than the original.

Expansion continued. McQueen introduced a made-to-measure menswear line at the Savile Row tailor H. Huntsman & Sons. In the summer of 2002, he opened his first boutique in the United States, in the Meatpacking District of New York, followed, in February 2003, by a new shop on Old Bond Street in London. Next up was Milan, in the Montenapoleone shopping quarter in the summer of 2003. On March 17, 2003—McQueen's thirty-fourth birthday—he launched his first perfume, Kingdom. In June, he learned that, like Galliano, he would be honored with a CBE from Queen Elizabeth II for his services to the fashion industry. The investiture would be in the fall.

Though he only had one company to worry about, instead of two jobs like when he was at Givenchy, McQueen found his workload relentless. His only respite were his two homes: an elegant three-story Georgian townhouse facing Victoria Park in Hackney, and an eighteenth-century stone farmhouse overlooking the English Channel near Hastings. Like the East End, Hastings had a dark history, having served as a smuggling port during the Middle Ages. "It's so quiet—desolate, really—but that's why I go," he said of the area, adding that the house "is like an old pirate's place."

THREE DAYS BEFORE the Dior fall–winter 2003–2004 haute couture show in July, Galliano's father died in Spain. "He was fine and then he just faded," Galliano later explained. Galliano didn't tell anyone in the atelier about his father's passing except for his inner circle and his bosses because he didn't want the team to lose focus. Arnault kindly lent Galliano the company's corporate jet to fly down to Gibraltar for the funeral. At forty-two, Galliano had never managed to tell his father that he was homosexual. "It was all very Latin and complicated between me and my father," he said.

Upon his return, Galliano conducted fittings with Bill Gaytten, Robinson, and the Dior atelier head Raffaele Ilardo throughout the night, as flamenco music blared on the sound system. "Flamenco music is always about somebody's pain," Galliano explained. "It never comes out okay in the end."

Though he went home well after midnight, he was up at dawn and went out for his usual three-mile run, followed by weightlifting and crunches. He showered, dressed in a shirt and worn jeans, and arrived at work looking worn out, sad, and numb. He went to his dressing room backstage, which was well appointed, including bouquets of flowers and a zebra rug on the floor, and he told his personal stylist: "I'm feeling very Spanish tango dirty creepy with oily black hair." The stylist understood and instructed the team on how to create a corresponding look.

The hairstylist attached a goatee to Galliano's chin and trimmed it to complement his pencil-thin mustache, and he curled Galliano's long, now-dark hair into a stringy mess. The makeup artist charcoaled Galliano's eyes to look like the devil's. He dressed in blue track pants with gray embroidery, a tight-fitting mesh tube top over a torn gray long-sleeved T-shirt, suede boots and a pair of hoop earrings, and he oiled up his muscled chest and face and smeared himself with dirt.

"This day is going to be hard," he admitted. "But I can deal with that later. Right now I need to focus on the show. I want people to forget about their electricity bills, their jobs, everything. It's fantasy time. My goal is really very simple: when a man looks at a woman wearing one of my dresses, I would like him basically to be saying to himself, 'I have to fuck her.' I think every woman deserves to be desired. Is that really asking too much?"

The models strode down a conventional catwalk in the dark, the backdrop and catwalk lighted in blinking colorful squares, like a giant piece of rainbow-colored graph paper. The clothes were the usual Galliano mixed bag of over-the-top madness: corseted Can-Can dresses; fluffy tulle ball skirts whacked mid-calf; long, loose flapper dresses with ample full-length furs, all in soft pastels and rich jewel tones like ruby and aquamarine. Everything was exaggerated, disheveled, torn, or seemingly unfinished, with strings dangling off hems like oversized threads. Stephen Jones's hats were equally fantastical: big furry horns in Popsicle colors and a Vegas showgirl plumed headdress in cotton candy pink.

For the finale, Healy served up the sound of flamenco dancing for the models' encore parade. Once they returned backstage, the room went dark, and as the thousand-plus crowd shouted and cheered Galliano came out to the wails of a male flamenco singer and marched purposefully, looking nearly demonic. After greeting editors, retailers, and celebrities backstage, including Jack Nicholson and Elizabeth Hurley, he finally erupted into tears. "That was for my father today," he said. "I hope I would have made him proud."

McQUEEN SPENT HIS AUGUST HOLIDAY in Ibiza. While there, he met up with Sebastian Pons. They hadn't spoken since Pons had left to work for Adrover in New York three years earlier. The job move had not gone well: after the September 11 attacks in New York, Adrover's backer, Pegasus, went belly-up, and Adrover was forced to close his company and lay everyone off.

Pons gave McQueen a big hug and was shocked at how thin he was. "All I felt was bones," Pons recalls. McQueen pulled up his shirt and showed Pons his liposuction scar. Pons was mortified. "He had paid a big price to be skinny," Pons says.

McQueen then shared some news he had recently received: he was HIV positive. Despite his taste for sex clubs, McQueen had been relatively careful when it came to STDs. "His idea was to have a boyfriend, get tested, and then they could have wild sex," Pons says. "He was really concerned about AIDS. He was not the sort to have unsafe sex." And yet, he had been infected and said he believed he'd contracted it from George Forsyth. He assured Pons that he was taking his meds and everything would be fine. But Pons could tell that everything was not fine with his old friend—not at all.

———————

McQUEEN'S SHOWS, LIKE GALLIANO'S, had always been somewhat auto-biographical. But in October 2003, he poured everything—his emotions, his work, his loves, his life, and, unbeknownst to most everyone, his diagnosis of HIV—into a show that still stands today as his masterpiece. He called it "Deliverance."

The inspiration was Sydney Pollack's monumental 1969 drama *They Shoot Horses Don't They?*, a film about Depression-era characters in a months-long dance marathon. It seemed to be an allegory for McQueen's life and career.

He hired dancer/choreographer Michael Clark, formerly of the Royal Ballet, to help with the show, which was staged on Friday, October 10, 2003, at the Salle Wagram, the old boxing hall that Galliano had used for his "Fili-bustiers" show in the early 1990s. It began with an emcee announcing the competition, with a half dozen couples—a mix of professional dancers and models, the men in muscle shirts and baggy, pleated trousers, the women in 1930s-style suits, day dresses, and delicate sequin and beaded bias-cut gowns—ballroom dancing across the wooden floor to Duke Ellington's "Take the 'A' Train." As the music amped up to a disco beat, so did the moves—tango, rhumba, fox-trot—the chiffon skirts swishing with each twirl.

After ten minutes, the lights briefly went down, signaling a second act. Out came the models and dancers—the men in tank tops, shorts, and sneakers, the women in flouncy floral day dresses and heels—and they ran as couples, arm in arm in a large oval, as if it were a track and they were in a race. They ran and ran, pushing each other and stumbling, until they were panting and col-lapsed in a heap.

Then came the closing act: the dance marathon finalists. The women dancers were visibly exhausted and disheveled, and began to flail about madly, their male partners holding them up, or dragging them off into the darkness. Eventually one remained, a redhead in a silver lamé column. She carried on, wobbling and lurching in the spotlights until she fell to the floor, crumpled and lifeless. The lights went dark.

XVIII

On the morning of October 29, 2003, McQueen put on his family's Scottish Highland dress and escorted his mother, dressed in a pink McQueen suit and Philip Treacy hat, and his father, in a Savile Row suit, to Buckingham Palace to receive the decoration of Commander of the Most Excellent Order of the British Empire from Queen Elizabeth II. McQueen was reluctant to accept the honor, and only did so at his mother's insistence. When he stood before the queen, he locked eyes with her, and told his parents that it was "like falling in love."

"How long have you been a fashion designer?" the queen asked.

"A few years, milady," he responded.

Then, he later recalled, "I looked into her eyes [and] it was obvious that she had her fair share of shit going on. I felt sorry for her. I've said a lot of stuff about the Queen in the past—she sits on her arse and she gets paid an awful lot of money for it—but for that instant I had a bit of compassion for her. So I came away feeling humbled."

THAT SAME DAY, *The New York Times* reported that Tom Ford and Domenico De Sole were in a power struggle with PPR management over who should run Gucci Group and could be forced to leave the company when their contracts expired the following April. McQueen had grown close to De Sole, dining informally at De Sole's home in London, or meeting with De Sole at the office to ask how business worked. He wanted to learn and De Sole was willing to counsel him.

Unfortunately, negotiations with PPR's new head, Pinault's son François-Henri, did not go well, and De Sole and Ford confirmed that they would indeed be leaving Gucci Group in the spring. McQueen was shattered by the news. As a consolation, young Pinault asked McQueen to replace Ford at Yves Saint Laurent—a job McQueen had fantasized about as a student at Central Saint Martins. McQueen thought seriously about it; he even asked a former staffer from Givenchy to join his Saint Laurent team. "It was almost a done deal," the assistant says.

Then it all fell apart. McQueen told the assistant the breaking point came when he insisted that all editorial credit should read "Alexander McQueen for Yves Saint Laurent," and when the PPR executives refused, he "threw the contract back at them and said no." McQueen later claimed he turned the job down because he was afraid he wouldn't be able to handle designing his own brand and Saint Laurent without one suffering.

The Saint Laurent job went to a then-unknown Gucci assistant named Stefano Pilati, who would be in principle far cheaper and easier to control than a star, and PPR promoted Gucci's in-house accessories designer Frida Giannini, also unknown, to replace Ford there. With those appointments, the power shift from the creative to the executive seemed complete. Stars like

Ford, Galliano, and McQueen made the brands they worked for famous—so famous that the marquee designers were no longer necessary; the brands could stand on their own recognition-wise as well as creatively. "We put an organization in place," a major luxury brand executive explained to me. "There were teams for every level and collection." The machine was humming; star designers were now expendable.

More surprising, however, was PPR's choice to replace De Sole: the company hired Robert Polet, a former Unilever executive who had previously run Häagen-Dazs and who quickly became known in fashion circles as "the Ice Cream Man." While kind and courteous, Polet knew little about the luxury fashion industry. What he did know about—his sole mission—was growth.

And McQueen's business grew, fast, under the guidance of his new CEO: thirty-seven-year-old Jonathan Akeroyd, a working-class–raised South Londoner who had worked his way up at Harrods from sales assistant to merchandising director. He implemented an ambitious new strategy for the company: In less than two years, the brand launched eyewear; menswear, which he showed in Milan; McQ, a younger, lower-priced line for men and women; and a second fragrance, My Queen. McQueen collaborated with Puma to create a special line of sneakers and received a lot of special orders for red carpet events and weddings. One was for his assistant Sarah Heard, who, in 2004, married fashion photographer David Burton, and became known as Sarah Burton. But McQueen didn't care about his job anymore: "I go in, do my business, do the parties, and leave," he said.

His shows evinced that disenchantment. They were still spectacular productions since he had pots of money, and, on occasion, biting commentaries on how he saw fashion, like "It's Only a Game," which he staged in October 2004 on a giant chessboard with the models lined up like chess pieces. But most felt like soulless exercises, such as "The Man Who Knew Too Much" in March 2005, a revisit of the Hitchcock theme, but in a far more literal sense than "The Birds" was a decade earlier; and "Neptune" in October 2005, which was named for the Roman god of the sea and was all white and gold like his first Givenchy show in 1997. The only thing notable about that show was McQueen taking his bow wearing a T-shirt that read "WE LOVE YOU KATE" to support model Kate Moss, who had recently lost several lucrative contracts after being filmed snorting cocaine.

McQueen's longtime friends and associates also noticed a definite shift in how his clothes were produced and marketed: what was on store sales floors had little to do with what he was showing on the runway. "They were rich-lady clothes and they didn't have any of his coolness, or his magic," says an observer. "They were just jackets, skirts, pants—supercommercial versions of his clothes. The rawness goes missing when things get slick and corporate."

Though McQueen reveled in his increased wealth—his art collection grew to include "lots of Chapman brothers, a bit of Warhol, lots of Joel Wit-kins, lots of Sam Taylor-Wood," he boasted—he became more socially with-drawn. Tiina Laakkonen remembers going backstage with Isabella Blow and Philip Treacy to see him after one of his shows: "He'd had a room built where no one was allowed to go," she says. "I was allowed in with Isabella and Philip to say hi, but he wouldn't let other people in there because he couldn't deal with any of that."

To cope, McQueen upped his narcotics consumption. He recognized he had a problem: in recent years, he had tried to quit a few times with profes-sional help. One time, he traveled to a rehab clinic in California, but once he got there, didn't like the place or its approach and turned around and went home. His staff was resigned to the situation, and rather than confront him or stage an intervention, they enabled him. When he went to New York to launch the new menswear line in 2004, Barneys invited him to host an event and party. To prepare for it, Barneys brass met with a McQueen PR assistant, who specified:

"Alexander will need a room . . . a room where he can do his drugs."

The Barneys executives were astonished by the request, and explained that not only were they uncomfortable with it, it was illegal. No, they responded, there would not be a room for McQueen to "do his drugs." The event went on as scheduled; though he was in New York, he was a no-show.

McQueen was so disenchanted with his life and his career that he started coming up with escape scenarios: jobs he'd rather do; places he'd rather live. He spent a fair amount of time in New York and rented a townhouse with the plan to move there for a few months—but he never did. He took more adven-turesome vacations, often with Annabelle Neilson. They'd go scuba diving in the Maldives or skiing in the Alps, or swimming with dolphins in Thailand. He went to Majorca to visit Pons, and bought a house on the spot. Pons was concerned about his old friend's state of mind. "He wasn't the same person as the kid in Hoxton Square doing thorn prints," Pons says. "He had a lot of money and a lot of pressure from work, and I could see he was not well. He was so far away from me—I didn't know how to help him and guide him."

IN EARLY JANUARY 2005, Valérie Hermann was poached from Dior and John Galliano by PPR to run Yves Saint Laurent. "She was really good," says a former Galliano assistant. "Talk about someone who could keep John in line—she could. She could."

Galliano did his best to keep going, and to keep up with his nonstop schedule: in January, he staged a well-received couture show based on Andy Warhol; in February, there was the Oscars with Charlize Theron in a Dior baby blue strapless ruffle gown; in March, at Dior, he showed a groovy 1960s Edie Sedgwick–inspired ready-to-wear collection of strong coats over filmy dresses; at John Galliano, a Cecil B. DeMille–like production with colorful suits galore and fireworks; and he put the finishing touches on the crystal-covered costumes he designed for Australian pop star Kylie Minogue's "Show Girl" tour; in May, he launched a new Dior perfume, Miss Dior Chérie, with an ad campaign starring Elvis Presley's granddaughter Riley Keough, and he attended the annual amfAR Cinema Against AIDS benefit gala and Naomi Campbell's birthday party at the Cannes Film Festival. He missed the CFDA Awards in June, where he won the Fashion Influencer award, because he was badly cut when his glass shower door at home shattered.

In July, there was couture again. And in September, he had a particularly important special order: a white tulle and sequin gown for Bernard Arnault's daughter Delphine's lavish $7 million marriage to Italian wine dynasty heir Alessandro Vallarino Gancia at Arnault's Château d'Yquem winery in Sauternes in September 2005.

In October, for his namesake brand during the spring–summer 2006 women's wear season, Galliano put on one of his most controversial shows ever: called "Everything Is Beautiful," it used as models a mix of giants, dwarfs, cross-dressers, transgenders, seniors, and children as well as the usual slim Caucasian fashion models, wearing gold party dresses, white cotton suits veiled with black tulle, evening gowns in torn chiffon, and Galliano's now-signature Galliano Gazette newsprint fabric. "It was fashion taking on some of its worst biases: fat, old and ugly," wrote *The Washington Post*'s Robin Givhan. "And it was uncomfortable."

Galliano was trying to make a grand commentary on fashion and society, but because of his voyeuristic method of presenting it and the camp makeup and hairdos that everyone wore, his message devolved into a carny-like pageant, embarrassing and insulting to those he was trying to honor.

More disturbing, at the end of the show, a stagehand walked out with a stringy-haired John Galliano marionette, which struck Galliano's rock star–like pose and took the bow.

It was apt: Galliano may have been creative director of Dior and John Galliano, but the companies' chief executive, Sidney Toledano, and chairman, Bernard Arnault, were without question the men in charge.

Weirdly, rather than embracing the notion of keeping enemies closer and trying to work in sync with Toledano and Arnault to get what he really wanted, Galliano built a fortress around him to keep the executives at a distance. It was as if he feared them like he feared his father, and he did whatever he could to avoid confrontation. Robinson was the go-between. Toledano admitted, "It bothers me, because I want to be sure of things." He added: "I understand [John's] genius [but] I still don't know him personally."

To contribute to the pressure, Arnault was increasingly attentive to what Galliano was doing at Dior, and communicating his growing dissatisfaction directly. In an e-mail on September 5, 2006, Arnault told Galliano that the runway show expenses were far too high and he chastised Galliano for soiling Dior's elegant image by embracing "eccentricity and extravagance" rather than "sophistication and refinement." Two weeks later, Arnault sent Galliano another critical e-mail, this time admonishing him for using cheap quality cloth.

Dior was growing steadily: in 2006, fashion and accessories sales were more than $800 million. And Arnault was raking in the dough: that same year, *Forbes* listed him the seventh-richest individual in the world with an estimated worth of $21.5 billion. But it wasn't enough: Dior's billion-dollars-a-year-in-revenues target still hadn't been met. Like McQueen, Galliano was starting to crack from the pressure of churning creativity at an assembly-line pace: between Dior and John Galliano, he was overseeing nearly two dozen collections a year.

He spent less time at the office. "He wouldn't come in at eight in the morning like the rest of us," says a Dior executive. "More like noon. In the morning, he was at home, attending to his personal matters and his workout with his coach. He would call Bill Gaytten or Steven, not because he had ideas but more to stress them out—'Why are you doing this or that?'"

He became obsessed with his backstage dressing room at shows and Dior did not oppose his requests. "It was decorated with fur rugs, flowers, chandeliers, and sofas and he had his own food," recalls Talley, who had seen his share of celebrity pampering during his years at *Vogue* and *Vanity Fair*. "The divadom. *The divadom*." Talley thought it was a "big sign of the spoiled over-the-top treatment of John. . . . I mean, people have those VIP corners, but his was almost like Gloria Swanson or something. It was just weird and creepy."

He was dressing up in increasingly strange costumes to take his bows—a habit that worried Talley. It had started innocuously enough: he came out at the end of a show wearing a top hat and tails, inspired by Charlie Chaplin. But the ritual had grown cartoon-like: at one show, he was dressed as an astronaut, another time like Napoleon.

His face was radically changing, and observers wondered if he was undergoing plastic surgery or using injectable cosmetic fillers such as Botox or Restylane. According to one report, he wore a Mark Traynor Isometric Beauty Band, a headband that pulls the face's skin tight and smooths out wrinkles.

And his physical regime seesawed between healthy and destructive. "He went off the wheels and then he picked up again and got better," says an assistant. "He'd get pumped up and get into something like gymnastics, which was great, then he'd go off the wagon. Then he went back on the wagon with whatever was the new obsession at the time. And off again."

MCQUEEN CONTINUED TO REPACKAGE old work. In March 2006, he revisited "The Highland Rape," with a show called "Widows of Culloden," which was inspired, he said, by the final battle of the Jacobite Risings and the widows of Scots who "got on a ship and moved to America"—escapist plan if there ever was one. This time, though, the clothes weren't tattered and torn and the models weren't bloodied and running scared. Far from it. The show felt like a beautifully executed Best of McQueen in the 1990s, with tailored

McQueen tartan suits (in a better quality cloth than what he bought off the barrow in Soho a decade earlier), tweed jackets, even a "Dante"-esque deer antler headdress draped with lace.

What wasn't a remake of vintage McQueen was a remake of vintage Galliano: McQueen was still fixated on Galliano's shellfish dress and sent out several variations of it, including one in ivory ruffled organza with a sheer torso and adorned with butterflies. The most stunning one, however, was the centerpiece of the closing tableau: in a giant glass pyramid, four cameras projected in the darkness a remarkable lifelike hologram by music video director Baillie Walsh of Kate Moss wearing the dress and floating midair like a ghost. "Lee McQueen got so obsessive about that dress that he actually made it better than John," Pons says. "John's [shellfish] dress is not that famous—fashion people know it—but the Kate hologram dress is a masterpiece. No one will ever forget it."

In May 2006, McQueen traveled to San Francisco to receive an honorary doctorate from the Academy of Art University's fashion department, where Simon Ungless worked. Ungless knew McQueen was HIV positive—Pons had told him—and he was worried about what sort of shape McQueen would be in.

After the ceremony and other official activities, Ungless and McQueen took off on a road trip to the Napa Valley wine country. During their drive to Calistoga, where they were going to a spa retreat for mud baths, McQueen blurted out:

"You know I'm HIV positive, right?"

"Yeah, I've heard," Ungless answered. "Are you okay?"

"Yeah, everything is fine."

McQueen didn't want to talk about what medicines he was taking to manage it, but assured Ungless that it was all under control.

McQueen's addictions, however, were not. Ungless noticed a book that McQueen brought with him: an idiot's guide to Buddhism. Ungless laughed out loud.

"Listen," he told his friend. "That's not going to work. If the rehabs aren't working, being a Buddhist is not going to stop you from taking drugs."

It didn't. McQueen was becoming less reliable in his work. Sometimes, says one Gucci Group executive, "he wouldn't show up for two weeks." Often that was during postshow downtime, when he was feeling low and burned out. But one season, just two weeks before the show, he went AWOL. Mc-Queen CEO Jonathan Akeroyd called a Gucci Group corporate head in a state: "We don't know where Lee is. It's a disaster." Sarah Heard (now Sarah Burton) managed to pull the collection together in time for the show—"magically," the executive says.

No one on the corporate level wanted to address—much less acknowledge—McQueen's drug abuse and emotional and professional instability. Most out of touch and hands-off was the group's chief executive, Robert Polet. According to a Gucci Group executive, Polet rarely spoke to the designers and he never asked his colleagues about McQueen, at least not at the corporate committee meeting every other Monday morning. McQueen's comportment, good or bad, "was never discussed," the executive says. Not that McQueen would have listened. "Mr. Polet was a nice guy but Lee didn't have huge respect for him," the executive says. "He didn't have huge respect for anyone in the group."

The only person from the corporate side that he put up with—may have even considered somewhat a friend—was Mimma Viglezio, Gucci Group's vice president of corporate communications. A strong Swiss-born woman, Viglezio was the Gucci Group version of Joyce McQueen, and McQueen affectionately called her Mimi. "He would go over budget by millions—he was useless with money that way," she says. "And when I would call and say, 'Lee, we can't afford this,' he would storm into the office and yell in his Cockney accent. He would pick up the phone and yell at everyone."

Viglezio would calmly explain to him how a publicly traded company worked, that budgets had to be respected, and if he spent too much on the show, the money had to come out of something else. "You can overspend by two million in every collection or you can have an advertising campaign," she'd tell him.

"But it's my company—I own fifty percent," he would howl. "Why can't I decide?"

Yes, you own fifty percent, Viglezio would say, but the other fifty percent is owned by shareholders and we must answer to them too. "I am the one in budget meetings where we have to cut this because you overspent there," she would tell him.

"I understand," he'd eventually admit. "I must remember I'm also a businessman."

"He was humble enough to accept it," she says, now. "Until it came up again."

IN EARLY APRIL 2007, Galliano went on vacation to the Caribbean. As usual, he asked Robinson to come along, but Robinson begged off this time. He had recently told Galliano that, after twenty years, he felt he had come to the close of their tenure together. He had been undergoing treatment for depression and he was burned out. He couldn't do any of it anymore.

Rather than escaping to a far-flung posh resort, Robinson told his colleagues that he would spend that weekend, which was Easter, at his apartment in Paris and then travel to England to see his parents. He left work on Friday, and bid everyone a happy holiday.

But instead of going home and having a restful couple of days, he called a Senegalese illegal immigrant named Alassane Seck, a souvenir seller at Paris tourist sites who was also a drug dealer to the rich and somewhat famous. Robinson wanted cocaine, a lot of it, immediately. Once he scored, he locked himself in his flat and went on a massive binge, which triggered a fatal heart attack. He was thirty-eight. People who knew Robinson well wonder if his overdose was intentional—if, in fact, he had committed suicide.

TEN DAYS LATER, Robinson's funeral was held at the American Cathedral in Paris, an Episcopal parish a couple of blocks from Dior's Avenue Montaigne headquarters. More than one thousand people attended. "It was packed," Howells recalls. "*Packed.*" Galliano was too upset to give a eulogy, but Stephen Jones read a Yeats poem, Toledano read from the Old Testament, and Howells read from *Winnie-the-Pooh*—"the part when all the animals come to say goodbye to Christopher Robin," he says.

Afterward, as with his father's death, Galliano didn't take any time off to grieve. He went straight back to work, conducting fittings for the couture show, which would be held at Versailles in eight weeks to celebrate Dior's sixtieth anniversary. "The death of Steven was very hard for John," Howells says. "Steven had been such a force and, in many ways, a protector of John—

he kept a lot of the crap away from John, corporate stuff—but also would sort of feed him with ideas and he was a constant friend." In the absence of Robinson, other assistants stepped in—most notably Bill Gaytten—to make sure collections were produced and deadlines were met.

ISABELLA BLOW WAS A MESS. She'd lost her job at the *Sunday Times*, and after a difficult time financially, landed a gig as fashion director at *Tatler*, where she had started her magazine career. In 2004, she and Detmar had split up and he took up with Stephanie Theobald, the society editor of British *Harper's Bazaar*. Isabella ran off with a Venetian gondolier, and later had a passionate love affair with banking heir Matthew Mellon. Eventually, she and Detmar reconciled, but she was—perhaps not surprisingly—diagnosed with bipolar disorder. Rather than treat it with medication, she elected to undergo electroshock therapy, which worked for a while, but eventually the rebounds were shorter and the depressions were darker and deeper.

She made several attempts on her life: she overdosed on sleeping pills; she jumped from an overpass in London and broke both ankles; she plowed her car into the back of a truck; she tried to drown herself in a lake; she took an excessive amount of horse tranquilizers. "People say, 'How are you?' and you say, 'Fabulous,'" Treacy said. "But not Isabella. She'd say, 'I'm suicidal.'"

In the spring of 2007, she seemed to rally. She invited McQueen for a weekend at Hilles, where she was living full time with Detmar. "Issie had organized a whole weekend—visits of houses, meals," Detmar says. "And he came with two lesbians to look after him and he stayed in bed, taking cocaine."

Eventually, McQueen emerged from his drug lair and he and Isabella sat down for a long heart-to-heart.

"You look so good," he told her. "You're not talking about death—no, are you?"

"No, no," she assured him.

Shortly after, Isabella went to see McQueen's mother in Essex for tea and gave her a few memento-like gifts. And she planned a nice spring weekend in early May at Hilles with all their friends. For it, she asked McQueen to make her an outfit. But it wasn't finished in time.

All of Isabella's nearest and dearest were expected, including her sister Lavinia Verney, and Philip Treacy and his partner, Stefan Bartlett. Vicki Sarge; Hamish Bowles; his partner, Peter Kent; and the gallery owner Thomas Dane were staying in a cottage on the property called Spoonfed Farm. The only one who was missing was McQueen, who was in Rome with Shaun Leane.

On Saturday, Isabella announced that she was going shopping.

Instead, she went into the garden and drank a sizable slug of the poisonous weed killer Paraquat—the same poison Detmar's father consumed when he killed himself at Hilles decades earlier. She called Lavinia and said she was ill. Lavinia rushed to the house and found Isabella collapsed on the bathroom floor.

When McQueen heard the news, he was inconsolable.

She died two days later. She was forty-eight.

ISABELLA'S FRIENDS PLANNED a funeral to befit her. McQueen chose her burial outfit: a couture gold embroidered pale green dress and colorful beaded coat trimmed in ocelot, both McQueen for Givenchy couture. Isabella had already decided ages beforehand which hat she would wear: the Pheasant, a Treacy favorite made of Chinese cock plumes. Her coffin was carried in a glass-sided Victorian carriage pulled by six black mane bays, each with a black plume on its crown. Atop the casket was a spray of white roses and lilies; nestled in the center was her and Treacy's most magnificent creation: the Ship, with a small fan hidden in the flowers blowing its sails.

Shortly before the service, McQueen called Treacy to ask him and her sisters to clip a chunk of her hair off for him. Shaun Leane was going to turn it into Victorian mourning rings for them. They agreed.

McQueen arrived in his traditional Highland dress, looking "like an old, sad widower," a friend remarked.

"He was aware that he broke her heart," says Tiina Laakkonen.

XIX

Following Isabella's death, McQueen traveled with Leane to India to spend a month reflecting on his life, career, and future. "The reason I got into this business is because I love what I do," he explained not long after the trip. "After I was at Givenchy, I lost that feeling. But after my friend [Isabella] died, I found a new love for it because she loved it and she found me because of what I was good at. I had to slap myself about the face and say, 'Pull yourself together. This is what you love doing, so do it properly.' It was a wake-up call, and I actually do love it more than I ever have."

When he returned to work in London, he launched what would turn out to be the most productive and powerful period of his career.

But first, he went to a psychic to see how Isabella was doing in the after-life. She was well, the medium told him—she was with her grandmother the adventuress and they were having a grand time together. She was, however, furious that Detmar had a new girlfriend, and worse, the woman was wearing her clothes. In response, Isabella swore that she would haunt Hilles for six hundred years. Last, she said that she wanted to be remembered as La Dame Bleue—the Blue Lady.

McQueen told Philip Treacy her wish. They decided to put a show on to-gether in her honor during the spring–summer 2008 fashion week, and they would title it "La Dame Bleue." McQueen's friend the artist Richard Gray designed the poster-size invitation: an illustration of Isabella wearing a Byzantine-like crown and sitting in a carriage pulled to heaven by a pair of winged white stallions representing McQueen and Treacy.

The overarching theme was birds, since, like McQueen, Isabella had a great love for them. The backdrop was a giant neon light hawk that flashed as if it were flying. McQueen worked the theme into his designs, like creating a black sheer shift with birdcage piping; a white origami-like dress with wing-trimmed cap sleeves; a macaw-inspired chiffon gown with rainbow plume open ruff; and a feather-covered gown with a Treacy-designed plumed head-dress.

Isabella also wore smart tailoring better than anyone, so McQueen sent out razor-sharp looks, such as a 1940s-style raspberry-dyed python sheath and a suite of chic gunmetal gray dresses and suits accented with scarlet obi sashes and belts. For one of the gray outfits, Treacy constructed a hat of silk netting with a crystal dragonfly; for another, he created a cloud of red monarch-like butterflies hovering around the head. McQueen and Treacy came out hand-in-hand to take their bow, Treacy obviously overcome with emotion.

A FEW WEEKS LATER, McQueen started working on his fall–winter 2008–2009 show, which he titled "The Girl Who Lived in the Tree." He came up with the idea while admiring the six-hundred-year-old elm that dominated his yard in Hastings, and from there concocted a tale about a girl who resided in it. "She was a feral creature," he explained, and "when she decided to descend to earth, she was transformed into a princess." He said that the princess was actually Queen Elizabeth as a young girl; it seems he had truly fallen in love. "I'll do this thing on the Queen, and I'll get the knighthood," he later joked. "I'll become Sir Alexander McQueen."

The collection was greatly informed by McQueen's trip to India—the clothing designs had a maharajah-like allure to them—and to up the opulence, he contacted the New York offices of Jaipur's famous Gem Palace to obtain real semiprecious stones for embroidery and styling.

Most important, McQueen called Treacy. Not every McQueen show had hats, but "The Girl Who Lived in the Tree" would have one. And only one.

"I want you to make me a bird," McQueen said.

"A bird?!" Treacy gasped.

Treacy was stumped. He loved challenges, but this was a doozy. Then he remembered a bag filled with bits of driftwood that he had scooped up off a beach in the Bahamas. At the time he found the wood, he didn't know what he could do with it, but it was impossibly beautiful, so he brought it back to London. With it, he constructed a delicate standing bird, with talons and a beak, and attached a giant sea fan, also from the Bahamas, as a tail, like a peacock. McQueen was nearly speechless when Treacy unveiled it. "This one you have to take home," he told his friend.

The show was held at the Palais Omnisports de Paris-Bercy. The set was quite simple: a reproduction of the giant elm wrapped in white tulle in the style of the environmental artists Christo and Jeanne-Claude; and the music was orchestral versions of Nirvana's "Come As You Are" and "Smells Like Teen Spirit." During the first half of the show, the models embodied the sad, lonely girl stuck in the tree by wearing Victorian gothic black dresses. In the second half, as she descended from the tree and became a princess, the models evoked the change by wearing glorious 1950s-style couture gowns in blood red and white silks and satins and embellished with sari ribbons and jewels, topped with maharani-like bejeweled headpieces. Treacy's exquisite, fragile peacock was the lone hat. It was a breathtakingly beautiful collection, one that rivaled Balenciaga, Fath, and Dior at their postwar heights.

McQueen invited Bobby Hillson to the show and she was so moved by it she wrote to him, telling him so. Unexpectedly, he responded with "such a sweet note" and a bouquet of roses, she recalls. "The sweetest thing about McQueen was [whenever he saw me] he always came up and said, 'You know, Bobby, I owe this all to you.'"

FOR HIS SPRING–SUMMER 2009 show in October 2008, McQueen looked to Charles Darwin's *On the Origin of Species* for inspiration. He titled the show "Natural Dis-Tinction Un-Natural Selection," and it was most likely the first time Darwin's mid-nineteenth-century treatise had been used as a creative and meditative source for a fashion show.

For the invitation, he used an illustration by his nephew Gary, who worked as a menswear assistant; it was a hologram portrait of McQueen that transformed into a skull. McQueen liked all things macabre, but since the company's introduction of a cranium-printed scarf in 2003, the skull had served essentially as McQueen's logo, like John Galliano's "Galliano Gazette" newsprint fabric. "We've done about a million [British] pounds of business just on that scarf," McQueen said with a laugh. "And it keeps on going."

Although McQueen received almost unanimous critical raves for his shows, he was still having a hard time selling his runway collection—and the reason was quite simple: it was hard to wear. "Those clothes were demanding," says a former colleague who regularly dressed in McQueen. "What mattered was how the silhouette looked, not how it felt." Happily, PPR's executives didn't mind too much: thanks to the robust sales of the skull scarf, as well as the success of McQueen menswear and the sporty McQ line, which McQueen was loath to work on, Akeroyd announced the company would make a respectable profit by year's end.

EVEN WITH HIS BUSINESS SUCCESS, McQueen was an emotional wreck and his addiction issues were still at the forefront. When he went out at night, he would get so intoxicated on drink and drugs that he'd forget where he'd parked the car. The next morning, his staff would have to locate it and drive it home.

He was obsessing on death more than before too. "He had researched Marilyn Monroe's suicide in detail on the Internet and read all the post-mortems," Archie Reed recalled. "He said to me, 'As I was powerful in life, I will be a god in death. And gays don't do old.'" Eventually, McQueen and Reed broke up for good—Reed claims because McQueen was "struggling with the idea of settling down"—and McQueen moved out of his Victoria Park house in the East End. He bought a 2,500-square-foot, three-bedroom flat in a handsome red brick Victorian townhouse on Dunraven Street in the elegant Mayfair neighborhood in central London. He had a couple, named César and Marlene Garcia, who ran the house for him.

Rather than find another steady beau, he started carrying on with various rough men, some he met online. One reportedly was a porn star named Mr. Stag. Another was an East End gangster. But none of them seemed terribly important to him.

If McQueen's shows were a commentary on what he was feeling or thinking at the moment of their conception, his fall–winter 2009–10 collection, to be presented in March 2009, was one of his most damning. He stated that it was about the horrid cycle of forced obsolescence in fashion and the hamster wheel he was running on at an insane pace to create that obsolescence and fill its void.

To tie the collection back to the absolute beginning of his career, he used the name of the East End pub where Jack the Ripper's final victim was last seen—the Horn of Plenty—as the title. It was as if McQueen was trying to bookend his career as well as to take a parting shot. He staged it at the Palais Omnisports de Paris-Bercy arena again, on a set dominated by a huge heap of car parts, old computers, junked televisions, and—most symbolically— leftover props from his previous shows. The catwalk was made of cracked mirrors—a swipe at fashion's self-obsession. He noted in the program that he dedicated the show to his mother, Joyce, who, unbeknownst to most everyone there, had been recently diagnosed with cancer. McQueen was three weeks shy of forty and his mother was ill—he was in a period of serious reflection and he was fearlessly telling fashion what he really thought of it.

He opened the show with a parody of Dior's New Look, and from there lampooned Yves Saint Laurent's soft wrap gowns and other recognizable silhouettes, to demonstrate how fashion had run out of ideas and contemporary designers kept reinterpreting classics rather than trying to come up with something new. He recycled his black bird prints, this time using an ever-thieving magpie in flight. Treacy added to the farce with clever hats made out of garbage bags and trashcan lids. Everything was exaggerated: the models' lipstick, which looked like giant red wax lips; the Prince of Wales print, with checks as big as playing cards; and the outfits themselves, with inflated bustles and immense ruffles. It was subversive and it was angry. Suzy Menkes seemed to understand the true message: "It was emotional to see McQueen push himself to the furthest reaches of creativity," she wrote, "as though it was [his] wild, last stand."

NOT LONG AFTER "The Horn of Plenty" show, McQueen telephoned Simon Ungless in San Francisco. Ungless was surprised by the call; he hadn't heard from his friend for a while. McQueen declared that he was ready for a life change.

"In his own words for it, he was 'burnt out,' 'fed up'—not with just being a designer, but with the industry as a bigger whole," Ungless says. "We'd started talking about him coming here [to San Francisco] and creating a very unique, small graduate program with him as a kind of captain of the team. If he needed to travel, I could step in. He wanted to do it here, or somewhere away from a supposed fashion capital."

In May, McQueen called Ungless to tell him he had put everything in motion, including renegotiating his contract with PPR so he would only have to provide the inspirations for the collections and work on the two women's wear runway collections each year; the rest would be on autopilot. "I've got Sarah," he said. "I can leave it to her. She's going to do everything. I can just go in and oversee." This would allow him to have extended time away so he could teach at the Academy of Art as well as work on other projects. He wanted to go to San Francisco at the end of the summer and start teaching in the fall. He was full of ideas and joy.

But Ungless was wary. "I could hear the level of energy and excitement was based on the drugs he was on," he says. "Unfortunately, I didn't know how bad it was."

That spring, McQueen had flown on a private jet with Annabelle Neilson to Majorca to see Pons. He brought his big dog, Callum, a Rhodesian ridgeback, with him.

"It's a South African dog that kills lions," McQueen told Pons.

"Why did you come on a private jet?" Pons asked.

"Because I had to bring the dog."

"Why?" Pons insisted.

"Because they want to kill me," McQueen responded. "You don't understand anything, Sebastian. I take the private jet, and I have to bring the dog, because they want to kill me, and that's that."

At the time, Pons's father was terminally ill, and Pons had a lot on his mind. He did his best to entertain his friend, but it was difficult.

"He was paranoid," Pons says. "He was scary."

While there, McQueen was doing a lot of drugs. At the same time, he had an HIV med regime that needed to be taken at specific times of the day. When it was time, Pons says, McQueen would be passed out, "and we would bang on his door, and shout, 'You need to take your pills!'"

Pons felt that McQueen's visit also had a strange vibe to it: a finality of sorts, as if this was his last trip to Majorca.

"He came to say goodbye," Pons says now. "I knew."

As he was leaving, McQueen told Pons:

"I've designed my last collection."

"What?" Pons responded, astonished.

"And in the collection, I kill myself."

"What do you mean?" Pons sputtered.

"Remember when I did the madhouse—the glass house—and we unveiled the woman?"

"Yes," said Pons.

"I'm going to redo it and I'm going to be in the box, and in the end, I'm going to shoot myself."

Pons was speechless.

McQueen left and flew back to London.

"I never saw him again," Pons says now.

Shortly after, Pons called McQueen's assistant in London to express his concern.

"I'm really upset," Pons told her. "He's not well."

"No, no," she responded. "He's fine."

Pons could see what was happening: "He was 'Alexander McQueen.' And all the people who surrounded him at his job just wanted to please him."

Pons tried a few times to get McQueen on the phone, but could never get through the barrier of assistants. He was always told that McQueen was in a meeting, or that he was busy. "We cannot disturb him now" was the refrain.

He'd leave messages but McQueen never returned the calls.

That same month, McQueen took an overdose of sleeping pills. Thankfully, he recovered, and in mid-June he went to Milan to put on his menswear show. It was inspired by Victorian rent boys and it was the hit of the season, which was important—by then, menswear accounted for 20 percent of McQueen's business.

He spent a lot of time on the phone with Ungless. He never mentioned anything about his mother's illness, but he was obviously wounded, and lost. "We were trying to work out a time when he'd be able to come to San Francisco, and it kept getting pushed back, and pushed back, and pushed back," Ungless says. "There was always something."

In July, McQueen OD'd again, this time on painkillers. His general practitioner, Dr. Mike Comins, suggested he seek psychiatric help and referred him to Dr. Stephen Pereira, a psychiatrist and cognitive behavior therapist known for treating work-related stress disorders. Pereira concluded that McQueen was not simply distressed by Blow's suicide; he had suffered from insomnia, anxiety, and depression since his appointment to Givenchy in 1997. The overdoses, he thought, were not serious suicide attempts but rather "cries for help."

Pereira noted McQueen's paranoia and found it difficult to get him to open up. "He was a very secretive person," Pereira said. "Over a period of time he had been let down by various friends who he felt were taking advantage of who he was. For that reason he was very guarded." Pereira prescribed antidepressants, but McQueen only took them for a week because they made him nauseous. Pereira also sent McQueen to see a clinical psychologist. McQueen didn't embrace the help that was being offered; he brushed off his doctors' medical advice and often skipped his appointments. His habitual excuse: he was too busy at work.

Finally, in mid-summer, there was a window of opportunity for McQueen to travel to San Francisco to firm up his exit plan from fashion—maybe even get it rolling for a fall start. But Leane cautioned Ungless against it: he said that McQueen's drug taking had reached epic proportions, he was suffering from drug-induced hallucinations, telling people that flashing lights would shoot out from underneath his bed, and he was still raving about a man sexually abusing him as he slept. Ungless was stunned. "There are all these people around him," he told Leane. "Can't somebody do an intervention? Couldn't they pluck him out and lock him up for a while? It can work."

No one in London did anything. McQueen started working on his spring–summer collection, with the idea that it would be his last full-time fashion collection and show ever. He titled it "Plato's Atlantis," after the fictional island in the classical Greek writer's works *Timaeus* and *Critias* that sinks to the bottom of the ocean. The show would be "metamorphic," McQueen explained. "The reversal of the one before . . . [on] Charles Darwin with the evolution of the species." Instead of Darwin's theory "that we come from the sea," he said, this would be about how we "go back into the sea."

For the core silhouette, he said, "I don't want to look at any shapes, I don't want to reference anything, a picture, a drawing. I want it all to be new."

He designed a uniform silhouette: an hourglass-shaped minidress with rounded shoulders and a bell-shaped skirt. It looked like a molded hybrid of a crustacean carapace and scuba wetsuit in Elizabethan proportions, and, as Burton says, it *was* "something new, without a reference." Each would be printed with a watery, organic swirl inspired by Swiss Surrealist H. R. Giger's work and photos of Australia's Great Barrier Reef. There were thirty-six prints, all circle-engineered to the body—meaning "a circle shape that sat in the middle of the bolt of fabric" and had to be exactly on the right place on the body to work, Burton explained. McQueen draped and cut more than half the dresses himself, and hardly made a mistake—a technical feat that few in fashion could achieve. "He came alive when he was fitting clothes," she later said. "He made you feel like you might as well pack your bags and go home."

McQueen was always looking for a different and more democratic way to reach the public. In September, he had started using Twitter to speak to his fans directly—his first tweet read: "STRESSED! Microwave head meltdown! Sparks flying out of my brain!"

To expand his reach beyond the same clique of editors, retailers, and bloggers, he enlisted his friend the photographer Nick Knight to stream the show live on Knight's nine-year-old fashion film Web site SHOWstudio. Shortly before the show, at the Palais Omnisports de Paris-Bercy arena, Lady Gaga tweeted that McQueen would premiere her new single—which triggered a surge on SHOWstudio.com and caused the site to crash.

The show went on as scheduled anyway. And it left critics gasping. Suzy Menkes called it "full-on techno revolution" and swooned over "the extraordinary beauty of these other-worldly" designs. She concluded: "The sophistication of the clothes, the intricacy of the workmanship and the ecological swell of the narrative were spellbinding."

"That was it," Ungless says. "He put everything into it."

By Christmas, it was clear that Joyce was dying and she was hospitalized. Her children decided to visit her there together—though McQueen had to be talked into going. "He fought against it because he was frightened and didn't want to see her so ill," his sister Janet said. "Eventually we persuaded him to come over but he really struggled. I think he knew it was the last time he would see her."

The start date for San Francisco was pushed back again, so he started working on his new runway collection, "Angels and Demons," to be shown in March. For it, he studied fifteenth-century sacred paintings of saints, angels, and Madonna with child to see if he could replicate their glowing, halolike light in clothing. There would be mystical showpieces constructed in gold and brocade and he and Burton created digital prints based on the paintings to be woven into silk jacquard.

McQueen called Treacy and asked him over to the new, larger studio on Clerkenwell Road in the East End to talk about hats. When Treacy arrived, he found McQueen alone, wrapping cloth around a model, cutting, draping, and pinning, until it took the form of a dress. Treacy had worked with many of the top designers in his twenty years in the business; never had he seen any of them work like this—such gifted magic. When Treacy remarked how special it was, McQueen shot back in his Cockney gruff: "What?"

McQueen told Treacy that he had always been fascinated by—obsessed with—the ship hat that Treacy had made for Isabella back in the 1990s and later adorned her casket. Treacy had long resisted making another because it was such a complicated project. But McQueen wanted one for "Angels and Demons," in white.

"A ghost ship," Treacy says.

He agreed.

IN MID-JANUARY, McQueen flew to Milan for his menswear show, and was pleased with how it turned out.

When he returned home, he called Polet at Gucci Group headquarters and asked if he could come by for an impromptu meeting in the afternoon. Polet said yes, of course.

He arrived wearing a gold and tan tweed suit.

"Wow, it looks great," Polet remarked.

"I'll make you one," McQueen replied.

Then he got to the point of his visit: "I am worried about the long-term sustainability of my business," he said calmly.

"What we have done over the last couple of years has transformed it from a business to a brand," Polet explained. "And as a brand it will live forever."

"The brand will live on?" he asked earnestly.

"Yep," Polet assured him. "Because it is real and has integrity and is well managed, the brand has a chance to have a very, very long life. You should be extremely proud that together in this joint venture we have achieved this."

McQueen seemed relieved. He thanked Polet for his time and went on his way.

JOYCE WAS FADING and McQueen was deeply distraught.

He called Treacy, who was in Ireland. "He sounded lonely," Treacy says.

On February 1, he posted a torrent of dispatches on Twitter, including:

from heaven to hell and back again, life is a funny thing. beauty can come from the most strangest of places even the most disgusting places

That evening, he and Annabelle Neilson went out on the town and dropped by a dinner party at Harry's Bar celebrating the premiere of Tom

Ford's feature film directorial debut, *A Single Man*. Ford invited them to join the party, but McQueen begged off. They had a drink together in the bar, and he and Neilson went on their way.

The next day, Joyce McQueen died.

Treacy went to see McQueen at the Green Street flat. McQueen confessed that he was having dark thoughts—that he was thinking of killing himself. Treacy got very upset. "Stop talking such rubbish," he told McQueen.

"I loved him," Treacy says now, his eyes welling up. "I loved him."

On Sunday, February 7, McQueen tweeted that he had been through an "awful week" but said, "my friends have been great." He added, "Now I have to some how [sic] pull myself together."

He rang his sister Janet. "We had a little chat and then he said, 'I love you,'" she recalled. "I thought it was strange as he was not a demonstrative person." He told Leane that he didn't want to go to the cemetery and see his mother interred. "We'll get through this together," Leane responded. He called Archie Reed and asked him to come over for comfort and company. But the conversation devolved into a fight. Reed said: "Take some sleeping pills and go to bed" and hung up.

He spent much of Monday with Annabelle Neilson. He gave her his wallet, saying he wanted a new one. He gave her a snapshot of him with one of his dogs and a few other items. She said she didn't want them, but he insisted, and she finally accepted them.

On Tuesday, he telephoned his sister Janet again, and he "sounded more upbeat," she said.

"I'm going to make Mum an old-fashioned pink winceyette nightgown and have it biked to the funeral parlor," he told her.

"I thought that he was slowly coming to terms with her death," Janet later said. "How wrong I was."

He went to the office and worked with Burton on the new collection, which was scheduled to be presented in Paris in three weeks. He told Verkade about Joyce's funeral, scheduled for Friday. Verkade offered to reserve a table for dinner afterward at J Sheekey Oyster Bar in Covent Garden for McQueen, Burton, Neilson, Leane, and herself. "Make it late," he advised her.

Later on that evening, he went to Shadow Lounge in Soho. Two of drag queen Trixie's friends ran into him there, and said he was taking copious amounts of cocaine and "drinking, drinking, drinking," Trixie says. "There was no one with him; he was all alone. He was totally on his own."

ON WEDNESDAY, FEBRUARY 10, he met up with Neilson again. He was blue. Besides losing his mother, dear Minter the mutt was dying of cancer. "He was running on an emotional deficit," Neilson later said. She spent much of the day with him and they planned their annual birthday trip together following his upcoming show.

She left at 3:00 A.M.

He locked all the doors and fastened the security chain on the front door. But instead of going to bed, he ingested what was later described as a "substantial" amount of cocaine, zopiclone sleeping pills, and the painkiller/tranquilizer midazolam.

He scribbled a note on the back of a book: *The Descent of Man*, a catalogue from a recent photography show by Darwin-inspired artist Wolfe von Lenkiewicz.

It concluded:

"Please look after my dogs. Sorry, I love you. Lee."

"PS Bury me in the church."

He rummaged through the kitchen and grabbed several knives, including a meat cleaver. He took them into the bathroom and tried to slice open his wrists, but it didn't work as he wanted. He went back in the kitchen to get a knife sharpener and a cutting board, returned to the bathroom, sharpened the knives and tried again. He bled, but not enough. He staggered into the bedroom and turned on his laptop. He opened the Yahoo page on the Internet and looked up: "When someone slits their wrists how long does it take for them to die?"

Frustrated, manic, and drowsy, he tried another tack: he yanked the belt from his bathrobe, tied it to the showerhead, and tried to hang himself. But the showerhead buckled under his weight.

He looked around the bedroom for another place to attempt again. His eyes were drawn to the closet. He removed the clothes, took his favorite brown belt, tied it to the rail and cinched it around his neck.

A few hours later, before ten in the morning—a damp, gray Thursday morning—McQueen's housekeeper César Garcia arrived at the Green Street flat and found the doors locked and the dogs whining. Garcia managed to get in through the utility room. He went into the master bedroom, which was a mess, but there was no sign of McQueen. He started to pick up a bit.

He walked into the guest bedroom and saw a candle burning on the floor. As he surveyed the room and its adjoining bath, he was stunned by the gory aftermath: an empty package of zopiclone next to the bed; a bloodied knife; blood all over the bathroom; the cutting board, carving knife, blade sharpener, and the cleaver in the shower; the bathrobe belt tied to the buckled showerhead.

He turned to the emptied closet and stopped cold: there, from the rail, hung McQueen, dead.

Hysterical, he called Kate Jones, the personal assistant of Shaun Leane. "He's gone," Garcia wailed. "He's gone for good."

He called the McQueen headquarters and stammered out what he saw to them.

He called the paramedics.

Garcia's wife, Marlene, arrived, and when she saw McQueen strung up in his closet, she started screaming uncontrollably too.

They called Shaun Leane again and spoke to him directly this time, but they were so overwrought, he couldn't figure out what they were saying. Leane said he'd be right over.

Verkade and Sarah Burton ran out of the Clerkenwell Road office, jumped into a black cab, and headed to Green Street. They stopped along the way to pick up Leane. When they told him what had happened, he couldn't quite process it and hoped they were all wrong—that there was still a chance to save his dear friend. "It's just a scare," he said. "He's going to be all right."

But when the taxi pulled up front, Leane knew everything was not all right. "As we walked toward the house there's a part of you that doesn't want to walk any further," he said. The ambulance and police were out front. Several members of the McQueen family arrived. Someone on the scene surreptitiously took photos of the dangling corpse; the pictures were never published.

Officials carried out a stretcher with McQueen in a burgundy body bag. A crowd of reporters was in the street and news photographers snapped pictures as the stretcher was loaded into a van.

"It was one of the saddest days of my life," Leane said.

Simon Ungless was in Manhattan, organizing the Academy of Art's student show for New York Fashion Week, when a text blipped on his phone from a friend how sad he was to hear the news about McQueen. When Ungless learned what the news was, he was bewildered.

"I knew he was really gearing up to—or wanted to—escape, but I didn't for a minute think the escape hatch was—" Ungless pauses. "I don't think he meant to kill himself. He knew how special he was. Do you know what I mean? He knew *that.*"

Michael McQueen went to the family home in Hornchurch, Essex, to tell their father, Ronald, what had happened.

"Dad," Michael sobbed, "Sorry. Lee's killed himself."

Stoic as ever, Ronald did not shed a tear.

"My poor boy," he said. "Why have you done this to me, Lee?"

XX

McQueen's family, friends, and colleagues were reeling. In the ultimate expression of his effective compartmentalization of his life,
his family insisted that they did not know he was suffering from
such psychological pain. "We'd all have been hammering on his door if we
had had an inkling something was wrong," his sister Janet said. His brother
Michael was confused by the suicide: "Why would someone who had so
much take his own life?"

The family held Joyce's funeral that afternoon as scheduled, since, as Michael said, "It [had] all been arranged."

Employees at the Old Bond Street store removed everything from the
front window and placed an announcement that McQueen had died. Fans
left notes and bouquets outside the McQueen boutiques in London, Milan,

Los Angeles, and New York. The designer Diane von Furstenberg was spotted adding one to the pile in front of his Manhattan shop. McQueen's death coincided with the opening of New York Fashion Week, and there were salutes to him in a number of the shows. The McQ show, which was scheduled to be presented there, was canceled.

Fashion players and celebrities flooded the press and blogosphere with their take on McQueen's talent and career—including Galliano. He told *Women's Wear*: "McQueen was daring, original, exciting. He shook up the establishment with his creativity and understood what it takes to be a great British ambassador for fashion. I admired him very much. He was a fashion revolutionary that, like me, made the journey from [Central] Saint Martins to Paris where he put his own unique mark on the industry. He will not be forgotten."

Pons flew from Spain to London and went straight to McQueen headquarters, without calling. "I was sick of people telling me when I called: 'He's fine,'" Pons says. "I walked straight in and saw Sarah. She was shocked. 'What are you doing here?!'" He told her how upset he was, that he had to see her, see everything.

They sat at her desk and talked about McQueen, his work, his last days.

Then she got up and showed him the unfinished collection.

"This is what he left," she told Pons.

McQueen had completed about 80 percent of "Angels and Demons." There was a fitted tailcoat made of antique gold-painted duck feathers with an open ruff collar, over a white tulle skirt, the hem embroidered in swirls of gold thread; a red silk short kimono coat printed with Tibetan tigers; a pale gray silk chiffon gown printed with birds in flight; a one-sleeved wrapped dress made of a silk printed with German artist Stefan Lochner's fifteenth-century *Altarpiece of the Patron Saints of Cologne*.

"Oh my God," Pons gasped. "It's a requiem."

ON FEBRUARY 25, McQueen's family and fashion friends gathered for the private funeral at St. Paul's, a Victorian Anglican church in Knightsbridge, followed by a reception at Claridge's hotel. Janet said it "was basically taken out of [the family's] hands. . . . We were asked for our preference in prayers and we had a family reading but other than that they took over. Although we were sitting at the front, I felt like an outsider. I didn't really know a lot of people there."

Several of the McQueen family members dressed in the family tartan. Daphne Guinness arrived wearing a black veil and the billowing black cape from the fall–winter 2002 show "Supercalifragilisticexpialidocious." Shaun Leane placed what remained of the lock of Isabella's hair and a letter in McQueen's coffin, which was decorated with a spray of pink and red roses and pink peonies. Annabelle Neilson read Edgar Allan Poe's poem "Annabel Lee." "I loved it because it was a tragic love story," she said. "He loved it too. Before he died he had the entire poem embroidered in gold thread onto a giant piece of cloth for me, which I still have. It's the most important thing I own."

Per his wishes, his ashes were buried in Kilmuir, Isle of Skye, in Scotland. "He had been there quite a few times over the years and felt a real connection to the place," his brother Michael said. "He wanted to return to the family home." The family marked the spot with a boulder sculpted by artist Andrew Tanser and inscribed with the Shakespeare line that McQueen had tattooed on his arm: "Love looks not with the eyes, but with the mind."

The house decided to show the sixteen completed looks of "Angels and Demons" to the press and retailers in a low-key presentation during Paris Fashion Week in the elegant Louis XV paneled salon of the former *hôtel particulier* of the Clermont-Tonnere family. To English baroque composer Henry Purcell's haunting opera *Dido and Aeneas*, which McQueen had listened to as he worked on the collection, the models came out looking like medieval madonnas, their faces powdered a ghostly white; and their heads wrapped in tight swaths of white or black bandages, like wimples. Some wore Mohawk-like crowns of gold feathers. *Vogue*'s Hamish Bowles called it "magisterial" and a "poignant coda to a career characterized by ceaseless invention, curiosity and lightning flashes of absolute brilliance."

McQUEEN HAD NAMED as executors of his estate Gary Jackson, an accountant, and David Glick, an entertainment attorney. They went to the McQueen home in Essex and read the will to the family. His estate was estimated at 16,036,500 pounds. He left 250,000 pounds to his five siblings and 50,000 pounds each to his nieces, nephews, and godson. His housekeepers, Marlene and César Garcia, were bequeathed 50,000 pounds for "long and faithful service" and he put 50,000 pounds in a trust to guarantee the upkeep of his three dogs for life. He donated 100,000 pounds to four charities: the Terrence Higgins Trust for HIV and AIDS issues, Battersea Dogs & Cats Home, the London Buddhist Centre, and the Blue Cross Sick Animal Centre in Burford, Oxfordshire.

The remainder was divided into two trusts: one for property, which included the three-bedroom apartment on Dunraven Street, the house on Victoria Park, the home in Hastings, the villa in Majorca, and two other holdings; and one for McQueen's charity, Sarabande, named after one of his shows. The charity's trustees were Glick, Jackson, and Verkade. The family suggested it set up scholarships at Central Saint Martins for students in need.

Sometime after McQueen's death, the executors of his estate sent a team to haul his belongings off to a storage facility in east London. The McQueen family was shut out almost completely from the process. "I did get a phone call saying that if we wanted Lee's bonsai trees, which he loved, we could pick them up from the garden," his sister Janet said, "but everything else had already been packed up—even his clothes. The executors may have behaved within the law but in our view they haven't behaved with any compassion. They didn't let us see his house before it was dismantled or pack up my brother's personal things, which is an essential part of the grieving process."

ON APRIL 28, the Westminster coroner, Dr. Paul Knapman, concluded the inquest and declared that McQueen "killed himself while the balance of his mind was disturbed." Knapman added: "It's such a pity for a man who, from a modest start, climbed to the top of his profession only to die in such a tragedy."

Among those who testified was McQueen's psychiatrist, Dr. Stephen Pereira. He told the inquest that McQueen had suffered from anxiety and depression for several years, and in his view, much of McQueen's mental anguish was due to the demands of his job. "He had been terribly let down in long-standing close relationships," Pereira added. "He was very close to his mother. I think on top of the grief he felt there was that one link that had gone from his life and there was very little to live for."

A month later, McQueen's ex-husband, George Forsyth, died of an overdose of dihydrocodeine, a painkiller, at the age of thirty-four.

On the morning of September 20, 2010, fans pressed up against metal barricades in front of St. Paul's Cathedral and gawked as more than twelve hundred mourners, most dressed in black, arrived for the memorial service in the thick of London Fashion Week.

Anna Wintour, wearing a McQueen-designed floral embroidered black satin frock coat, gave the eulogy: "There was no containing his contradictions. Even his final collection was a literal fight between dark and light." But, she said, "He taught us that the runway was a place where dreams become reality."

Suzy Menkes also spoke. She called him "an artist who just happened to be working with clothing" and "a designer with an unparalleled vision of the future who was dragged down by visions of his past."

Shaun Leane said, "It was your personality we loved. You were always true to who you were, when we laughed we laughed until we cried and when we argued we argued with you until we cried. But that was the beauty of your extremes."

Treacy and two of McQueen's nephews, Mark McQueen and Gary Huyler, led prayers and read from the Bible, and the collection benefited the Battersea Dogs & Cats Home. The London Community Gospel Choir sang a vibrant version of "Amazing Grace," and Björk, wearing a pair of wings that McQueen had made for her, performed "Gloomy Sunday," a song about suicide made popular by Billie Holiday. The service concluded with bagpiper Donald Lindsay playing the pipe motif from *Braveheart*, followed by a marching band of pipers dressed in mourning kilts and McQueen tartan sashes.

Noticeably missing from the memorial service was John Galliano. Since the death of Steven Robinson, he had put on a stoic public face. He went directly back to work after the funeral, because of the upcoming Galliano and Dior menswear shows as well as another monumental couture show in the Orangerie at Versailles—this time for Dior's sixtieth anniversary and Galliano's ten-year mark at the house—in less than two months.

In June 2010, he received the Chevalier—or Knight—of the Legion of Honor from French president Nicolas Sarkozy at the Elysée Palace. That summer, he skipped his goddaughter/niece's wedding in Gibraltar—though he did make her Dior bridal gown—and went on vacation with Alexis Roche, as he had every August for several years, in the jet-set Riviera resort Saint-Tropez, where Bernard Arnault also has a summer home.

"Some people fall apart when they lose someone that close, but John didn't," says his show producer Alexandre de Betak. "He stayed on the treadmill and he kept going."

But privately, Galliano was barely holding it together. He wouldn't show up to the office for four or five days, which "[meant] he went on a bender," says one assistant. "It had happened before."

In May 2008, he was invited to the Savannah College of Art and Design (SCAD) to receive the André Leon Talley Lifetime Achievement Award. (Talley is a board member at the school.) Galliano first flew to New York; from there, SCAD arranged to fly him to Savannah on a private jet for the event. Talley had organized a glorious visit of the Southern town for his friend, beginning with a gospel choir to welcome him on the tarmac. "I was on my way to the airport when I got the phone call," Talley recalls. It was Katherine Ross, senior vice president of public relations and communications for LVMH in New York.

"I'm so sorry but I have bad news," Ross told Talley, "I can't wake John up."

"What do you mean you can't wake John up?!"

"He won't answer the door. He won't get out of bed."

Talley was crushed, and saddened.

Ross flew to Savannah to receive the award on Galliano's behalf.

A week later, Anna Wintour told Talley, "Why didn't you call me? I would have come and accepted the award for him."

"Everyone was aware" of Galliano's alcohol abuse issues, his former assistant insists. "Come on, you don't show up for five days [and] call drunk on the phone like a complete idiot? Everyone knew the kind of state he was in because he never spent a day without calling. Everyone, *everyone* got a phone call. 'I want this for the show' or 'I heard this'—it could be anything. We played along with it; it's a shared responsibility. We were all responsible. All of us."

Over the years, employees and friends had suggested to Galliano that he go to rehab. "Oh yeah, many times," the assistant confirms. "He never wanted to." Instead, he would go for cures at spa-like establishments—"He loved them," the assistant says—while Robinson and Gaytten made sure everything at work continued to run smoothly.

No one, including Galliano, ever brought it up with Toledano. And because Dior's executive suites were on a different side of the building, with a separate entrance, and Galliano rarely went to the Dior studio anymore, Toledano didn't see the descent firsthand. When Toledano would remark that Galliano was absent, his personal assistant at home would simply say: "He's not well."

At the same time, fashion sales at both Dior and Galliano were less robust than before, in part because of the economic crisis of 2007, which affected the luxury business across the board, but also in part because Galliano's designs simply weren't selling as well as they once had. Anna Wintour reportedly wrote to Galliano suggesting he let go several members of his studio team and bring in new blood because Bernard Arnault's daughter Delphine—the one for whom Galliano had designed the exquisite wedding dress and who was said to be as cunning in business as her father—had been brought by Dior allegedly to find his replacement. Eventually, Robinson's former assistant Vanessa Bellanger was hired as collections director, studio director, and style director at the John Galliano brand.

It needed her help. Women's wear sales in the United Kingdom were slim, and in the United States they were nonexistent, despite support by the glossies, especially American *Vogue*, which continued to photograph Galliano's designs and report on his shows. "No retailers in the U.S. were carrying Galliano women's wear," a then-Galliano executive says, "Not Barneys or Fred Segal or Jeffrey's or Ikram or Saks or Bloomingdale's." Not even long-supportive Bergdorf's; it dropped the line in 2007.

Overall, the Galliano brand had fifty points of sale worldwide—a pittance compared with other LVMH brands—and most were for the secondary line, which was simply called Galliano and then produced by Ittierre in Italy. Its target audience was eighteen-to-twenty-five-year-olds—"the *Gossip Girl* demographic," the former Galliano executive says. "It was tacky, with 'Galliano' written big across the chest, like high-fashion Abercrombie. There were nearly zero [retail outlets] for the runway line." The executive pauses for a moment, then amends that last statement:

"Qatar. There were stores in Qatar."

In November, Galliano threw a fiftieth birthday party for himself at the Savoy hotel in London, with a cabaret performance by impersonators, but guests say he appeared wan and unusually quiet.

A few days later, he traveled to New York with his Dior personal assistant and three people from the haute couture studio, to do research for the couture collection in January. Toledano wasn't always so keen on Galliano's "research" trips. Sometimes, such as when Galliano went to China, he would come back genuinely inspired and with a plethora of ideas. But often the trips would turn into vacations on the company dime, or there would be problems "of comportment in hotels," as a Dior executive explained.

In the middle of the night Paris time, Toledano received a frantic call from Galliano's assistant at the Mercer Hotel, where the team was staying.

"Mr. Toledano, he is banging on my door," she wailed. "He's called me a thief and says I stole money out of his room. I'm in my room, and he is banging on my door, creating a scene. I don't know what to do."

He assured her he would handle it.

He called the hotel and asked security to be sent up to calm Galliano down. He called Galliano and told him to return to Paris immediately. Galliano refused, saying he was fine and wanted to stay in New York and complete his research.

"No, John, in this state, you cannot stay."

Toledano wrote an e-mail to Galliano, copying Galliano's lawyer Stéphane Zerbib, ordering Galliano to return to Paris.

"You are on a mission for the company," Toledano wrote. "It is over and now you must return to Paris. This is an order."

Toledano then called Roche, who was in Paris, and dispatched him on a commercial flight to New York to fetch Galliano and bring him home.

Once Galliano was back in Paris, Toledano convoked him to Dior headquarters to discuss what had happened. But Galliano never showed up—he and Roche flew to Thailand for vacation instead. Upon his return in January, Toledano invited him to lunch in the private dining room on the executive side of Dior headquarters. Galliano told Toledano's assistant beforehand what he would eat and not eat—he still insisted on a very strict diet. When he arrived, Toledano remarked that Galliano was calm and assured, rather than nervous and perspiring, as he often still could be in stressful situations. They sat down at the table, Galliano with a plate of lentils and chickpeas, specifically cooked to order, and water with lemon, before him. Toledano had fish, and the waiter offered him a glass of wine. Toledano accepted.

"Not good, Sidney," Galliano scolded him. "You should pay attention to what you eat, what you drink."

He then launched into a monologue about his trip: he'd met with Buddhist monks who told him that cells rejuvenate, not only physically, but also spiritually. "It was amazing!" he exclaimed.

"We have to talk about what happened in New York," Toledano said. "It's not normal behavior, and you should seek psychological counseling. Go see a psychiatrist. It's not because you're crazy, but you have ups and downs, and stress, and anxiety. Sometimes we all need some professional help to cope. And you have a lot going on."

"No, Sidney, I'm okay," Galliano responded. "I'm okay."

"Think about it," Toledano counseled. "I know you go see doctors when you aren't well. But it's hard to sort it all out and you might benefit from counseling."

He added that if Galliano wanted to lighten his workload, or take a sabbatical for a few months, that would be fine.

"We are organized here," Toledano assured him. "You can come and give the brief and leave. We don't need you here every day. We have a strong team."

Galliano sloughed off the proposal. His cells were going to regenerate, he insisted, therefore he would be fine.

Toledano didn't buy it. There was obviously something profoundly wrong, Galliano needed professional help to sort it out, and no one in his entourage had the courage to confront him. "We were scared," admits one. "You know how addicts are. You never know how they will react. We were really scared."

Though self-harm and addiction were completely foreign notions to the quietly restrained Arnault, he was willing to do what he could to help Galliano, as he had supported Louis Vuitton designer Marc Jacobs through his two rehab stints for drug addiction. Toledano and Arnault called Galliano in for a meeting in the executive suite at Dior, sat him down, and told him it was time for him to check into a rehab facility for however long he needed to get sober.

"If you keep drinking, you will kill yourself," Arnault told him. "You are going to commit suicide."

"What are you talking about?" Galliano retorted.

"If you want to stop for a while, take the time you need," Arnault said. "Take a break and seek out help."

Galliano insisted he was fine. To prove his point, he stood up, ripped open his shirt, showed off his tan, buff, hairless torso, and declared:

"Does this look like the body of an alcoholic?"

A FEW WEEKS LATER, Toledano hosted a reception at Dior where he received the Officer of the Order of Merit award from French minister of finance Christine Lagarde. Galliano arrived at the evening reception wearing black sunglasses, but otherwise seemed fine. Toledano went to Milan a few days later to attend the Fendi women's wear show—he was helping oversee that LVMH brand too. Before he left, he called Galliano's assistant and said he would like to meet with Galliano upon his return.

When he arrived in Paris, he rang the assistant to confirm the appointment. Galliano was sick, the assistant said. He was in bed with the flu and had a doctor's note confirming it and instructing Dior to give him the week off to recover.

Instead, on Thursday night, Galliano went to La Perle and was arrested for fighting with Géraldine Bloch and Philippe Virgitti.

Toledano knew nothing about any of it until he walked into the office shortly before nine on Friday morning: his assistant flagged him on what she had read online about the La Perle incident. Toledano felt sick. How could his longtime employee utter such hateful statements, especially knowing that he was devoutly Jewish? "Mr. Toledano wasn't nasty or angry," says an observer. "Just very sad."

Dior communications director Olivier Bialobos instructed the John Galliano team to say nothing publicly or to the press. After much discussion, Arnault and Toledano concluded that the right response was to suspend Galliano pending the police investigation. The Dior press office issued a release that announced Galliano's suspension and quoted Toledano as stating that the house "has an unequivocal zero-tolerance policy regarding anti-Semitism and racism."

OVER THE WEEKEND, Toledano received calls from people who claimed they had been verbally harassed by Galliano during the week. He also learned about a telephone video of Galliano drunk at a café, spewing anti-Semitic remarks. Apparently, it was being peddled to media outlets. Rupert Murdoch's British tabloid *The Sun* picked it up and published it on its Web site on Monday, February 28, 2011:

WOMAN: Are you blond?

GALLIANO: No. But I love Hitler. People like you would be dead today. Your mothers, your forefathers, would all be fucking gassed, and fucking dead.

WOMAN: Oh, my God! Do you have a problem?

GALLIANO: With you? You're ugly.

WOMAN: With all people. You don't like peace? You don't want peace in the world?

GALLIANO: Not with people who are ugly.

WOMAN: Where are you from?

GALLIANO: Your asshole.

That afternoon, Galliano had an appointment at the police station for a follow-up investigation. He arrived with his face concealed by a wide-brimmed black hat tacked with a sprig of pink and white flowers. He underwent several hours of questioning and denied all the accusations against him. According to police files, he told the questioning officer, "How would I know she's Jewish? It isn't written on her forehead." (Bloch is not Jewish.) "It's clear that I'm neither a racist, nor an anti-Semite, nor a misogynist," Galliano continued. "It's possible this lady and her friend would like to profit from this chance [and] get some money and publicity in a sordid way." In fact, Bloch's suit demanded a fine of a symbolic one euro plus court costs and she complained that she had been hounded by paparazzi and Galliano fans ever since the news broke.

French officials said a hospital test after the incident showed Galliano had 1.1 grams of alcohol per liter of blood (about 0.11 percent blood alcohol content), more than twice the legal limit to drive in France.

Toledano met with Arnault, and Arnault's two adult children, Delphine and Antoine, both LVMH executives, at Dior to discuss what to do. Arnault wanted his children to be a part of the conversation, since they were being groomed to eventually take over the company. The foursome decided that Galliano's offenses were inexcusable. The following day—Tuesday—Dior issued a press release that stated it had "begun firing procedures against him."

THE PUBLIC CONDEMNATION of Galliano was swift and harsh. "As the daughter of a Holocaust survivor, I find what he said was absolutely unacceptable," Diane von Furstenberg, the designer and head of the Council of Fashion Designers of America, said. The actress Natalie Portman, who had recently signed on as the advertising face for Dior's new perfume, Miss Dior Chérie, issued a statement declaring, "As an individual who is proud to be Jewish, I will not be associated with Mr. Galliano in any way." Saks Fifth Avenue announced it would discontinue carrying the Galliano menswear line. "We have values like I hope everyone else has," the department store flagship's general manager Suzanne Johnson said. "What happened was not right, and we would not want to carry his merchandise in honor of our customers and my employees that work in the store."

Those who had long known and worked with Galliano couldn't believe he had uttered such offensive statements. "Oh, I was saddened," Joan Burstein says. "I thought: 'What has made this man do that? That's not the man I know.'"

"I'm personally convinced that he's not anti-Semitic," says Alexandre de Betak, who is one of Galliano's many close Jewish business associates and whose grandparents were Holocaust survivors. "He's a master of provocation and a punk in the sense of fighting back, contradiction, arrogance. I think he was being the lousy punk he can be."

Some of Galliano's inner circle blamed themselves for his implosion. "We didn't get there soon enough," Stephen Jones says. "We were all guilty."

ARNAULT AND TOLEDANO were determined to stage the Dior show. The tent was already up at the Musée Rodin, and the invitations had been printed. And as Betak explains, "We wanted to show the talent of the house of Dior apart from its designer—the fact that the house of Dior is an entity; it's a responsibility. It makes millions of people dream. We had to not only respect that dream, but its audiences, and look to the future and not erase history, because you shouldn't erase history."

Toledano decided it was necessary to address what had happened, and that he would speak to the audience before the show. He also came up with the idea of having the atelier hands take the bow in the place of Galliano.

The mood was surprisingly solemn for a fashion show—nearly funereal.

As the lights went down, Toledano came out, elegant as always, stepped into the spotlight and read his prepared statement in French. Then, to Jeremy Healy's soundtrack, out came the sexy 1970s-inspired clothes—jewel-tone velvet hip-huggers, smock tops, baby doll dresses, leather knee-high boots, frock coats, capes, and floppy felt hats—though it was questionable how much of it Galliano actually worked on given how little he had been in the studio in the previous three months.

The crowd exploded into applause, some into tears—of sadness and of loss. Delphine Arnault, seated in her absent father's usual front row spot, visibly wept. Italian designer Carla Fendi, who had flown in from Rome for it, sat for twenty minutes in her seat, too emotional to leave. An exciting and vibrant era of creation in fashion had come to an abrupt end right there before them. As guests walked back out into the bleak afternoon light, they passed a fan out front who was dressed in gold, Roman-like robes and towering platform shoes and carrying a sign. It read: "THE KING IS GONE."

XXI

A year after McQueen's death, his family was still shut out of his estate and legacy. Janet e-mailed Gary Jackson, the accountant who was one of the executors, to find out about donations made in McQueen's name to students or other charities, and Jackson responded that he could not tell her because it was confidential. "I just wanted to know that [Lee's] money was being spent wisely," Janet later said. "I didn't bother to contact them again." Instead, the family hired lawyers to force the executors to allow the family access to McQueen's personal effects.

Finally, in October 2011, Janet was granted permission to visit the storage facility in the East End where everything had been kept since his death and go through a small selection of boxes that were deemed appropriate for family review. There, in a poorly lit room, she cried as she combed through two dozen cartons piled up among furniture, art, and other items he had accumulated during his flush years and found some of his good clothes riddled with moth holes. "I just got this horrible feeling in the pit of my stomach," she said. "I had gone there on my own to get a little bit back of my brother but I ended feeling really upset and alone."

Missing among the items and not given to the family by executors was McQueen's Commander of the British Empire decoration.

In May 2010, Gucci Group officially appointed Sarah Burton as creative director of Alexander McQueen. "Having worked alongside Lee McQueen for more than fourteen years, she has a deep understanding of his vision, which will allow the company to stay true to its core values," McQueen CEO Jonathan Akeroyd said in a statement. Gucci Group chairman and CEO Robert Polet added, "Sarah has a real talent, a close understanding of the brand, and the vision necessary to take it forward. We will be giving full support to Sarah and the team in the coming years." Polet left the company a year later, his duties taken over by PPR chairman and CEO François-Henri Pinault, the forty-eight-year-old son of PPR founder François Pinault.

For her first show, in October 2010 in Paris, Burton respected McQueen's fierce aesthetic, but she softened it with her more feminine point of view. She said there would always be what she called "McQueen elements." But, she added, "you have to stay true to yourself. That's what Lee drummed in to me: you have to be able to stand behind your work."

A FEW WEEKS LATER, Prince William announced his engagement to his longtime girlfriend, Catherine Middleton. Once the wedding date of April 29 was set, the next big question was: which designer would Middleton choose to design her gown? After all, the wedding dress of Prince William's mother, Princess Diana, became one of the most famous dresses in modern history and gave its designers, a relatively unknown young pair named David and Elizabeth Emmanuel, a much-needed boost. Middleton's gown, which would be seen by an estimated two billion people on television and via the Internet—

twice as many as had watched Princess Diana walk down the aisle—was bound to have an even more powerful effect on whichever brand she chose. The commission would be the greatest publicity a company could wish for.

Unbeknownst to the public and press, Middleton went to see British *Vogue* editor Alexandra Shulman for advice. Shulman urged Middleton to hire McQueen. She did, and kept the decision to herself. Most of the employees at McQueen didn't know they were working on the royal wedding dress; they were told it was a movie costume. When rumors that the house was making the gown popped up in the press, the house categorically denied them.

When Middleton stepped out of the Rolls-Royce in front of Westminster Abbey in her McQueen gown, the fashion world gasped a sigh of relief: she had chosen not only the house of a tragic British talent but what many in fashion now believe was one of the greatest couturiers ever.

The gown was both lovely and complex: a long-sleeved lace bodice over an ivory and white satin gazar corset, with a full skirt that the palace press office described as "in the shape of an opening flower." Much of the lace was made by the Royal School of Needlework at Hampton Court Palace. The hips were padded and the silhouette was based on Victorian corsetry, both McQueen signature elements. And the back had fifty-eight gazar- and organza-covered buttons, a small, modern bustle, and a nine-foot-long chapel train.

Three days later, the Metropolitan Museum of Art staged its annual gala to celebrate the opening of "Savage Beauty," the retrospective dedicated to Alexander McQueen. The exhibit of more than one hundred pieces, beginning with his postgraduate show and up through his last collection, showed McQueen's profound creativity, deft cutting skills, and darkly romantic voice.

GALLIANO CONTINUED to pop up in headlines too.

Not long after he got out of rehab, the board of his namesake company convened in Paris and voted to fire him.

On the afternoon of June 22, 2011, he arrived at the Tribunal Correctionnel de Paris in the Palais de Justice accompanied by his lawyer. He looked thin and pale. He was dressed in a black three-piece suit, without a shirt, and his hair was a conservative dark blond, shoulder length and straight. He crossed through the waiting crowd of gawkers and protesters, television cameras trailing him, and entered the gold-trimmed wood-paneled courtroom for his hearing. The gallery was filled with both fashion and news reporters seated on wooden benches.

During the seven-hour-long proceedings, Galliano stood before the panel of three judges and said in a barely audible voice that he remembered nothing of the incident at La Perle in February, because of his "triple addiction"—to alcohol, barbiturates, and sleeping pills. "After every creative high, I would crash and the drink would help me to escape," he testified. "I started to have panic attacks and anxiety attacks, and I couldn't go to work without taking Valium. My body was becoming used to the pills, so my intake increased to an amount that I actually can't remember how many I was taking. Sometimes I was taking sleeping pills during the day." He added: "I have only just discovered since after rehab what a lethal mixture I was taking."

He described himself to the court as a "recovering alcoholic and a recovering addict," and, sounding contrite, he said he had undergone two months of rehabilitation, in Arizona and in Switzerland. Following the death of Robinson and the 2008 economic crisis, he claimed his workload increased. "I had two children," he said. "One was Dior, the other was Galliano. . . . They kept me very busy." In response, he said he had more panic attacks and his addictions escalated. "Dior is a big machine," he explained, "and I didn't want to lose Galliano."

He insisted that what he allegedly said was out of character, pointing out that as a gay man, he had endured discrimination himself. "We moved to South London when I was six years old and aware that I was gay. I was sent to a difficult English boys' school and you can imagine that children can be cruel. . . . I never had these views all my life," he said. "These are not the sentiments of John Galliano."

The court gave him suspended fines totaling 6,000 euros ($8,400) plus court costs.

He later sued Dior and John Galliano for wrongful dismissal. In November 2014, the court rejected his claim.

ARNAULT AND TOLEDANO APPOINTED Galliano's former assistant Bill Gaytten as creative director of the John Galliano brand as well as interim studio director for Christian Dior as they searched for a permanent replacement. "I worked very closely with John and Steven over the years—it was always teamwork," Gaytten told me. "So I'm just carrying on." Gaytten's Dior work was savaged by the critics—particularly his attempts at couture—but he quickly found a good rhythm at John Galliano. Stephen Jones was put in charge of John Galliano accessories.

At Dior, the search committee of Arnault, his daughter Delphine, and Sidney Toledano were having a difficult time finding a new creative director. The problem, a former LVMH executive confided to me back then, was "when they chose John fifteen years ago, it was a bold move, and they are scared to do it again. Now Dior is a serious business, and they are permanently turning in circles around what to do. They are afraid. Really afraid. There is too much money in play."

Finally, a full year after firing Galliano, Dior hired Raf Simons, a critically lauded Belgian designer who had been recently let go by the Jil Sander brand when Sander wanted her old job back. The critics were far more sympathetic toward Simons than they had been to Gaytten.

In August 2012, a full eighteen months after his termination, news broke that newly elected French president François Hollande suddenly stripped Galliano of his Chevalier of the Legion of Honor decoration. A month later, Britain's Foreign and Commonwealth Office announced that Bernard Arnault would be made a Knight Commander of the Most Excellent Order of the British Empire.

Occasionally, a rumor would surface that Galliano was orchestrating a fashion comeback: that he was going to be creative head of Schiaparelli, the long-shuttered Parisian couture house that was going to be revamped by its new owner, Tod's founder Diego Della Valle; that he was working out some sort of deal with Topshop owner Philip Green to either design a capsule collection or start a new company; that he was negotiating to buy back his own brand; that he was moving to Los Angeles and getting into the film costume business. At one point, he was overheard telling *Vogue* creative director Grace Coddington at lunch in New York that he was "thrilled" about something brewing. In July 2012, he was photographed having lunch with Anna Wintour at the Ritz in Paris. *Women's Wear Daily* reported that Wintour was thought to be "lobbying on Galliano's behalf with major fashion houses."

Finally, in mid-January 2013, *Women's Wear* broke some real news: Galliano would be a designer "in residence" at Oscar de la Renta, the New York fashion company known for its demure, ladylike clothes. De la Renta invited Galliano for a three-week internship of sorts in his midtown Manhattan studio. "I think John is one of the most talented men I've ever met," de la Renta told *New York* magazine shortly after the announcement. "The years I was doing Balmain in Paris, I went many times with Anna [Wintour] to his shows. . . . So when Anna asked me if I would have John in my studio, I said yes."

The show featured signature elements from both designers. Galliano watched it on a monitor backstage, and at the end, only de la Renta came out for a bow. The applause was full but not ecstatic. No one was allowed backstage—not even Talley. "John had so many bodyguards and they didn't know who I was," he says.

The reviews were respectful. *Women's Wear* called it "a tale of two designers [that] had mystery, suspense, harmony, beauty, optimism—and some truly great clothes."

But what dominated the press the next morning was a photo of Galliano on the front page of the *New York Post*, with the headline: "SCHMUCK! JEW-BASH DESIGNER'S COSTUME MOCKS FAITHFUL." Just before the de la Renta show, photographers had snapped Galliano coming out of the downtown brownstone where he was staying, dressed in a long black coat, knickers, black Doc Marten-style boots, and a black homburg hat, his hair styled in long, tight curls similar to *payot*, or side locks worn by some Orthodox Jewish men.

Galliano's spokeswoman, Liz Rosenberg, responded: "Regarding his attire yesterday: As you well know, John has worn big hats and long coats for many, many years. He indeed has long curly hair, and I can understand people/the *New York Post* misinterpreting his look at the show. But I can assure you there was no intent to dress in a Hasidic style, to present himself as an homage to the Hasidic community or to insult the Jewish culture or pay tribute to people in seventeenth-century Poland on John's part—consciously or unconsciously. His attire included a Stephen Jones hat, Yohji Yamamoto trousers, Brooks Brothers shirt, Dolce & Gabbana vest. In other words—fashionable. The last thing on John's mind would be to do anything that would offend the Jewish community."

It became obvious that Galliano was not going to be able to return to mainstream fashion for the moment—he was too hunted by the paparazzi, hated by too many people—to be fully forgiven for his anti-Semitic outbursts. To shift public opinion to a more forgiving position, he launched an apology tour in the media, including an hour-long appearance on the American talk show *Charlie Rose*. He arrived for the program taping dressed in a navy blue suit and light blue button down shirt sans necktie, his hair slicked back in a neat ponytail—the way his mother used to groom him—and put forth the overworked-self-medicated argument in what felt like a very rehearsed script. When Rose showed the *Sun* clip of him saying he loved Hitler, he looked humiliated.

"How could you say that?" Rose asked.

"No one was more shocked than myself, Charlie," Galliano responded, his voice quiet and evenly timbered. "I just saw that footage you showed and it threw me quite. At that point in my career I had become what is known as a blackout drinker. It's where one can't transfer short term memory into long-term memory. So I have no memory of that event."

The campaign seemed to work somewhat. There was talk in fashion that it might be time to let Galliano return. In July, Kate Moss married her rocker beau, Jamie Hince, in an ethereal *Great Gatsby*–inspired gown designed by Galliano. "Creating Kate's wedding dress saved me personally because it was my creative rehab," he said. "She dared me to be me again." When Moss's father, Peter, gave his speech at the reception dinner and thanked Galliano for the dress, the three hundred guests stood up and gave Galliano an ovation.

In October 2014, Renzo Rosso, president of the Only the Brave (OTB) fashion group, announced that he had hired Galliano as creative director of Maison Martin Margiela—the house where McQueen first went looking for a job twenty years earlier. The first show would be during couture week in January 2015. "John Galliano is one of the greatest, undisputed talents of all time—a unique, exceptional couturier for a *maison* that always challenged and innovated the world of fashion," Rosso told *Women's Wear*. "I look forward to his return to create that fashion dream that only he can create."

IN THE THIRTY YEARS since Galliano presented his breakthrough degree collection and started his tiny company, with two primarily handmade collections a year, fashion has grown into a monolith that has no time or patience for imaginative young designers or small businesses. He and McQueen undertook parallel professional journeys: lauded degree collections at the same school; independent and financially unstable early years that were brilliantly inventive and critically acclaimed; and corporate-backed superstardom that eventually drove them to emotional and creative burnout and self-destruction. They changed fashion—demanded more from it, gave more than most followers could begin to absorb or digest—and their departure from the scene left a creative void.

Today, a fashion show lasts an average of twelve minutes, and as soon as the last model steps out, the front row dashes off to its waiting fleet of chauffeured sedans to whisk it to the next one. Brands unveil new collections almost monthly. Designers are hired hands charged with interpreting the house's codes, and few outside the industry know their names. And all they can come up with on their ever-demanding design schedule are "vintage this and accessible that . . . repackaged and presented as the Hot New Thing," as *New York Times* fashion critic Vanessa Friedman recently lamented.

Fashion's stars today are bloggers and Instagrammers who have hundreds of thousands of followers and earn more than a million dollars a year in kickbacks and "gifts" from brands for shamelessly flacking products in their posts.

The McQueen brand now reaps bountiful profits, thanks in large part to the skull design McQueen used to laugh about; today it graces everything from sweaters to umbrella handles, as well as that blockbuster scarf.

After a four-year forced sabbatical, will Galliano be able to fit into this new reality? How will his elaborate clothes look in a far more sober and commercial landscape? Will anyone care what he has to say?

Young designers have learned from the mistakes and the self-destruction of McQueen, Galliano, and their confreres: "A big part of making this work has been learning to let go," thirty-year-old Alexander Wang, who runs his own company in New York and also holds Ghesquière's old job at Balenciaga in Paris, recently told *The New York Times*. "It was very hard, because I was used to being involved in everything. But while this is my passion and I have devoted myself to it, I am not going to kill myself for it."

Wang and his fellow designers accept that fashion now is about consumption, not creation.

That there is no place for "The Birds" or the São Schlumberger show.

That there is no poetry. No heart. No angst.

It's just business.

ACKNOWLEDGMENTS

Thanks to my many sources—more than 150, including:

The most connected man in fashion, Robert Forrest; the kindest man in fashion, Philip Treacy; the always elegant Stephen Jones; the ever-debonair Hamish Bowles; and the extraordinarily helpful and supportive André Leon Talley. All the early Galliano assistants, supporters, and friends, most notably Richard Cook, Johann Brun, Gail Downey, Deborah Bulleid, William Casey, Limpet O'Connor, Neil Mersh, and Tom Mannion; the early McQueen supporters and staff, including Detmar Blow, Lavinia Verney, Lucy Birley, Ruti Danan, Tiina Laakkonen, Sebastian Pons, Annabelle Neilson, Simon Costin, Lise Strathdee, Eo Bocci, Kim Blake, Karen Maher, Derek Anderson, Andrew Groves, and Nicholas Townsend.

Galliano's Passage du Cheval Blanc team, including Jacqui Duclos, Mesh Chhibber, Dietmar Schloten; McQueen's Paris team, especially Leslie Johnsen and Nicolas Jurnjack; executives Domenico De Sole, Marianne Tesler, Valérie Hermann, and Dawn Mello; designer Tom Ford; June Flett for welcoming me into her home, telling me stories about her son, and letting me paw through his archives and photo albums; everyone who spoke to me on background; and most important, Simon Ungless, who kindly trusted me and responded to my relentless barrage of questions, even when it caused him profound heartache. Without him, this book would not be what it is.

I wouldn't have had any background reporting without Deborah Heard of *The Washington Post*, Amy Spindler at *The New York Times Magazine*, and Christopher Dickey at *Newsweek*'s Paris bureau, who all green-lighted monumental and uncompromising profiles on Galliano and McQueen in the 1990s and gave me the time and encouragement to dig for the truth. Spindler's instruction to "go for it" still rings in my ears.

Thanks to *Details* magazine founder Annie Flanders, who graciously opened her home and personal *Details* archives to me; Mitchell Owens for design expertise and covert ops; Stan Friedman at the Condé Nast library for helping me track down old clips; Deborah Needleman, Whitney Vargas, Margaret Russell, and Stephen Wallis for giving me the time off I needed; Andre Balazs and Philip Pavel at Chateau Marmont in Los Angeles, Tricia Rosentreter at the Peninsula in New York, and everyone at Hazlitt's in Soho, London, for looking after me and providing a home away from home to report and write.

My many readers and cheerleaders, including Sarah Christie, Marina Zenovich, and P. G. Morgan; Cathy Nolan, Laurie Sprague, Shellie Holubek, Evan Roth, Jenny Sullivan, Delores Downs, and Don Ashby. My former *Newsweek* Paris colleagues Jacqueline Duhau, whose clipping files were a godsend, and Ginny Power, who, with Alessandro Zuffi, wrangled the photos.

I've had a team of sharp and dedicated research assistants and fact-checkers, including Julia Lefkowitz, Lauren Seligman, Cynthia Cotts, Mike Elkin, Karen Fragala-Smith, and the indefatigable Chantel Tattoli, who thought she was signing on for a three-month internship and three years later is now a part of the family. I'd like to thank Paula Wallace and James Lough at the Savannah College of Art and Design (SCAD) for inviting me to Savannah as a writer-in-residence and assigning Chantel as intern. I don't know what I would have done without her.

Thank you to photographer Filep Motwary for a beautiful catalogue picture, and the gifted Michael Roberts for a gorgeous, happy author's portrait, many a lunch, and a lot of laughs.

My editors, Helen Conford and Virginia Smith at Penguin, who understand that one year actually means three, and whose deft touch made the manuscript sing. If there were an annual Max Perkins Award, I would most certainly nominate them. Maybe we should start one?

My agent, Tina Bennett, who has stuck by me through all the ups and downs, represents me with utmost integrity, and always telepathically knows when a supportive note or phone call is needed.

And to my husband, Hervé, and our daughter, Lucie Lee—I have no words except love.

SELECTED BIBLIOGRAPHY

Ballard, Bettina. *In My Fashion.* New York: David MacKay, 1960.

Beckett, Andy. *When the Lights Went Out: What Really Happened to Britain in the Seventies.* London: Faber and Faber, 2009.

Blow, Detmar, and Tom Sykes. *Blow By Blow: The Story of Isabella Blow.* London: Harper Collins Publishers, 2010.

Blow, Isabella, and Philip Treacy and Hamish Bowles. *Philip Treacy: When Philip Met Isabella.* New York: Assouline, 2002.

Bolton, Andrew. *Alexander McQueen: Savage Beauty.* New Haven: Yale University Press, 2011.

Brassaï. *The Secret Paris of the 30's.* New York: Pantheon, 1976.

Broackes, Victoria, and Geoffrey Marsh. *David Bowie Is The Subject.* London: V&A Publishing, 2013.

Burchill, Julie, and Tony Parsons. *The Boy Looked at Johnny: The Obituary of Rock and Roll.* Winchester, Mass.: Faber and Faber, Inc. 1987.

Capote, Truman. *Portraits and Observations: The Essays of Truman Capote.* New York: Random House, 2008.

Carter, Graydon, and Cullen Murphy. *Anderson & Sheppard: A Style Is Born.* London: Quercus, 2011.

Coopey, Richard, and Nicholas Woodward. *Britain In The 1970s:*

Troubled Economy. London: UCL Press Ltd., 1996.

Cosgrave, Bronwyn. *Made for Each Other: Fashion and the Academy Awards.* London: Bloomsbury, 2008.

Crowe, Lauren Goldstein. *Isabella Blow: A Life in Fashion.* New York: St. Martins Press, 2010.

Doe, Tamasin. *Patrick Cox: Wit, Irony, and Footwear.* New York: Watson-Guptill, 1988.

Doonan, Simon. *The Asylum.* New York: Blue Rider Press, 2013.

Fairchild, John. *The Fashionable Savages.* New York: Doubleday & Company, Inc., 1965.

Forden, Sara Gay. *The House of Gucci: A Sensational Story of Murder, Madness, Glamour, and Greed.* New York: Perennial, 2001.

Gleason, Katherine. *Alexander McQueen: Evolution.* New York: Race Point, 2012.

Glinert, Ed. *East End Chronicles.* London: Allen Lane, 2005.

Levine, Joshua. *The Rise and Fall of the House of Barneys.* New York: Morrow, 1999.

London, Jack. *The People of the Abyss.* London: Thomas Nelson and Sons, 1919.

Markman, Sidney David. *Jewish Remnants in Spain.* Mesa, Ariz.: Scribe, 2003.

McDowell, Colin. *Galliano: Romantic, Realist, Revolutionary.* New York: Rizzoli, 1998.

Mulvagh, Jane. *Vivienne Westwood: An Unfashionable Life.* London: HarperCollins, 1999.

O'Byrne, Robert. *Style City: How London Became A Fashion Capital.* London: Frances Lincoln Limited, 2009.

Pochna, Marie-France. *Christian Dior: The Man Who Made the World New Again.* New York: Arcade, 1996.

Smith, Graham. *We Can Be Heroes: London Clubland 1976-1984: Punks, Poseurs, Peacocks and People of a Particular Persuasion.* London: Unbound, 2011.

Smith, Sally Bedell. *Diana: The Life of a Troubled Princess.* New York: Random House, 2002.

Steele, Valerie. *The Berg Companion to Fashion.* New York: Berg, 2010.

Talley, André Leon. *A.L.T.: A Memoir.* New York: Villard, 2003.

Watt, Judith. *Alexander McQueen: Fashion Visionary.* London: Goodman Books Limited, 2012.

Webb, Iain R. *Blitz: As Seen in Blitz—Fashioning '80s Style.* London: ACC Editions, 2013.

Wilcox, Claire. *Vivienne Westwood.* London: V&A Publications, 2004.

NOTES

INTRODUCTION

1 **"Your voice is":** http://www
.vogue.co.uk/news/daily/110225-
john-galliano-arrested-in-paris-for
.aspx.

1 **The drunk man's bodyguard:**
Christopher Dickey and Tracy
McNicoll, "The Galliano Dossier,"
Newsweek, June 19, 2011.

1 **Before she could:** Peter Allen,
"John Galliano Called Me 'A Jewish
Whore . . . with Ugly Eyebrows,'"
Daily Mail, February 27, 2011.

3 **"Everything John":** Amanda
Harlech, interview with the author,
by telephone, 1999. All Harlech
quotes are from this interview unless
otherwise indicated.

3 **"He created":** Alex Fury, "Lady
Amanda Harlech: 'I Really Like
Getting My Hands Dirty,'"
Independent, January 22, 2012.

4 **"What the hell":** Michael
Roberts, interview with the author,
London, November 16, 2012. All
Roberts quotes are from this
interview unless otherwise indicated.

4 **"a new way":** Joan Juliet Buck,
interview with the author, by
telephone, 1995.

4 **"I wanted to":** Andrew Bolton,
Alexander McQueen: Savage Beauty
(New York: Metropolitan Museum
of Art, 2011), p. 53.

5 **"Alexander McQueen is":** Alix
Sharkey, "The Real McQueen,"
Guardian Weekend, July 6, 1996,
p. T38.

5 **McQueen and Galliano "were":**
Eugene Souleiman, interview with
the author, by telephone, August 8,
2013. All Souleiman quotes are
from this interview.

5 **"John's a hopeless":** Bridget
Foley, "The Alexander Method,"
Women's Wear Daily, August 30,
1999.

5 **"fashion wasn't":** Rifat Özbek,
interview with the author, London,
December 7, 2011.

6 **"I've made a rope":** Alice
Rawsthorn, *Yves Saint Laurent: A
Biography* (London: HarperCollins,
1996), p. 141.

7 **Bernard Arnault landed:** http://
www.forbes.com/profile/bernard-
arnault/.

8 **French designer Christophe
Decarnin:** "Christophe Decarnin
Misses Balmain Bow, Reportedly
Suffering from Nervous
Breakdown," *Huffington Post*,
March 4, 2011; Eric Wilson, "Star
Designer Leaves Balman House,"
New York Times, April 6, 2011.

8 **"You're only":** "John Galliano,
Designer," *Charlie Rose*, June 12,
2013.

8 **"Fashion is fast":** Dana Thomas,
"Under Pressure, Some Top
Designers Crack," *Washington Post*,
March 12, 2001.

8 **As Bernard:** Antoine Arnault,
interview with the author, Paris
June 20, 2013.

8 **"Fashion doesn't":** John
McKitterick, interview with the
author, by telephone, March 5,
2013. All McKitterick quotes are
from this interview unless otherwise
indicated.

9 **In 1996, a reporter:** William
Middleton, "Three's Company," *W*,
June 1996, p. 105.

9 **"With Galliano":** Claire Wilcox,
interview with the author, by
telephone, September 24, 2014.

9 **it had more than:** Eric Wilson,
"McQueen: The Final Count," *New
York Times*, August 8, 2011.

I

11 **"thronged with the phantoms":**
Mark Twain (Samuel Clemens),
The Innocents Abroad (New York:
Wordsworth Classics, 2010).

11 **"the days slide by":** Truman
Capote, *Portraits and Observations:
The Essays of Truman Capote* (New
York: Random House, 2008), p. 51.

11 **"The souks, the markets":**
http://designmuseum.org/design/
john-galliano.

12 **Galliano was born:** Gibraltar
birth certificates of John Charles
Galliano, No. 54318, Vol. 24, p. 75;
Rose Marie Galliano, No. 54321,
Vol. 22, p. 372; and Maria
Inmaculada Galliano, No. 54319,
Vol. 24, p. 374.

12 **"came from":** Carol Price, "I
Always Liked Looking Cool," *Times*
(London), July 4, 1992.

12 **"They were renowned":** Ibid.

12 **13, Serfaty's Passage:** Gibraltar
Birth Certificate of John Charles
Galliano, No. 54318, Vol. 24, p. 75.

12 **Galliano was baptized:** Alice
Mascarenhas, "Galliano's Splash
of Flamenco for Gib Family
Wedding," *Gibraltar Chronicle*,
August 2, 2010.

12 **"bright alleyways":** Price,
"I Always Liked Looking Cool."

12 **"to depart with three":** Ibid.

13 **"In a decade":** "Great Britain:
You Can Walk Across It on the
Grass," *Time*, April 15, 1966.

13 **"On tabletops":** Michael
Specter, "The Fantasist," *New
Yorker*, September 22, 2003, p. 168.

13 **"I knew pretty":** Price, "I
Always Liked Looking Cool."

13 **John Joseph:** Grace Bradberry,
"From Streatham to Dior," *Times*
(London), October 15, 1997.

13 **"I would sometimes":** Price,
"I Always Liked Looking Cool."

13 **"People are always":** Specter,
"The Fantasist," p. 164.

13 **Galliano's mother:** Paul Frecker,
interview with the author, London,
May 3, 2012. All Frecker quotes are
from this interview unless otherwise
indicated.

14 **Throughout the home:** Richard
Cook, interview with the author, by
telephone, October 5, 2012.

14 **"Other boys' houses":** Price, "I
Always Liked Looking Cool."

14 **As in Gibraltar:** Simon Gage, "Lean Mean Fashion Machine," *Arena*, July 2001, p. 68.
14 **He was particularly:** Paul Frecker, "John Galliano Interview," *Blitz*, never published, August 1991.
14 **For his first:** Price, "I Always Liked Looking Cool."
14 **Galliano readily:** Ibid.
14 **His father "was pretty":** Ibid.
14 **"If I went":** Ingrid Sischy, "Galliano in the Wilderness," *Vanity Fair*, July 2013, p. 78.
14 **"I flew into":** Price, "I Always Liked Looking Cool."
15 **"what the whole":** Ibid.
15 **He wasn't much:** Richard Cook, phone, October 5, 2012.
15 **"I developed cunning":** Sischy, "Galliano in the Wilderness," p. 78.
15 **"into my own":** Price, "I Always Liked Looking Cool."
15 **"Some of the boys":** http://www.bbc.co.uk/news/entertainment-arts-12642163.
15 **in 1975, inflation:** http://www.inflation.eu/inflation-rates/great-britain/historic-inflation/cpi-inflation-great-britain-1975.aspx.
15 **accepted financial aid:** Jane Mulvagh, *Vivienne Westwood: An Unfashionable Life* (London: HarperCollins, 1999), p. 90.
16 **The epicenter:** Ibid, p. 108.
16 **For Galliano:** Ian Hyland, "When Cindy Met Johnny," *Sunday Mirror*, April 4, 1997.
17 **"whatever I had":** Price, "I Always Liked Looking Cool."
17 **a Saturday morning job:** Heather Lambert, interview with the author, London, November 12, 2012.
17 **Once he did arrive:** Lynne Franks, interview with the author, London, September 18, 2012.
18 **"sort out in":** Frecker, "John Galliano Interview."
18 **"was giving education":** Hamish Bowles, interview with the author, New York, January 5, 2012. All Bowles quotes are from this interview unless otherwise indicated.
18 **"You could move":** Colin McDowell, *Galliano*, (London: Weidenfeld & Nicolson, 1997), p. 74.
18 **"a quiet little mouse":** Sheridan Barnett, interview with the author, by phone, December 6, 2011. All Barnett quotes are from this interview.
18 **"with a quiff":** John Cahill, interview with the author, by telephone, April 1999.

18 **Galliano was "terribly":** Bobby Hillson, interview with author, London, September 16, 2011. All Hillson quotes are from this interview.
18 **Galliano studied graphics:** Frecker, "John Galliano Interview."
18 **"Phenomenal":** Sara Livermore, interview with the author, telephone, 1995.
19 **"Only the coolest":** Mitzi Lorenz, interview with the author, London, November 18, 2011.
19 **"It was red-and-white":** Fiona Dealey, interview with the author, by telephone, April 27, 2012. All Dealey quotes are from this interview.
20 **"You'd have Clark":** Steve Dagger, interview with the author, London, May 3, 2012. All Dagger quotes are from this interview.
20 **"It was important":** Boy George, interview with the author, by telephone, July 21, 1999. All Boy George quotes are from this interview.
20 **Taboo "was the place":** Specter, "The Fantasist," p. 166.
21 **"Any kid in":** Ibid.
21 **Of Jewish descent:** June Flett, interview with the author, Blyth, England, March 13, 2013.
21 **When he and his:** John Puddephatt, interview with the author, by telephone, January 10, 2013. All Puddephatt quotes are from this interview.
22 **Another classmate:** Deborah Bulleid, interview with the author, London, December 8, 2011. All Bulleid quotes are from this interview unless otherwise indicated.
22 **Soon, Galliano:** Sara Livermore Freegard, interview with the author, London, May 1, 2012. All Livermore quotes are from this interview unless otherwise indicated.
22 **"I would be":** Specter, "The Fantasist," p. 168.
22 **Fellow dresser:** Ralph Mills, interview with the author, London, November 14, 2012.
23 **In addition to his duties:** Bradberry, "From Streatham to Dior."
23 **"I was looking":** Specter, "The Fantasist," p. 168.
23 **"My tutor Sheridan":** Sarah Mower, "Empire's Maid," *Guardian*, February 5, 1987, p. 11.
24 **"I wanted":** Mulvagh, *Westwood*, pp. 144–45.
24 **Her shows were:** Ibid., pp. 172–73.

24 **In March 1984:** Ibid., p. 187.
25 **"I knew I had":** Price, "I Always Liked Looking Cool."
25 **"Every detail":** Sara Livermore, phone, 1995.
25 **While Galliano:** Frecker, "John Galliano Interview."
26 **The atmosphere was:** Joan Burstein, interview with the author, London, September 15, 2011. All Burstein quotes are from this interview unless otherwise indicated.

II

29 **"Wheeled it through":** Liz Jobey, "John Galliano: Romantic Hero," British *Vogue*, February 1988, p. 150.
29 **"Buckingham Palace":** Michael Gross, "In London, the 'Design Wars,'" *New York Times*, January 10, 1987.
30 **Galliano realized:** McDowell, *Galliano*, p. 87.
30 **"Looking back":** Ibid.
30 **a junior fashion editor:** Middleton, "Three's Company," p. 102.
30 **A friend:** Amanda Harlech, e-mail, March 13, 2012.
30 **"What was meant":** Middleton, "Three's Company," p. 102.
31 **"My feelings were":** Ibid.
31 **handsome, twenty-four-year-old:** Johann Brun, interview with the author, London, December 7, 2011. All Brun quotes are from this interview unless otherwise indicated.
31 **"We were clearly":** McDowell, *Galliano*, p. 91.
32 **"Would you, could":** Middleton, "Three's Company," p. 102.
32 **"all very ad hoc":** McDowell, *Galliano*, p. 91.
32 **The next morning:** Richard Buckley, e-mail, February 3, 2013.
33 **"I like the idea":** McDowell, *Galliano*, p. 91.
33 **"My clothes are":** John Duka, "Fashion in London: Rebels With Causes," *New York Times*, October 17, 1984, p. C12.
33 **Excited by what:** Roberta Wagner, interview with the author, by telephone, March 28, 2012.
33 **"fundamental re-thinking":** McDowell, *Galliano*, p. 91.
34 **Neimark and Mello:** Dawn Mello, interview with the author, New York, March 14, 2012.
34 **"Behind the scenes":** Andrew Basile, interview with the author, by telephone, March 28, 2012.

35 **Galliano found a muse:** Sibylle de Saint Phalle, interview with the author, by telephone, 1999.
35 **"One gas":** Bill Gaytten, interview with the author, Paris, September 22, 2011.
36 **"A Brueghel":** Richard G. Buckley, "London Calling: John Galliano," *Daily News Record*, March 27, 1985, p. 10.
36 **"Imagine a":** Michael Gross, "Center Stage, from the Creative Fringe," *New York Times*, October 14, 1987.
37 **The day before:** William Casey, interview with the author, London, November 15, 2012. All Casey quotes are from this interview.
37 **For a last-minute:** Deborah Bulleid, interview with the author, London, May 1, 2012.
38 **"London's":** Buckley, "London Calling: John Galliano," p. 10.
38 **"Galliano never":** Bill Cunningham, "Fall Fashion: The Search for the Quintessential Eighties Woman," *Details*, September 1985, p. 140.
38 **"was a mob":** Gail Downey, interview with the author, Isle of Wight, September 19, 2012.
39 **John Flett:** Lowri Turner, "Designer Flett, 27, Dies of Heart Attack," *Evening Standard*, January 22, 1991, p. 12.
40 **"I am quite":** Frecker, "John Galliano Interview."
40 **"John would":** Fury, "Lady Amanda Harlech: 'I Really Like Getting My Hands Dirty.'"
40 **"Galliano was":** Vicki Sarge, interview with the author, London, December 9, 2011.
41 **As "Fallen":** Patrick Cox, interview with the author, London, May 1, 2012. All Cox quotes are from this interview unless indicated.
41 **"People thought":** Gross, "Center Stage, from the Creative Fringe."
42 **"looked like":** Suzy Menkes, "Sex, Sensuality, and the Bashful British," *Times* (London), October 15, 1985, p. 11.
42 **"This presentation":** Bernardine Morris, "From London, a New Accent on Simplicity," *New York Times*, October 14, 1985, C15.
42 **"a ghostly tribe":** Sarah Mower, "Big Top Brits," *Guardian*, October 17, 1985.
42 **Most troubling:** Richard G. Buckley, "London Shows: John Galliano," *Daily News Record*, October 22, 1985, p. 17.

42 **"John cried":** Mulvagh, *Westwood*, p. 347.
42 **"When fashion":** Patricia Shelton, "The British Are Coming," *Chicago Sun-Times*, August 24, 1986.
42 **"We got talking":** Louisa Young, "Women: Dear (Oh Dear) Diana—It Was the Fashion Event of the Year. And the Fashion Mistake," *Guardian*, December 12, 1996, p. 5.
43 **"I don't want":** Johann Brun, interview with the author, London, May 1, 2012.
44 **Galliano worked:** Sarah Mower, "Style: Loves Me, Loves Me Not," *Guardian*, February 27, 1986.
44 **"He is a volatile":** Ibid.
45 **"It was very":** Gross, "Center Stage, from the Creative Fringe."
45 **"If John":** Bill Cunningham, *Details*, September 1986, p. 110.
46 **Brun went:** Brun, interview, May 1, 2012.
46 **In June 1986:** James Fallon, "Galliano Plans Line Despite Split with Backer," *Daily News Record*, June 24, 1986, p.13.
46 **he talked:** Downey, interview, September 19, 2012.
46 **"I wish I'd":** Frecker, "John Galliano Interview."

III

47 **Galliano was so broke:** Saint Phalle, phone, 1999.
47 **He was briefly:** Freegard, interview, May 1, 2012.
48 **"[Bertelsen] was":** Jobey, "John Galliano: Romantic Hero," p. 207.
48 **Bertelsen told Galliano:** Peder Bertelsen, interview with the author, by telephone, 1995.
48 **"I didn't alter":** Jobey, "John Galliano: Romantic Hero," p. 207.
48 **An Aguecheek:** "UK's Aguecheek Signs Pact to Finance Galliano's Collection," *Daily News Record*, July 1, 1986, p. 4.
49 **He cleaned up:** Gross, "Center Stage, from the Creative Fringe."
49 **"It's then passed":** Colin McDowell, "Haute Society," *Sunday Times* (London), February 2, 1997.
50 **"A lot of women":** Joyce Caruso, "Innocence by Design," U.S. *Elle*, March 1987.
50 **The British fashion:** Liz Smith, "Showing Style to Win Exports," *Times* (London), March 12, 1988.
50 **"The moment":** "Tell it to the Birds," *Harpers & Queen*, no date.
51 **The New York Times:** Michael Gross, "Notes on Fashion," *New York Times*, October 13, 1986.

51 **The tone of:** Limpet Barron, interview with the author, London, November 14, 2012.
51 **Another night:** Ibid.; Simon Doonan, *Confessions of a Window Dresser: Tales From a Life in Fashion* (New York: Viking Studio, 1998), p. 112; Middleton, "Three's Company," p. 105; Barron, interview, November 14, 2012.
51 **O'Connor figured:** Barron, interview, November 14, 2012.
52 **"I did":** Sean Dixon, interview with the author, London, December 8, 2011.
52 **In early 1987:** Ibid.
52 **Galliano also had:** http://thelondoni.com/?p=375.
53 **"The funniest":** Jasper Conran, interview with the author, by telephone, 1995.
53 **Galliano cracked:** Deborah Bulleid, interview with the author, London, December 8, 2011.
54 **"You know":** Gail Downey, interview with the author, Isle of Wight, November 13, 2012.
54 **She would ride:** Suzy Menkes, "Lady Harlech's Album," *New York Times Magazine*, August 15, 1993.
54 **and keep her:** Sarah Mower, "Tough Romantic: Amanda Harlech," *Vogue*, August 2002.
55 **"If I do":** "The Muse Who Leads a Double Life," *Scotland on Sunday*, March 16, 1997.
55 **He had no idea:** Downey, interview, November 13, 2012.
56 **When she took:** Sarah Crichton, interview with the author, London, May 3, 2012.
57 **Conran's curiosity:** Lorraine Piggott, interview with the author, London, September 17, 2012.
57 **In addition:** Ibid.
58 **Finally came:** Crichton, interview, May 3, 2012.
58 **Liz Smith of:** Liz Smith, "Shining Star," *Times*, October 13, 1987.
58 **Sarah Mower—the:** Sarah Mower, "London Follows Galliano," *Observer*, October 18, 1987, p. 53.
59 **When interviewed by:** Robert O'Byrne, *Style City: How London Became a Fashion Capital* (London: Frances Lincoln Ltd., 2009), p. 99.
59 **Ever shy in:** Nadine Frey and Christopher Petkanas, "Westwood: Eclectic Finale for London," *Women's Wear Daily*, October 13, 1987.
59 **Barker went:** Joan Burnie, "Take Three Brides," Times *Magazine* (London), no date.

59 **By the end:** James Fallon, Peder Bertelsen's Ups and Downs," *Women's Wear Daily*, February 8, 1989, p. 26.

60 **As a result:** Steven Robinson, interview with author, Paris, April 1999. All Robinson quotes are from this interview unless otherwise indicated.

61 **To protect himself:** Downey, interview, September 19, 2012.

61 **His spring–summer:** Bernadine Morris, "In London, Simplicity (Mostly) Reigns," *New York Times*, October 17, 1989.

61 **and Liz Smith:** Liz Smith, "The Glittering Prizes," *Times* (London), October 17, 1989.

61 **Peder Bertelsen:** Morris, "In London, Simplicity (Mostly) Reigns."

IV

63 **Among these is:** Graydon Carter and Cullen Murphy, *Anderson & Sheppard: A Style Is Born* (London: Quercus, 2011), p. 35.

63 **It is best:** Ibid., p. 23.

64 **It was,** *Vanity:* Ibid., p. 18.

64 **"We taught":** John Hitchcock, interview with the author, London, December 9, 2011. All Hitchcock quotes come from this interview.

64 **He was born:** Birth Certificate of Lee Alexander McQueen, General Register Office, England, Application No. 4958958-1, certificate no. 356.

64 **the last of six:** Booth Moore, "Alexander McQueen Dies at 40," *Los Angeles Times*, February 12, 2010.

64 **Soon after:** Sharkey, "The Real McQueen," p. T38.

64 **The East End:** Ed Glinert, *East End Chronicles: Three Hundred Years of Mystery and Mayhem* (London: Allen Lane, 2005), p. viii.

65 **Friedrich Engels:** Friedrich Engels, "May 4 in London," *Arbeiter Zeitung*, May 23, 1890.

65 **The area had:** Glinert, *East End Chronicles*, p. 256.

65 **"Beaten":** Foley, "The Alexander Method."

65 **They married:** England & Wales, Marriage Index, 1916-2005, p. 243.

65 **"When Dad was":** Claudia Joseph, "The Lonely Suicide of Alexander McQueen and Family's Anger at Mystery of £16 Million Legacy," *Mail Online*, November 23, 2013.

65 **By the time:** Richard Pendlebury, "The Inspiring Truth About the Self-Styled Yob of Fashion," *Daily Mail*, January 30, 1997.

65 **Later, when:** Sharkey, "The Real McQueen," p. T38.

66 **When they arrived:** http://www.dazeddigital.com/music/article/15910/1/bowie-mcqueen.

66 **"But I wanted":** Lynn Barber, "Emperor of Bare Bottoms," *Observer*, December 15, 1996, p. D7.

66 **A visual learner:** Pendlebury, "The Inspiring Truth About the Style-Styled Yob of Fashion."

66 **"I got the piss":** Sharkey, "The Real McQueen," p. T38.

66 **"I survived":** Kathryn Samuel, "New Kid on the Block," *Telegraph*, February 24, 1994, p. 17.

66 **One time, he:** Simon Gage, "Alexander McQueen," *Arena*, December 2000, p. 100.

66 **He knew his:** Barber, "Emperor of Bare Bottoms," p. D7.

67 **His sister Jacqui:** Ibid.

67 **She may have:** Pendlebury, "The Inspiring Truth About the Style-Styled Yob of Fashion."

67 **When he did emerge:** Jess Cartner-Morley, "Boy Done Good," *Guardian*, September 18, 2005.

67 **bird watching:** Sharkey, "The Real McQueen," p. T38.

67 **"That's why":** Gage, "Alexander McQueen," p. 100.

67 **"My mum was":** Foley, "The Alexander Method."

67 **Looking back:** Joseph, "The Lonely Suicide of Alexander McQueen and Family's Anger at Mystery of £16 Million Legacy."

67 **He grew up:** Stephanie Theobald, "Alexander the Great," *Harpers & Queen*, April 2003.

68 **"He fucking stole":** Detmar Blow, interview with the author, Hilles, November 17, 2011.

68 **"There's a breaking":** Sharkey, "The Real McQueen," p. T38.

68 **At fifteen:** Avril Mair, "McQueen Meets Knight," *i-D*, July 2000, p. 88.

68 **"I was the only":** Mimi Spencer, "McQueening It," British *Vogue*, June 1994, p. 125.

68 **"Just, you know":** Cartner-Morley, "Boy Done Good."

68 **"I had to draw":** Barber, "Emperor of Bare Bottoms," p. D7.

68 **Janet was the:** Gary James McQueen, interview by telephone, May 29, 2013. All Gary McQueen quotes from this interview.

69 **To appease family:** Pendlebury, "The Inspiring Truth About the Style-Styled Yob of Fashion."

69 **"Dad said I":** Samuel, "New Kid on the Block," p. 17.

69 **"Why don't you":** Sharkey, "The Real McQueen," p. T38.

69 **"In a working class":** Foley, "The Alexander Method."

70 **"was like Dickens":** Barber, "Emperor of Bare Bottoms," p. D7.

70 **"I sat for two":** Samuel, "New Kid on the Block," p. 17.

70 **"He kept his":** Derrick Tomlinson, interview with author, by telephone, May 29, 2013.

70 **He later claimed:** Katie Webb, "Alexander McQueen," *Sky*, March 1993.

71 **After an acute:** Barber, "Emperor of Bare Bottoms," p. D7.

71 Sharkey, "The Real McQueen," p. T38.

71 **"[It was] just":** "Fashion's Hard Case," *Forbes*, September 16, 2002.

72 **By the time:** Barber, "Emperor of Bare Bottoms," p. D7.

72 **that he ran:** http://collections.vam.ac.uk/item/O15677/jacket-koga-yuzun/.

72 **Working at Tatsuno:** Sharkey, "The Real McQueen," p. T38.

72 **Lee was so":** Victoria Fernandez, interview with the author, Paris, January 25, 2012.

73 **"You weren't just":** McKitterick, phone, April 16, 2013.

74 **"Italian designers":** Bernadine Morris, "Fashion; A Many-Splendored Spring: Dressing for Every Mood," *New York Times*, October 4, 1988.

74 **He landed there:** Sharkey, "The Real McQueen," p. T38.

74 **his parents:** Luke Leitch, "Wherefore Art Thou, Romeo Gigli?" *Telegraph*, September 5, 2012.

74 **"From the start":** Holly Brubach, "In Fashion: Between Times," *New Yorker*, April 24, 1989, p. 101.

75 **Gigli was:** Susannah Frankel, "The Real McQueen," *Independent* fashion supplement, September 18, 1999.

75 **On his first:** Watt, *Alexander McQueen*, p. 18; Lise Strathdee, interview with the author, by e-mail, December 17, 2012. All Strathdee quotes come from this interview.

75 **They hustled:** Watt, *Alexander McQueen*, p.18; Strathdee, e-mail, December 17, 2012.

75 **Gigli looked:** Romeo Gigli, interview with the author, Milan, September 21, 2012. All Gigli quotes are from this interview.

76 **"We did tedious":** Carmen Artigas, interview with author, by telephone, December 12, 2012.
77 **"It's going to get":** Ibid.
78 **He surreptitiously:** Simon Ungless, interview with the author, San Francisco, January 20, 2012. All Ungless quotes are from this interview or follow-up e-mails and telephone calls.
79 **In 1969, she:** http://www.vogue.co.uk/spy/biographies/bobby-hillson.
80 **After McQueen left:** Watt, *Alexander McQueen*, p. 23.
80 **As it happened:** Heller, "Fashion's Hard Case," *Forbes*, September 16, 2002.
80 **"She saw the designs":** Barber, "Emperor of Bare Bottoms," p. D4.
80 **When she was told:** Pendlebury, "The Inspiring Truth About the Style-Styled Yob of Fashion."
80 **In October:** Central Saint Martins MA 1992 flyer.
81 **"What I really":** "British Style Genius," BBC, 2009.
82 **"There was always":** Joseph, "The Lonely Suicide of Alexander McQueen and Family's Anger at Mystery of £16 Million Legacy."
82 **McQueen was aghast:** Foley, "The Alexander Method."
83 **Back then students could pay:** Jane Rapley, interview with the author, London, September 16, 2011.
84 **On a Sunday night:** Sophie Anderson, "Shaun Leane: From Catwalk Showstoppers to Ready-to-Wear Diamonds," *JQ*, July 1, 2005.
85 **When it came time:** William Middleton, "The World of McQueen," *Harper's Bazaar*, April 2003, p. 184.
85 **And though they:** Watt, *Alexander McQueen*, pp. 25–26.
86 **McQueen added all:** Ibid, p. 25.
86 **One fabric—a rich pink:** Ungless, e-mail, October 13, 2014.
86 **The structural leitmotif:** John Brodie, "Hanging by a Thread," *GQ*, September 2002, p. 361.
87 **When McQueen picked:** Costin, e-mail, October 16, 2014.
87 **The Central Saint Martins M.A.:** Central Saint Martins MA Fashion Show Invitation.
87 **As the graduation:** Central Saint Martins MA Degree Fashion Show video.
87 **In his program notes:** Lee Alexander McQueen Program Notes, Central Saint Martins MA Degree Fashion Show, March 16, 1992.

V

89 **"London was dead":** McDowell, *Galliano*, p. 165.
90 **On Wednesday:** Bernadine Morris, "Even More, Paris Is the Place to Show," *New York Times*, March 17, 1990.
90 **Bernadine Morris:** Ibid.
90 ***Women's Wear Daily:*** "London Comes to Paris in French RTW Opener," *Women's Wear Daily*, March 15, 1990, p. 11.
90 **"I knew":** McDowell, *Galliano*, p. 165.
90 **and *Details* fashion:** Bill Cunningham, *Details*, September, 1986, p. 111.
91 **On the evening:** Nunzio Carbone, interview with the author, by telephone, March 10, 2013.
91 **Flett's obituaries:** "John Flett," *Daily Telegraph*, January 28, 1991, p. 19.
91 **Galliano felt:** Frecker, "John Galliano Interview."
91 **Instead, Aguecheek:** "John Galliano Returning to Paris for October Shows," *Women's Wear Daily*, July 3, 1991, p. 12.
92 **The jeans were:** Frecker, "John Galliano Interview."
92 **Instead the company:** "John Galliano Returning to Paris for October Shows," p. 12.
92 **That summer:** Frecker, "John Galliano Interview."
93 **Galliano was determined:** "John Galliano Returning to Paris for October Shows," p. 12.
93 **Galliano told Amor:** Fayçal Amor, interview with the author, by telephone, July 6, 2012. All Amor quotes come from this interview unless otherwise indicated.
93 **Paris designer:** Azzedine Alaïa, interview with the author, Paris, December 21, 2012.
94 **"There is no reason":** Bernadine Morris, "Voyages into Uncharted Waters," *New York Times*, October 19, 1991.
94 **"Maybe after all":** Cathy Horyn, "Fashion Notes: Galliano's Girls," *Washington Post*, October 20, 1991.
94 **"John's market":** John Fallon, "Aguecheek No Longer Financing John Galliano," *Women's Wear Daily*, November 26, 1991.
95 **The day after:** "Galliano Will Go Ahead with Spring/Summer Lines," *Women's Wear Daily*, November 27, 1991, p. 22.

VI

97 **One of the:** Central Saint Martins MA Fashion Show Invitation.
97 **An associate editor:** Lauren Goldstein Crowe, *Isabella Blow: A Life in Fashion* (New York: St. Martins Press, 2010), p. 117; Samuel, "New Kid on the Block," p. 17.
97 **"She was like":** Detmar Blow with Tom Sykes, *Blow by Blow* (London: HarperCollins, 2010), p. 153.
98 **"It was obvious":** Sharkey, "The Real McQueen," p. T38.
98 **"No one spotted":** Shane Watson, "Mad as a Hatter," *Evening Standard*, July 1, 2002.
98 **When she got:** Blow, *Blow by Blow*, p. 153.
98 **A true English:** Edward Helmore, "Final Blow," *Vanity Fair*, September 2007, p. 384.
98 **their mother moved:** Crowe, *Isabella Blow*, p. 47.
98 **Isabella used fashion:** Blow, *Blow by Blow*, p. 187.
99 **"Issie understood":** Amy Larocca, "The Sad Hatter," *New York*, July 15, 2007.
99 **"Severity with a":** Stephen Doig, "Hats Off: a Tribute to Isabella Blow," *South China Morning Post*, September 7, 2007.
99 **There was also:** Larocca, "The Sad Hatter."
99 **or when she:** Watson, "Mad as a Hatter."
99 **And she never:** Blow, *Blow by Blow*, p. 74.
99 **He opened it:** Isabella Blow, Philip Treacy, and Hamish Bowles, *Philip Treacy: When Philip Met Isabella* (New York: Assouline, 2002), p. 5.
99 **"I'd never seen":** Crowe, *Isabella Blow*, p. 13.
100 **"I couldn't":** Blow, Treacy, and Bowles, *Philip Treacy: When Philip Met Isabella*, p. 15.
100 **"Issie could":** Ibid., p. 7.
100 **When he:** Ibid., pp. 7–8.
100 **Treacy accepted:** Larocca, "The Sad Hatter."
100 **to break the rules:** Crowe, *Isabella Blow*, pp. 12–15, 119.
100 **Upon seeing:** Ibid., p. 117.
101 **When he returned:** Hamish Bowles, "Blow Up," *Vogue*, September 1996, p. 256.
101 **He resisted:** Sharkey, "The Real McQueen," p. T38.
101 **Finally he gave:** Bowles, "Blow Up," p. 256.

101 **She arrived:** Ibid.
101 **She tried on:** Sharkey, "The Real McQueen," p. T38.
101 **"That's a lot":** Blow, *Blow by Blow:* p. 154.
101 **For years, Blow:** Watt, *Alexander McQueen*, p. 27.
101 **What is for:** Blow, *Blow by Blow*, p. 154.
101 **Then the pair:** Philip Treacy, interview with the author, London, September 18, 2013.
101 **Treacy was fine:** Ibid.
101 **Despite Isabella's:** Alexander McQueen, interview with the author, Paris, March 1997.
103 **Hilles is a:** Eve MacSweeney, "Over at Hilles and Far Away," British *Vogue*, November 1992, pp. 186–91.
103 **She convinced Hamish:** Bowles, e-mail, May 16, 2013.
103 **"I went to south":** Jada Yuan, "Hamish Bowles Was 'Terrified' When He First Met McQueen," nymag.com, May 4, 2011.
104 **Blow introduced:** Lucy Birley, interview with the author, London, December 8, 2011.
104 **Through Blow, McQueen:** Cecilia Burbridge, interview with the author, by telephone, May 29, 2013.
105 **When McQueen went:** Pendlebury, "The Inspiring Truth About the Style-Styled Yob of Fashion."
107 **Lee, because:** Blow, *Blow by Blow*, p. 157.
107 **In fact, McQueen:** Heath, "Bad Boys, Inc.," *The Face*, April 1995.
107 **He had an idea:** Bolton, *Alexander McQueen*, p. 35.
107 **For his first labels:** Ibid.
107 **The recession had:** Lucinda Alford, "London Burning," *Observer*, October 17, 1993, E12.
107 **To give it:** Iain R. Webb, "Something to Show for Themselves," *Times* of London, March 8, 1993, p. 12.
107 **To qualify:** Nilgin Yusuf, "Shaping Up; London Fashion Week," *Sunday Times*, March 7, 1993, p. 3.
108 **Since he had no money:** Lucinda Alford, "The Real McQueen," *Observer*, March 21, 1993, p. B56
108 **All the while:** http://www.harpersbazaar.co.uk/latest-news/MMoA-mcqueen-savage-beauty-exhibition.
108 **There were a:** Yusuf, "Shaping Up; London Fashion Week," p. 3.

108 **Officially, it was:** Alford, "The Real McQueen," p. B56.
108 *The Times* **of:** Yusuf, "Shaping Up; London Fashion Week," p. 3.
108 **"A lot of people":** Burbridge, phone, May 29, 2013.
108 **In a review that:** Alford, "The Real McQueen," p. B56.
109 **"Tiina, you":** Tiina Laakkonen, interview with the author, by telephone, July 21, 2013. All Laakkonen quotes are from this interview unless otherwise indicated.
109 **"No, really":** Tiina Laakkonen, interview with the author, Amagansett, N.Y., July, 19, 2013.
109 **"They wouldn't":** Larissa MacFarquhar, "The Mad Muse of Waterloo," *New Yorker*, March 19, 2001.
110 **The effect was:** http://www.dazeddigital.com/music/article/15910/1/bowie-mcqueen.
112 **When the show:** Katherine Betts, "London Time," *Vogue*, April 1994, p. 178.
112 **Many of the models:** Amy Spindler, "A Mostly Minimal Look in London," *New York Times*, October 20, 1993, p. C13.
113 **"[McQueen's] was a":** Ibid.
113 **"As such, his clothes":** Marion Hume, "McQueen's Theatre of Cruelty," *Independent*, October 21, 1993.
113 **The** *Evening Standard's:* David Hayes, "A Jekyll and Hyde Finale," *Evening Standard*, October 19, 1993, p. 4.
113 **The retailer response:** Samuel, "New Kid on the Block," p. 17.
114 **Shulman wanted her:** Crowe, *Isabella Blow*, pp. 134–35.
114 **"Until we put them on":** Ibid., p. 135.
114 **"the emergence of":** Helmore, "Final Blow," p. 392.
114 **Within months, she was off:** Crowe, *Isabella Blow*, pp. 133–34.
114 **He moved into:** http://markcoflaherty.wordpress.com/1994/05/12/alexander-mcqueen-april-1994-the-pink-paper/.
114 **Though his mother:** Alford, "The Real McQueen," p. B56.
115 **Early in the New Year:** McKitterick, e-mail, April 8, 2013.
115 **As a central theme:** http://thefashionarchive.blogspot.fr/2010/03/alexander-mcqueen-archive.html.
115 **"I think quite":** http://www

.dazeddigital.com/music/article/15910/1/bowie-mcqueen.
115 **"People who are":** http://markcoflaherty.wordpress.com/1994/05/12/alexander-mcqueen-april-1994-the-pink-paper/.
115 **McQueen believed:** Ibid.
116 **"He loved the shock":** Macdonald, e-mail, July 12, 2013.
116 **whom McQueen:** Samuel, "New Kid on the Block," p. 17.
116 **which one reporter:** Spencer, "McQueening It," p. 125.
117 **"My aim is":** Samuel, "New Kid on the Block," p. 17.
117 **"That's the way":** Samantha Murray-Greenway, "Alexander McQueen," *Dazed & Confused*, September 1994, p. 36.
117 **McQueen was one of twenty-nine:** Samuel, "New Kid on the Block," p. 17.
117 **Everyone who helped out:** Michael Roberts, "Alexander McQueen (1969-2010)," Vanityfair.com, February 11, 2010.
117 **worked for free:** Samuel, "New Kid on the Block," p. 17.
117 **"They're not going":** http://markcoflaherty.wordpress.com/1994/05/12/alexander-mcqueen-april-1994-the-pink-paper/.
117 **"All the girls":** Plum Sykes, "25 Years of London Fashion Week: Plum Sykes on Modeling for Alexander McQueen," Vogue.com, September 21, 2009.
118 **The model Tizer Bailey:** Ibid.
118 **"Let's go!":** http://markcoflaherty.wordpress.com/1994/05/12/alexander-mcqueen-april-1994-the-pink-paper/.
119 **"He let Isabella":** Roberts, "Alexander McQueen (1969-2010)," February 11, 2010.
119 **"an eclectic mix":** http://markcoflaherty.wordpress.com/1994/05/12/alexander-mcqueen-april-1994-the-pink-paper/.
119 **team ignored both:** Laakkonen, interview, July 19, 2013.
119 **"I can do it":** http://markcoflaherty.wordpress.com/1994/05/12/alexander-mcqueen-april-1994-the-pink-paper/.
120 **"Among the Scotch tape":** Betts, "London Time," p. 178.
120 **He also talked:** "Scoops: Shock Talk . . . Temper, Temper, Part

Two . . . Tough Sell," *Women's Wear
Daily*, April 12, 1994.
120 **They were knocked out:** David
Livingstone, "Raw, Ribald and
Experimental," *Globe and Mail*,
August 11, 1994, p. D2
120 **"I have seen the future":**
Derek Anderson, interview with
author, by telephone, July 12, 2013.
All Anderson quotes are from this
interview.
121 **Bocci liked:** Eo Bocci,
interview with the author, Paris,
March 3, 2013. All Bocci quotes are
from this interview.
122 **They took the train:** Andrew
Groves, interview with the author,
London, September 18, 2012. All
Groves quotes are from this
interview.
123 **From a fashion aspect:** Suzy
Menkes, "Cool Energy from Hot
London," *International Herald
Tribune*, October 11, 1994, p. 9.
123 **McQueen chose to interpret:**
Menkes, "Cool Energy from Hot
London," p. 9.
124 **Not long after:** Groves, e-mail,
August 5, 2013.
124 **"I've got the feeling":** Murray-
Greenway, "Alexander McQueen,"
p. 36.
125 **McQueen had a new stylist:**
http://showstudio.com/contributor/
katy_england.
125 **"I'd seen her":** Rebecca
Lowthorpe, "The Court of
McQueen," *Observer*, February 23,
1997, p. 108.
126 **Backstage before the show:**
Karen Maher, interview with the
author, by telephone, October 20,
2013. All Maher quotes are from
this interview.
126 **Blake had to work:** Kim Blake,
interview with the author, London,
September 16, 2013. All Blake
quotes are from this interview.
126 **"If they offered me":**
Murray-Greenway,
"Alexander McQueen,"
p. 36.
127 **The New York Times's:** Amy
M. Spindler, "Reviews/Fashion; In
London, Designers Are All Grown-
Ups," *New York Times*, October 11,
1994.
128 **"filled with raw sex":** "London:
Plenty to Look At—But Not Enough
to Rave About," *Women's Wear
Daily*, October 10, 1994.
128 **"Thanks to Alexander
McQueen":** "New Designers,"
Women's Wear Daily, October 17,
1994.

VII

129 **Galliano needed a new
backer:** Godfrey Deeny, "Societe
Amor to Back Galliano's RTW
collection," *Women's Wear Daily*,
August 12, 1992, p. 19.
130 **Robinson filled:** Andrew
Billen, "Can He Really Cut It?"
Observer, February 28, 1993, p. B24.
130 **The deal was announced:**
Deeny, "Societe Amor to Back
Galliano's RTW collection," p. 19.
130 **The women are saved:** Billen,
"Can He Really Cut It?" *Observer*,
p. B24.
131 **"One hundred and three
minutes":** Cathy Horyn, "In a
Toga, in a Trance," *Washington Post*,
October 16, 1992, p. D1.
131 **The show was an endless
parade:** "Paris Plays On," *Women's
Wear Daily*, October 16, 1992, p. 21.
131 **"It is fun":** Bernadine Morris,
"In Many Guises, A Supple Charm,"
New York Times, Oct. 17, 1992.
132 **Amor took Galliano:** Billen,
"Can He Really Cut It?" p. B24.
132 **"There are sewing machines":**
Roger Tredre, "Galliano Meets His
Maker," *Independent*, August 13,
1992.
132 **"He was so practical":**
McDowell, *Galliano*, p. 165.
132 **In his downtime:** Amy M.
Spindler, "Patterns," *New York
Times*, March 8, 1994.
132 **A fervent:** André Leon Talley,
A.L.T. (Villard, 2003: New York),
pp. 112–13.
132 **Vreeland not only:** Ibid, p. viii.
132 **"They were both":** Middleton,
"Three's Company," p. 102.
132 **A few years later:** Ibid, p. 104.
132 **During the three:** André Leon
Talley, interview with author, Paris,
June 28, 2013. All Talley quotes are
from this interview unless otherwise
indicated.
133 **I thought they were:**
Middleton, "Three's Company,"
p. 104.
133 **"She's got":** Heidi Lender,
"Galliano the Great," *Women's Wear
Daily*, October 11, 1993, p. 4.
134 **It was funded:** Heidi Lender,
"The Adventures of Dapper John,"
W, November 1993, p. 71.
135 **"Worse orders":** Julie Gilhart,
interview with the author, by
telephone, August 13, 2013.
135 **He had been:** "Paris Scoop,"
Women's Wear Daily, January 18,
1994, p. 9.
135 **was sleeping on:** Talley, phone,
1999.

135 **"she makes you":** Cathy
Horyn, "Citizen Anna," *New York
Times*, February 1, 2007.
136 **Her Father:** Peter Preston,
"Charles Wintour," *Guardian*,
November 5, 1999.
136 **his manner with:** Michael
Leapman, "Obituary: Charles
Wintour," *Independent*, November
5, 1999.
136 **In 1983, she joined:** Horyn,
"Citizen Anna," February 1, 2007.
136 **"I thought he was a designer":**
Anna Wintour, interview with the
author, by telephone, 1999.
136 **"I was invited to amazing
parties":** Maryellen Gordon, "John
Galliano: The New
Constructionist," *Women's Wear
Daily*, June 13, 1994, p. 16.
137 **Talley was eager:** Cathy
Horyn, "Mental Breakdown,"
Washington Post, February 13, 1994,
p. F3.
138 **According to an American:**
Memo from Patrick O'Connell,
Vogue Director of Public Relations,
June 14, 1999.
138 **"We hadn't time":** McDowell,
John Galliano, p. 170.
138 **"Nineteen-forties":** "Galliano's
Theatrics," *Women's Wear Daily*,
March 7, 1994, p. 7.
138 **The jewelry would be:** Ibid.
139 **To give it:** Specter, "The
Fantasist."
139 **Galliano and his assistants:**
Ibid; Duclos, February 10, 2014.
139 **The morning of the shows:**
Marion Hume, "Galliano Glamour
Outs the Grunge," *Independent*,
March 6, 1994.
140 **"It was brilliant":** Cathy
Horyn, "In Paris, Fall Shows Get
Star Treatment," *Washington Post*,
March 7, 1994, p. C1.
140 **London's Sunday:** Paula Reed,
"Shows of Strength; Paris Fashion,"
Sunday Times, March 13, 1994, p. 32.
140 **orders rolled:** Godfrey Deeny,
"Galliano in High Gear," *Women's
Wear Daily*, October 6, 1994, p. 10.

VIII

145 **For a night at:** Nicholas
Townsend, interview with the
author, London, November 12,
2012. All Townsend quotes come
from this interview.
146 **she was "like a disease":**
MacFarquhar, "The Mad Muse of
Waterloo."
147 **"That's a lot":** Ashley Heath,
"Bad Boys Inc.," *The Face*, April
1995, p. 102.

147 **a petite Israeli woman:** Ruti Danan, interview with the author, London, June 26, 2013. All Danan quotes come from this interview unless otherwise indicated.

147 **"England's rape":** Bolton, *Alexander McQueen*, p. 122.

149 **He called on Julien:** Gemma Ainsworth, interview with the author, by e-mail, September 27, 2013.

149 **a cool English redhead:** Lowthorpe, "The Court of McQueen," p. 108.

150 **"I've been called":** Heath, "Bad Boys Inc.," p. 102.

150 **"you've got to":** Ibid.

150 **The catwalk was strewn:** Cathy Horyn, "London's Bright Idea Is Color," *New York Times*, September 22, 2010.

150 **The show was:** Hamish Bowles, "Blow Up," *Vogue*, September 1996, p. 256.

151 **While the models:** Barber, "Emperor of Bare Bottoms," p. D7.

151 **For his preshow:** David Livingston, "The Scottish Force of Fashion," *Globe and Mail*, March 23, 1995, p. D1.

151 **"The Scottish Highlands":** Livingston, "The Scottish Force of Fashion," p. D1.

151 **"brushed by the":** Amy M. Spindler, "From Young Designers, Familiar Echoes," *New York Times*, March 14, 1995.

152 **"an obvious ploy":** Ibid.

152 **"Rape victims":** Marion Hume and Tasmin Blanchard, "A Little Bit of Fancy," *Independent*, March 17, 1995.

152 **"It is McQueen's":** Katherine Gleason, *Alexander McQueen: Evolution* (New York: Race Point, 2012), p. 32.

152 **"People were so":** Bolton, *Alexander McQueen*, p. 122.

152 **"crucified me":** Rob Tannenbaum, "Drama McQueen," *Details*, June 1997, p. 149.

153 **His neighbor upstairs:** Mira Chai Hyde, interview with the author, by telephone, December 22, 2013.

153 **"Your first project":** Sebastian Pons, interview with the author, by telephone, September 29, 2013. All Pons quotes are from this interview.

155 **"He was obsessed":** Rati Danan, interview with Chantel Tattoli, London, November 27, 2013.

155 **"Oh, I've got an idea":** Macdonald, interview, June 26, 2013.

156 **In truth, McQueen:** Ungless,

e-mail, November 6, 2013; Dante Credit Sheet.

156 **McQueen instructed:** Watt, *Alexander McQueen*, p. 57.

157 **Retailers placed:** Sharkey, "The Real McQueen," p. T38.

157 **"Alexander McQueen":** Iain R. Webb, "Simply Cool for Summer," *Times* of London, October 25, 1995.

157 **"[McQueen] offers the:** Amy M. Spindler, "In London, Straining for Consistency," *New York Times*, October 24, 1995.

157 *Sunday Times Magazine:* Colin McDowell, "Divided We Rule," *Sunday Times*, October 29, 1995, p. 9.

158 **They quickly became:** Neilson, "Annabelle Neilson Remembers Alexander McQueen."

159 **"about war and peace":** "Fashion: Absolutely Fabulous Four," *Observer*, February 25, 1996.

159 **McQueen contacted McCullin's:** Simon Costin, interview with the author, London, March 18, 2013. All Costin quotes come from this interview unless otherwise indicated.

161 **Joseph Corré:** Spindler, "In London, Blueblood Meets Hot Blood," *New York Times*, March 5, 1996.

161 **Vicki Sarge:** "Dante" Credit Sheet.

161 **"I think religion":** "Europe Goes on Maneuvers," *Women's Wear Daily*, March 4, 1996.

162 **He said his:** Lowthorpe, "The Court of McQueen," p. 108.

162 **Verkade persuaded:** Maher, phone, October 20, 2013; "Dante" Credit Sheet.

162 **Backstage:** Simon Chaudoir, interview with the author, by telephone, November 7, 2013. All Chaudoir quotes come from this interview.

162 **As the two:** Maher, phone, October 20, 2013.

162 **Shortly before:** Ibid.

162 **McQueen wouldn't:** Amy M. Spindler, "In a Time of Shadow, Two Sparklers," *New York Times*, March 30, 1996.

162 **The makeup:** Lowthorpe, "The Court of McQueen," p. 108.

163 *"life-threatening crush":* "Europe Goes on Maneuvers," *Women's Wear Daily*, March 4, 1996, p. 6.

164 **"Alexander McQueen went":** Ibid.

164 **Earlier in the week:** Suzy Menkes, "The Macabre and the

Poetic," *International Herald Tribune*, March 5, 1996.

164 **she deemed:** Spindler, "In London, Blueblood Meets Hot Blood."

164 **"Our success":** Treacy, interview, September 18, 2013.

164 **Bocci restricted:** Jessica Kerwin, "The McQueen of England," *Women's Wear Daily*, March 28, 1996, p. 5.; Bocci, interview, March 3, 2013.

164 **The collection:** Sharkey, "The Real McQueen," p. T38.

164 **half of:** James Fallon, "McQueen Signs Pact with Gibo," *Women's Wear Daily*, May 14, 1996.

164 **McQueen's influence:** Maher, phone, October 20, 2013.

166 **"It was chaos":** Mimi Avins, "A New Star in the World of Artifice," *Los Angeles Times*, April 4, 1996, p. 8.

166 **And McQueen walked:** Spindler, "In a Time of Shadow, Two Sparklers," *New York Times*, March 30, 1996.

167 **From below she:** Laakkonen, interview, July 19, 2013.

167 **"At the age of only":** Spindler, "In a Time of Shadow, Two Sparklers."

167 **He went to Japan:** James Fallon, "McQueen Signs Pact with Gibo," *Women's Wear Daily*, May 14, 1996.

168 **"After that you":** Sharkey, "The Real McQueen," p. T38.

IX

171 **"I am very shocked":** "Ferre In, Bohan Out at Dior," *Daily News Record*, May 11, 1989.

171 **Simonin came up:** Richard Simonin, interview with the author, Paris, September, 1995.

172 **Simonin asked:** Jenny Capitain, interview with the author, New York, March 12, 2012.

172 **New York designer:** Cathy Horyn, "Just a Glimpse of the Glad Rags," *Washington Post*, June 14, 1994, p. C2.

172 **"John understood":** Dawn Mello, interview with the author, New York, March 14, 2012.

172 **"John was locked":** Jacqui Duclos, interview with the author, Paris, April 20, 1999. All Duclos quotes are from this interview.

172 **Rubenstein rang up:** Hal Rubenstein, "John Galliano's Wicked, Wicked Cut," *Interview*, September 1994, p. 151.

173 **"John has the spirit":** Simonin, interview, September 1995.

173 **"What I want":** Godfrey

Deeny, "Galliano in High Gear," *Women's Wear Daily*, October 6, 1994, p. 10.

173 **"the grit and grim"**: "Galliano's Camp Glamour," *Women's Wear Daily*, October 14, 1994.

174 **Usually she**: Talley, phone, 1999.

175 **As a final touch**: Fury, "Lady Amanda Harlech: 'I Really Like Getting My Hands Dirty.'"

175 **For the invitations**: Holly Brubach, "Enter Galliano," *New York Times Magazine*, November 27, 1994, p. 85.

176 **Misia Diva**: Press Notes, "Misia Diva," John Galliano S.A., October 12, 1994.

177 **I spotted Madonna**: Madonna, interview with the author, Paris, October 12, 1994.

178 **Marion Hume**: Marion Hume, "Galliano Shows How to Dress Like a Star and Dance All Night," *Independent*, October 14, 1994.

178 **"brilliantly crafted"**: Suzy Menkes, "Funky '50s, Dangerous Liaisons," *International Herald Tribune*, October 14, 2014.

178 **"The clothes were"**: Dawn Mello, interview with the author, by telephone, April 1999.

178 **When he finally**: John Galliano, interview with the author, Paris, October 14, 1994.

180 **For a profile**: Hilton Als, "The Only One," *New Yorker*, November 7, 1994, pp. 98, 100.

180 **"You had to be"**: Sarah Mower, "Genius Galliano," *Harper's Bazaar*, January 1995, p. 104.

181 **"If last season's"**: Amy M. Spindler, "Review/Fashion; Four Who Have No Use for Trends," *New York Times*, March 20, 1995.

182 **Galliano found Arnault**: John Galliano, interview with the author, Paris, July 1995.

182 **"[Arnault's] main concern"**: Ibid.

183 **"We spoke about it"**: Simonin, interview, September 1995.

184 **"That was so touching"**: Pamela Harriman, interview with the author, Paris, July 1995.

184 **He was touched**: Hubert de Givenchy, interview with the author, Paris, July 1995.

184 **"It's the biggest"**: André Leon Talley, interview with the author, Paris, July 1995.

184 **Not everyone**: Sally Brampton, "Second Front: Cutting a Dash," *Guardian*, July 12, 1995.

185 **Galliano chain-smoked**: Galliano, interview, July 1995.

X

188 **"Lentils and fish"**: Sally Brampton, "Flight of Fantasy," *Guardian*, February 3, 1996, p. 12.

188 **On the rare occasions**: Specter, "The Fantasist."

188 **"Really a breath"**: Maria Herrera-Jeuffrain, interview with the author, by telephone, December 20, 2013.

188 **Galliano was more succinct**: Brampton, "Flight of Fantasy," p. 12.

189 **He fell out**: Bruno Barbier, interview with the author, by telephone, April 1999.

190 **Galliano had great respect**: Avril Groom, "A Clash of Cultures Puts Creativity on the Catwalk," *Financial Times*, January 20, 1996.

191 **"It's like suddenly"**: John Galliano, interview with the author, Saint-Denis, January 20, 1996.

191 **McLaren told me**: Malcolm McLaren, interview with the author, Saint-Denis, January 20, 1996.

191 **Joan Collins said**: Suzy Menkes, "Galliano's Theatrics at Givenchy," *International Herald Tribune*, January 22, 1996, p. 1.

191 **Of the India-style gowns**: Martha Duffy, "The New Kid in Town," *Time*, February 5, 1996, p. 65.

191 **Menkes called it**: Menkes, "Galliano's Theatrics at Givenchy," p. 1.

191 **Galliano champion Sally Brampton**: Sally Brampton, "Remembrance of Things Past," *Guardian*, January 25, 1996, p. A10.

191 **"Fabulous. Is it"**: Amy M. Spindler, "Investing in Haute Couture's Lower-Brow Future," *New York Times*, January 22, 1996.

191 **"It's always along"**: Ibid.

192 **"Before, everything"**: Middleton, "Three's Company," p. 106.

192 **"Yes, yes"**: Ibid.

193 **Harlech described it**: William Middleton, "Anything Goes," *Women's Wear Daily*, March 12, 1996, p. 3.

193 **"Could that possibly"**: Amy M. Spindler, "Was That Phantasm by Galliano a Dream?" *New York Times*, March 16, 1996; "Paris: Two Shining Moments," *Women's Wear Daily*, March 15, 1996, p. 11.

193 **Women's Wear said**: "Paris: Two Shining Moments," *Women's Wear Daily*, March 15, 1996, p. 11.

193 ***The Guardian*'s Susannah Frankel**: Susannah Frankel, "Foreigners Storm Paris Catwalks," *Guardian*, March 16, 1996, p. 9.

194 **"The Paine Webber Inc"**: Suzy Menkes, "Galliano Shines with Mohican Motif," *International Herald Tribune*, March 16–17, 1996, p. 17.

195 **As with his eponymous show**: Trish Donnally, "Galliano Redecorates Givenchy's House," *San Francisco Chronicle*, March 18, 1996, p. D1.

195 **Janie Samet of *Le Figaro***: Janie Samet, "Givenchy: C'est Gagné," *Le Figaro*, March 18, 1996, p. 13.

195 **Menkes said the clothes**: Suzy Menkes, "A Neat, Cool Take on Couture for the Fall," *International Herald Tribune*, March 18, 1996.

195 **"The collection will be"**: "The Month in Fashion," *W*, August 1996.

195 **"He was so looking"**: "Suzy," *W*, August 1996.

195 **He did eventually**: Mitchel Owens, "He Likes Couture When It Sizzles," *New York Times*, September 12, 1996.

196 **Galliano, in Arnault's opinion**: Holly Brubach, "And Luxury for All," *New York Times Magazine*, July 12, 1998.

197 **For a couple of years**: Catherine Ostler, "Curse of the Harlechs," *Mail on Sunday*, September 11, 1994, p. 37.

197 **"I didn't want to get"**: Lynn Barber, "My Brilliant Career," *Observer*, August 18, 2007.

197 **"She's crazy and she's so"**: Duclos, interview, April 20, 1999.

198 **Meanwhile, the fashion press**: Amy M. Spindler, "What's New in Couture? Nothing," *New York Times*, July 16, 1996.

198 **Arnault fueled the debate**: Suzy Menkes, "For Dior, a Giant Sword of Damocles," *International Herald Tribune*, July 9, 1996, p. 12.

199 **"I did not have"**: http://www.vogue.co.uk/spy/biographies/sarah-burton.

199 **"[And] he would talk"**: Bolton, *Alexander McQueen*, p. 226 and p. 228.

200 **"No other queen in the world"**: Tannenbaum, "Drama McQueen," p. 148.

200 **McQueen adored Arthur**: Barber, "Emperor of Bare Bottoms," p. D7.

200 **He regarded Hilles**: Ibid.

200 **"I felt like I've lived"**: Ibid.

200 **At the end of July 1996:** "Spitzer Named Givenchy President," *Women's Wear Daily*, July 12, 1996.

200 **"When I contacted him":** Georges Spitzer, interview with the author, Paris, March 1997; McQueen, interview, March 1997.

200 **He thanked Spitzer:** Cartner-Morley, "Boy Done Good."

201 **"To do Dior as well":** Janet Ozzard, "The Galloping Galliano," *Women's Wear Daily*, September 9, 1996.

201 **For head decoration:** Dai Rees, interview with the author, by telephone, May 26, 2014.

203 **"I'm proud of my heritage":** Debra Shaw, interview with the author, Paris, December 7, 2011.

204 **"It threw a lot of people":** http://www.dazeddigital.com/music/article/15910/1/bowie-mcqueen.

204 **"It's about refining":** "London Takes the Lead," *Women's Wear Daily*, September 30, 1996.

205 **McQueen told his mother:** Suzy Menkes, "The British Designer Alexander McQueen," *International Herald Tribune*, October 8, 1996.

205 **"You can be":** Barber, "Emperor of Bare Bottoms," p. D4.

205 **"They haven't made":** Ibid.

206 **"And he expressed great":** Arno Klarsfeld, interview with the author, by telephone, August 18, 2014.

207 **Anna Wintour arrived:** Fatna Moktari, interview with the author, Paris, 1999.

207 **Unbeknownst to the crowd:** Sidney Toledano, interview with the author, Paris, April 1999.

207 **Galliano "always turns":** Suzy Menkes, "Galliano Strikes Out," *International Herald Tribune*, October 14, 1996.

207 **Then he told her loudly:** "Galliano's Muse May Join Rival Chanel," *Toronto Star*, November 21, 1996, p. L6.

208 **"The example of what happened":** Janie Samet, "Chez Givenchy: God Save Mac Queen," *Le Figaro*, January 16, 1997.

208 **But by the next morning:** "McQueen Signs with Givenchy," *Women's Wear Daily*, October 11, 1996, p. 7.

208 **"We needed her":** Treacy, interview, September 17, 2013.

208 **"It made me feel like":** Amy M. Spindler, "Zut! British Infiltrate

French Fashion," *New York Times*, October 15, 1996.

208 **Then he stormed out:** Isabella Blow, interview with the author, Paris 1999.

208 **On the way out:** Crowe, *Isabella Blow*, p. 144; Vassi Chamberlain, "Lean, Mean McQueen," *Tatler*, February, 2004.

208 **McQueen was apprehensive:** Barber, "Emperor of Bare Bottoms," p. D4.

209 **"I mean I like to live":** http://www.dazeddigital.com/music/article/15910/1/bowie-mcqueen.

209 **"He is an emerging talent":** Georges Spitzer, interview with the author, Paris, 1996.

209 **"He could have taken":** Spindler, "Zut! British Infiltrate French Fashion."

209 **"They are killing fashion":** Sally Brampton, "Paris Awaits the New Master of Dior," *Guardian*, October 9, 1996, p. 11.

210 **"We don't produce designers":** *Alexander McQueen*, p. 67; Tamsin Blanchard, "Fashion McQueen," *Independent*, October 14, 1996.

210 **London seemed so hip:** Stryker McGuire and Michael Elliott, "London Reigns," *Newsweek*, November 4, 1996.

210 **"Our country has taken over":** http://www.johnmajor.co.uk/page856.html.

210 **"Fuck off!":** David Kamp, "London Swings! Again!" *Vanity Fair*, March 1997.

210 **"Anyway, if you give":** Suzy Menkes, "Of Clothes, Sing Heavenly Muse!" *International Herald Tribune*, December 7, 1997.

210 **"She hoped":** Treacy, interview, September 18, 2013.

210 **"Devastated" is how:** MacFarquhar, "The Mad Muse of Waterloo."

210 **"He finally had money":** Macdonald, interview, June 26, 2013.

211 **"Oh, she would":** Ibid.

211 **She arrived wearing:** William Middleton, "Karl's New Lady," *W*, January 1997, p. 60.

211 **She confided her disbelief:** Barber, "My Brilliant Career."

211 **Desperate, she rang up:** Ibid.

211 **"Take this contract":** Ibid.

212 **"And they rang back":** Ibid.

212 **"But I had the impression":** Lisa Lockwood, "Fashion's Great Raids," *Women's Wear Daily*, January 6, 1997.

212 **When the news broke:** "Flight

of a Muse," *Women's Wear Daily*, November 14, 1996.

212 **But Galliano saw her departure:** Barber, "My Brilliant Career."

212 **"Mr. Arnault was more":** John Galliano, interview with the author, Paris, April 1999.

XI

213 **"The Givenchy position":** Heller, "Fashion's Hard Case."

214 **"It's the house":** Crowe, *Isabella Blow*, p. 144.

214 **"It's nice to walk down":** Pendlebury, "The Inspiring Truth About the Style-Styled Yob of Fashion."

214 **"Because I prefer people":** Barber, "Emperor of Bare Bottoms," p. D7.

214 **One was Saint:** Saint Phalle, phone, 1999.

214 **He set immediately to work:** Barber, "Emperor of Bare Bottoms," p. D4.

215 **"I said, 'This is couture'":** Mimi Spencer, "Animal Magic," *Evening Standard*, July 8, 1997.

215 **But he surprised the old-timers:** Samet, "Chez Givenchy, God Save Mac Queen," *Le Figaro*.

215 **"He went on his hands":** Herrera-Jeuffrain, phone, December 20, 2013.

215 **"But then when we saw":** Katherine Betts, "Agents Provocateurs," *Vogue*, April 1997, p. 284.

215 **"a true technician":** Middleton, "Will It Sizzle?" p. 6.

215 **"All these people":** Ibid.

216 **He assured them:** Lisa Armstrong, "Galliano Cleans Up," *Times* of London, March 13, 2000.

216 **were a middling:** Christian Dior Annual Report, 1999, p. 9.

216 **"There were Dior rice":** Stephen Jones, interview, December 8, 2011.

216 **There were shelves:** McDowell, *Galliano*, p. 18.

216 **Dior came from:** Stanley Karnow, *Paris in the Fifties* (New York: Times Books, 1997), p. 265.

216 **Upon graduating from:** Ibid, p. 266.

216 **He was demobilized:** Ibid.

216 **He partnered with Marcel:** "Dictator by Demand," *Time*, March 4, 1957.

217 **Though Lelong declared:** Bettina Ballard, *In My Fashion* (New York: David MacKay, 1960), pp. 232–33.

217 **"It was a nostalgic voyage":** Dana Thomas, *Deluxe: How Luxury Lost Its Luster* (New York: Penguin, 2007), p. 28.

217 **There was Passe-Partout:** Marie-France Pochna, *Christian Dior: The Man Who Made the World Look* (New York: Arcade Publishing, 1996), pp. 131–36.

217 *Vogue's* **Bettina Ballard:** Ibid., p. 135.

218 **Dior and Boussac:** Francine du Plessix Gray, "Prophets of Seduction," *New Yorker*, November 4, 1996, p. 84.

218 **They came up with the idea:** Palmer White, *The Master Touch of Lesage, Embroidery for French Fashion* (Paris, Editions du Chêne, 1987), p. 80.

218 *Time* **put the still-portly designer:** Gray, "Prophets of Seduction," p. 87.

218 **"My dear," cried one:** Ibid.

219 **Not all the gems were there:** McDowell, *Galliano*, p. 23.

219 **She tied a scarf around her wrist:** Ibid., p. 33.

219 **She denounced socialites:** Ibid., p. 33.

219 **She dispensed advice to women:** Middleton, "Will It Sizzle?" p. 6.

219 **"Upon studying pictures of the tribe":** Karl Plewka, "Eureka! It's John Galliano," *Interview*, April 1997, p. 104.

220 **Arnault immediately named:** Bridget Foley, "The Global Brand," *Women's Wear Daily*, July 22, 1997, p. 26.

220 **A few years later:** http://www.dior-finance.com/en-US/Documentation/InformationsReglementees/01,02_RapportsFinanciers.aspx/.

220 **"All these zombies":** Ashley Heath, "McQueen of England," *The Face*, November 1996, p. 84.

221 **"If you can imagine":** http://www.dazeddigital.com/music/article/15910/1/bowie-mcqueen.

221 **Vivienne Westwood declared:** Alex Bilmes, "The Interview: McQueen," *GQ*, May 2004.

221 **"We called him 'The Fly'":** Ben Griffiths, "Alexander McQueen Blew £8 Million on Drugs," *The Sun*, June 22, 2014.

221 **They reconnected in 1996:** Archie Reed, interview with the author, by telephone, July 28, 2014.

221 **"It was then I realized":** Griffiths, "Alexander McQueen Blew £8 Million on Drugs."

221 **Though Reed was married:** Reed, phone, July 28, 2014; Wendy Lee, "Scorn of 'Stitch Bitch' Alexander McQueen," *Mail Online*, July 26, 2014.

222 **"Here are your horns":** Treacy, interview, September 18, 2013.

222 **McQueen called the ritual:** Ibid.

222 **Jurnjack recalls:** Nicolas Jurnjack, interview with the author, by telephone, April 25, 2012. All Jurnjack quotes are from this interview.

222 **The event, with a dinner:** Sally Bedell Smith, *Diana: The Life of a Troubled Princess* (New York: Random House, 2007), pp. 318–19.

223 **During the cocktail:** Grace Bradberry, "Princess Slips In for a Model Role with the Fashion Crowd," *Times* of London, December 11, 1996, p. 7.

223 **which included former:** Brenda Polan and Tony Gallagher, "A Couture Conundrum by Dior and a Debacle at the Dance," *Daily Mail*, December 11, 1996, p. 3.

223 **as well as Bernard:** "Les 50 Ans de Dior Eblouissent New York," p. 38.

223 **She was whisked out:** Allan Hall, "Princess Diana Stuns New York Party with Galliano Nightie Dress," *Daily Mirror*, November 12, 1996, p. 1.

223 **and was ferried back:** Judy Wade, "Princess Diana Wows New York in a John Galliano Dress at the Party of the Year," *Hello!*, December 21, 1996, p. 17.

223 **"I paid all":** Polan and Gallagher, "A Couture Conundrum by Dior and a Debacle at the Dance," p. 3.

223 **The headline in the *Daily*:** Smith, *Diana: The Life of a Troubled Princess*, p. 318.

223 **The British press:** Louisa Young, "Women: Dear (Oh Dear) Diana—It Was the Fashion Event of the Year. And the Fashion Mistake," *Guardian*, December 12, 1996, p. 5.

223 **"And it's an inescapable fact":** Polan and Gallagher, "A Couture Conundrum by Dior and a Debacle at the Dance," p. 3.

224 **As British writer Lynn:** Barber, "Emperor of Bare Bottoms," p. D4.

224 **McQueen planned on spending:** Ibid., p. D7.

224 **"We were so tired":** Betts, "Agents Provocateurs," p. 286.

224 **"It's like a meditation":** Claudie Van Gelder, "L'extravagant Mr. Galliano," *Paris Match*, January 1997.

224 **This may have been couture:** Betts, "Agents Provocateurs," p. 286.

224 **Most were wigs:** McDowell, *John Galliano*, p. 136.

225 **"'Why can't we?'":** Ibid., p. 63.

225 **In the weeks:** Betts, "Agents Provocateurs," p. 286.

225 **"It was great fun:** Gelder, "L'extravagant Mr. Galliano."

225 **He was less pleasant:** Betts, "Agents Provocateurs," p. 284.

226 **The newsweekly *L'Express*:** "McQueen, Prince Charment de Givenchy?" *L'Express*, January 16, 1997, p. 33.

226 **"Compared with him":** Kate Muir, "Diary," *Times Magazine* (London), March 8, 1997, p. 5.

226 **But she couldn't manage:** Janie Samet, "Chez Givenchy: God Save Mac Queen," *Le Figaro*, January 16, 1997.

227 **"I don't expect":** "The Ups and Downs of Paris," *Women's Wear Daily*, January 21, 1997, p. 8.

227 **Isabella Blow took her seat:** "Dior's Golden Age," *Women's Wear Daily*, January 21, 1997, p. 6.

227 **She did not help out:** Crowe, *Isabella Blow*, p. 145.

227 **She explained that:** Pendlebury, "The Inspiring Truth About the Style-Styled Yob of Fashion."

227 **The show started:** Hilton Als, "Gear," *New Yorker*, March 17, 1997, p. 88.

227 **After the first look:** Betts, "Agents Provocateurs," p. 291.

227 **"If he continues":** Hilton Als, "Gear," *New Yorker*, March 17, 1997, p. 88.

228 **"The distinctly *now*":** Ibid.

228 **"Overwrought showmanship":** "The Ups and Downs of Paris," *Women's Wear Daily*, January 21, 1997, p. 8.

228 **"This was basically":** Amy M. Spindler, "Among Couture Debuts, Galliano's Is the Standout," *New York Times*, January 21, 1997.

228 **"I'm Alexander McQueen":** "Coo-coo-couture," *Interview*, April 1997, p. 126.

229 **A team of 146 workers:** Middleton, "Will It Sizzle?" p. 6; McDowell, *Galliano*, p. 39.

229 **There were fifty models:** McDowell, *Galliano*, p. 39.

229 **This was his chic new look:** William Middleton, "Johnny Be

Good," *Women's Wear Daily*, December 9, 1996.

230 **"I kept waking up":** John Galliano, interview with the author, Paris, January 20, 1997.

230 **"They aren't going":** Author notes, January 20, 1997.

230 **"That, and with the":** Shaw, interview, December 7, 2011.

230 **The front row:** Suzy Menkes, "Divine Madness," *International Herald Tribune*, January 21, 1997, p. 10.

230 **former French president:** Gerard Lefort, "Galliano, Union Libre Avec Le Prince-de-Galles," *Libération*, January 22, 1997; Betts "Agents Provocateurs," p. 291.

230 **When the show:** Suzy Menkes, "Divine Madness," *International Herald Tribune*, January 21, 1997, p. 10.

231 **It was over:** McDowell, *Galliano*, p. 39.

231 **"this conservative house":** Nan Kempner, interview with the author, Paris, January 1997.

231 **It was as if:** McDowell, *Galliano*, p. 39.

231 ***Quelle* extravagance":** "Dior's Golden Age," *Women's Wear Daily*, January 21, 1997, p. 6.

231 ***International Herald Tribune*'s Suzy Menkes:** Menkes, "Divine Madness," p. 10.

231 **Many of the orders:** McDowell, *Galliano*, p. 39.

231 **In response, he liked:** Sarah Raper, "The Tower and the Glory," *Women's Wear Daily*, December 6, 1999.

231 **At the end of February:** http://flavorwire.com/78245/41-facts-about-alexander-mcqueen.

232 **"Fashion is a jungle":** Tannenbaum, "Drama McQueen," p. 147.

232 **Gainsbury's team:** Ibid, p. 148.

233 **Three days before:** Melanie Rickey, "England's Glory," *Independent*, February 8, 1997.

233 **The place smelled:** Tannenbaum, "Drama McQueen," p. 146.

233 **Katy England, dressed:** Ibid., p. 147; Rickey, "England's Glory."

233 **And he let out his manic:** Tannenbaum, "Drama McQueen," p. 146.

233 **As he fondled the hair:** Ibid., p. 147.

233 **The clothes were supposed:** Rickey, "England's Glory."

233 **He shouted at England:** Tannenbaum, "Drama McQueen," p. 149.

233 **Finally, at 2:00 A.M.:** Rickey, "England's Glory."

233 **"I have mood swings":** Tannenbaum, "Drama McQueen," p. 149.

234 **"bruisy eyeliner":** Rickey, "England's Glory," February 8, 1997.

234 **The Harrods team:** Grace Bradberry, "McQueen's Vision of Chaos," *Times* of London, February 28, 1997.

234 **Some of the youths were throwing:** Tannenbaum, "Drama McQueen," p. 150.

234 **Finally, McQueen was so fed up:** Ibid.

235 **"Someone is going to get killed":** Ibid.

236 **"No matter what happens":** Amy M. Spindler, "In London, the Scene Has Final Say," *New York Times*, March 4, 1997.

237 **"That's what a lot of people":** McQueen, interview, March 1997.

XII

240 **"like a dignified":** Amy M. Spindler, "Designing as a Collective Effort," *New York Times*, March 12, 1997.

240 **Robinson readily:** Robinson, interview, April 1999.

240 **"It increasingly feels":** Amy M. Spindler, "Replacing the Raw with the Refined," *New York Times*, March 15, 1997.

240 **"It's kind":** Als, "Gear," p. 88.

240 **"Frenchified'":** Spindler, "Replacing the Raw with the Refined."

241 **"[When] I":** Tannenbaum, "Drama McQueen," p. 150.

241 **"playing the star":** Middleton, "Will It Sizzle?" p. 6.

243 **"It takes a":** Amy M. Spindler, "Chanel and Givenchy Transitions," *New York Times*, March 14, 1997.

244 **"What the herd":** Katherine Betts, "Diary of a Fashion Insider," *Vogue*, July 1997, p. 58.

245 **Kidman became:** Dana Thomas, "Eyes Wide Open," *Harper's Bazaar Australia*, March 1998.

245 **In the winter:** Bronwyn Cosgrave, *Made for Each Other: Fashion and the Academy Awards* (London: Bloomsbury, 2008), pp. 218–19.

245 **There was one hitch:** Ibid., pp. 218–23.

245 **When Kidman:** Ibid., p. 223.

245 **"I couldn't believe that dress":** Thomas, "Eyes Wide Open," March 1998.

245 **The night after:** "Model Behavior," *Women's Wear Daily*, March 18, 1997, p. 4.

248 **"Some things over the years":** Eric Wilson, "John Galliano," *Women's Wear Daily*, September 19, 1997, p. 7.

249 **In the early 1990s:** Suzy Menkes, "Refurbished Dior Boutique Sees the Light of the Future," *International Herald Tribune*, October 14, 1997, p. 11.

249 **He suggested a soaring rotunda:** Ibid., p. 11; Thomas, *Deluxe*, p. 89.

249 **Arnault approved wholeheartedly:** Thomas, *Deluxe*, p. 88.

249 **However, it was the first:** Saori Masuda, interview with the author, by telephone, April 25, 2012.

250 **According to the Chambre Syndicale:** Dominique Savidan, "Un Deuxième Souffle," *Le Figaro*, July 7, 1997, p. 18B.

250 **"Not in terms of dresses sold":** Sarah Raper, "Haute Hype," *Women's Wear Daily*, July 7, 1997, p. 7.

250 **The star attractions:** Savidan, "Un Deuxième Souffle."

250 **"The classic couture customer":** Raper, "Haute Hype," p. 7.

250 **"Even if I sold zero dresses":** Ibid.

250 **His business partner:** Ibid.

251 **"Others choose a reliable model":** Ibid.

252 **Everyone discovered:** Alessandra Greco, by e-mail, May 27, 2014.

252 **"It was an interesting blend":** Mira Chai Hyde, interview by telephone, December 22, 2013.

252 **For the set:** Watt, *Alexander McQueen*, p. 86.

252 **"In terms of showmanship":** William Middleton, "Here Comes Couture," *Women's Wear Daily*, July 3, 1997.

253 **"It's a lie":** "Couture Scoop," *Women's Wear Daily*, July 7, 1997.

253 **She explained that:** Suzy Menkes, "McQueen's Dance of the Macabre," *International Herald Tribune*, July 8, 1997, p. 10.

253 **"It was like being":** Amy M. Spindler, "New Word in Couture: Fun," *New York Times*, July 9, 1997.

254 **he hired Michael:** Michael Howells, interview with the author, London, September 15, 2011.

254 **"Incredibly international":**
Middleton, "Here Comes Couture,"
July 3, 1997.

254 **"We waited more than":**
Raper, "Haute Hype," p. 7.

254 **Many sported smart straw:**
Suzy Menkes, "Taking Dior into
Wonderland," *International Herald
Tribune*, July 9, 1997, p. 11.

254 **Lucy Ferry was there:** Raper,
"Haute Hype," p. 7.

255 **He added that it:** Phil Collins,
interview with the author, Paris,
July 8, 1997.

255 ***Women's Wear* decried it:**
"Beautiful Dreamers and Glitzy
Gals," *Women's Wear Daily*, July 9,
1997, p. 6.

255 **Spindler proclaimed that:**
Spindler, "New Word in Couture:
Fun."

255 **The problem was:** Janie Samet,
"Galliano Chez Dior: Éblouissant,"
Le Figaro, July 9, 1997, p. C15.

256 **This was the life:** Deborah
Ball, *House of Versace* (New York:
Crown, 2010), pp. 208–9.

256 **When asked how he felt:**
Bridget Foley, "Haute Couture: The
Trickle-Down Theory," *Women's
Wear Daily*, July 22, 1997, p. 10.

256 **"the same budgets":** Costin,
March 18, 2013

257 **"Everyone at the London":**
Amy M. Spindler, "In London, a
Newfound Maturity," *New York
Times*, September 30, 1997.

257 **McQueen slapped the stories:**
Foley, "Haute Couture: The Trickle-
Down Theory," p. 10.

257 **"One is a prim, proper":**
Lauren Ezersky, "Lunch with Laure:
Alexander McQueen," *Paper*,
November 1999.

258 **And they could do:** Spindler,
"In London, a Newfound Maturity."

258 **But McQueen's sponsors**:
Watt, *Alexander McQueen*, p. 97.

258 **He staged it in an old bus:**
Grace Bradberry, "Sparks as
McQueen Goes Down a Storm in
Chelsea," *Times* of London,
September 29, 1997, p. 11.

259 **"It's just as simple":** Cathy
Horyn, "Alexander McQueen's Final
Bow," *New York Times*, April 3, 2010.

259 **It took three months:** Jennifer
Asiama, "Shape of Things to Come,"
Sunday Times, January 9, 2000.

259 **McQueen had taken
Galliano's:** Spindler, "In London, a
Newfound Maturity."

259 **Every minute of it:** Ibid.

260 **who came in from London**:
Thomas, "Eyes Wide Open."

260 **"John Galliano had his":**
Suzy Menkes, "At Dior, Galliano
Fluffs It—Gorgeously,"
International Herald Tribune,
October 15, 1997, p. 8.

260 **"People always make":** Sarah
Raper, "New Dior Prototype Set to
Open," *Women's Wear Daily*,
October 13, 1997, p. 8.

260 **Galliano didn't attend:** Eric
Wilson, "John Galliano," *Women's
Wear Daily*, September 19, 1997,
p. 7.

261 **In his remarks:** Grace
Bradberry, "Fashion's Strangest
Muse?" *Time* of London, November
21, 1996.

261 **He spoke lovingly of London:**
Maher, phone, October 20, 2013.

261 **"If that hadn't happened":**
"The New Surrealists," *Interview*,
September 1998, p. 95.

261 **A few weeks later:** Yvette Vega,
e-mail, May 28, 2014.

261 **"Charlie trusts Anna":** Yvette
Vega, e-mail, July 30, 2014.

261 **During the twenty-minute:**
http://www.thedailybeast.com/
videos/2010/02/11/alexander-
mcqueen-on-charlie-rose.html.

262 **"Once is enough":** Charlie
Rose, "A Look Back at Alexander
McQueen," *Charlie Rose*, season 18,
episode 30, directed by Iain Softley,
aired November 17, 1997
(Bloomberg Television Studios, NY:
PBS, 1997), DVD.

XIII

266 **Arnault's fashion adviser:**
Dominick Dunne, "Paris When
It Sizzles," *Vanity Fair*, May 1998,
p. 246.

267 **There were "lots":** Ibid.,
p. 204.

267 **Valentino, who had just:**
Robert Galbraith, "Italian Group
Eager to Sell Off Valentino," *New
York Times*, January 15, 2002.

267 **Some elegantly smoked:**
Dunne, "Paris When It Sizzles,"
p. 248.

267 **She lost her pet boa:** http://
www.marchesacasati.com/bio.html.

268 **"We love that":** William
Middleton, "Paris: Here Comes
Couture," *Women's Wear Daily*,
January 15, 1998, p. 8.

268 **He and Robinson decided:**
"Let 'em Eat Cake," *WWD/Global*,
January 1998, p. 10.

268 **with the models:** Middleton,
"Paris: Here Comes Couture," p. 8.

268 **To create the sort:** Dunne,
"Paris When It Sizzles," p. 247.

268 **Dior reportedly paid:** Ibid.,
p. 246.

269 **Behind Arnault sat:** Ibid.

269 **"It's a happening":** Ibid.

269 **For Debra Shaw:** Shaw,
interview, December 7, 2011.

269 **"For him, no":** Dunne, "Paris
When It Sizzles."

269 **And the trade scolded:** "Let
'em Eat Cake," p. 10.

270 **"One could hear":** Dunne,
"Paris When It Sizzles," p. 248.

270 **"Alexander is much":** Ibid.,
p. 248.

270 **"There's a new erogenous":**
Ibid.

271 **McQueen would have:**
Samantha Conti with James Fallon
and Melissa Drier, "Gibo: Pinning
Its Future on the Young and the
Risky," *Women's Wear Daily*,
January 28, 1998, p. 54S.

271 **Again McQueen was the
closing:** Grace Bradberry,
"American Guns Turn Out in Force
for Week of Big Name Hunting,"
Times of London, February 21,
1998, p. 9.

271 **"Britannia, it seems:** Sally
Brampton, "Britannia Rules the
Raves," *Times* of London, February
21, 1998.

271 **She revealed to reporters:**
Grace Bradberry, "McQueen Gets
Kate McQueen on Board for the
Oscars," *Times* of London, March
12, 1998, p. 9.

272 **"It's kind of good":** Ezersky,
"Lunch with Laure: Alexander
McQueen."

272 **Ralph Lauren was doing:**
Katherine Betts, "Rumbling in the
Ranks," *Vogue*, April 1998, p. 322.

272 **"If at the end of this century":**
Ibid., p. 321.

272 **He didn't know how:** Émilie
Lanez, "John Galliano Sure Le
Divan de Boris Cyrulnik," *Le Point*,
June 5, 2014, p. 65.

273 **Finally, on March 13:**
Katherine Weisman, "Toledano
Appointed Dior Head," *Women's
Wear Daily*, March 16, 1998.

273 **Arnault understood:** Katherine
Weisman, "Baufumé Expected to
Give Date for Retirement at Dior,"
Women's Wear Daily, March 13,
1998.

274 **His mother was:** Cathy Horyn,
"Man of the House," *New York
Times*, September 16, 2007.

274 **In 1984, he:** http://www.juf
.org/news/arts.aspx?id=60674.

274 **LVMH counted immensely:**
Thomas, *Deluxe*, pp. 83–84.

274 **In fact, Arnault:** Holly Brubach, "And Luxury for All," *New York Times Magazine*, July 12, 1998.

274 **But fashion and accessories:** http://globaldocuments.morningstar.com/documentlibrary/document/73bfe2421fe6e902.msdoc/original.

275 *Women's Wear* **adored:** "Paris Couture: Toujours Glam," *Women's Wear Daily*, July 20, 1998, p. 6.

277 **The trunks came from:** Agathe Godard, "Jocelyne Wildenstein et Mouna Ayoub Prennent Le 'Diorent Express,'" *Paris-Match*, no date.

277 **During a preview:** Suzy Menkes, "Galliano's Diorient Express Runs Out of Steam," *International Herald Tribune*, July 21, 1998, p. 11.

277 **Dolled-up haute couture:** Agathe Godard, "Jocelyne Wildenstein et Mouna Ayoub Prennent Le 'Diorent Express.'"

277 **As with every Galliano:** Amy M. Spindler, "In Paris Couture, the Spectacle's the Thing," *New York Times*, July 21, 1998.

278 **"Whoa there":** Menkes, "Galliano's Diorient Express Runs Out of Steam."

278 **"Season after":** "Paris Couture: Real or Surreal?" *Women's Wear Daily*, July 21, 1998, p. 6.

278 **"It was an embarrassment":** Talley, phone, 1999.

XIV

280 **"His idea is also":** Miuccia Prada, "1990s," American *Vogue*, November 1999, p. 543.

280 **"To read that must":** Miles Socha, "The Level-Headed McQueen," *Women's Wear Daily*, September 18, 1998, p. 15.

280 **He explained that the:** "Speaking English," *Women's Wear Daily*, September 29, 1998, p. 6.

281 **"And put in the context":** Suzy Menkes, "McQueen Brings Poetry to Britpop Showmanship," *International Herald Tribune*, September 29, 1998, p. 12.

281 **The morning after:** Cathy Horyn, "Man of the House," *New York Times*, September 16, 2007.

281 **And he did not keep:** Miles Socha, "What Price Creativity?" *Women's Wear Daily*, February 18, 1999, p. 1.

281 **"Despite what people think":** Ibid.

281 **"This time, the":** Ibid.

281 **But quietly, Galliano was:**

Suzy Menkes, "At Dior, a Victory for the People," *International Herald Tribune*, October 14, 1998.

282 **"These clothes do not":** Ribin Givhan, "In Paris, John Galliano's Pure Fantasy," *Washington Post*, October 17, 1998.

282 **Dior "requires him":** Suzy Menkes, "The Faustian Syndrome," *International Herald Tribune*, October 17, 1998.

283 **"We're not the foreign":** Cathy Horyn, "For Couture, the Show Will Go On," *New York Times*, January 26, 1999.

284 **Galliano came out:** Susannah Frankel, "Enter the Back-to-Front Jacket as Galliano Adds Touch of Surrealism," *Independent*, January 19, 1999.

284 **"It was actually":** Aguiar, phone, September 14, 2012.

285 **"No one needs":** Suzy Menkes, "Couture in Euroland," *International Herald Tribune*, January 19, 1999.

286 **The idea, McQueen:** Suzy Menkes, "An Icy Showcase for McQueen's Shining Moment," *International Herald Tribune*, February 25, 1999.

287 **Another gem was:** Gleason, *Alexander McQueen*, pp. 66–67.

287 **She called the show:** Menkes, "An Icy Showcase for McQueen's Shining Moment."

287 **Blanchett said she'd:** Cosgrave, *Made for Each Other*, p. 230.

288 **"Why don't we":** Ibid.

288 **"It was her idea":** Ibid., p. 231.

288 **The "most fantastic":** Ibid., pp. 232–35.

288 **Menkes found it:** Suzy Menkes, "Givenchy's Glitzy Space Odyssey," *International Herald Tribune*, March 11, 1999.

288 **and** *Women's Wear:* "Free Spirits and Future Shock," *Women's Wear Daily*, March 11, 1999, p. 8.

288 **A few days:** Dana Thomas, "Brawling for Beauty," *Newsweek*, April 4, 1999.

290 **One night that spring:** Lee, "Scorn of 'Stitch Bitch' Alexander McQueen."

290 **"I think he felt":** Tom Ford, interview with the author, by telephone, November 13, 2013.

290 **"He was never really":** Macdonald, interview, June 26, 2013.

291 **"It was quick and":** "Alexander

McQueen: Liposuction," *Evening Standard*, January 18, 2002.

291 **It sucks up:** Ibid.

XV

293 **"Some practically doubled their":** Sidney Toledano, interview with the author, Paris, April 1999.

294 **Dior, he concluded:** Bernard Arnault, interview by fax, June 25, 1999.

294 **"It's not inexpensive":** Dawn Mello, interview with the author, by telephone, April, 1999.

294 **"Valérie was an excellent":** Katherine Weisman, interview with the author, by telephone, June 29, 2014.

294 **"Steven calls the":** Talley, phone, 1999.

297 **"With anyone as":** Galliano, interview, April 1999.

297 **Shortly after our lunch:** "Dior Extends Galliano Pact for Three Years," *Women's Wear Daily*, April 20, 1999.

297 **"The windows, the ads":** "Fashion Flash," *Women's Wear Daily*, July 19, 1999, p. 13.

297 **"So much for restraint":** "Galliano to Show Dior Fall Couture at Versailles," *Women's Wear Daily*, July 2, 1999.

298 **"The show masqueraded":** Suzy Menkes, "But Chanel Stays Cool for 2000," *International Herald Tribune*, July 21, 1999.

298 **"Ludicrous":** Cathy Horyn, "Is There Room for Fashion at the Paris Haute Couture Shows?" *New York Times*, July 25, 1999.

298 **"It's for the media":** Menkes, "But Chanel Stays Cool for 2000."

298 **But given:** Horyn, "Is There Room for Fashion at the Paris Haute Couture Shows?"

299 **"McQueen is to be":** "Puttin' on the Glitz," *Women's Wear Daily*, July 19, 1999, p. 11.

299 **The problem was that:** Suzy Menkes, "Givenchy's Automated Models: Museum Drama from McQueen," *International Herald Tribune*, July 20, 1999.

299 **but it didn't dissuade:** http://www.dazeddigital.com/fashion/article/15910/1/bowie-mcqueen.

300 **"I thought it would":** Heller, "Fashion's Hard Case."

300 **He asked to stage:** Mark Inglefield, "Alexander McQueen: Diary," *Times* of London, September 13, 1999, p. 18.

300 **The storm "will add":** Lisa Armstrong, "Fashion Show

Stands Its Ground as Hurricane Threatens New York," *Times* of London, September 17, 1999, p. 9.

300 **"There's something perversely":** "High Energy, High Wires and Calvin's Class Act," *Women's Wear Daily*, September 21, 1999, p. 4.

301 *The New York Times*'s **Horyn:** Cathy Horyn, "McQueen's Audacity, Beene's Impishness," *New York Times*, September 18, 1999.

301 **"The clothes didn't break":** Ibid.

301 *Women's Wear* **concluded:** "High Energy, High Wires and Calvin's Class Act," p. 4.

301 **In recent months:** Wendy Hessen and Sarah Raper, "LVMH Agrees to Buy Chaument, Ebel," *Women's Wear Daily*, October 21, 1999.

301 **and the two-hundred-year-old:** http://news.bbc.co.uk/1/hi/business/522664.stm.

301 **Tom Ford planned:** Suzy Menkes, "Gucci Moving to Buy Yves Saint Laurent, Fashion's Biggest Prize," *International Herald Tribune*, October 9, 1999.

302 **The** *New Yorker* **architecture:** Paul Goldberger, "Dior's New House," *New Yorker*, January 31, 2000, p. 88.

302 **Arnault's personal wealth:** Sarah Raper, "The Tower and the Glory," *Women's Wear Daily*, December 6, 1999.

XVI

303 **Galliano found the:** Specter, "The Fantasist."

304 **They also studied mid-century:** Bridget Foley, "Dior: The Saga Continues," *Women's Wear Daily*, January 28, 2000.

304 **he told me that he:** "Homeless Isn't Chic," *Newsweek.com*, February 7, 2000.

304 **"John Galliano has more":** "From Hobos to Ho-Hum," *Women's Wear Daily*, January 18, 2000.

304 **The French media:** Cathy Horyn, "Fashion Review: Offstage, Paris Fusses About Dior," *New York Times*, January 23, 2000.

305 **He added:** Foley, "Dior: The Saga Continues."

305 **Galliano scoffed:** Susan Chandler, "Homeless Don't Want Their Fashions on Runway," *Chicago Tribune*, February 5, 2000.

305 **A gust of genius:** Sarah Raper,

"A Protest in Paris—and Dior's the Target," *Women's Wear Daily*, January 28, 2000.

305 **"It's fantastic":** Maureen Dowd, "Haute Homeless," *New York Times*, January 23, 2000.

306 **"But we want their":** "Homeless Isn't Chic."

306 **They got it:** Raper, "A Protest in Paris—and Dior's the Target."

306 **What set folks:** Suzy Menkes, "Hot or Haute, Image Is the Value That Drives Demand," *International Herald Tribune*, January 17, 2000.

306 **"Nobody told me":** "Couture Scoop," *Women's Wear Daily*, January 18, 2000.

306 **"I'm just a romantic":** Lisa Armstrong, "McQueen's Back, and He's Dynamite," *Times* of London, January 31, 2000, p. 36.

307 **"I'd never heard":** Will Payne, "The Crazy World of Alexander McQueen, by His Ex-Husband," *Daily Mirror*, February 14, 2010.

307 **"Until then I'd only":** Laura Collins, "Alexander McQueen's Ex-partner Throws a Disturbing Light on the 'Hangers-on' Who Lionised Him, but Who Never Truly Knew Him," *Daily Mail*, February 14, 2010.

307 **"It'll always be":** Watt, *Alexander McQueen*, p. 113.

307 **Tribalism had long been:** Ibid., p. 115.

307 **American** *Vogue* **said:** Sally Singer, "Blue-Chip Dressing," *Vogue*, June 2000, p. 99.

308 *The New York Times*'s **Ginia:** Ginia Bellafante, "In London, Executing Triple Axel Jumps," *New York Times*, February 20, 2000.

308 **"Some in the audience":** Ibid.

308 **As everyone danced:** "Fair Game," *Women's Wear Daily*, June 6, 2000, p. 3.

309 **"This is my kind":** Heller, "Fashion's Hard Case."

309 **"I didn't like the":** Ibid.

309 **McQueen was intrigued:** Ford, phone, November 13, 2013.

310 **In fact, LVMH:** Robert Murphy, "Dior Sales Rise 42 Percent for First Half," *Women's Wear Daily*, July 18, 2000.

310 **"It has to be":** Sarah Mower, "Rebel Designer: John Galliano," *Vogue*, November 2001, p. 222.

310 **"And I agree even":** Sarah Raper, "The Tower and the Glory," *Women's Wear Daily*, December 6, 1999.

310 **The show opened with:** André Leon Talley, "Let Them

Eat Cake," *Vogue*, October 1, 2000, p. 248.

311 **"To make light of":** Suzy Menkes, "Fetishism on the Runway: Chic or Sick?" *International Herald Tribune*, July 10, 2000.

311 **"It's Kate Moss":** Payne, "The Crazy World of Alexander McQueen, by His Ex-Husband."

311 **"It was all party":** Collins, "Alexander McQueen's Ex-partner Throws a Disturbing Light on the 'Hangers-on' Who Lionised Him, but Who Never Truly Knew Him."

311 **The vows were performed:** Gage, "Alexander McQueen," p. 102.

312 **"It was a perfect":** Collins, "Alexander McQueen's Ex-partner Throws a Disturbing Light on the 'Hangers-on' Who Lionised Him, but Who Never Truly Knew Him."

312 **"I was never given":** Christa D'Souza, "McQueen and Country," *Observer*, March 4, 2001.

312 **In September, he:** Susannah Frankel, "McQueen: The Diary of a Dress," *Independent*, October 25, 2000.

312 **"about nature":** Ibid.

312 **Another aha:** Ibid.

313 **By then, McQueen:** Mair, "McQueen Meets Knight," p. 91.

313 **"[I design for] intelligent":** Gage, "Alexander McQueen," p. 100.

313 **Galliano didn't have:** Gage, "Lean Mean Fashion Machine," p. 68.

314 **"And, if you can":** Lauren Milligan, "Fashion Flashback: McQueen's Asylum Show," Vogue.co.uk, August 7, 2014.

314 **"The shells":** Ibid.

314 **"Fucking hell":** MacFarquhar, "The Mad Muse of Waterloo."

315 **Horyn called:** Cathy Horyn, "In London, Ho-Hum Ends in Smash Finale," *New York Times*, October 1, 2000.

315 **Instead of confronting them:** D'Souza, "McQueen and Country."

316 **The deal was reportedly:** *Women's Wear* says he did $10 million in sales. Samantha Conti, "Gucci's Sneak Attack," *Women's Wear Daily*, December 5, 2000, p. 1.

316 **"I don't think Arnault:** D'Souza, "McQueen and Country."

316 **A Gucci spokesman pointedly:** Jay Rayner, "Absolute Designer Chic," *Observer*, December 10, 2000, p. 18.

316 **"Otherwise I could not":** D'Souza, "McQueen and Country."

316 **"He's always complaining"**: Sara Gay Forden, *The House of Gucci: A Sensational Story of Murder, Madness, Glamour, and Greed* (New York: Perennial, 2001), p. 339.

317 **"Everybody else got contracts"**: Cathy Horyn, "The Woman No Hat Could Tame," *New York Times*, May 10, 2007.

317 **With the Gucci money:** Adam Rapoport, "Alexander the Great," *GQ*, September 2004, p. 398.

317 **"I want to have"**: Gage, "Alexander McQueen," p. 102.

317 **He also went on:** Payne, "The Crazy World of Alexander McQueen, By His Ex-Husband."

318 **During an interview:** D'Souza, "McQueen and Country."

320 **"Some of it is fun"**: Suzy Menkes, "McQueen Musters Leather and Braid for Gucci Camp," *International Herald Tribune*, February 23, 2001.

XVII

321 **"I'm very proud"**: http://www .dailymail.co.uk/news/article -86496/Designer-Galliano-collects -CBE.html.

323 **"It was a tour"**: "Magnificent Madness," *Women's Wear Daily*, January 22, 2002.

323 **"So far he has"**: Miles Socha, "Dear John," *W*, April 2002, p. 215.

323 **Dior executives:** Specter, "The Fantasist."

323 **The shows were:** "Vive La Difference," *Women's Wear Daily*, October 8, 2002, p. 4.

324 **"Lee was so"**: Collins, "Alexander McQueen's Ex-partner Throws Disturbing Light on the 'Hangers-On' Who Lionised Him, but Who Never Truly Knew Him."

324 **"Lee was very"**: Griffiths, "Alexander McQueen Blew £8 Million on Drugs."

324 **He said he:** Samuel, "New Kid on the Block," p. 17., "Fashion's Hard Case," *Forbes*, September 16, 2002.

324 **"We are going"**: Gilhart, phone, October 28, 2013.

324 **"It makes me believe"**: Maggie Davis, "The Boy Is Back in Town," *Evening Standard Magazine*, January 2002, p. 12.

324 **"Myself and others would"**: Griffiths, "Alexander McQueen Blew £8 Million on Drugs."

325 **"How much is"**: Serge Weinberg, interview with the author, Paris, December 6, 2013.

325 **"I know what I"**: Maggie Davis, "The Boy Is Back in Town," *Evening Standard Magazine*, January 2002, p. 12.

326 **On March 17, 2003:** "In the Running," *Women's Wear Daily*, June 2, 2003, p. 24S.

326 **"It's so quiet"**: William Middleton, "The World of McQueen," *Harper's Bazaar*, April 2003, p. 184.

327 **"He was fine"**: Cavendish, "I Ask If He Can Design a Dress for Me. His Eyes Linger on My Breasts. 'No,' He Says Sadly. 'I'm Afraid Not.'"

327 **"It was all very"**: Specter, "The Fantasist," p. 162.

327 **"It never comes out"**: Ibid, p. 169.

327 **He went to his:** Ibid.

327 **"I think every woman"**: Ibid., p. 163.

328 **"I hope I would"**: Ibid., p. 171.

XVIII

332 **"So I came away"**: Alexander McQueen and Joyce McQueen, "Meeting the Queen Was Like Falling in Love," *Guardian*, April 20, 2004.

333 **And McQueen's business:** McKee, interview, November 18, 2011.

333 **"I go in"**: Rapoport, "Alexander the Great," p. 396.

334 **Though McQueen reveled:** Cartner-Morley, "Boy Done Good."

334 **One time, he traveled:** Ungless, interview, January 20, 2012.

334 **When he went:** Simon Doonan, *The Asylum* (New York: Blue Rider Press, 2013), pp. 252–55.

334 **He spent a fair:** Cathy Horyn, "McQueen: the Backstory and Beyond," *New York Times*, April 5, 2010.

334 **They'd go scuba diving:** Neilson, "Annabelle Neilson Remembers Alexander McQueen."

335 **Galliano did his best to keep going:** "Cherie Harkens Back," *Women's Wear Daily*, May 20, 2005, p. 6.

336 **"And it was"**: Robin Givhan, "Citizen Models," *Washington Post*, October 11, 2005.

336 **Toledano admitted:** Cathy Horyn, "Man of the House," *New York Times*, September 16, 2007.

336 **Two weeks later:** Joelle Diderich, "Galliano Case to Head Back to Labor Court," *Women's Wear Daily*, November 28, 2013.

337 **According to one report:** David James Smith, "The Secret Torments of Galliano," *Sunday Times*, August 21, 2011.

339 **The only person:** Mimma Viglezio, interview with the author, by telephone, November 26, 2013.

340 **In early April:** Smith, "The Secret Torments of Galliano."

340 **Ten days later:** Howells, interview, September 23, 2001.

341 **"But not Isabella"**: Larocca, "The Sad Hatter."

341 **"No, no," she:** Bridget Foley, "Hail McQueen," *W*, June 2008.

342 **he was inconsolable:** David James Smith, "Stitch Bitch," *Sunday Times Magazine*, May 23, 2010, p. 13.

342 **Shaun Leane was going:** Horyn, "Alexander McQueen's Final Bow."

342 **They agreed:** Crowe, *Isabella Blow*, pp. 2–6.

XIX

343 **It was a wake-up:** Adam Tshorn, "In a New Light," *Los Angeles Times*, April 6, 2008.

344 **Last, she said:** Treacy, interview, September 17, 2013.

344 **McQueen's friend the artist:** Ibid.

345 **"She was a feral"**: Watt, *Alexander McQueen*, p. 187.

345 **"I'll become Sir"**: Foley, "Hail McQueen."

346 **"We've done about"**: Adam Tshorn, "In A New Light," *Los Angeles Times*, April 6, 2008.

346 **Happily, PPR's executives:** Cathy Horyn, "General Lee," *T*, September 11, 2009.

346 **"The next morning, his"**: Griffiths, "Alexander McQueen Blew £8 Million on Drugs."

347 **Eventually, McQueen and Reed:** Reed, phone, July 28, 2014.

347 **He bought a 2,500:** Stuart Woledge, "An Apartment Fit for McQueen,' *Mail Online*, August 31, 2013.

347 **One reportedly was a:** Horyn, "General Lee."

347 **But none of them:** Horyn, "Alexander McQueen's Final Bow."

347 **He stated that:** Watt, *Alexander McQueen*, p. 195.

348 **Suzy Menkes seemed:** Suzy Menkes, "Creative to the Extreme," *International Herald Tribune*, March 12, 2009

350 **"The overdoses, he"**:

Sam Jones, "Alexander McQueen Hanged Himself After Taking Drugs," *Guardian*, April 18, 2010.

350 **His habitual excuse:** Smith, "Stitch Bitch," p. 15.

351 **Instead of Darwin's theory:** Godfrey Deeny, "Alexander McQueen: The Final Interview," *Harper's Bazaar Australia*, March 8, 2010.

351 **"I want it all":** Bolton, *Alexander McQueen*, p. 229.

351 **It looked like:** Ibid.

351 **"He made you feel":** Ibid, p. 230.

351 **"Sparks flying out":** http://jezebel.com/5469572/alexander-mcqueens-disturbing-final-tweets.

352 **She concluded: "The":** Suzy Menkes, "Techno Revolution," *International Herald Tribune*, October 8, 2009.

352 **"I think he knew it":** Joseph, "The Lonely Suicide of Alexander McQueen and Family's Anger at Mystery of £16 Million Legacy."

352 **When Treacy remarked:** David James Smith, "Alexander McQueen," *Sunday Times Magazine*, May 23, 2010, p. 17.

353 **He agreed:** Treacy, interview, September 18, 2013.

353 **He thanked Polet:** Robert Polet, interview with the author, by telephone, December 23, 2013.

353 **"He sounded lonely":** Treacy, interview, September 18, 2013.

354 **"Stop talking such":** Ibid.

354 **"I loved him":** Ibid.

354 **He added, "Now I":** http://www.fernandoirigoyen.com/resources/THE%20LAST%20TWEETS%20OF%20MCQUEEN.jpg.

354 **"I thought it was":** Joseph, "The Lonely Suicide of Alexander McQueen and Family's Anger at Mystery of £16 Million Legacy."

354 **"We'll get through":** Horyn, "Alexander McQueen's Final Bow."

354 **Reed said: "Take":** Griffiths, "Alexander McQueen Blew £8 Million on Drugs."

354 **She said she didn't:** Neilson, "Annabelle Neilson Remembers Alexander McQueen."

354 **"How wrong I":** Joseph, "The Lonely Suicide of Alexander McQueen and Family's Anger at Mystery of £16 Million Legacy."

354 **"Make it late":** Horyn, "Alexander McQueen's Final Bow."

355 **"He was running":** Neilson, "Annabelle Neilson Remembers Alexander McQueen."

355 **She left at:** Horyn, "Alexander McQueen's Final Bow."

355 **But instead of going:** Smith, "Stitch Bitch," p. 13; Jones, "Alexander McQueen Hanged Himself After Taking Drugs.

355 **"PS Bury me":** Jones, "Alexander McQueen Hanged Himself After Taking Drugs."

355 **He removed the clothes:** Judith Thurman, "Dressed to Kill," *New Yorker*, May 16, 2011, p. 116.

356 **He walked into the guest:** Jones, "Alexander McQueen Hanged Himself After Taking Drugs."

356 **He turned to the emptied closet:** Smith, "Stitch Bitch," p. 14.

356 **"He's gone for good":** Ibid.

356 **He called the paramedics:** Horyn, "Alexander McQueen's Final Bow."

356 **Garcia's wife, Marlene:** Smith, "Stitch Bitch," p. 13.

356 **"He's going to be all":** Horyn, "Alexander McQueen's Final Bow."

356 **"It was one of the":** Ibid.

357 **Michael McQueen:** Joseph, "The Lonely Suicide of Alexander McQueen and Family's Anger at Mystery of £16 Million Legacy."

XX

359 **His brother Michael:** Ibid.

359 **The family held Joyce's:** Simon Perry, "Without Mom, Alexander McQueen 'Could Not Face the Future,'" *People*, February 12, 2012.

360 **The McQ show:** Rebecca Camber, Michael Seamark, and Sara Nathan, "Alexander McQueen's Family Makes Agonizing Decision to Hold His Beloved Mother's Funeral the Day After His Suicide," *Mail Online*, February 12, 2010.

360 **"He will not be forgotten":** "Alexander McQueen, a True Master," *Women's Wear Daily*, February 11, 2010.

361 **"I didn't really know":** Joseph, "The Lonely Suicide of Alexander McQueen and Family's Anger at Mystery of £16 Million Legacy."

361 **"It's the most important":** Neilson, "Annabelle Neilson Remembers Alexander McQueen."

361 **"He wanted to return":** "How Alexander McQueen's Skye Ancestry Shaped His Fashion Legacy," *Scotsman*, April 24, 2011.

361 **Some wore Mohawk-like:** Hamish Bowles, "Nobel Farewell," *Vogue*, July 1, 2010, p. 142.

361 *Vogue's* **Hamish Bowles:** Ibid.

361 **His housekeepers, Marlene:** "Fashion Designer Alexander McQueen Leaves £50,000 of £16m Fortune from His Beloved Dogs," *Daily Mail*, July 27, 2011.

362 **The family suggested it:** Joseph, "The Lonely Suicide of Alexander McQueen and Family's Anger at Mystery of £16 Million Legacy."

362 **"They didn't let us see":** Ibid.

362 **On April 28:** Jones, "Alexander McQueen Hanged Himself After Taking Drugs."

362 **A month later, McQueen's:** George Joseph Forsyth-Griffiths, death certificate, Application Number 5238262-1 CJL (October 23, 2010), London Borough of Islington, London, England.

363 **But, she said, "He":** Isabel Wilkinson, "Inside Alexander McQueen's Memorial," *Daily Beast*, September 20, 2010.

363 **"But that was the beauty":** Emma Hallett, "Fashion Elite Told of McQueen's Career of Dreams and Demons," *Herald*, September 21, 2010.

363 **Treacy and two:** Jess Cartner-Morley, "Alexander McQueen: Family and Fashion Royalty Pay Tributes at St. Paul's," *Guardian*, September 20, 2010; Hamish Bowles, "A Service of Thanksgiving to Celebrate the Life of Lee Alexander McQueen, CBE," Vogue.com, September 20, 2010.

363 **That summer, he skipped:** Mascarenhas, "Galliano's Splash of Flamenco for Gib Family Wedding."

363 **went on vacation:** http://new.ftv.com/video/double-karl-lagerfeld-john-galliano-vip-room-saint-trope_124170.html.

364 **"He stayed on the treadmill":** Alexandre de Betak, interview with the author, Paris, December 17, 2013.

365 **Anna Wintour reportedly wrote:** Smith, "The Secret Torments of Galliano."

365 **Not even long-supportive:** Mallory Andrews, interview with the author, e-mail, July 28, 2014.

366 **In November, Galliano:** Smith, "The Secret Torments of Galliano."

368 **The Dior press office:** http://www.forbes.com/sites/hannahelliott/2011/02/25/full-statement-from-dior-about-john-gallianos-arrest/.

369 **"Galliano: Your asshole":** Sischy, "Galliano in the Wilderness."

369 **In fact, Bloch's suit:** Dickey and McNicoll, "The Galliano Dossier."

370 **The following day:** "Dior Fires Designer Galliano over Praise of Hitler," Associated Press, March 1, 2011.

370 **"As the daughter of a Holocaust survivor":** Jenny Barchfield, "Galliano Scandal Overshadows Paris Fashion Week," Associated Press, March 1, 2011.

370 **The actress Natalie Portman:** Jenny Barchfield and Jamey Keaten, "Fashion Provocateur Galliano Sacked by Dior," Associated Press, March 1, 2011; Doreen Carvajal, "Video Raises Questions for Designer," *New York Times,* February 28, 2011.

370 **"What happened was not":** "Dior—yes, Galliano—no," *New York Post,* March 15, 2011.

370 **"I think he was being":** Betak, interview, December 17, 2013.

370 **"We didn't get there":** Stephen Jones, interview with the author, London, December 8, 2011.

371 **"We had to not only":** Betak, interview, December 17, 2013.

371 **Delphine Arnault, seated:** Suzy Menkes, "At Dior, Tears and Applause," *International Herald Tribune,* March 7, 2011.

XXI

374 **"I had gone there":** Joseph, "The Lonely Suicide of Alexander McQueen and Family's Anger at Mystery of £16 Million Legacy."

374 **"We will be giving":** http://www.vogue.co.uk/spy/biographies/sarah-burton.

374 **"That's what Lee drummed in":** Ibid.

375 **And the back had fifty-eight:** Dana Thomas, "Kate's Choice Was a Mod Nod To Tradition," *Washington Post,* April 30, 2011, p. C01.

376 **"Sometimes I was taking":** Joelle Diederich and Alex Wynne, "'Too Much Pressure,' Galliano Tells Court," *Women's Wear Daily,* June 23, 2011.

376 **"Dior is a big machine":** Ibid.

376 **"These are not the sentiments":** Doreen Carvajal, "Designer Galliano Says He Can't Recall Speaking Slurs," *New York Times,* June 22, 2011.

376 **The court gave him:** Sischy, "Galliano in the Wilderness."

376 **He later sued:** Joelle Diderich, "Labor Court Rules Against John Galliano," *Women's Wear Daily,* November 5, 2014.

377 **"So I'm just carrying":** Gaytten, interview, September 22, 2011.

377 **In August 2012:** Miles Socha, "John Galliano Stripped of Legion of Honor," *Women's Wear Daily,* August 24, 2012; Belinda White, "John Galliano Stripped of Legion of Honour Following Anti-Semitic Abuse Conviction," *Telegraph,* August 28, 2012.

377 **A month later:** Miles Socha, "Bernard Arnault to Receive British Knighthood," *Women's Wear Daily,* October 5, 2012.

377 ***Women's Wear Daily*** **reported:** Marc Karimzadeh, "Oscar de la Renta Opens Studio to John Galliano," *Women's Wear Daily,* January 18, 2013.

378 **"So when Anna":** William Norwich, "Oscar de la Renta on Taking in Galliano, the Women He's Known and Loved, and Why He Once Tried to Hit Cecil Beaton," *New York,* February 18, 2013.

378 ***Women's Wear*** **called it:** "Oscar de la Renta RTW Fall 2013," *Women's Wear Daily,* February 12, 2013.

378 **Just before the de la Renta show:** "Schmuck!" *New York Post,* February 13, 2013, p. 1.

378 **The last thing:** Bridget Foley, "Galliano, a Judgment Call," *Women's Wear Daily,* February 14, 2013.

379 **his anti-Semitic outbursts:** Eric Wilson, "A Tentative Step by a Fallen Start to Come Back," *New York Times,* February 13, 2013.

379 **"She dared me":** Sischy, "Galliano in the Wilderness."

379 **When Moss's father:** Özbek, interview, December 7, 2011.

379 **"I look forward to":** Miles Socha, "John Galliano Joins Maison Martin Margiela," *Women's Wear Daily,* October 6, 2014.

380 **And all they can come up:** Vanessa Friedman, "Behind Jean Paul Gaultier's Goodbye," *New York Times,* September 23, 2014.

INDEX